Intimacy

Intimacy

The complete illustrated guide to love, sex and living together

Edited by Dr Rosalie Burnett

Salem House Publishers
Topsfield, Massachusetts

CONTRIBUTORS

VOLUME EDITOR

Dr Rosalie Burnett
Course Tutor in Social Psychology,
The Open University, UK

DISTINGUISHED CONSULTANTS

Dr Jack Dominian
Director, Marriage Research Centre,
Central Middlesex Hospital, London, UK

Professor Elaine Hatfield
Professor of Psychology,
University of Hawaii, USA

ADVISORY EDITORS

Professor Steven W Duck
Daniel and Amy Starch Research
Professor in Communication Studies,
University of Iowa, USA

Dr Barbara M Montgomery
Associate Professor of Communication
Studies, University of New
Hampshire, USA

KEY TO AUTHORS

AA   Professor Anne-Marie Ambert
Professor of Sociology,
York University,
Toronto, Canada

ALW   Dr Ann Weber
Associate Professor of Psychology,
University of North Carolina at
Asheville, USA

AS   Dr Andrew Stanway
Psychosexual and Marital Physician,
Surrey, UK

ATJ   Ms Anne T Jewell
Department of Psychology, Wake
Forest University, USA

BB   Dr Bram Buunk
Associate Professor of Psychology,
University of Nijmegen, The Netherlands

BCM   Professor Brent C Miller
Professor of Family and Human
Development, Utah State
University, USA

BvD   Drs Barry van Driel
Department of Social Psychology,
University of California at
Santa Cruz, USA

BMM   Dr Barbara M Montgomery
Associate Professor of Communication
Studies, University of
New Hampshire, USA

DE   Dr Diane Ehrensaft
Psychology Professor, The Wright
Institute, Berkeley, California, USA

DMN   Dr David M Newman
Assistant Professor of Sociology,
University of Connecticut, USA

EAB   Dr Elizabeth A Bankoff
Department of Psychology,
Northwestern University, USA

EH   Professor Elaine Hatfield
Professor of Psychology, University of
Hawaii, USA

FD-M   Dr Fran Dickson-Markman
Assistant Professor in
Communication, University of
Colorado at Boulder,
USA

JD   Dr Jack Dominian
Director, Marriage Research Centre,
Central Middlesex Hospital, London, UK

JS   Ms Julie Serovich
Department of Child and Family
Development, University of
Georgia, USA

JT   Dr John Triseliotis
Director of Social Work Education,
University of Edinburgh, UK

LKA   Dr Linda K Acitelli
Program Coordinator/Research
Psychologist, Center for Research on
Learning and Teaching, University of
Michigan, USA

MBA   Dr Mara B Adelman
Assistant Professor of Communication
Studies, Northwestern University, USA

MDN   Dr Michael D Newcomb
Associate Professor of Counseling
Psychology, University of Southern
California at Los Angeles, USA

MLH   Dr Michael L Hecht
Associate Professor of Communication,
Arizona State University, USA

MRL   Dr Mark R Leary
Associate Professor of Psychology,
Wake Forest University, USA

PCM   Professor Patrick McKenry
Professor of Family Relations and
Human Development, Ohio State
University, USA

PG   Dr Patricia Gillan
Consultant Psychologist, North Wales
Medical Centre, UK

PHW   Professor Paul H Wright
Professor of Psychology, University of
North Dakota, USA

PJM   Dr Peter J Marston
Assistant Professor of Speech
Communication, California State
University at Northridge, USA

RB   Dr Rosalie Burnett
Course Tutor in Social Psychology,
The Open University, UK

RLR   Professor Richard L Rapson
Professor of History, University of
Hawaii, USA

RMC   Professor Rodney M Cate
Professor of Child and Family Studies,
Washington State University, USA

SD   Professor Steven W Duck
Daniel and Amy Starch Research
Professor in Communication Studies,
University of Iowa, USA

SJP   Professor Sharon J Price
Professor of Child and Family
Development, University of
Georgia, USA

TC   Ms Tricia Casey
Department of Counseling, University
of Southern California, USA

WHB   Dr William H Bergquist
President, The Professional School of
Psychology, San Francisco, USA

PROJECT EDITOR

Sally Carpenter

TEXT

Editors
Hilary Dickinson
Nancy Duin
Ann Hunter
David Lambert
Joanne Lightfoot
Michael March
Pamela Mayo
Mary Melling
Vivienne Richardson

Research consultant
Richard Newnham

Indexer
Fiona Barr

Typesetting
Reina Foster-de Wit

Word-processing
Lyn Murphy
Ann Richardson
Nicola Whale

PICTURES

Research coordinator
Thérèse Maitland

Researchers
Celia Dearing
Suzanne Williams

ART

Art editor and layout
designer
Chris Munday

Additional layout designers
Martin Anderson
Patricia Burrows
Michael Grendon

Artists
Martin Cox
Simon Driver
Mary Ann Le May

SERIES EDITOR
Stuart McCready

First published in the United States
by Harper and Row Publishers, 1989,
10 East 53rd Street,
New York, NY 10022

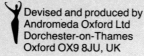 Devised and produced by
Andromeda Oxford Ltd
Dorchester-on-Thames
Oxford OX9 8JU, UK

Copyright © Andromeda Oxford Ltd
1989

ISBN 0-06-018198-2

Library of Congress
Cataloging-in-Publication Data

Intimacy: the complete illustrated
guide to love, sex, and living
together.
1. Marriage – Psychological
aspects 2. Mate selection
3. Intimacy (psychology)
4. Interpersonal conflict
I. Burnett, Rosalie, 1946- II. Title
HQ734.I65 1989 646.7'7 89-10244

Originated by Scantrans,
Singapore

Printed and bound in Spain by
Grupo Nerecan - Tonsa, San Sebastian

MOST OF US learn about relationships simply by having them. And most of us learn the hard way – by repeated trial and error. When, in time, we come to what is usually the central, most important relationship of adult life – an enduring partnership with a member of the opposite sex – we are all too often ill-prepared.

Personal relationships are so much part of human existence that we have a natural tendency to take them for granted. How many couples ever stop to think – *really think* – about their relationship: what it amounts to, how it is developing, how they could improve it? Far too few. Most, as a result, deny themselves reachable joys – the deep satisfaction that wholehearted commitment brings, and the high-points of happiness and self-fulfillment that come with true intimacy.

Sound information about making the most of a couple relationship is hard to acquire casually. Couples with problems do not often talk about them with others who could learn from their experience. And happy couples, thoughtful though they may be, seldom formulate principles that they could pass on to others in conversation. And even if they do, there is no guarantee that their particular secrets of success will work for others.

However, relationships in general and couple relationships in particular have lately become a focus of new research. And more and more couples are becoming aware of the value of absorbing the newly available information. *Intimacy* is specially designed to make it easy – and pleasurable to do so. Part One – COUPLES – will help you find out more about the couple relationship and how it works. It will also help you explore your own intimate relationship to advantage. The main focus in Part Two – GREATER INTIMACY – is on practical ways of enriching the partnership.

Intimacy has been written by a panel of experts nearly all of whom are well known, widely experienced and actively engaged in relevant research. They skillfully combine the best established findings of social scientists with the practical insights of marriage counselors and sex therapists. And in doing so they make liberal use of photographs and diagrams that bring much of what they say dramatically to life. **RB**

SUMMARY CONTENTS

Contents: Part One *7*, Part Two *9*
Subject Guides *10*

1 : NEEDING A SPECIAL PERSON *16*
2 : WHAT MAKES A COUPLE *24*
3 : FINDING, MATCHING AND ATTRACTING *30*
4 : PAIRING OFF *40*
5 : LOVE AND COMMITMENT *48*
6 : MAINTAINING INDIVIDUALITY *54*
7 : OPTING FOR MARRIAGE *62*
8 : HOW COUPLES HAVE CHANGED *70*
9 : MAKING LOVE *76*
10 : THINKING OF PARENTHOOD *86*
11 : EXTRAMARITAL AFFAIRS *94*
12 : FALLING OUT *102*
13 : CONTEMPLATING DIVORCE *110*
14 : STARTING AGAIN *120*
15 : THE MATURE YEARS *126*
16 : A SENSE OF INTIMACY *134*
17 : IDEALS AND REALITIES *138*
18 : EXPECTATIONS OF THE OPPOSITE SEX *148*
19 : SUSTAINING YOUR RELATIONSHIP *156*
20 : BETTER COMMUNICATION *164*
21 : UNDERSTANDING EACH OTHER *172*
22 : A SOUND AND HAPPY MARRIAGE *180*
23 : MANAGING TOGETHER *188*
24 : THE DIFFICULT PARTNER *196*
25 : GETTING THERAPY *204*
26 : ENJOYING SEX *214*
27 : ROOM FOR OTHER PEOPLE *224*
28 : SHARED PARENTING *234*
29 : REVITALIZING YOUR RELATIONSHIP *242*

Further Reading and Sources *248*
Acknowledgments *252*   Index *254*

PART 1 – COUPLES

Part 1 describes the complete cycle of forming and ending an intimate partnership and the choices and challenges met at each stage.

We need to make a success of relationships with *many* people. What are we looking for as we try to do this, and why do people put so much value on having one *special* relationship?
TURN TO CHAPTER 1

How is being a couple different from being just good friends?
TURN TO CHAPTER 2

Not just anyone will do as an intimate partner, but almost everyone finds someone. How do they do it?
TURN TO CHAPTER 3

Initial attraction does not usually lead to an instant lifelong commitment. We first court each other for a time. This allows us to explore the possibilities for building on a deeper and more meaningful attraction, and it allows us to develop a joint management style.
TURN TO CHAPTER 4

Does the way you feel really mean that you are in love? What is involved in committing yourself to a relationship?
TURN TO CHAPTER 5

Is a couple relationship the right thing for you? If you do form a partnership, does it mean the end of your identity as an individual?
TURN TO CHAPTER 6

Matrimony is not the only destination that a developing relationship can aim for, yet the great majority of people marry. Why do they?
TURN TO CHAPTER 7

Tradition is still one of the most influential marriage guides and one of the easiest to consult. However, its strength is waning.
TURN TO CHAPTER 8

How much should we expect of the sexual side of an intimate relationship?
TURN TO CHAPTER 9

How does having children affect the parents' relationship?
TURN TO CHAPTER 10

Why do people have extramarital affairs? Is it folly to take back a partner who has strayed?
TURN TO CHAPTER 11

Does arguing mean incompatibility? What are the signs of an approaching breakdown?
TURN TO CHAPTER 12

Is it worth struggling with an unhappy marriage? What would divorce be like?
TURN TO CHAPTER 13

After a break-up, what does the future typically hold in store for those who stay single and for those who try once more with a new partner?
TURN TO CHAPTER 14

For those whose relationships survive the often stressful early and middle years of marriage, will old age bring a disappointing loss of passion?
TURN TO CHAPTER 15

1 *Needing a Special Person* 16

2 *What Makes a Couple* 24

3 *Finding, Matching and Attracting* 30

4 *Pairing Off* 40

5 *Love and Commitment* 48

6 *Maintaining Individuality* 54

7 *Opting for Marriage* 62

8 *How Couples Have Changed* 70

9 *Making Love* 76

10 *Thinking of Parenthood* 86

11 *Extramarital Affairs* 94

12 *Falling Out* 102

13 *Contemplating Divorce* 110

14 *Starting Again* 120

15 *The Mature Years* 126

PART 2 – GREATER INTIMACY

Part 2 is about enhancement of the relationship between a committed couple. How can they meet the challenge of staying together for the rest of their lives, when so many of those around them are parting?

———▼———

Intimacy should be recognized as imposing burdens and risks as well as offering excitement and fulfillment.
TURN TO CHAPTER 16

Not only are the ideals of intimacy elusive, but also the realities – relationships never achieve everything we want them to and we often underestimate what we do achieve.
TURN TO CHAPTER 17

Most couples assume that a distinctly masculine man and a distinctly feminine woman are the ideal pattern. But exaggerated sex differences conflict with other ideals – intimacy and equality.
TURN TO CHAPTER 18

Relationships that coast do not maximize the benefits of intimacy. It helps to take a conscious interest in developing the partnership.
TURN TO CHAPTER 19

Positive, open and well-managed communication is at the heart of any successful relationship.
TURN TO CHAPTER 20

Helping each other to feel understood is one of the greatest benefits that partners can exchange. How is it done?
TURN TO CHAPTER 21

Stability is essential but it is not everything. What else does a happy marriage need?
TURN TO CHAPTER 22

Sharing a life intimately involves less romance than it does joint management of the more mundane aspects of life. How can this be done effectively?
TURN TO CHAPTER 23

Most partners will seem difficult to live with at times. How much difficulty should we tolerate?
TURN TO CHAPTER 24

Going to a relationship therapist with your marriage problems does not have to be the desperate measure it might seem.
TURN TO CHAPTER 25

How can a couple enliven sex that has become dull, or increase confidence in their ability to please each other?
TURN TO CHAPTER 26

How much room should a couple make in their life for friends, relatives and in-laws?
TURN TO CHAPTER 27

Except for single parents whose former partners never see the children, parenthood is always shared to some extent. Some couples find that the greater the sharing, the more their relationship benefits.
TURN TO CHAPTER 28

When boredom sets in, techniques are available for renewing interest – for bringing fresh excitement into a relationship you have taken too much for granted.
TURN TO CHAPTER 29

CONTENTS PART 2

16 *A Sense of Intimacy* 134

17 *Ideals and Realities* 138

18 *Expectations of the Opposite Sex* 148

19 *Sustaining Your Relationship* 156

20 *Better Communication* 164

21 *Understanding Each Other* 172

22 *A Sound and Happy Marriage* 180

23 *Managing Together* 188

24 *The Difficult Partner* 196

25 *Getting Therapy* 204

26 *Enjoying Sex* 214

27 *Room For Other People* 224

28 *Shared Parenting* 234

29 *Revitalizing Your Relationship* 242

USE this alphabetical guide to find the main subjects in Part One, *Couples*. A single reference is given for each, indicating the page or beginning page of its fullest treatment.

For a guide to Part Two see page 8.
For a wider reference to a subject and for a more extensive list of subjects, see the index at the end of the book.

Adjusting to divorce 120

Adoptive parenting 92

Adulthood and marriage 70

Advertising for a mate 36

Age patterns in marriage 32

Aging and sexual activity 128

AIDS 99

Alimony 118

Assessing love and commitment 52

Attraction 30

Baby bonding 18

Benefits of children 86

Betrothal 67

Childlessness 91

Children and divorce 119

Cohabitation 71

Cohabitation partners 28

Commitment 48

Commuter couples 75

Companionship 50

Conflict 102

Contraception 85

Couple relationships 24
Courtship 40
Courtship and roles 45
Dating 40
Divorce 110
Divorce and health 60
Engagement 67
Equality in marriage 72
Eternal triangle 100
Events that changed couples 74
Expectations of marriage 65
Extramarital affairs 94
Families 73
Feminism 74
Fertilization 78
Fidelity 50
Finding a partner 30
Flirting 97
Friendship 24
Health and marriage 60
Health and relationships 20
Individuality 54
Industrialization and marriage 73
Infertility 90
Infidelity 94
Intimacy and independence 54
Introduction services 38
Jealousy 101
Living together 71
Loneliness 21
Love and commitment 48
Love in mature years 126

Lovemaking 76
Loving styles 51
Marriage bureaus 36
Marriage ceremony 62
Marriage decisions 57
Marriage patterns 58
Marriage roles 70
Marriage squeeze 33
Marriage as a turning point 66
Married status 62
Masturbation myths 83
Matchmaking 38
Mate-swapping 97
Meeting potential partners 34
Modern family 73
Money conflicts 104
Money and marriage 64
Need for love 22
Open marriage 97
Orgasm 78
Pairing off 40
Parenthood 86
Passion 50
Perils of intimacy 102
Personal growth 19
Premarital sex 46
Privacy 55
Qualities that attract 31
Reasons for marrying 57
Relationship assessment 43
Relationship breakdown 106
Relationship formation 30

Relationship rewards 17
Religion and divorce 112
Remarriage 122
Role conflict 105
Romantic expectations 30
Romantic love 48
Romantic love and commitment 53
Self-esteem 18
Self-knowledge 23
Separation 111
Sex and aging 128
Sex drive 76
Sexual intercourse 78
Sexual myths 83
Sexual problems 81
Showing love 49
Single mothers 32
Singles 55
Social change and marriage 70
Social pressure and marriage 62
Solitude 55
Standards in relationships 26
Starting a sexual relationship 46
Stepparenting 124
Swinging Sixties 72
Taboo subjects 42
Typical couple 29
Ways of getting closer 40
Wedding customs 68
Well-being and relationships 19
Women and career ambitions 55
Women's marriage expectations 33

SUBJECT GUIDE TO PART 2
Greater Intimacy

USE this alphabetical guide to find the main subjects in Part Two, *Greater Intimacy*. A single reference is given for each, indicating the page or beginning page of its fullest treatment.

For a guide to Part One see page 6. For a wider reference to a subject and for a more extensive list of subjects, see the index at the end of the book.

Adolescence and parents 136
Androgyny 153
Arousal 216
Assessing intimacy 135
Better communication 164
Better mutual understanding 178
Boredom 242
Celebrating the relationship 160
Change within relationships 142
Choosing marriage partners 180
Co-parenting 234
Communication about sex 222
Communication breakdown 208
Communication styles 164
Confidence-boosting 183
Conversation habits to avoid 168
Conversation skills 244
Decision-making 191
Difficult partner 196
Disability in a partner 203
Domestic division of labor 194
Drinking and violence 199
Economics of living together 188

Emotional intimacy 135
Emotional support 158
Empathy 179
Erotic holidays 221
Expectations of each other 148
False assumptions 183
Family intimacies 136
Family leisure 232
Fantasies 217
Fathering 235
Female emotional styles 149
Female and male perspectives 176
Femininity 154
Fighting 166
Flirting 159
Friendship and couples 226
Happy and unhappy couples 183
Honesty 162
Humor 166
Ideal relationships 138
Idealizing your partner 147
Illness of a partner 202
Illusions 145
Images of partnership 138
Immaturity 196
Individuality and relationships 246
Intimacy 134
Intuitions 178
Leisure sharing 233
Love and marriage 182
Love-hate relationships 199
Lovemaking settings 220

Maintenance strategies 156
Male emotional styles 150
Marital enrichment therapy 205
Marital power 192
Marriage styles 186
Marriage therapy 204
Masculinity 154
Media images of couples 138
Mental illness in a partner 202
Misunderstandings 173
Money management 188
Mood recognition 185
Mother guilt 237
Mutual masturbation 218
Mutual problem-solving 197
Mutual sexual discovery 214
Neighbors 232
Openness 170
Parents-in-law 231
Personality problems 196
Physical intimacy 135
Play and relationships 245
Problem-solving 160
Real-life relationships 143
Reconciliation 196
Relationship centeredness 176
Relationship growth 244
Relationship maintenance 156
Relationship readjustment 142
Relationship revitalization 242
Relationship rituals 160
Relatives and couples 230

12

Repair and reconciliation 196
Role expectations 140
Role-sharing 239
Self-disclosure 183
Self-knowledge and understanding 178
Sensitivity to feelings of partner 163
Seven-Year Itch 142
Sex differences in parenting 236
Sex roles 151
Sex therapy 212
Sexual anatomy and arousal 216

Sexual equality 148
Sexual intercourse 220
Sexual pleasure 214
Sexually explicit material 222
Singles and couples 227
Socializing 224
Stability in marriage 180
Stagnation in a relationship 242
Stimulation therapy 215
Taboo subjects 170
Talking treatment 209

Therapy 204
Therapy programs 206
Thinking styles 153
Understanding 172
Unemployment and marriage 202
Violent relationships 199
Work and relationships 190
Wife-battering 199
Wild Man syndrome 150
Work-centeredness 176
Working women and marriage 189

13

1

COUPLES

PART ONE

Needing a Special Person

ALMOST everyone spends some periods of their adult life single – either before finding a partner or after a relationship has ended. These may be times of welcome freedom. Someone who places a high value on independence and privacy may consciously choose to live separately and so much distress in life is associated with relationships going wrong that it may be worth asking if you would be better off alone (see *Ch 6*). However, many singles are lonely – not just for friends (they may already have many) – but lonely for one special person who can share their life intimately.

Overwhelmingly, we choose to form twosomes. Sexual attraction is an important part of what draws us together, but most of us are looking for a long-term relationship – in spite of its emotional complications – not simply for sexual encounters. About 90 percent of adults marry. Their motives include wanting to have children and the practical advan-

tages of a shared household, but, even in countries where most marriages are formally arranged, partners are attracted too by the opportunities for emotional intimacy. This is also a motive for couples who are involved with each other sexually and depend on each other emotionally without ever having matrimony or offspring as objectives. It is a motive for most long-term same-sex couples, unofficially married couples and couples living together in trial marriages.

What we gain from relationships

Many are disappointed, for having a partner is not an absolute guarantee against loneliness: people who feel close at first often grow apart emotionally without ending their union; some never achieve a hoped-for intimacy in the first place. What is it that they sense they are missing and what is it that those who find fulfillment in a relationship

16

■ **Feeling alone in a crowd.** *Loneliness is a yearning for the rewards of love and companionship. "Social loneliness" is a longing for friends and a social network. "Emotional loneliness" is a longing for a particularly close relationship – a need for a special person. Only a tiny proportion of people desire neither friends nor an intimate partner, and the great majority want both.*

■ **Displays of togetherness** *confirm what our relationships mean to us – how much and in what ways we need each other.*

RIGHT The security of a long-standing partnership allows two people to enjoy just being together. Totally at ease in each other's company, they show their mutual affection in a relaxed way.

LEFT The eagerness of a less established couple reaffirms to both partners that each is an object of passionate excitement to the other.

Why does an intimate partnership matter so much? ■ *When couples make a success of intimacy, mutual support is more complete – and there is a fuller mutual acceptance – than in any other close relationship.*

actually gain from teaming up with another person?

Even those who choose a single life still need to be close to somebody: they rely on their relationships with friends and relatives for many of the same benefits intimate partners receive from each other with greater intensity. People without friends and relatives benefit, to a much less intense degree, by personalizing contacts with shopkeepers or fellow commuters they see regularly, or else they make cherished friends of their pets. They may keep former relationships alive by imaginary dialogs. They may look forward to the appearance on the screen of a favorite television personality they have adopted as a friend as much as they would look forward to a visit from a real-life acquaintance.

Each of us by some combination of friends, acquaintances, relatives – and usually an intimate partner – tries to meet a long list of basic human needs. Relationships are a main channel for practical information, for example, and for useful introductions and help with material problems. We turn to friends, relatives or a partner for advice, and they take the trouble, often uninvited, to inform us about things that affect our interests, and to introduce us to people they know and whom it may be worth *our* while knowing. It helps to give you peace of mind to know you can borrow a tool from a neighbor, ask a friend to watch the children, get money from a relative if you are really in trouble, divide the household tasks with a partner and rely on their income.

Relationships reinforce our sense of belonging and identity. An important part of my answer to the question "Who am I?" is that I am a member of a certain family or of a

certain community. Claims to belong will seem very hollow if I do not have any relationships with others who also belong. Thus, it is not the physical fact of living in my street that makes me part of a neighborhood community – it is the courtesies and favors that I exchange with others.

Similarly, my sense of belonging to a family would be greatly weakened if I had no more than a biological link with my parents, brothers and sisters. If you are the intimate friend, husband or wife of someone, this will usually also be a positive part of your identity – we tend to choose partners we are happy to have people link with us when they think of who we are. Usually a partner also connects you with a family, a community and a circle of friends.

It is through relationships that we acquire most of our self-esteem. The fact that others *give* us their attention – for example, taking an interest in our plans and how we spend time – helps us to believe that we are *worthy* of attention. Friends, a partner and the relatives we get along with best, moreover, tend to share our beliefs and show respect for our opinions and the way we make sense of the world. If we need someone to see our point of view, we go to someone close to us for understanding. People with whom we form close friendships also tend to be the ones who appreciate our personalities, our tastes and our sense of humor.

Because we feel so well accepted by them, and also

THE FIRST RELATIONSHIP

■ *We are biologically built for personal relationships with people who cannot be easily replaced. The pattern emerges clearly in most babies before their first birthday. They show attachment to their caregivers and a mistrust and avoidance of others. This selectivity helps to sustain a bond they will need throughout the long period of infant dependency in humans, and it provides early experience of the pleasures of intimacy.*

Many problems can arise if the infant is separated from the special person or persons to whom it has become attached. If the separation period is especially long and combined with deprivation of other needs such as attention and kindness, the child may grow into an adult who has difficulty with relationships.

Developmental psychologists have closely analyzed videos of mother and child interaction, and have discovered that every movement and response of the child is finely tuned to every movement and response of the adult. Mother and child engage in a kind of rhythmic dance, each matching head movements and eye contact to synchronize and balance with the other. This kind of rhythmic response is missing in the case of autistic babies, who grow up unable to respond and relate in the usual way and remain withdrawn in a locked world of their own.

In a frame-by-frame analysis of videos, Martin Richards at Cambridge University, England, confirmed that mothers talk to their babies as if the infants are able to make reasoned choices and have goals and preferences. Parents think on behalf of their babies. In a way, the parents relate to a child of their own invention rather than the child as it really is, because they attribute to it capacities it does not yet possess. This provides a kind of relationship structure, which the child is able to build on in order to develop its own personality and understanding.

Researchers call this process "physical symbiosis." One person fills in gaps for the other. In biology, a symbiotic relationship between two organisms is where one lives in or on the other, but both benefit. Some theorists argue that a kind of symbiosis applies to all personal relationships. Everyone depends on other key persons in order to become more whole. No one is a fully rounded human being: we are all defective in some way, and personal growth seems to result from intimate, mutually dependent, interaction.

18

▲ **The one most enduringly special person** *for most people is the person with whom they formed the first relationship of their life. It is from her, in the first place, that we learned how to* be close and how to reciprocate caring. For most of us, the relationship will continue to be close until one of us dies.

"Who are my friends?" is part of my answer to the question "Who am I?" ■ *Your sense of identity and worth is strengthened by belonging to a family, a community, a circle of friends and one person who finds you special.*

because they share our interests, we can express our individuality when we are with the people who are close to us. We have more fun when we are with them than when with strangers, and we may feel a greater freedom to develop opinions we would not otherwise voice. Because we trust them to take us seriously and to be sympathetic, we can ask them to clarify our confusions and give us constructive criticisms.

All of this helps our personal growth – the development of life skills and personal potential (see p58).

Because friends, relatives and a loving partner value us, they express affection and admiration. Because they care for us, they are prepared to go to great inconvenience to help us emotionally when we face a crisis. They listen to us, touch us, hold us, make us understand that we are not to blame, when we need to cope with tensions, frustrations, disappointments and grief.

How relationships affect well-being

Experts use the term "social support" when they refer to the material help, advice, esteem, love and emotional comfort that we exchange with others. We do not receive exactly

▲ **Making a special person of a pet** *is something that many animal lovers do, whether or not they have other friends and loved-ones. The unconditional affection that pets offer can be especially valuable for those who find it hard to form other relationships.*

◄ **Tête à tête.** *We learn the skills of friendship earlier in life than the skills of pairing off into intimate partnerships. Once this later stage of social life arrives, it is a mistake to neglect friendships: broadly based social support is invaluable.*

the same kinds and amounts of support from any two people, and in different kinds of relationships it is typical to find different intensities of support. Those who are on good terms with their neighbors give and receive practical help in small matters, and benefit from the sociability of having people to stop and talk to in the street. Most people, however, ask little from their neighbors unless they are also close friends. People often expect to have more fun with friends and receive more support for their opinions from friends than they do from relatives, but they may feel more comfortable about asking relatives for material and emotional support at times of great crisis.

From intimate partners, we usually hope for a higher intensity and a wider variety of material and emotional support than from anyone else. The fact that most people feel a strong sense of needing a special person may in part reflect the amount of support such a person can provide – in fact hardly anyone expects that their needs could be fully met without one.

Medical statistics reflect in a dramatic way the importance to our well-being of the more intense levels of social support, but they do not show unequivocally that an intimate partnership is what we need.

People who have no friends and no close relationships with relatives or an intimate partner are more at risk from every illness. From the common cold and every other infection through every form of cancer, every kind of system malfunction (such as heart attacks, asthma, Alzheimer's disease), and every mental disturbance from depression to schizophrenia, it has been found that without people who care, the prognosis is worse. Facing the common stress of life alone is difficult, and when people cope badly with

> *Why are our expectations so high in couple relationships?* ■ *Couples are more committed to each other than friends* ■ *They spend more time together, taking more opportunities to grow close and to become interdependent* ■ *Sharing sexual intimacy can strongly intensify a couple's mutual trust and openness.*

emotional stress, they feel the stress more intensely: high levels of stress hormones disrupt the immune system as well as creating wear and tear on other bodily systems.

Psychologically, single people who have never married fare worse than married people (see *Ch 6*). However, this does not prove that getting married or forming some other long-term intimate relationship is essential for mental health: the statistics do not discriminate between people who suffer the stress of loneliness and those who are happy to rely on friends and relatives.

▲ **Fingering her wedding ring,** *a woman contemplates a man who is emotionally part of her. Long-term stability is a reward for couples who can cope with the strains of intimacy. This stability may offer them a more secure and reliable social life than any other kind of relationship.*

◀ **Because they are so often together,** *couples have more opportunity than friends to grow close and to support each other in every way.*

The stress of loneliness – especially a sense of loneliness due to loss – is very acute among the divorced and the bereaved, and they, as groups, have even poorer health than never-married singles. Many writers on relationships warn that you should avoid depending too exclusively on an intimate relationship – you should keep up a network of close friends and relatives who can cushion you against the loss of your partner. This advice is especially important for men, since, despite the friendly relations they have with people at work and with neighbors, so many feel close only to their wives. Widowers as a group are more vulnerable to illness and death in the year following bereavement than widows.

Investigation also shows that it is not the number of relationships you have, but the quality that improves well-being. A wide circle of acquaintances is not as likely to benefit you as much as a small network of close friends. And medical records show better health in married people who report that they are happy with their relationships than in those who are dissatisfied.

Why are couple relationships so close?

Expectations are commonly disappointed, but there *are* reasons to expect a more rewarding intimacy within a couple relationship than in other kinds. First, most couples are drawn close by feelings of sexual passion. Second, this kind of relationship usually involves a higher level of commitment, and commitment can help intimacy to flourish.

Sexual acts can be performed in a very impersonal way. It is even possible to have a long-term sexual relationship in

which two partners perform dutifully but mechanically. Most couples, however, release passion together during sex in a way that takes them past a threshold of caution and defensiveness that they maintain with other people – sex is a part of their life where it is safe to be emotionally and physically uncontrolled. Being accepted and rewarded when revealing your most unguarded self is profoundly gratifying, and it allows a vigorous intensification of the trust and openness that are vital if intimacy is to thrive.

21

loved and needed in ways that can enrich sexual interaction. This special person has insights about us which a temporary partner has no chance to learn and may be unmotivated to attempt. Such understanding enables each to ask for and do more than can readily be expected from someone less familiar.

Sexual experience in a special, committed relationship is enhanced by the strength of positive feelings we have for each other. People who are in love take a kinder view if anything goes wrong and are strongly motivated to be appreciative. Also, the goals of sex are extended. Physical pleasure and showing of our feelings become combined, so that erotic exchanges between loving partners are more richly communicative.

WHY HAVE ONLY ONE SEXUAL PARTNER?

■ *A strong, continual wish for erotic love is at the center of our need for a partner. Sexual arousal, of course, is frequently not dependent on having a relationship with, or even knowing, the person who is the object of desire. The mere sight of someone who is sexually appealing can stir libidinous feelings.*

You can satisfy the desire without being linked in a permanent or settled arrangement with another person. Masturbation is the least complicated way. Casual or short-term partnerships, formed only for sex, however, compare favorably with masturbation, by providing some element of human contact. Some would argue that a further attraction of satisfying sexual needs in occasional, time-limited relationships is the novelty value of multiple partners.

The possibility of catching or passing on a sexually transmitted disease, however, is a major disincentive for such brief encounters. For many, there are moral objections too. Casual sex is contrary to religious and ethical views that require sexual activity to be linked to love and commitment.

Disease and morals apart, sharing a sex life with one chosen partner is arguably still the most effective way to satisfy sexual desires. A partner chosen to share life is

Even when they do not live together, couples spend more time with each other than friends do. It would show a lack of commitment to the relationship if they did not. Spending so much time together, they learn more about each other than they do about anyone else – if you have been together for a few years, it is probable that no one else knows you so well as your partner, and for this reason alone your partner may be better placed than anyone to make life what you, in particular, need life to be. Being together so often also means that your partner is probably more readily available than anyone else to support you materially and emotionally as your needs occur.

Because the couple relationship involves a high level of commitment, we are highly motivated to sustain it, and this can make it a very reliable source of support. If a friend is promoted and moves to another city, we do not change jobs in order to stay with them and we do not make complex arrangements for spending every weekend together. If a friend gradually drifts away emotionally we are less likely to look for reasons and solutions than when our partner becomes distant. Friendships usually cannot survive as easily when one party begins to make demands that seem unreasonable; intimate partners try harder to accommodate each other. We are also more prepared to make subtle adjustments in our personalities, lifestyles and expectations as each of us gradually changes with time.

Needing to be loved

So much talk about the benefits of a relationship makes it sound as though loving someone amounts to no more than wanting them to make your own life easy and comfortable. Of course, a relationship involves give-and-take, but do partners only give in order to receive?

Some social scientists suggest that we enter and maintain a relationship such as friendship or marriage only for as long as we find the rewards of the relationship an adequate

Do partners only give in order to receive?
■ *Giving and taking have to be about equal in a happy relationship, but giving what? – Any person could wash your socks or earn income*
■ *What makes a partner irreplaceable is the way that being part of each other's lives makes you feel that your life makes sense.*

return for what we invest in it. The balance-sheet approach is known as Exchange Theory.

The giving and the taking have to be about equal: if one person is giving more than the other, efforts are made to correct the imbalance. Other relationships – past and present, real and imagined – provide a standard of fair exchange, and the relationship is likely to end if the gains are assessed as falling short.

An exception to this, though, is when a great deal has been invested – time, hope, love and other emotions, work and wages. The level of investment itself helps to persuade us that the relationship is valuable.

Exchange Theory has been criticized for making an intimate relationship sound too much like an impersonal marketplace transaction. As an explanation of what makes a happy relationship, furthermore, it puts the cart before the

horse. Those who are happy together will generally treat each other fairly.

An extra insight is introduced into this discussion, however, by the American psychologist Paul Wright. Most of what a friend or partner does for you is not especially important; more than by anything else, the relationship is sustained by very special benefits that could never be bought or sold, and that only a friend or loved one can supply. Any person could wash your socks, make your dinner, dig the garden and so forth, without this making you feel emotionally close to them, although you might feel grateful. However, only a person who knows you extremely well is in a position to strengthen your self-knowledge and provide feedback to assure you that you are a worthwhile person – on the right track. Such a person cannot simply be replaced. Thus the most important rewards of a personal relationship are inseparable from that relationship: they depend on that special person. **RB**

"YOU ARE PART OF ME"

■ *In an intimate relationship your partner becomes vital to the sense that you make of yourself and your life. They know you extremely well and are in a unique position to strengthen your self-knowledge by providing feedback and assurance that you are worthwhile. Such a person cannot be simply replaced by another. They become an extension of yourself, and for this reason the*

relationship becomes self-sustaining – its continuation does not depend on any ordinary balancing of the costs you bear by committing yourself to the relationship, against the benefits you gain. You come to feel attached to your partner not because of what they do for you, but because of who they are.

What Makes a Couple

COUPLES often express satisfaction with their relationship by comparing it favorably with friendship: "We're not only husband and wife, we're each other's best friend." On the other hand, people commonly speak of friendship to make it clear that they are definitely *not* a couple: "There's nothing really serious between us; we're just friends." In a survey of 250 Americans, including both married people and singles, 27 percent said that their "best" friend – who was not a romantic partner – was of the opposite sex. More claimed "close" friends of the opposite sex: 56 percent of the men and 44 percent of the women.

A genuine couple relationship seems to be friendship plus something more. What exactly are the extra ingredients and how can you tell whether your relationship has them?

What makes people close?

To begin with, what is it that sets apart *all* close personal relationships (not just couples) from those that are impersonal? First, they involve an individualized interest and concern. Friends, close family and couples respond to one another as unique and irreplaceable individuals (see p23). Close sisters, for example, go beyond merely fulfilling the duties customarily owed to someone who occupies the role

of sister – they become involved with each other out of deep affection. They feel a personal loss if the other dies or moves away.

Second, in personal relationships people are more open and less guarded with each other than they are in impersonal encounters. When interacting with someone close, we feel more like we are reacting to the person, less like we are reacting to the social situation, as we would, for example, when dealing with strangers while shopping, visiting the dentist or applying for a job.

Third, in personal relationships, we maintain a noticeable level of interdependence – we commit time to each other and allow our lives to overlap in such a way that the plans, the decisions and the day-to-day activities of the one are influenced to some degree by those of the other. Normally, the closer the relationship, the more our lives overlap.

Fourth, personal relationships provide several important rewards (see *Ch1*). These rewards are available to us in relationships we do not think of in terms of coupleness in addition to those we do. A good friend may be just as willing and able as our spouse or fiancé to do us favors or help us out when we are in trouble; to respond with sensitivity and encouragement if we need a boost in our morale; or do or

24

■ **Are we – will we be – a couple?** *This question may tantalize a newly developing relationship or haunt a long-established, slowly evolving one. It arises because we hesitate to say that we are "genuinely" a couple unless we are sure that the relationship lives up to the standards we consider ideal, and because there are basic differences between being a couple, even in a minimal sense, and just friends, or being a couple and being two people who happen to live in the same house.*

Friendship and much more besides ■ *What are the extra ingredients that will make two companions add up to one couple?* ■ *Sexual attraction springs quickly to mind, but more goes into the equation* ■ *A sense of permanent – and in many ways exclusive – involvement with each other is essential.*

say just the right thing to help us shore up our sense of identity in periods of self-doubt.

Because the lives of a couple are so closely intertwined, there are times when a close friend or a trusted sibling is better at providing some of these rewards than a spouse or fiancé. For example, one partner in a marriage may be weighing the pros and cons of a dramatic change – such as a career move or a return to university – that is bound to affect the other, possibly in disruptive ways. In such cases, a good friend will often find it easier to be genuinely supportive.

Friendship plus sex?

You may feel that you are *very very* close friends – and add "very" as many times as you like – but this still does not amount to saying you are a couple: it is not just a matter of the degree of closeness. An obvious suggestion about what

does make the difference is that couples, unlike "just friends," have a heavy dose of physical attraction and sexual passion thrown in.

The erotic element is prominent in the idea of a couple relationship and not in the idea of friendship. However, it is not just sex which distinguishes couples from friends. To complicate the comparison some friends do share sexual intimacy while considering themselves just friends and without being regarded as a couple by others. It is only when two people share a commitment to making their sexual relationship exclusive that their sexual intimacy contributes clearly to their being a couple. Then again, not all couples are sexual partners. But sexual exclusivity is a central theme – even when it is an ideal not lived-up to. And, even in the case of open marriages (see *Ch11*) each partner is, by agreement, still the *primary* partner of the other, even though they are compromising the ideal of exclusiveness.

The exclusiveness that helps to make a typical couple, however, concerns much more than sexual intimacy. We tend to be preoccupied and *fascinated* with a partner, especially during the formative stages of the relationship, even giving attention to them and thinking about them when

Being a couple typically means

Being close companions

Regarding the relationship as exclusive and permanent

Being sexually attracted

25

we should be doing something else. Other relationships, too, can have an element of exclusiveness: only one person can be your best friend; and Fred must choose Barney as his bowling partner, or else upset the sense of what their friendship means. But we give a couple relationship *priority* over most of our others. The element of exclusiveness is crucial even to the most minimal couple – such as two strangers out on their first date. They are only a couple in the barest sense, that of showing an initial attraction to each other as potential partners, but if one of them spends most of the evening talking to a best friend they are no longer a couple in even this sense, and the occasion is hardly a date.

A committed couple

Being committed to a couple relationship typically means much more than treating it as exclusive. It also means expecting a high level of mutual assistance. Couples expect to count on each other in times of need, trouble or personal distress.

Research has found people to regard this as just as essential to friendship as to being a couple, and both friends and couples are expected to stand up for each other's rights, interests and reputations – to be each other's advocate; however, there is a stronger expectation that couples will do their utmost for each other in difficult situations, and couples expect and are expected generally to count on each other more.

Another commitment for couples is permanence. They are expected – and themselves expect – to remain intact, if not "till death do us part," at least for a long time. More than close friends, they are expected to maintain their relation-

> *Couples are exclusive in much more than sexual attentions* ■ *You are preoccupied and fascinated, especially with a new partner* ■ *For this person, more than for anyone else, you are probably prepared to do your utmost.*

ships in spite of changing circumstances such as long-distance moves, shifts in careers, and changes in their values and their lifestyles.

Relationship standards

The conventional expectations surrounding different kinds of relationships help to define them – by enshrining commonly accepted ideals of how they should be conducted and what their aims should be. When one person says to another "I want to be your friend," "I want to be a *real* father to you," or "I want us to be a couple," the two of them usually share a sense of the commitments that the person who is speaking thereby undertakes and expects the other to undertake, and the standards of friendship, fatherhood or couplehood that they will try to live up to.

As closeness and communication develop, terms are clarified: differences of expectation are discovered and adjustments are made. For example, by "friendship" one person might have mainly understood having fun together, another might have mainly understood helping each other with loans and weekend jobs around the house. The two people may also arrive at spoken or unspoken agreements that personalize their ideas about how they should behave toward each other. They add their own rules for their relationship to what they accept as the principles for their *kind* of relationship. For example, two friends might feel they are letting their relationship slide if they do not meet every Wednesday for lunch.

26

◄ **How exclusively devoted to each other does a couple have to be?** *Each partner in a couple relationship expects the other to give them priority in their affections, consideration and concern. Being securely a couple means having confidence that your partner's attentions to someone else represent social affability, not really a neglect of the relationship. Similarly, and increasingly, in the age of two-career families, it means knowing that your partner would do what is best for the partnership, faced with a choice between it and the temptation to become "married" to a job.*

■ **Signaling that they are a couple**. *LEFT* Two people stroll out in a choice of apparel and colors that leave an unmistakable impression of harmonized togetherness without uniformity. *RIGHT* A distinctive style of interlocking advertises emotional interdependence. *TOP* The world passes by, signaling non- involvement and acceptance of a couple's exclusiveness by giving a characteristically wide berth to a public display of intimacy.

Most kin relationships are more highly regulated than friendship – for example, there is a stronger expectation that you will remember family birthdays than there is that you will remember friends' birthdays, and a stronger expectation that you will keep up family contacts if you move away.

We feel our highest levels of obligation in couple relationships. Society in general, as well as our parents, siblings, grandparents, in-laws, preachers, priests, rabbis and other people who are important to us have much to say about how the relationship should be conducted and what its aims should be. And most of us are strongly influenced by them.

Standards for couples

Besides exclusiveness and commitment, ideals for couples include interdependence. As already mentioned, this is crucial for any closeness. However, because what one does affects and is of concern to the other, it is a common view that couples need to make more joint decisions, coordinate more of their activities, cooperate more in long-range planning and keep closer track of each other's comings and goings.

Couples also expect high levels of emotional expression. Lovers spend a great deal more time in self-conscious and open expressions about their mutual love than do friends about their friendship. There is usually more emotional expression in women's than in men's friendships. Even so, it normally occurs less than in a couple relationship. Research finds that enjoyment of each other's company is a stronger characteristic of couples than of friends.

Honoring commitments and meeting standards can call for effort and sacrifice. Consequently, research finds that people perceive slightly less trust, understanding and spon-

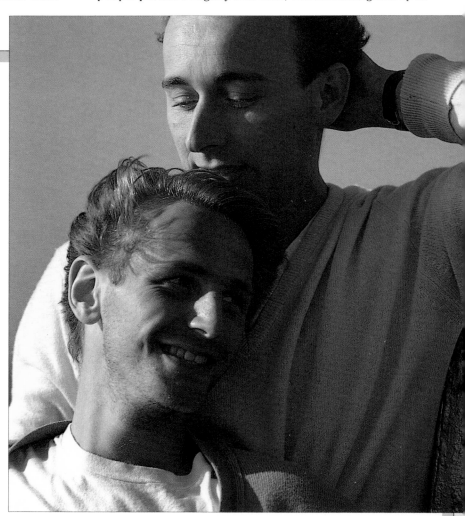

ARE COHABITATION PARTNERS COUPLES?

■ *Nonmarital cohabitation and homosexual love relationships are becoming more common – or at least more open and visible. Do the partners involved in either of these kinds of relationship constitute a couple? According to available research, such relationships typically include interdependence, emotional sharing, intimacy and passion. But do other standards of coupleness apply to them? Do the partners themselves consider their relationship exclusive? Do they consider it permanent? The answer seems to be that some of them do, and some of them do not. Because of this, the coupleness involved has to be considered on a case-by-case basis. In some cases, both partners agree to a relationship that is exclusive and, barring unforeseen changes in circumstances, permanent. In other cases, the understanding is that the relationship is open and nonexclusive, and that it will eventually be dissolved, for example, when the job begins that one of the partners has been promised in another city.*

There is at present a lack of consensus about what cohabitation and homosexual relationships are "supposed" to be like. Therefore, there can be unwitting disagreement between the partners about what they are committing themselves to. One of them may expect the relationship to be exclusive and permanent while the other does not. Unless the partners are careful to come to an early mutual understanding, their relationship is likely to be especially vulnerable to conflict, insecurity and instability. To know where you stand you need to know what being a couple means to each of you.

▲ **Are they a couple?** *It will depend on their sense of permanence and exclusiveness, not on their being of two different sexes.*

> *To be a couple you do not need to be the perfect couple* ■ *Very vital relationships at times combine close companionship with high levels of passion and commitment, but all couples experience ebbs and flows of all these.*

taneity in couple relationships than in friendships. Conflict and discussions about how to manage the relationship are more frequent, and stability is lower.

Although divorce and breaking up are everyday occurrences, however, the fact that permanence is one of a couple's chief commitments and one of society's standards means that ending a marriage or engagement is never as easy as breaking off a friendship.

The typical couple: how do you compare?

Being a couple involves close companionship, passion and commitment that goes beyond that of friendship. To combine a good measure of each of these three elements in

one relationship is not an impossible dream. Many couples do it happily, maintaining a highly vital partnership.

However, we all know of marriage partners, at the other extreme, who are couples in name only. They have long since lost the passion and closeness they may have once shared, but maintain a commitment to the relationship for the sake of the children or to avoid the stigma of separation.

If, like most couples, you fall somewhere between – having begun with a very vital relationship which has now become less intense, or never having had a very exclusive or interdependent relationship – you are still a couple, of course: it just means you match up less well to the criteria of a classic couple. You may find it informative, however, to explore the subject of relationships and explore the untapped potential that your own has for contributing to your happiness and your partner's.

If permanence is a standard of coupleness, are engaged partners a couple? The answer is "Yes, usually." Legally and socially, marriage is more permanent than engagement. However, studies show that once two people have become officially engaged, they almost always consider their relationship just as permanent as marriage. In fact, this is often true even of couples who are merely "pinned," "going steady," or "engaged to be engaged."

But many romantic partners who experience mutual passion and intimacy do not consider their involvement exclusive or necessarily permanent – they still "date around" or "play the field." They have not reached the point of decision and commitment.

Lack of exclusiveness makes it difficult to think of them as couples, but they are more than noncouples. They are, at the very least, potential couples. **PHW**

▲ **"Are we just friends?"** *Having the sense of permanence that makes a couple depends not so much on whether the relationship will in reality last, as it does on sharing a belief that it will.*

▶ **"Are we just going through the motions?"** *Most established couples sense a loss of the excitement they felt when first attracted to each other. Idealization of the romantic phase of the couple relationship, however, may unjustly undervalue its later potential to provide contentment.*

Finding, Matching and Attracting

IT IS A myth that for every man and woman there is the perfect partner and one day the two are bound to meet. Films, songs and television continually portray two people discovering each other in a random and unexpected encounter engineered by "fate," – at a bus stop, in a restaurant or hitchhiking across country.

The mythology starts as early as childhood in bedtime stories such as *Cinderella* or *Snow White*, where the hero and heroine suddenly meet in the most unlikely of circumstances and "live happily ever after." It leaves a prevailing expectation that affects the way we idealize and project our own notions that someday *our* prince(ess) will come. We start believing in these romantic visions rather than in strategy or routine as the way to meet someone special.

In reality, we are far more likely to meet that someone in our everyday dealings with other single people at home, work and school, and through familiar contact among friends. Apart from meeting people through our immediate social circles, our chances of finding a partner can depend on larger social trends such as the general availability of suitable people and the ways we go about looking for them.

The sudden attraction that develops between two people of the opposite sex has often been seen as inexplicable "chemistry," but it has in fact been the subject of extensive research. Social scientists have found that just how we meet depends on a complex interplay of factors ranging from physical attraction to how far we conform to some very common social expectations.

Magnetism, the attractive force?

We all have our own theories about what brings two people together. We say "like attracts like," "opposites attract" or refer to the excitement of "being drawn together." Another cliché for finding the right person is that you both have a lot in common. There is obviously more chance of meeting someone of the same background and education because those are the people you will mix with. As for having similar interests and personalities – finding out what you have in common is all part of the fun of dating.

Although everyone fantasizes about their ideal partner, we are usually most interested in people who have an equivalent degree of physical attractiveness and similar social characteristics. This is a way of protecting ourselves from rejection and disappointment.

While we try to pair off with the most attractive person we can, it is realistic to limit the search to someone likely to be attracted to us. If someone is a great deal more attractive, richer or more intellectual than us, we will probably not pursue our interest in them.

Every society decides how much importance to attach to physical attributes when choosing a partner. Although good

IS THERE A RAPPORT BETWEEN YOU?

■ *When people choose their partners they look for someone with whom they can feel comfortable. We may not be conscious of some of the influences at work during the period of getting closer and deciding a person is right for us.*

Everyone missed out on something when they were growing up. No one can hope to accomplish everything. As a result, we all have limitations. In choosing a partner, we seek someone who has strengths that will mirror or complement our own. The right person helps you to believe in yourself despite inevitable imperfections and gaps in your development. Perhaps you grew up in a family where it was frowned upon if you showed anger – so you suppressed your anger. Or perhaps you grew up in a family where no one was ever flippant – so you did not make jokes. In each case, a partner who gets angry, or a partner who is always cracking jokes may make you feel awkward. So you try again – until you find someone who seems to fit.

Matching allows us to find someone with whom we can feel relaxed about our biases and quirks and about those aspects of us that others might find hard to accept. People whose personalities match in this way are on a similar wavelength. It is easier for them to establish a rapport. **RB**

◄ **Compatibility attracts.** *Mutual attraction passes through stages in which we reveal more and more of ourselves and progress to greater understanding. We are more likely to advance to a deeper level of attraction when we discover that we each know* *what the other means, can confirm that their thoughts and feelings are acceptable and valuable and can interpret the world in a similar way. Personality support like this is one of the main reasons why we need intimate relationships.*

Is there already a perfect partner for you, just waiting to be found? ■ *Probably not – partners are not perfect – but it does make sense to look for someone whose own strengths and weaknesses match and complement yours.*

looks are valued and praised in most industrial societies, clearly there are other important factors that influence choice. We take account of various attributes in a person and compare them with those of other possible partners. For example, are there other people available who are affectionate, considerate, kind, cheerful, easygoing, more intelligent or with a better sense of humor?

Qualities that first attracted us may seem less important as the relationship progresses. What ultimately makes a person attractive to us is the extent to which they see the world in the same way. Having a shared perspective is vital for an effective long-term relationship. Attitudes are only part of this. We do not all make sense of the world in the same way. Someone who construes events in a similar way and who understands our interpretations is more rewarding to be with than someone who has opposing ideas. Relationships with like-minded people affirm our own opinions, require less work and make it more likely that we will get along. Seeing eye-to-eye is a good foundation for developing a stable relationship.

This does not mean that dissimilarities are always unattractive. On the contrary, we may come to like someone we initially disliked, but this is only likely to happen if we are often in their company and can discover some other common ground or reason for our differences. By the same token, similarity in itself may not be a good enough reason to like someone, especially if the quality we have in common is something we dislike in ourselves. Shy people, for example, may admire social extroverts and avoid introverts.

What makes an ideal partner?

Studies on what we look for in a potential partner show that men are more likely to value female physical attributes such as youth, beauty and slenderness and women are also likely to be interested in material and expressive qualities such as earning power, education and openness.

There are two ways of explaining these differences. From an evolutionary point of view, potential partners look for attributes that ensure the survival of their genes. Since a woman's childbearing capabilities are linked to age and health, attractive physical qualities such as vitality and a good figure are probable cues to her reproductive capacity. Because male fertility is not linked to age, women will look for the ability to provide for the family materially. Assets such as high income and education are indicators that men will be able to fulfill the role of provider. However, this role

■ **Initial fascination**. *We are excited superficially by an attractive appearance, more profoundly by the idea that behind the appearance lies a uniquely desirable personality.*

"IT WAS LOVE AT THIRD GLANCE"

■ *"Before I met John, I decided to stop dating. Constantly meeting new people, starting new relationships, and ending mediocre ones was just too much trouble. Then a friend introduced me to someone very special. When I met John, it wasn't love-at-first-glance, more like love-at-third-glance."*

is being challenged as an increasing number of educated single women are materially able to provide for their children alone. In Britain, recent statistics show that 15 percent of births are to single women.

Another explanation is that because women have been severely restricted in obtaining economic and political power in the past, they have traditionally gained upward mobility by marrying men of higher social and economic status. The male attraction to a woman's physical beauty reflects the cultural value attached to youth and good looks in most societies. One way for a man to enhance his status among other men is to have an attractive partner.

What you look for in a partner will have a bearing on the success of the relationship and how long it will last. If you continually choose partners for their looks or for their money or with whom you are competitive in attractiveness or economic power, the consequence may be a series of unstable relationships.

If you are looking for a long-term and lasting partnership, consider the durable and intrinsic qualities of the other person – not just their pretty face or expensive car. Beyond looks and status is a complicated human being. If the two of you discover that you share thoughts, attitudes and perceptions, then these are better clues to discovering if you are really right for each other.

Marriage can wait

When and where you will meet your life's partner are affected by social trends. For example, people now marry later. Census data in the United States show that in 1970 the average age at first marriage was 22.5 years for men and 20.6 years for women and in 1983 the averages had risen to 24.4 years for men and 22.5 years for women. This trend seems to have continued through the eighties, with people begin-

32

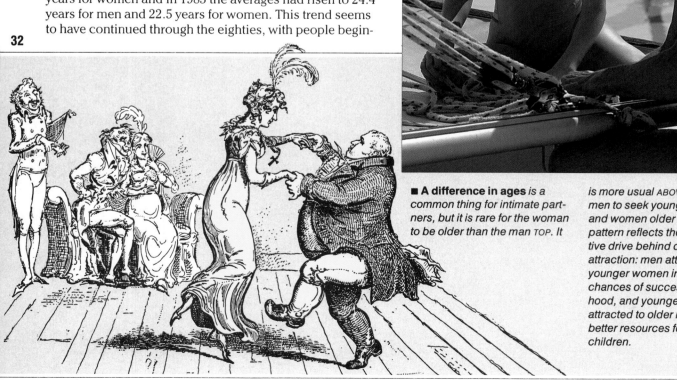

■ **A difference in ages** is a common thing for intimate partners, but it is rare for the woman to be older than the man TOP. It is more usual ABOVE and LEFT for men to seek younger partners and women older ones. This pattern reflects the reproductive drive behind opposite-sex attraction: men attracted to younger women improve their chances of successful fatherhood, and younger women attracted to older men secure better resources for their children.

Your chances of finding a partner depend partly on social trends ■ *In the past wars – today the rising expectations of better educated and better paid women – have upset the balance of suitable, available candidates.*

ning to look seriously for a partner in the surroundings in which they find themselves in their early or mid-twenties rather than their late teens.

Although these figures could partly be the result of people living together before deciding to marry, the postponement may also be caused by the fact that women are placing much greater value on education and career development (see *Ch 8*). Women are now likely to defer thoughts of marriage in favor of other achievements. They are also

becoming more selective in choosing whom they marry. Generally speaking, women have tended to marry men who are two or three years older and who have a comparable or better education and income. Now that there are more professional and educated women earning high salaries, there are fewer males in this category to go round.

The marriage squeeze

The discrepancy in the numbers of available men and women has led newspapers and magazines to refer to a "marriage squeeze." There are two ways of accounting for this. One explanation claims that men tend to reject women

THE MARRIAGE SQUEEZE

Opportunities to marry

Most men do not want to marry women who are more mature, earn more money and have a better education.

Most women are now more mature, earn more, have a better education. They still want to marry men who are at least their equals.

▶ **Breaking through barriers**. *In 1977, at the age of 25, Ellen K Lee became an assistant vice-president of a national investment and brokerage house and the first woman ever to represent such a firm on the floor of the New York Stock Exchange. The trend toward careers for women in finance and investment accelerated in most countries throughout the 1980s, with many single young women earning salaries far in excess of what the great majority of young men could match.*

33

of higher or even comparable status (for example, in age, income and education), and this leaves many mature, achievement-oriented single women without partners. A second explanation, however, points to the fact that such professional women are becoming more selective: they are unwilling to marry men who are not as well-educated as them or earn less than they do, and so they remain single. Also, evidence suggests that it is less acceptable for a woman to marry down than it is for a man. A man might marry his secretary but his female President is unlikely to marry him.

However, all is not lost. As the pool of available men and women of the same age and status decreases, it seems that the acceptable age-range for a potential partner may be widening. Recent books about women with younger partners suggest that what was once only acceptable for men, is becoming increasingly acceptable for women too. This may be true only up to a certain age, as men who want to have children will presumably look for a woman still young enough to bear them. Nevertheless, as women outlive men by an average of 7-8 years, selecting a much younger partner could ensure that a woman is less likely to be left a widow.

Where do people meet?

School and college used to be the common meeting places, but because people are now putting off marriage until their mid to late-twenties, the range of venues for finding a partner has expanded. Where can people find each other?

The greater the opportunity for face-to-face contact with others, the more likely the chances of developing a relationship. Physical proximity not only gives two people the direct opportunity to meet each other, it also allows them to observe and learn more about each other. Classic involve-

ments such as the boss-secretary affair can usually be accounted for by the two people's close proximity at work, which promotes familiarity. It is more likely to be the mundane chit-chat of daily encounters than the brief, intense whirlwind affair that builds the foundation for a serious relationship.

It is not uncommon to find marriage partners who met because they lived in nearby houses or in the same street. So, if you are actively looking for a partner you should perhaps consider working and living somewhere where you will have regular contact with other single people of the opposite sex. Since it is not always possible to arrange these conditions, other useful ways of meeting people are through activities such as involvement in sports clubs or special-interest groups – anything that encourages ongoing social contact.

Meeting through friends and work

Once they have left school or college, people do not have easily accessible ways of meeting other people with similar interests. Groups of relatives and friends will gradually make all the potential introductions among their members, exhausting any possibility of new dates. As mutual friends

HOW SINGLES TRY TO MEET

■ A study of 482 unmarried Canadian adults from urban areas, with average ages in their lower 30s, found that, overwhelmingly, they wished they had better opportunities to meet. Mainly, they met people through introductions by mutual friends, by going to parties, and through contact at work and in recreational activities. Less commonly used, and also considered inadequate by those who used them, were dating and advertising services, church and singles clubs.

Most common ways:

92%	Introductions by mutual friends
90%	Parties
82%	Workplace
80%	Activities, hobbies, sports

Least common ways:

10%	Dating services
20%	Advertisements
26%	Church groups
27%	Singles clubs

"I JOINED TO MEET MEN"

■ When I was a teenager I dated anything that moved. Selectivity was not a word in my vocabulary. But as I furthered my education and developed my own career – well, pressures of time and desire for quality relationships began to alter my social life. I decided that if I wanted to meet quality men, I had to look for quality situations. Because I strongly supported a local

Will your social network find you a partner?

■ *Friends and relatives may without success introduce you to all the possible matches they know* ■ *Married friends and those left behind when you move with your work may help little.*

■ **With a little help from your friends.** *LEFT Same-sex friends go together for moral support to a St Valentine's Day party in a London club. TOP Friends arrive on the doorstep with flowers and blind date.*

▶ **Meeting at work**. *With more women in the workforce and with job mobility leaving more people cut off from family and old friends, on-the-job self-introductions are becoming an increasingly important way for single people to meet.*

politician I got involved in his campaign, worked on various committees, attended several social events and met people from various walks of life. About two months ago, I met a really nice man in another political campaign and now we're dating. Although I consciously joined the campaign to meet men, it felt really great to be involved in something I believed in."

marry they provide less help to single friends in meeting new people: friendships between single and married people are difficult because couples tend to mix with other couples, children get in the way, arranging mutually free time is a problem and sometimes the single person does not get on with one of the partners (see *Ch 27*).

Also, people often move away from family and old friends as job mobility increases. The problem of isolation is made worse by the heavy demands some jobs place on young professionals. Long working hours, traveling and professional commitment can make it difficult for them to plan their free time and to socialize.

Employed people are likely to spend more time and meet more people at work than anywhere else. It is not surprising, therefore, that there are a large number of love relationships between colleagues. A relevant factor here is the increased number of women in the workforce and changing attitudes toward this type of relationship.

One study revealed that 31 percent of people had been involved in at least one romantic relationship at work. Although women in particular may find that their professional life is jeopardized by an office affair, there is some evidence to show that individual and teamwork performance can be improved by these relationships. Other col-

leagues are likely to show more disapproval and concern where the two people involved are of unequal status.

Seeking someone

A large population of older single people are still looking for partners and a courtship industry has grown around their needs. New technology has expanded the traditional methods of finding a companion. As well as advertisements and introduction agencies, computer dating bureaus and video services are available. Telephone companies also

SINGLES BARS ARE GREAT IF YOU WANT TO STAY SINGLE.

I don't. And I want a lady who doesn't either. So if you'd like to meet and get together, just send a picture and a short note to

Michael
℅ GPO Box 2331,
New York City,
New York 10017

■ **How to advertise.** *Michael Block* LEFT *may be too busy in his career as a New York advertising executive to get out and attract the attention of women in more time-honored ways* TOP, *but his profession gives him the know-how to make his need for a partner known. If you decide to advertise, try reading other people's advertisements first and learn from the wording of* those you think people would answer. Do not specifically mention marriage, but show that you are looking for a serious relationship. Be honest but not negative about yourself. Choose a newspaper or magazine read fairly exclusively by the kind of person you are looking for.

WHY ADVERTISE?

20% Advertising was a last resort		8% I had just moved to the city
33% Preferable to singles bars		61% Advertising is convenient

Most commercial introductions do not lead to relationships ■ Many who use the services are looking for too ideal a partner ■ A minority find that the counseling services of good agencies help them reconcile expectations and reality.

operate "chat lines" where you can speak to other subscribers and make new contacts. In France, the Minitel public computer system enables people to advertise for and connect up with other people also looking for a relationship. In Britain, in 1989, the main telephone company stopped offering a personal contact service after accusations that the company was encouraging lonely people to run up excessive telephone bills.

Personal advertisements have a long and respected tradition in countries such as India, and pioneer farmers in Australia and the United States used to advertise for wives to join them. However, until fairly recently, advertising for a partner was confined to fringe publications in most Western countries. That situation has changed drastically and now major newspapers and magazines such as the *National Review* and *New York Review of Books* carry a personal section. In Britain in 1988 three magazines – *Time Out*, *Private Eye* and *Singles* – between them published over 30,000 lonely hearts advertisements and forwarded over half a million replies. A feature article on marriage advertisements recently appeared in an issue of *Soviet Life*.

The effectiveness of this sort of advertising is increased by the target marketing of the magazines themselves. In New York there is a publication called *Chocolate Singles* that helps blacks meet other blacks and one called *Mother Earth* that brings together people who value rural living. A great many other publications around the world are aimed at specific religious, educational, ethnic and sexual preferences.

Is advertising an admission of defeat?

Are the advertisers in the personal columns lonely or just well-organized? Many people still consider this approach as either an admission of defeat or as sexually deviant, but research into the new wave of advertisers indicates that they

---

USER-FRIENDLY DATING

■ *Do you want to be systematic about choosing a partner? Computer dating could be the answer. Fill in the questionnaire about your interests and your personality, and the computer will supply you with a list of possible partners with matching traits. It could not be simpler. But be warned. Relationships are complex. People need to match their thinking and emotions. Finding out if you are attracted in these extra ways takes time. The best a computer can do is introduce you to possible partners. Only the two of you, by learning how to interact, and learning about each other in a detail that you yourselves will find difficult to express, can discover if a relationship is possible.* **RB**

▼ Reasons people give for advertising: *the motives of 52 men and 45 women using the personal columns of a Canadian newspaper. They also valued advertising for allowing them to screen candidates while remaining anonymous.*

13% due to shyness
23% lack of time
35% did not meet people
in daily routine

54% I have difficulty meeting people

It is a good way to meet people

▲ "Women needed for the purpose of marriage" *was the straightforward advertisement in two regional newspapers that led to this and other engagements in the north-eastern* Spanish village of Plan. Men of the village advertised after a female migration to urban centers left a total of 142 bachelor farmers and shepherds with only three single women of marriageable age to court. In three busloads, 150 prospective wives visited the village as guests at a bachelor's party.

are fairly representative of the whole single population. Some people believe this way of meeting someone to be more rational than waiting for a random encounter with the "right" person, especially given the constraints on time posed by a busy professional life.

An analysis of the content of heterosexual singles advertisements reveals that most of them are looking for a genuine and serious relationship. A Canadian study of 98 advertisers aged between 30 and 39 found that 46 percent were looking for a long-term relationship and 29 percent wanted friendship. A study of gay magazines found that 53 percent of the advertisers sought faithful, lasting relationships.

Most personal advertisements have a numerical code and do not give names or addresses. In this way the advertisers can remain anonymous and can screen the replies. People who have used this type of service usually report that even if they do not meet their special person, they do expand their contact with other people and make new friends.

Matchmakers and introduction agencies

It is not uncommon for people to claim that they are a "matchmaker" for their family and friends, yet few of these people would ever think of charging money for their help in bringing two mutual acquaintances together. However, there are commercial organizations that perform much the same function on a large scale. These are the "introductory services" whose creative organizational names include the subtle and the more explicit – *Intimates*, *Partners*, *Connections*, *Moving Singles*, *Old Friends* (for the over 40s). Their services range from nonselective arrangements whereby

"WHY I MATCHMAKE"

■ *"I drive my husband crazy. Yes, another dinner party, one more call, an invitation to a concert. I'm always trying to fix up my single friends, my divorced friends, my widowed friends. Sometimes, I lose friends this way. Sometimes they get insulted or embarrassed by my choices and refuse to speak to me again. When this happens, my husband tells me, "See – I told you so. It's none of your business." This is the risk. But what's really funny is that occasionally mismatches convert into romance. And when my instincts are on target I can almost predict a marriage. This is the reward. In my day, parents tried to make arrangements."*

"WHY I USE AN INTRODUCTION SERVICE"

■ *"I'm a romantic like anyone else. But quite frankly, I've exhausted all my friends for blind dates and there are few women to meet at my job. I imagine meeting "her" while picking out grapefruits in my local market. But that's a million-to-one chance and I don't have the time for random chance.*

Joining an introduction service at least puts me in the ballpark and although I haven't met that special someone, I have met some very nice women. Sure it's a bit awkward, but I'm not into the bar scene anymore. Anyway, in the nontraditional approaches your intentions are clear, and hopefully so are hers."

■ **International marriage travel agency**. At this German agency ABOVE clients begin their search by stating the nationality they prefer in a partner. RIGHT After exchanging photographs and letters, a first meeting at Frankfurt Airport.

Introduction agencies say that unrealistic expectations are the main cause of disappointment with the results of their services.

Are the advertisers in the personal columns lonely losers, or well-organized? ■ *They are representative of the whole population* ■ *Many busy professionals argue that this is a more rational, less random, way of looking for a match* ■ *About half of the advertisers are genuinely looking for a long-term relationship.*

clients simply mail in their request, to highly screened, in-depth interviews with individual clients.

The services offered by these organizations vary from arranging weekend dates to finding the client a permanent partner. The personnel adopt a variety of approaches from the old-fashioned, "godmother" image to semi-therapeutic "counselors," "consultants" and "directors."

An investigation into a nonprofit-making Jewish introduction service showed that out of 157 applicants, 43 percent were in their twenties, 44 percent were between 30 and 35 and the remaining 13 percent were older. The service caters to professionals. Far from being loners and losers, these people have strong social ties, numerous personal interests and are very involved in their professions. Why do they go to a matchmaker?

Some clients come to the service at times of seasonal change such as holidays or following family reunions or weddings. These seem to be times for reassessing their romantic status.

Other people use the service when they change jobs or cities, after a period of traveling or when they have successfully achieved a career goal.

These reasons are closely linked to the fact that many clients use the service when there is a change in their existing relationship such as divorce or when they realize that they are not meeting potential long-term partners from among their current dating partners.

Designer dating

Enlisting the aid of a matchmaker is viewed by many as a form of consulting. Young professionals value the efficiency of the approach and they use the "consultant" in their private lives just as they do in their professional lives. They even describe the procedure in marketplace metaphors – "like going to a broker to invest," doing "target marketing" and "finding a headhunter."

These young people find many advantages in going to a matchmaker. They see it as a way of exercising control over their lives and not leaving everything to chance. They also find it helpful to talk over with a third party just what they are looking for in a partner.

Meeting new people helps them develop social skills and build self-confidence, and some contacts lead to an increased social circle.

There are disadvantages, however. There is always the risk of rejection and disappointment and some people feel a sense of futility after several months of introducing themselves to new people, always hoping that this time they have found *the* person.

According to one matchmaker it is these unrealistic expectations that lead most often to disappointments – many people find it difficult to reconcile their ideal partner with the real partner, and as a result, most introductions do not lead to subsequent dates. The same source feels it is critical for people seeking a partner for life to assess their own personal strengths and weaknesses honestly and have clear, reasonable, attainable priorities for what they are looking for in that partner. **MBA EAB**

▶ **AIDS-free introduction service.** *Many people who use dating services see them as a way of exercising control over their lives – for example, making sure that everyone at the cocktail party they attend has had a negative result in a recent test for the AIDS virus. Introduction services providing this kind of screening are multiplying, but you should be aware that people can be infected with the virus for six weeks to nine months before producing a positive blood-test result.*

Pairing Off

WHEN couples pair off, a special kind of relationship begins to form – a private one that concerns two people to the exclusion of all others. At this stage it is noncommittal. Dating and interacting as a pair gives us the opportunity to learn about each other and decide how seriously to consider the prospect of a deeper relationship. If closeness develops, it may lead to genuine courtship.

The question that is uppermost in our minds might be "Will we fall in love?" In practical terms, however, we are pairing off to see whether we have enough in common to get along together; to see whether we match up to each other's and society's ideals of the benefits we should provide to each other as a couple; to see whether we will be able to agree, if we settle permanently with each other, on the way

we will make decisions and share out such roles as that of breadwinner or cook.

The relationship is special to the couple, but not out of the ordinary. When dating we tend to conform to society's expectations about couples, even at the serious courtship stage. Two people who are deeply in love but only 20 years old may break off their relationship because everyone thinks they are too young to get married. Two other people, aged 28 but with less depth of emotion, may decide to get married simply because all their friends are married.

Dating and courtship also have a built-in failure rate. It is a time for experiment, when we test whether we think we could form a permanent relationship with our current partner. Few tests are successful at first and we must occasion-

▲ **Experiments in pairing off.** *On a bright summer's day out adolescents explore experimental couple relationships. Commitment is low but interest is high – there is curiosity, excitement and uncertainty about the possibility of becoming close.*

SEVEN WAYS OF GETTING CLOSER

■ *Researchers have identified seven strategies that people use to make others like them and feel closer to them.*

"I'm someone special." Show that you are in control – make decisions, take the initiative and act generously toward your partner. Make an effort to look your best and be interesting when you are with them

"Let's trust each oth» Show that you can be trusted by being open thus encouraging the other person to share confidences with you. Always keep promises

How do you move from meeting someone to loving them? ■ *Dating and courtship teach us how to become close and show us with whom we are likely to stay close* ■ *Longer courtships are the most useful.*

ally expect relationships not to be satisfactory – by the age of 22, the average American student has had between three and four serious "love" relationships.

Looking beyond appearances

When we date someone we constantly test them to see if they share our own attitudes and values and if we have compatible personalities. To begin with we check the similarity of their background to our own, then we move on to discuss our views on certain key issues that we find important. Although we will probably first have been attracted to our

▲ **A shoulder to lay your head on.** *Having become a couple, this Romanian pair find that opportunities for becoming closer occur again and again, simply because they spend so much time together.*

■ **Sharing our interests and our pleasures** *draws us together. At the fair or the beach couples test whether they can enjoy each other's company and enthusiasms.*

41

ow it's your turn." your partner take ntrol – do not interrupt ir conversation, and pond with interest to at they are saying

"Let's have fun together." Include your partner in your social activities and make your encounters as positive as possible. "I belong to a sports club. Why don't you come with me?"

"See how much I care." Be supportive and sensitive. Listen to your partner. Bolster their self-confidence and take their side in arguments

"See how close we are." Try to include yourself in your partner's interests and activities. Hint that you are closer to your partner than might actually be the case

"Birds of a feather flock together." Show your partner how alike you are, and that you feel at ease in their company. Point out things to your partner that you have in common

partner by their looks, these soon become less important than their beliefs and how we get on together.

It seems that the longer people date each other before marriage, the greater their chances of having a happy and stable life together. The longer the partners are together the more time they have to develop communication skills.

We can use these skills even when telling each other about negative feelings (see *Ch20*). Research into pre-marital relationships has shown that the amount of conflict a couple experiences during dating and the way they express their negative feelings will set the pattern for their future relationship. We learn during dating that a certain amount of disagreement is an inevitable part of any rela-tionship and we are able to practice communicating oppo-site points of view and negative emotions. It is a good time to acquire problem-solving skills and to learn that we can disagree without damaging our relationship.

Handling taboo subjects

Is the dating phase of your relationship the right time to see how open you can be with each other? Even though many people are completely open with their partner, many others hold back information. Taboo topics are usually those that we feel might damage or give misleading im-pressions about our relationship. One particular topic that we are most likely to avoid is how we feel about the state of the relationship. This is quite surprising because this infor-mation might be helpful. For example, John may be afraid to tell Jane that he is not happy with their sexual relationship

There are ways of finding out whether the relationship is going somewhere ■ *Ask someone your partner confides in, or who knows them well and understands their moods* ■ *How does your partner react to public displays of affection?* ■ *Does separation make your partner's heart grow fonder?*

in case he drives her away, even though if Jane knew this was how he felt, she might be able to discuss with him how they could improve the situation.

We also tend to avoid talking about other things we fear might damage our relationship – what we do when we are not together, how we feel about the way we should treat each other and previous relationships – in fact, anything that might cause a disagreement. This is very shortsighted: it is possible that if we avoid these subjects when we are dating we will never resolve them. If they come up again later – when we are married or living with our partner and we have to face them – the consequences could be serious. Issues that we shied away from will have had time to fester into problems that might even cause breakdown and separation.

The costs of ending an established relationship are far greater than they would have been at the dating stage. It is much easier to disagree with your partner during courtship when the most you have to lose is a companion. The same problem in a marriage could lead to divorce, separation from children, loss of income and home and a host of other traumatic experiences (see *Ch12*). It is much better to try to talk over problems and difficult issues as soon as they arise.

◀ **Testing reactions** to a public show of affection is one way that uncertain couples gauge how their relationship is going. Will your partner draw away, accept your gesture noncom-mittally, or reciprocate – show-ing a readiness to allow the two of you to be linked in other people's minds as a couple? Will your friends' reactions reinforce or discourage your decision to choose this partner?

Is it getting serious?

If you cannot discuss openly with each other how you are getting along together, just how do you find out if the relationship is working? Many people use a variety of less direct ways to get feedback on the state of their relationship. One common way is to ask mutual friends or acquaintances if they know how your partner feels about you. If the friends say "He told me that he really enjoys being with you," or "She feels she is seeing too much of you at the moment," it gives you a clue as to where the relationship is going. Another sign comes from physical contact. You can often get an idea of how comfortable your partner is with you by their reaction to the way you touch them. If they move away, then perhaps they do not feel as close to you as you do to them or perhaps they do not feel ready for such a level of intimacy. Their reaction allows you to consider whether or not you want to increase your involvement with them.

A further way to test the state of the relationship is to observe your partner's reaction to a public display of affection. If, when you introduce your partner to a group of friends as "my boyfriend/girlfriend," they are not happy with your definition of how things stand, you should be able to tell from the way they react.

Some people use more negative means of testing their relationship. One of these is to deliberately criticize themselves in the hope of getting reassurance or a compliment from their partner. They might say something like "Oh, I can't do anything right," expecting their partner to reply

■ **Who is more in earnest,** *the couple in the photograph* LEFT *or in the engraving* TOP? *The couple in the photograph may not know either. Although they are close, the freedom of today's customs may leave them uncertain of each other's intentions. They may learn about these in a less explicit way than the old-fashioned couple in the engraving, who are more likely to be involved in a consideration of serious commitments, which rules and traditions require them to discuss explicitly, once the relationship reaches a definite point.*

43

THIS TIME IT'S FOR REAL

■ *There are three basic patterns of courtship. All of them suggest that courtship is an important period in the success or failure of the eventual marriage.*
Rocky-road relationships. *The partners take a relatively long time to reach commitment with frequent "ups and downs" along the way. There is a high level of conflict and questioning "Is this relationship really for me?" The partners are often young and may also face opposition from parents to the marriage.*
Fast-worker relationships. *The partners progress from dating to commitment in just a few weeks or months. (These relationships are not likely to lead to the best marriages.) The partners are older than other couples and are more likely to feel parental or social pressure to get married. They communicate less and seem less involved with each other. They never learn before marriage how to have a constructive argument and may have less stable and less happy marriages in the long run.*
Cautious partners. *The partners seem to be wary of getting too involved to begin with but once they feel secure they move rapidly to commitment. The partners are often somewhat older than most couples when they meet.*

They are very aware of the costs of making a mistake. Their initial caution allows them to weigh up the relationship and they proceed with little conflict to marriage. **RMC**

"Don't be stupid, I think you're wonderful." Others will test their relationship by spending time apart. If the separation makes their hearts grow fonder, they are likely to believe that the relationship is strong.

Many people use tests of faithfulness in order to assess the strength of their liaisons. They watch the way their partner behaves toward other potential partners. If their partner shows signs of being attracted to another person, it indicates to them that their partner is not fully committed. **RMC**

The time of courtship

In Western cultures, we have come to expect that before marriage there will be a period of courtship. We see this as a stage between casual dating and full commitment in which we can test that we are sufficiently well-matched to make a successful marriage. We tend to spend a relatively fixed amount of time in courtship – somewhere between nine months and two or three years is "about right." We expect courting couples to be young rather than very old – when two 85-year-olds get married, it is thought unusual enough to rate a news story. Courting couples are usually of a similar age, so the story of the 65-year-old who courts a 19-year-old also hits the headlines.

People who marry for a second time do not always have lengthy courtships. Second courtships are unlikely to last

■ *If the relationship is failing, they may decide to break up*

COURTING CONFLICT

A dating couple learn about their own and their partner's personalities – a testing ground

A married couple can assess the seriousness of the problem and put it into perspective

C O N F L I C T

The couple may use conflict to re-evaluate their relationship

But learning to discuss problems can create a rapport – the basis for a stable marriage

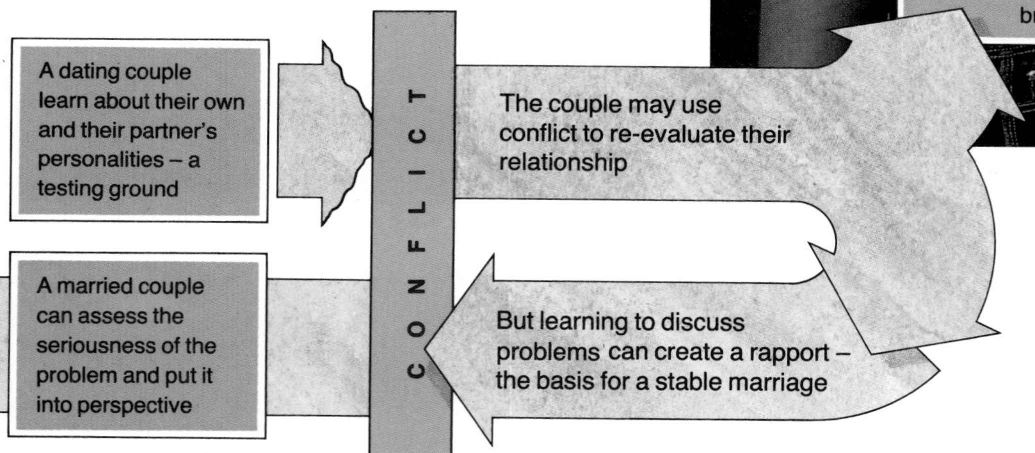

■ *When a couple is dating, the more they air disagreements the better. Learning how to argue without anger or resentment can improve the relationship and time together will not have been wasted. But if the problem is serious they may consider parting. Couples who go on to marry, hoping that taboo subjects will disappear, could face a much more painful breakup in the future.*

■ *Couples react to conflict in different ways according to the stage of their relationship. The courting couple constantly need to assess the health of their relationship – they need to discuss problems to see how things are going between them. They may see conflict as a reason for ending the relationship or as a reason for re-evaluating its progress.*

However, when a dispute arises *between married partners, they do not always talk about it. Having experienced many disagreements, they know that conflict is bound to arise from time to time in their partnership and they are able to judge whether or not the problem is a serious one. Past experience has shown them that conflict is not necessarily a threat to the relationship and they feel secure enough to let some quarrels ride.* **RMC**

44

After the decision to get serious, a time for serious reconsideration ■ *Courtship is a time for learning how you would handle conflicts and for learning what roles your partner will expect each of you to play in the long run.*

longer than six months. They are also more likely than first courtships to have been arranged through a special meeting method such as dating services, singles' bars or personal advertisements. It seems from this that the second time around, people have learned how to take shortcuts through the stages of the courting process.

Some things are worth fighting about

Couples use courtship as a way of filtering each other through a series of screening processes. This is a crucial period in their relationship when they can take important decisions about their future life together. At an advanced stage of the filtering process, the two partners will be trying to sort out joint beliefs about particular problems – namely who does what and how. They are working out the roles of "husband" and "wife" and trying to match their own expectations with those of their partner (see *Ch23*). If there is any one time in a long-term relationship to establish exactly what each partner expects of the other, this is it. Clearly, for the marriage to work, the couple must reach agreement about these two pivotal roles and how they fit together.

It is a common fallacy that courtships are based purely on love and that they will only succeed if they are free from conflict. The truth is more that some kinds of conflict are actually good for the eventual marriage (see *Ch12*). A dispute about roles, for example, can be dealt with in a positive way and the couple can successfully resolve their original differences. If they can do this they know that they can cope with other disagreements. Such conflict will not only be rewarding, it will have a beneficial future effect.

Couples in serious courting relationships are often quite remarkably similar in background. They usually come from the same socioeconomic group, have had the same sorts of educational experiences, often share the same religious beliefs, have more or less similar political views, are usually of the same race and within about four years of each other in age (see *Ch3*).

Some people also believe that couples are usually made up of partners who have similar personalities and that these people tend to have happier marriages than those who are not similar. But it is difficult to know whether these couples find that they are similar during courtship and therefore get married, or whether people who get married gradually grow more like each other with time.

Other people are convinced that opposites attract and that it is important for couples not to be too alike. One American study found that couples tended to be made up of

45

◄ **Intensifying your shared interests** *helps a relationship grow. A couple enjoy a visit to the Metropolitan Museum of Art in New York. Not only will they enjoy learning from each other by seeing through each other's eyes, but they will learn about each other, discovering how compatible their opinions and attitudes are likely to be in the long run. Couples with similar tastes grow close, and couples who want to be close develop similar tastes.*

a dominant and a submissive partner or a supportive and a dependent partner. The success of their relationships came from the balance between their characteristics. **SD**

"Will sex harm or help our relationship?"

It is often claimed that the 20th century has seen a "sexual revolution" among unmarried people with more and more couples having sexual relationships before marriage. However, a closer look at the surveys reveals that if there has been any such revolution, it has been a revolution mainly for women. Since the 1960s when oral contraceptives became widely available, the percentage of men who had intercourse before marriage has not changed drastically but there has been a dramatic increase in the number of women who have chosen to have premarital intercourse. This does not necessarily mean that women are being more promiscuous. In fact, researchers find that most American women have had only one sexual partner before marriage. Although men generally have more premarital sexual partners than women, there is no evidence to suggest that their premarital sexual activity should be uniformly seen as promiscuous.

▲ **Conflicts about sex** may arise when it becomes a bargaining issue, a young man demanding sexual intimacy as a sign that he is valued, a young woman demanding a strong long-term commitment in return. Conflict may increase after sexual intimacy has been established simply because the couple feel more confident about speaking openly.

DECIDING ABOUT SEX

■ *The personal experiences of four young women are representative of four basic patterns of transition to a sexual relationship.*

Instant lovers. *"I met my current boyfriend at a fraternity party and was immediately attracted to him. Afterwards we went up to his room and we got to kissing and touching a little. Maybe it was just hormones, but I could feel an energy flowing between us! I was so attracted to him and I was sure he was attracted to me. So, I told him I didn't have any reservations and wanted to go to bed with him."* Only a small percentage of lovers have sex on their first date.

Little-by-little lovers. *"The first time I met him I wasn't attracted to him. Over a three-month period we got to know each other better but nothing was happening physically. After we had been seeing each other for another couple of months our physical relationship began to grow. At first all we did was kiss and caress each other. During the next few months he began to want to do more physically intimate things. Then one night as we were kissing and caressing we decided that having intercourse was the logical next step for our relationship."* These couples move step-by-step to increased levels of intimacy. As the relationship becomes more serious they will have intercourse.

Hesitant lovers. *"I've been dating my present boyfriend for about six months. We were working in the same place, which allowed us to get to know each other pretty well. Then he asked me out to a movie but nothing happened physically. In fact, only after going out for more than two weeks, did he finally kiss me goodnight. When we talked about sex it was evident that he was quite experienced, while I was rather naive on the subject. We dated at a casual level for four more months without much physical interaction but we realized that we meant something special to each other. When my parents loaned us their beach house for a weekend, we had intercourse for the first time."* These couples usually do no more than kiss on the first date, then indulge in fondling and petting during casual dating. They dramatically increase their sexual involvement to include intercourse at the stage of commitment.

Reluctant lovers. *"I first met my boyfriend at a college church function. On our next date we went bowling. When he walked me to the door that night, he gave me a small kiss on the cheek. After that, we dated for three years and became quite close emotionally, but not sexually. I also had strong religious convictions and knew that having sex was not the right thing to do. On our wedding night we had intercourse for the first time."* Many of these couples do not even kiss on the first date, although they are usually kissing during casual dating. By the time they are dating seriously they will often indulge in petting but will not have intercourse until they are married. **RMC**

Will premarital sex affect the success or the failure of a courtship? ■ *Not measurably* ■ *Practice at good communication and joint management is a more important groundwork than practice at love-making* ■ *You are just as likely to stay together or part whether or not your courtship includes sex.*

Many considerations come into a person's decision whether or not to have sex before marriage. They may or may not have moral or religious objections; they may or may not be particularly attracted to their partner. A secondary concern is likely to be the question of whether or not having sex will work against the relationship. One study of couples who were dating found that whether a couple had sex early in a relationship, late in a relationship or not at all, did not affect whether they stayed together over a two-year period. This confirms something that family scientists have suspected for years – the quality and stability of a relationship is based on much more than sex, although sex is an important part of any committed relationship.

An investigation of whether having sex during dating affects the relationship if the couple gets married, drew the

same conclusions. In a study of adolescents over a seven to ten-year period, researchers found that the age at which people first had intercourse was not related to their later sexual adjustment. Over half of these people were married at the end of the study. It is factors other than sex, such as communication and problem-solving skills, that form the firm foundation for good permanent relationships.

How sex can lead to conflict

Many couples start to argue more when they start going "all the way" together sexually. In some cases this conflict may be caused by a bargaining situation, where the woman thinks "I'm not going to have sex with this guy until he shows that he's serious about me," while the man is thinking "If she wants me to be committed to our relationship, she should be willing to have sex with me." When each partner realizes what the other is thinking, it is easy to see how a quarrel might arise. For other couples, though, this increased fighting and bickering may be a spin-off from their increased intimacy. They may now feel close enough to begin bargaining and talking about everything. **RMC**

▲ **Once the decision to have sex is made**, what effect will it have on the future of the relationship? Studies have found that the age at which people first have intercourse does not affect their later sexual adjustment, and whether a couple have sex early, later or not at all during a two-year period does not affect the likelihood of their staying together for this time.

47

Love and Commitment

MOST OF US like to think of our love for our partner and our commitment to them as inseparable. We usually view love as the main basis for a romantic commitment and, conversely, we often regard commitment as a "test" of our love. On the other hand, love and commitment are clearly separable in many cases. Love does not always result in a long-term commitment, for example, and most of us have had at least one relationship where our feelings of love carried on long after commitment had been abandoned.

Romantic love has been discussed by philosophers through the ages, from the time of Plato onward. It is only in the last 20 years, however, that it has been the subject of research in the social sciences. Indeed, since the mid-1970s there has been a virtual explosion of psychological and sociological investigations of love, from the most technical university studies to the enormous variety of self-help books now available. Psychologists and sociologists believe that by defining love and commitment, and the ways in which they interact, they can help us to understand better our own romantic relationships.

What is love like?

You may decide you are in love because you actually feel physically different. A warm glow or the conviction that colors are brighter and emotions more intense or the feeling of being more alive than ever before are common experiences. "Love is the elation you feel when you've made your partner happy," says one woman. Another may say that she feels beautiful, vibrant, more healthy than she did before she met her partner. Not all physical reactions to love make you feel so good, though; lovers often speak of negative responses, such as feelings of nervousness, butterflies in the stomach or loss of appetite.

In addition to these feelings, there is also a great variety of

attitudes that you may associate with love, such as: your physical desire to be with your partner, your emotional concern for them, and your wish to share your life with them. One way of considering your love for your partner is to look carefully at each of these attitudes – attachment, caring and intimacy – and examine its role as a component of your love.

When you are in love you may not bring particular feelings and attitudes together in the same way as someone else might – or even the way your lover does. Loving is a matter of individual experience. For instance, it may be vital to you that your partner is attractive, whereas your friends may not care so much about their partners' looks. They may insist on someone who can make them laugh, or brings out the best side of them, or gives them a warm glow of affection.

DOES LOVE LAST?

■ RIGHT Carving their initials on a tree is this young couple's way of affirming their commitment to love each other always. If the relationship does last, they may in the end love each other in ways that they did not at first expect. Passion and attraction tend to be intense in the early days of a romantic attachment, but in some surveys, romantic and passionate behavior – exchanges of compliments, saying "I love you," sharing emotions and sexual intercourse – decline by about a third in the first year of marriage. FAR RIGHT A more companionable and practical love may begin to take over, however, and commitment to this less romantic sharing may increase with the years, as stability comes to be valued over passion. In marriages that last, partners show little decline between the early years following the honeymoon and old age, in either the passion or the friendship they feel for each other (see Ch15).

What is the meaning of love? How committed are you to your own? ■ *Should your love be analyzed, classified, defined?* ■ *By unraveling the complexities of this key experience, social scientists hope to help us find happiness.*

Another way of looking at love is from the outside rather than the inside: in other words, how you behave. This may be the way you show your physical attraction to your partner, the way you express your friendship and intimacy, or the games you play – like "playing hard to get" or being secretive about past relationships. Your love may involve just one of these types of behavior or a combination.

How do people show their love?

Love also involves communication. For example, we tell our partners that we love them, talk out problems and share emotions and feelings. Communication is not merely a way of expressing our love, it is also an important part of the love itself. Lovers often talk about their thoughts and feelings and concentrate on each other. More so than friends, lovers spend time just being together, sharing their lives. They communicate in subtle ways (see *Ch 2*).

Many lovers communicate their love for each other through nonverbal signals. It is evident in the sound of their voice, the look in their eyes, or the way they smile or dress. This way of expressing love – which is sometimes known as an intuitive style of loving (see p51) – although difficult to define exactly, remains an important part of the love experience for many lovers.

Should your love be classified?

Sometimes, categorizing the kind of love you feel helps you to make sense of it (see, for example, the six categories on p51), but you cannot always tidy your feelings away so easily. For instance, you may not always experience love in the same way. You may feel intuitive love with one partner and then, in another relationship, experience collaborative love.

A variation like this is possible even within one relationship as it develops over time. Also, a love experience may be a combination of various different ways of loving. This is not surprising as love is an experience that involves our complete self. In fact, combinations are more likely than not and we should expect them.

An added complication is that within the partnership, the two people involved may have different ways of experiencing love. Although it does seem that collaborative and expressive lovers would be most compatible with similar partners, this is not necessarily true of the other types.

Love and the way we communicate it are both complex processes and no list of six love patterns can adequately

account for the success or failure of individual relationships. Nevertheless, if we can identify which groups we belong to, we may find it easier to solve our relationship problems. For example, we may understand why we are incompatible with certain partners.

How committed are you?

If love is difficult to define, commitment is equally so. What do we mean by commitment? Two questions spring to mind: Commitment to what? For how long?

One aspect of commitment is the stability of a relationship over time. When we commit ourselves to our partner,

we often mean that we will do whatever we can to ensure that the relationship will continue, and that we will not abandon it when problems arise.

The other aspect of commitment for most of us is that we promise fidelity. We tell our partner that we will not get involved in romantic or sexual activities with anyone else. It seems that in spite of the sexual revolution, exclusiveness is still an important part of commitment in most relationships.

Commitment is complex, and stability and fidelity may take different forms. Many patterns of behavior, thought and emotion are possible and, as in romantic love, they may exist in different combinations in different relationships.

IS YOUR LOVE PASSIONATE OR COMPANIONATE?

■ *Researchers have defined two basic forms of love – passionate and companionate. Passionate love is spontaneous, emotionally intense and focused on physical attraction. Companionate love is more stable and relaxed, and focused on deep friendship and concern.*

How can you determine whether your feelings are passionate or companionate? One area to consider is whether you express your love for each other openly. Passionate partners generally display their love publicly – for example, embracing or holding hands while walking in the street. Companionate partners are less emotionally expressive.

Passionate partners often refer to "love at first sight." Their initial attraction is likely to be sudden and based on physical appearance. Companionate love develops more slowly and partners are unlikely to remember a particular moment of "falling in love."

Your attitudes are also significant. If you tend to idealize your partner, focusing on their good points and minimizing their faults, your love is passionate. If, however, you see your partner as being "special" rather than perfect, your feelings are probably companionate – you may exaggerate your partner's good points but are also aware of their weaknesses.

While companionate lovers are happy to develop separate interests, passionate partners tend to view independent activities as potentially threatening to the relationship. They are likely to make statements such as "I couldn't live without you," and may experience jealousy or suspicion. Companionate partners feel more trust and cope better with separations. They more often remain friends if the relationship breaks up.

Most couples experience a combination of passionate and companionate love. And, since relationships are not static, the degree to which you experience each kind of love may change over time.

Research suggests that men feel more passion than women, and women feel more friendship than men. This contradicts the image of women as the romantic ones. There is also some evidence that passionate partners – men or women – are most willing to accept traditional sex-role distinctions.

Is your partner "special," or perfect? ■ *If you merely exaggerate your partner's good points, while accepting that they have weak points, your love is probably "companionate," a sounder base for a long-term commitment than passion.*

The most common way of expressing commitment is the pledge or vow. Before they make the public and formal commitment of wedding vows many lovers will exchange private informal pledges. They will say "I'll never leave you" or "I'll always care." What you talk about may also reveal your commitment to each other. You may discuss your future together, for example, having children or what you will do when you are older.

It is not only the way you act with your own partner but how you behave with other people that reflects your commitment to a relationship. For instance, if you go to a party and spend the whole evening flirting with your partner's best friend, your commitment may not be very deep. If you

SIX WAYS OF LOVING

Collaborative love *is shown by supportiveness and negotiation between partners. The help and support you give makes you both stronger and more powerful — a combined force. As one lover put it: "Love gives me energy (too much!) and keeps my heart racing whenever I think of him."*

Active love *shows itself through increased confidence and social participation. Active lovers do lots of things together. Their feeling of activity was highlighted when active lovers were asked to describe their love in terms of a rhythm. They frequently said that their love was erratic or moving faster.*

Intuitive love *involves a high level of nonverbal communication. Intuitive lovers can show their love without having to express it in words. They use eye contact, facial expressions, a certain tone of voice to reassure each other that they care. "I can see she loves me, she doesn't have to say anything."*

Committed love *involves some kind of agreement between partners that they will stay together. Committed lovers will spend time with each other and will discuss and plan their future together. "It's wanting to be with that special person no matter what you ought to be doing."*

Expressive love *is communicated. You know you are in love at the moment you have the urge to say "I love you"; when you do special things for your partner; when you discuss your feelings; and when you negotiate your differences. As one lover says: "To me, love is all the little signs of love we make to each other."*

Traditional romantic love *causes partners to feel more beautiful and more healthy. They feel committed to building a future together. This love is called traditional and romantic because it seems to reflect the idealized notions of love that have always been common in art and literature.*

51

WHAT KIND OF LOVE DO YOU FEEL?

■ *TOP Classifications of ways of loving may provide you with some insight into your own relationship. Do not be surprised if you do not exactly fit one of these patterns. Every love is unique. The first and the second times you are in love can be very different, and a love that lasts seldom stays the same.*

■ *RIGHT Love can be analyzed into feelings, thoughts and acts of love, but many people would say that the whole experience is greater than the sum of these parts.*

◄ **Feeling the excitement of passionate love** *is one of the most important ways we have of knowing that our relationship is not just friendship, but something more special. However, happily married couples report that their partner is also their* *friend – the most rewarding and most stable couple relationships are those that meet a wide range of the participants' needs, including not just the need for romance but the need for affection and loyal companionship.*

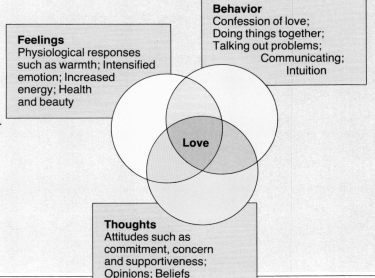

Feelings
Physiological responses such as warmth; Intensified emotion; Increased energy; Health and beauty

Behavior
Confession of love; Doing things together; Talking out problems; Communicating; Intuition

Love

Thoughts
Attitudes such as commitment, concern and supportiveness; Opinions; Beliefs

In spite of the sexual revolution, we still expect commitment ■ *Most people want their partners to make the relationship last and to avoid becoming romantically or sexually involved with someone else.*

actually have sex with another person, your commitment is even more doubtful.

Commitment can also involve thoughts and attitudes. The most important of these is the value you attach to feeling that you should stay together, and that you should go on to make new commitments to each other. When you want a relationship to continue or when you would like to extend it further – such as taking on the responsibilities of having children – you may say that you are becoming more committed to that relationship. Along with the commitment as it stands, there is your expectation of where it is going. You expect your relationship to continue and your partner to remain faithful. Again, as expectations about the future of a relationship increase, so does the degree of commitment that you feel to that relationship.

If you have ever been committed to a partner you will probably be no stranger to feelings of despair and fear when you are separated from them for some reason, or if something threatens your relationship. Conversely, you feel content when your partner is nearby and your relationship seems solid. Another negative feeling that commitment may bring is guilt. Some people are made aware of their commitment only when they feel guilty about being physically attracted to someone else and this guilt assures them of their commitment to their partner.

Because we are all individuals, however, different people will probably experience their commitment in different ways. One person may be very strongly committed to their partner in terms of their thoughts and feelings, and yet the way they behave may seem to be at odds with how they feel. Someone else may behave in a way suggesting commitment but may not feel the emotions that we generally associate with commitment. Another person may think, feel and act in a committed way. There is no one sign that can indicate whether you and your partner are committed and no one experience that is common to all committed relationships.

Love with and without commitment

Not all forms of love include commitment. Some people feel and show love through a sense of commitment, others have different styles of loving where that commitment is either missing or not a central part of their love. The man who feels and expresses deep love but cannot conceive of monogamy is a common hero, or antihero, of film and fable. However, even when it is not acted on, commitment is usually part of the ritual of love. Saying "The way I feel for you now, I never want to be with anyone else again," is commitment behavior. This is one way expressive lovers talk to their partners. Active lovers may also see commitment as part of their love because they see that love in terms of being together.

Many love affairs have run their course without the partners ever being committed to each other, but this is unlikely if the original feelings are to stand the test of time. It is quite possible to be in love and not be committed; it is less likely that a love relationship will last without a show of commitment at some stage. Romantic love is, after all, at the mercy of threats from within and without. Conflict, a sense of routine, or a loss of attraction are the dangers within; the

---

ASSESSING LOVE AND COMMITMENT

■ *How can understanding different styles of love and commitment help us deal with relationship problems?*

During his relationship with Lisa, Jeff has found himself very outspoken about his feelings. He repeatedly asserts his love by telling her "I love you" and often does special things for her, such as leaving cards on her desk at work. He feels committed to Lisa and is saddened that she does not tell him that she loves him. Although he does not want to marry, he has told Lisa on many occasions that he will never leave her.

Lisa relies almost exclusively on nonverbal behavior in her awareness and communication of love. She sees Jeff's affection in the look in his eyes when they are together and hears it in the sound of his voice when they speak on the telephone. When Jeff tells her that he loves her, she often responds simply with an affectionate look or a brief kiss. At some point, she would like to marry Jeff and she is concerned that Jeff's distaste for marriage is a sign that he will never really make a commitment to her.

For Jeff and Lisa to make better sense of the nature of love and commitment in their relationship, they need to do two things. First, they should not project their own particular way of loving as the only "true" way. Jeff shows his love by expressing it, whereas Lisa relies on intuition: Jeff should sense she loves him, even if she does not say it in so many words. This difference need not prohibit their relationship working, but they both need to recognize and accept the other's way of loving.

Second, in examining areas of compatibility and incompatibility Jeff and Lisa must be able to recognize the various clues – thoughts, actions, words – associated with their ways of loving and being committed. Otherwise, it is too easy to jump from a specific issue of compatibility (eg "Jeff, I feel hurt when you say you don't want to get married") to the relationship as a whole (eg "Jeff, I guess you don't really love me"). Since love and commitment are such ambiguous terms, we need to understand better what each involves before we can deal effectively with our relationships.

attraction of other possible partners or separations due to work or family, are the threats from without. Making a commitment helps to counteract these threats and allows partners to feel that they can keep on a stable footing.

Romantic love and commitment are both experiences that are difficult to understand fully, especially as they apply to you and your partner. One moment you may feel confident that you have a clear understanding of your love for someone and you are certain of your commitment to them. The next, your feelings may change and your assurance is threatened. That is the nature of love relationships: being in love is not a constant state, it is something that develops, ebbs and flows.

However, you will understand love and commitment far better if you recognize that there are many different ways of loving and many types of commitment, each a different complex of thoughts, feelings and actions. There is no one right way of loving. **PJM MLH**

WHY BECOME COMMITTED?

■ Making a commitment is a deliberate decision and we are right to ask the question: "Why should I become committed?" One reason is that commitment helps us reduce our uncertainty about our partner and our relationship. ABOVE Choosing the ring is a firm sign that you feel committed.

When you marry in church you promise to stay together in sickness and poverty, even "Till death us do part," to show your belief in the relationship itself. Our vows make us feel secure, even if uncertainty develops later. Commitments do not all need to be as formal as the marriage vow. When your partner promises they will never leave you, you may feel more certain of your relationship.

Many of us cannot live up to these promises, however. RIGHT Events and pressures that fragment commitment include infidelity, lack of communication, a fear of becoming vulnerable to another person.

Suspicion of occasional uncharacteristic behavior

Being afraid to make yourself vulnerable to another

Wanting the stability of commitment without exclusivity

Lack of communication — judging partner by only a few actions

Mistrust because of experiences in childhood or youth

WHAT CAN FRAGMENT YOUR COMMITMENT?

Maintaining Individuality

WE ALL admire and most of us would like to be people who have something individual to contribute. We sense within us a potential to achieve goals and express ourselves in ways that reflect our own judgment, talents and tastes. However, it is not easy to fulfill this potential. It requires a clear sense of identity – you have to know who you are, not merely in terms of group membership ("I am a Johnson," "I am a Catholic"), but in terms of the ways in which you are unique. And you need the freedom to develop your talents and your personality – for example, you cannot effectively develop individuality if all of your attention is taken up by basic needs, such as getting enough to eat.

The couple relationship is usually the most intense group membership to which we commit ourselves. Like every other membership it demands conformity to shared goals and standards. This in itself can make our identities seem less distinct. And the aims that are typical of the most typical couple relationship – marriage – include many that may limit our freedom to develop. In the daily struggle to meet mortgage payments, keep children fed, clothed and out of danger and meet each other's basic emotional needs, partners may find little room for independent growth.

To be individual, is it better to stay single? What are the prospects for being individual *within* a relationship?

Our conflicting needs

Two of our basic needs – for intimacy and for independence – easily come into conflict. We want someone to care for us, yet we shun dependency. We want to belong, and we define our identity in terms of the groups we are part of and the people we are attached to; yet we consider ourselves as special and as having a separate identity from anyone else. We want to have control over, and expect a lot from, our lives, but we also want to be loving and giving. Someone who is alone may long for a partner (see *Ch1*); an attached person may at times feel tied down and want to be free to pursue new goals or pursue old goals more effectively.

The need for intimacy pulls you in the direction of joining in with others to find security as part of the whole. The need for independence pulls you in the opposite direction to take charge of yourself, be strong and stand alone. At different stages of our lives the pull of one or the other of these needs may be stronger. For instance, in youth your first concern may be to show that you can cope independently. Soon after, finding a mate might involve pulls in the opposite direction. Having a close relationship is likely to be more important to us at some stages in our lives than at others. Life does not stand still, and nor do we. And, in any case, people are different. Some do not feel such a strong need for

▲ **Time for yourself** *is easier to find when you are single. Maintaining a relationship in a happy condition will mean giving attention to your partner and devoting energy to joint activities and goals.*

▶ **Time for each other,** *to express your sense of individual specialness as a couple, is easier to find when the more demanding phases of the relationship are past. The most time-consuming phase is midmarriage, with partners absorbed in the basic tasks of earning, homemaking and raising children (see Ch10).*

To be a truly individual person, do you have to remain uncommitted? ■ *For some people, staying single is the best policy* ■ *Partners in a relationship can jointly decide to be different from each other while still needing each other* ■ *A genuinely supportive relationship provides an excellent environment for individual growth.*

"I WANT TO BE ALONE"

■ *Everyone needs some time to be alone. Solitude, like sleep, meditation and prayer, helps you to clarify your ideas and think things through. In particular, creative, original thinking demands solitude. Being alone – whether by choice or accident – forces you to make your life meaningful without the help or distractions of an intimate partner. Works of genius have resulted from enforced solitude – the need to do something to fill the void left by a loved one. Others came about by the artist consciously and deliberately excluding anything or anyone that might interfere.*

People with exceptional talent or a strong vocation often find an intimate relationship too demanding. While they need support and encouragement, a close, loving relationship and the responsibilities of caring for another may make too many claims on their time and their energies. The heroine of Robert Graves's "The White Goddess" faces just such a dilemma. A gifted poet, she takes a vow of chastity after falling in love, afraid that commitment to the relationship might damage that which she prizes above all – her talent.

Professional people with career ambitions – women in particular – sometimes also have to decide whether settling down to a shared life is right for them. Of those with high educational qualifications holding important positions in business or industry, the women are more likely to be single than the men. This suggests that the women have had to make the choice between marriage and career. Because of childbearing potential and social conditioning about sex roles, this dilemma belongs much more to women. Of course many women do manage to combine career and family, often aided by their partner's commitment to shared domestic responsibilities. One possible compromise solution is for women to marry but to opt for a career instead of children. Other women may choose to stay single and not mind being alone with their career.

▲ **The need for solitude** and privacy is something that we all experience, some more than others. If you enjoy working hard all week and then savor weekend activities that allow you to be alone, it is well worth considering whether you really want to include an intimate partner in your life. If you do want a partner, you may be happier with one who will be equally glad of chances to be alone and to pursue unshared interests.

FOLLOWING THE MASSES

■ *RIGHT A joint wedding, organized by a company specializing in this kind of event, unites 41 couples in Singapore. Almost everyone marries – and doing what everyone does may not seem like a way of developing an individual character. However, our individuality benefits from the self-esteem and emotional strength we acquire through building sound relationships, and for many it is the marital relationship that provides the best opportunity for such personal growth.*

intimacy, preferring a greater degree of detachment and independence in their relationships, and perhaps finding their motivation more in their career or leisure activities. Staying single may be their best solution to the problem of staying individual. Other people need a close relationship, achieving self-expression through helping and caring for each other and finding ways of being unique while belonging.

Is it immature to remain single?

According to one view, single people are immature because they refuse to accept the responsibilities of a permanent relationship. Moreover, it is said, this will cause them to remain that way – they will lack the opportunity to develop their personality further through meeting the challenge of sharing life with a partner.

Of course, many singles disagree. They believe that being single gives you greater freedom to explore ways of developing your potential as an individual and to achieve your goals without having to compromise either yourself or your objectives for the sake of another. For instance, having a permanent partner, or being married with a family, makes enormous demands upon your time and upon your financial and emotional resources. To make matters worse, arguments in the home are an almost inevitable part of family life and they often cause pain and distress.

An emotional life with ups and downs does not appeal to everybody. If, for example, since childhood you have always been interested in science and have pursued that interest through university and beyond, it may be your work as a scientist that gives you the most satisfaction in life. Consciously deciding not to marry, you invest all your energies in your desire to explore your chosen discipline and, through contributions to research journals, to communicate your discoveries to others in your field.

Singles do not necessarily underestimate the importance that interpersonal relationships can have for their personality development and general well-being. However, they may find it sufficient to draw social support from a number of close friendships and family relationships without committing themselves to one intense involvement. Intimacy is only one possible route to personal fulfillment, and not necessarily the best for everyone.

Who is single?

There is no longer the stigma attached to being single that there once was. People who do not marry are not considered to be "left on the shelf" or undesirable as partners. We accept that many men and women may choose to lead a "bachelor life" – though between the ages of 30 and 50 they are still in the minority. Most of us are single for at least part of our adult life, whether before, after or instead of marriage. Sociologists have identified several categories of singles, including young and older singles who have never married, divorced singles, widows and widowers who have not remarried, and single parents.

Are there more singles today than there used to be? Certainly singles are more conspicuous, if only for the reason that, as an identifiable group, they are more socially

SINGLES: MYTHS AND REALITIES

■ *Researchers have classified common views about singles into the following sets of myths and realities. The remarks in parentheses report what was found about* singles *in a comparison of singles and couples in a randomly selected group of 400 people in Ohio.*

MYTHS
- *Singles are tied to mother's apron strings.*
  (Not really: there is little difference in singles' and marrieds' relations with parents.)
- *Singles are selfish.*
  (Not really.)
- *Singles are rich.*
  (Not really: marrieds on average have more money.)
- *Singles are happier.*
  (Not really: they feel more anxious, despondent and worthless, and get more depressed than marrieds.)
- *Singles are increasing in numbers.*
  (Not really: there are literally more, but the percentage of singles is lower than between 1900 and 1940.)
- *Being single is acceptable.*
  (Not really: marriage continues to be a preoccupation, and the majority anticipate they will marry.)
- *There is something wrong with singles.*
  (Not really.)

REALITIES
- *Singles are different.*
  (Yes: between the ages of 30 and 50 singles are in the minority. They perceive themselves, and are perceived, as deviating from the normal pattern.)
- *Singles have more time.*
  (Yes: they give more time to their leisure activities.)
- *Singles have more fun.*
  (Yes: they have more social outings, and are more self-indulgent.)
- *Singles are more promiscuous.*
  (The majority are not promiscuous, but they have generally had more partners than marrieds.)
- *Singles are lonely.*
  (Yes: they are more likely to be lonely than marrieds, especially divorced singles.)
- *Life for singles is changing for the better.*
  (Yes: singles are better catered for. There are more opportunities and the single lifestyle is improving.)

Life for singles is changing for the better

■ *They are on average more lonely and less wealthy than married people, but instead of being socially downgraded, are now catered to by an industry devoted to their needs.*

accepted. Instead of being socially downgraded, singles are now catered to by a whole industry that has grown up around their needs. Singles have their own bars, their own clubs, their own housing and their own holiday resorts. The number of singles has grown over the past two decades. However, census figures show that proportionally there are fewer of them now than there were before the Second World War. Then, First World War casualties were still having an impact on statistics about the number of older women who had partners, and the economic hardships of the Great

Depression were forcing many young couples to postpone marriage. Today's increase in numbers of singles is due to a combination of the baby boom of the immediate postwar years, a later marrying age and an increase in the number of divorces.

In the future, the proportion of singles to marrieds is likely to increase because of changes in the composition of the population. People in the advanced countries are living longer, so that today older people account for a greater share of the population than they once did. With that increase, the ratio of men to women is falling. Of those people aged 75 or over, nearly two-thirds are women. In Australia and the United States more and more women

TO MARRY OR NOT TO MARRY

■ *The American sociologist Peter Stein identifies these pushes and pulls toward married life and single life RIGHT based on an investigation of 165 singles in their twenties and early thirties. Freedom and excitement ABOVE are among the main pulls toward the single status. Desire for a family ABOVE RIGHT is a chief pull toward marriage.*

TOWARD BEING SINGLE

PUSHES

Restrictions within relationships: suffocating one-to-one relationships, feeling trapped; obstacles to self-development; boredom, unhappiness and anger; traditional role expectations too restricting.

Poor communication.
Sexual frustration.
Lack of friends, isolation, loneliness.
Limited mobility.
Limited opportunity for new experiences.

TOWARD BEING MARRIED

Pressure from parents.
Desire to leave home.
Fear of independence.
Loneliness.
Cultural expectations.
Guilt over singlehood.
Lack of alternatives.

PULLS

Career opportunities.
Variety of experiences and plurality of roles.
Self-sufficiency.
Sexual freedom.

Exciting lifestyle.
Freedom to change.
Mobility.
Time for friendships.
Independence.

Approval of parents.
Desire for a family.
Example of peers.
Romanticization of marriage.
Physical attraction.
Emotional attachment and love.
Security, social status, prestige.
Wanting a sexual partner.

coming of age will not find a male partner because the women so outnumber the men. Studies of marriage patterns have shown that, generally, women "marry high"; that is, husbands tend to be older, taller, better educated and more highly paid than their prospective wives. Consequently, there are likely to be more unmarried women at the upper end of the socioeconomic scale and more unmarried men at the bottom (see *Ch3*).

To live happily ever after?

From childhood we are brought up to see our future in terms of finding a partner and settling down. Just think how many fairy stories end up with the words "...and they lived happily ever after." If by the time you reach your mid-to-late twenties or thirties you are still single, you are probably consciously resisting what was at one time a virtual marriage imperative.

When singles in a New York survey were asked why they were still unmarried, many said they believed that people often got married not so much to please themselves as to please their parents. Being single did not mean that they would always remain so, but at least it avoided the pitfall of rushing into what might turn out to be a calamitous marriage.

We are more aware today, from the statistics on divorce, and possibly from our own experiences or those of our friends, of how often marriages go wrong. Trial marriage or living together as a couple is now more socially acceptable, allowing either partner to walk away if the relationship does not work out (see *Ch8*).

To many singles, any idea of being tied or settling down is unthinkable. Some believe that it is unrealistic to expect one person to satisfy all your needs throughout the whole of your life (see *Ch11*). You change, your partner changes, but

monogamy makes no allowance for the possibility of people growing apart as they get older.

Being single places fewer demands on your time and on your person, avoids the jealousy and recrimination that can arise between couples, and provides more opportunities for exploring new relationships and new friendships, as well as keeping up old ones.

Many singles have tried marriage or cohabitation and found the experience stifling. The responsibilities of home, partner, perhaps children, and regular household expenditures inevitably involve compromise, and the compromises may compare unfavorably with your former independence and freedom.

Before setting up home together and starting a family, couples in which both partners are career-minded often have to choose who is to be allowed to continue to work.

IN SICKNESS AND IN HEALTH

■ *Advantages of being married include greater mental and physical health, but available statistics do not compare people who choose to be single and those who are single but would prefer to have a partner.*

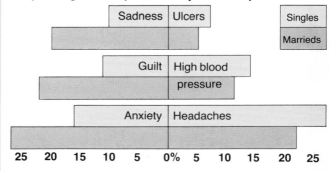

Psychological complaints   Physical complaints

Sadness	Ulcers		Singles
			Marrieds
Guilt	High blood pressure		
Anxiety	Headaches		

25   20   15   10   5   0%   5   10   15   20   25

INTIMACY AND GROWTH

■ *A successful relationship has therapeutic qualities. Partners give each other emotional support and self-esteem by accepting each other as they are and seeing the worth that others might not. Carl Rogers teaches that the same considerations apply as in a healthy psychotherapist/client relationship. He is a founder of the "humanist" approach to psychology (which emphasizes the study of what makes us well, in place of the study of what makes us ill). The humanist approach to relationships works like this:*

IF...
I can create a relationship in which I am:
genuine and open,
warmly accepting and appreciative of the other person's individuality,
sensitive to their view of themselves and the world,

THEN...
the other person will:
experience and understand aspects of themselves that they had repressed,
become more complete as a person,
become more like the person they want to be,
be more self-directing and self-confident,
become more self-expressive and individual,
be more understanding and more tolerant,
be better able to cope with life's problems.

A chance to grow may be the finest gift you can make to your partner ■ *By accepting and appreciating each other as you are you give each other the confidence to become more like the people you most want to be.*

Thus for some – usually women – getting married means putting the relationship before their profession. In later years they may regret the sacrifice unless an understanding partner encourages them to resume their career, or they have something else to do that is equally rewarding. However, not all women find it easy to switch from work to family and back to work again. Single career-minded women, whatever else they may be missing, often consider themselves lucky in not having to take on the added responsibilities of being a wife and mother.

Staying individual in a relationship

Being single, however, has its own psychological drawbacks. Singles are generally less happy and more prone to feelings of stress than marrieds, and indeed lonelier, which often prompts them eventually to give up their single status. In some cases, singles may even find it harder to develop their individuality. As one of a couple you look to your partner for reassurance when necessary, and probably respect

SELF-EXPRESSION AND COMMITMENT

■ *Devotion to a religious commitment LEFT does not stifle self-expression. Similarly, devotion to each other and to the children they produce together can be a central part of what gives a couple's lives meaning. TOP Devoted relationships leave room for more individualistic forms of self-expression as well. Which of this pair is responsible for making their flower garden* *so distinctive? Both, in fact, have contributed, sharing a taste for invention. In another relationship, an unusual garden might result from the cheerful indulgence by one partner of the other's eccentricity. In marriages that encourage personal growth for both partners, each takes pleasure in seeing the other develop individual talents and interests.*

their judgments above those of outsiders. Without such support, singles may succumb more easily to outside pressures and become more conformist in their attitudes and behavior than marrieds.

Staying individual depends on self-knowledge, self-expression and personal achievement. Involvement in happy and secure relationships is a prerequisite for this. The couple relationship may be the right kind of relationship to give this support to your own individuality. The distinctive roles of man and woman within the couple relationship may help each to develop a greater sense of identity and individual worth. When partners value the fact that they have complementary – rather than identical – personalities, they reinforce each other's individuality.

Is being married better for your health than being single and therefore a safer framework in which to pursue your individuality? Certainly, partners can give each other better social support than singles receive. However, a straight comparison between the two groups does not tell the whole story. Each group contains subcategories (eg never-married, separated, remarried, childless) and the position is different for men and women.

Researchers have found that people who are divorced or separated, especially men, have more psychological and physical health problems than the never-marrieds. Single women are healthier and better adjusted than single men, but on the whole less so than married women. Marrieds have more headaches, ulcers and high blood pressure, but experience less mental illness.

How close do you need to be?

To couples who have just fallen in love, even a brief separation can be intolerable. A crisis such as an accident or a serious illness, or, on the night when the loved one is late coming home, the thought that for some reason they may never return, threatens to shatter their whole world. Popular songs with lyrics like "I only live for you" or "You are my everything" convey this intensity of feeling very well. Cynics may say that if your whole existence really does depend on another person then you must lead an otherwise rather empty life. Others may point to a loving relationship as a substitute for religion in a secular age, as something that can give meaning to life.

Devoting yourself to another person suggests self-sacrifice, but, provided that the commitment is freely made,

INDIVIDUAL SOLUTIONS

■ *The fact that Julian and Freda have separate addresses does not place any emotional distance between them. They depend on each other very much, but find that the arrangement allows them to function more as individuals rather than just a couple.*

After years of a difficult marriage, Victor has found fulfillment living alone and tending his garden. Now, happier, more outgoing and more relaxed, he still sees a lot of his family and has widened his circle of friends.

Karen had a bright future as an accountant before her, but today she cheerfully spends her time at home as a wife, and the proud mother of two children. For her, the world of high finance held fewer attractions than the intimate world of husband, home and family.

A WORKING RELATIONSHIP

■ *One way to express your individuality is through work, particularly work that demands initiative, skill and knowledge.*

Traditional marriages, with a male breadwinner, have thus enhanced the individuality of men, but not necessarily of women. His work is what matters most; her role is a supportive one. He is work-centered; she is relationship-centered.

Today women are less predictably relationship-centered than in the past. They too now have more opportunities to derive satisfaction from their work. To complement this change, men are less exclusively anchored to their jobs. In a survey of American men and women either married or cohabiting, about a quarter of them said they were equally committed to their work and to their relationship. The rest displayed more traditional attitudes.

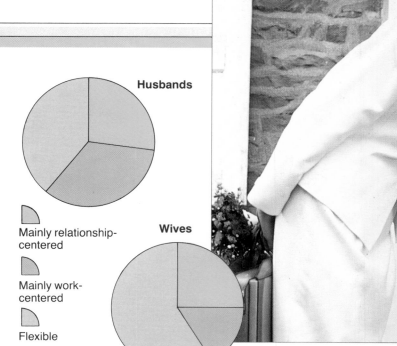

Husbands

Mainly relationship-centered

Mainly work-centered

Wives

Flexible

A good relationship is one plus one ■ *A close and loving relationship can give both partners an extra dimension, releasing individual potential because each values what is unique and worthy of development in the other.*

this need not be the case. Just as a career may be a means to self-fulfillment, commitment to a partner, and to children if there are any, may bring with it a wide scope for self-development.

However, some couples need to be more independent of each other to make their relationship work – even to the extent of living apart. That way, though they may visit each other frequently, each can be boss in his or her own house and indulge their own idiosyncratic tastes in furniture, food or music. Other couples may live together but prefer to take separate holidays.

Making a point of being yourself

The necessity of having personal relationships can be overstated. The arts, nature, creative pursuits and even the everyday objects around us may be equally worthy of our attention as possible sources of satisfaction. Indeed, some people who are separated or divorced find greater fulfill-ment and scope for development, both personally and creatively, in following a hobby or intellectual interest, than they ever did in marriage.

Many of us, at different points in our lives, see within our-selves the possibility of becoming another kind of person, or living another kind of life. Sometimes circumstances – work or perhaps friends – may push us in that direction, another time it may be largely left to us to choose. If, out of

fear or refusal to make the effort, we shun those opportuni-ties, we perhaps deny ourselves the chance to develop in new directions.

A couple who understand each other well, in a close and loving relationship, will not normally deny each other such opportunities. On the other hand, you will feel a more urgent need to explore new possibilities if your one-to-one relationship is proving unsatisfactory.

Whether as one of a couple or as a single, the key to self-fulfillment is to be yourself, that is, to live your life as you want to live it, not as others would have you do. To many – but not all – the way to achieve this is through a happy, loving relationship with a partner. The individuals who make up such couples assist each other to become, so to speak, more themselves, combining their respective strengths to work as a team. We are all lacking in some respects, but with the right partner to give to and take from we perhaps have a better chance of coming closer to com-pleteness. A good couple relationship is one plus one – a combination that releases individual potential. **RB**

▲ **Independence and self-reliance** *make you feel like a genuine individual. Inevitably, becoming part of a couple relationship means becoming dependent on a particular person in special ways, and it means accepting the principle* *of relying on each other. The challenge of retaining a sense of individuality in a relationship is one of making your mutual interdependence a constructive and complementary one.*

Opting for Marriage

WHY DO PEOPLE get married? Most of us are now in a position to choose whether or not we marry, live together or live separately: yet, despite the rising divorce rate, the acceptance of cohabitation and the increasing independence of women, over 90 percent of people in the United States and Europe will get married at least once. Typical reasons for getting married are that we want to settle down, have our own home and raise a family. In the past, marriage was the *only* option for couples who wanted to enjoy sexual intimacy and have children. It is now more socially acceptable for them to do this outside institutionalized marriage, so by deciding to get married rather than live together, a couple is making a choice.

Marriage as affirmation

People marry for many reasons, but in Western cultures most of us believe that young couples should only marry when they feel a love that is intense, romantic and passionate. Many couples see their marriage as making a public statement that they love each other and use the event to announce their change in status from two single people to a pair. Couples who do not marry have no similar way of publicly making their affection known – there are no cohabitation ceremonies or living together greetings cards.

Some people use the marriage ceremony as a mutual affirmation of their love. It is the strongest way they have of saying that they have committed themselves to loving the other person for life. The ceremony consists largely of promises and making these promises to each other in public gives them more weight and meaning.

In most religions marriage is a sacrament and those couples who have a strong religious faith believe that they cannot form a true partnership without the approval of that faith. Even people only nominally belonging to a religion often prefer to have the blessing of its marriage service. In the United States 85 percent of marriages are religious services. The religious ceremony is a solemn occasion during which the couple make vows to each other in the sight of their god. This has the same force as taking an oath in court – we use the Bible or the presence of God as a totem against breaking our vow. The couple is also asking for a spiritual blessing. The words of the Christian ceremony include promising to love and support each other in adverse circumstances – this is a recognition that marriage is a difficult relationship with problems and pitfalls. The knowledge that we have promised in the sight of God to overcome them is supposed to encourage us to succeed.

The pressure of society

Society is geared toward the idea of a couple being married (see *Ch 8*). Up until a hundred years ago, the meaning of marriage centered not on emotional fulfillment but on economic survival and social status. In 17th-century England, the status of "husband" was a privileged position which gave a man power over his wife, his children and his servants. The wife gained status from becoming "dame" in her own household.

Marriage is still the norm and we assume couples will get married in preference to living together. We are all influenced by what our friends and family expect and accept. At a certain stage in our lives when our friends are marrying and starting families, there is a social momentum that carries us along and we will probably do likewise.

Society differentiates between the married couple and a couple who are living together. Married men and women are accepted as their partner's companion in a way that unmarried partners are not and families will treat their son- or

▲ **Affirming their commitment** to each other, a Bangladeshi couple participate in a traditional ceremony of marriage.

A wedding announces changes in the partners' social status. For many couples it is also a public celebration of their love.

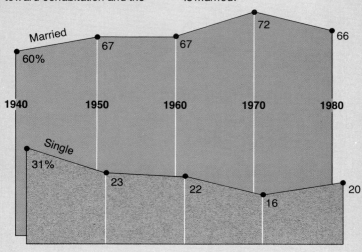

▼ **Marriage is a favored way of life**. *Despite increasing divorce rates, greater tolerance toward cohabitation and the* *fact that people are now marrying later, well over half the adult population of the United States is married.*

Married
60% — 67 — 67 — 72 — 66

1940 — 1950 — 1960 — 1970 — 1980

Single
31% — 23 — 22 — 16 — 20

You do not have to marry to live together but most people still do ■ *Why do people pursue marriage, even in the face of serious obstacles?* ■ *Lovers, parents, the church and the taxman all help to keep it popular.*

▲ **A wedding in the rubble**. *For most people marriage represents emotional security and this can seem even more important when external circumstances are threatening, as in this scene from Beirut. A partner provides emotional support – someone who will help you cope with everyday frustrations as well as major stresses.*

daughter-in-law differently from the way they treat an unmarried family member. Getting married means not having to explain your relationship.

On the whole, married couples receive more consideration from the outside world than do cohabiting couples. For example, a husband is allowed time off work to help his wife when she has a baby and employers are understanding if a wife has to stay home to look after a sick husband. If the couple is not married there might be more resistance. Many employers prefer to hire married men. Some studies have suggested that this may be because employers believe that the responsibilities of supporting a family make husbands more serious about being successful.

Marrying for money

Some people choose to get married for financial reasons and there are certain benefits that make marriage an attractive option. For example, married couples often receive tax incentives and some companies will include a married partner in medical schemes or pay for husbands and wives to go together on business trips. Unmarried partners are unlikely to be included in this way. Many organizations pay a married person's living allowance but would not consider paying for a cohabitee.

It is no longer common for couples to marry in order to protect family finances or land, but they still need to safe-guard their economic position. Unless a couple makes very careful and detailed provision for their financial and legal situation (see *Ch 8*), they will not have the same sort of rights and obligations as those accorded by the marriage ceremony. The legal side of marriage, symbolized by the signing of the register, has always been society's way of

CAPTURING THE PRIZE

■ *When primitive man wanted a wife, he seized a woman by force. As society became more developed, capture became more symbolic and some societies incorporated sham dramatic "captures" of the bride by the groom and his friends into the marriage ritual. In 16th and 17th century England one ritual called for the groom and his companions to ride to the home of his intended bride to demand her in marriage. Their progress was traditionally obstructed by her family who set up a series of barriers. Once at the house the groomsmen engaged in a verbal contest with those defending the house and eventually "forced" entry. As the men disputed, the bride lamented her fate and mustered fake tears to add to the drama. The idea of capture survives today in the custom of the groom carrying the bride over the threshold of their new home.*

FORMALITIES OF UNION

■ *Signing the marriage documents in the synagogue. When two people marry, each acquires a legal status in relation to the other. Marriage contracts reflect the laws of the country and sometimes the requirements of religion. They are also usually a formal and binding expression of the couple's own wishes.*

The rights of couples who live together without marrying are less clear. For example, in the famous "palimony" award against the American actor Lee Marvin, the court ruled that there was no reason to take note of whether the couple had intended to keep their earnings separate. *In many other countries, by contrast, an unmarried woman separating from a common-law partner is unlikely* to be awarded a substantial share in joint assets such as a house unless she formally is a co-owner or can prove that she helped to buy them. To avoid unexpected material losses, it is advisable to make a formal contract.

Marriage is good for you – it improves your public image and keeps you healthy ■ *But do we expect too much of marriage?* ■ *A little give-and-take is essential if you want to avoid asking too much of your partner* ■ *If you are too demanding you may end up changing your partner as often as you change your car.*

ensuring that assets are owned and divided legally, that disputes can be settled by the courts, that the rights of inheritance are protected and that a couple's duties toward each other and their children can be enforced. When a couple is considering how they will form their partnership for life, they may well feel that the complications of trying to cover every legal eventuality are so great as to make the marriage ceremony the more attractive option. By getting married they automatically acquire a legal status.

Other personal reasons for marrying are to do with the way we see our roles. Some women like the idea of being cared for and protected; some men want to provide for their wives and families. People may well feel that these roles are only possible within the framework of a legal marriage. Being married gives many people a sense of security that is almost mystical. This makes them more willing to take risks such as having children, buying a house and changing jobs to fit in with their partner's plans. All of these things are

possible outside marriage but are probably thought about more warily with a great deal more weighing up of the pros and cons.

What do we expect marriage to provide?

Marriage often gives a couple ready-made roles and expectations. They have made a commitment that carries with it explicit and implicit guidelines on such issues as fidelity and permanence. There are no such rules for living together and the cohabiting couple will have to work these out for themselves.

Marriage represents both giving up and gaining. We expect to give up certain important things such as sexual freedom, privacy, independence, personal control and time; and we expect to gain security, companionship, sexual fulfillment, a confidant and social support. Obviously, in view of the popularity of marriage, most people consider that the gains far outweigh the losses.

We look for many kinds of emotional support from marriage. We hope to gain a balance of personal fulfillment from sharing experiences and values. We want someone to help bring up our children and build a family and we expect our marriage to be a source of financial, sexual and personal security. Married people clearly benefit from such personal fulfillment – they live longer and are emotionally better adjusted than single people.

■ **Personalizing the ritual.** *While most people prefer to follow established traditions and enter marriage as a totally religious sacrament in a church, mosque, synagogue or temple, others like to create more individualized ceremonies. A ceremony can reflect the feelings, views and beliefs of the partners: they marry each other out of personal choice as a statement of commitment and* *often choose a setting that is associated with their special circumstances and interests. The text of the ceremony may express to each other and those around them a very personal statement about their relationship.*

65

In modern marriage this expectation of emotional support can often lead us to place a tremendous emotional burden on a partner to supply all our needs (see *Ch 8*). We may even use them as a target for displaced aggression from dissatisfaction with work or our inability to find some personally meaningful activity. This strong emphasis on emotional support and constant gratification may jeopardize rewards traditionally associated with marriage, such as long-term companionship, and may lead to "serial monogamy," that is, when we find our current partner no longer satisfying, we replace them in the hope of obtaining the personal gratification we have come to expect from a partner. A good marriage supplies each partner with a readily available source of human reinforcements but it also represents a compromise in which we accommodate ourselves to another person and give up some of our autonomy. By getting married we gain a companion who is interested in our life but who will also expect us to take account of their needs.

Because marriage is a public partnership the two partners are able to share in each other's achievements. They expect to have a part in whatever the other does as well as in what they do together. This reflected glory can add enormously to each person's self-esteem. We like to be proud of those close to us and to receive praise, warmth and congratulations on their behalf. Major family events are also rewarding for the married couple. When we get married we look

> *Self-sacrifice is just as bad as selfishness when it comes to organizing a marriage* ■ *"Me" has got to learn to become "us"* ■ *A successful partnership depends on a delicate balance between the individual and the couple.*

forward to being together for a long time. Important dates like silver and golden wedding anniversaries that bring the whole family together can add to the couple's sense of shared achievement and satisfaction (see *Ch 15*).

Marriage changes your life

Getting married represents one of the most radical life transitions, perhaps second only to becoming a parent. It can create vast changes in virtually every area of our life – some hoped-for and desirable, others stressful and unexpected. The changes usually affect our roles, self-perception, responsibilities, behavior, finances, social relations and family connections. If we are able to cope successfully with these upheavals, we will establish a firm foundation upon which to build a lasting and happy marriage.

The fundamental change brought about by marriage is the joining of two separate and distinct individuals into a single entity called the married couple. Newly-married people have to transform concerns about goals for "my" life to goals for "our" life. They have to share everything including possessions. We all know couples who insist on referring to "my" stereo and "her" car. If this extends to every aspect of their life, then they are not adjusting well to being a pair. There has to be something that we consider as "ours."

From "living together" to "married"

Not all couples experience the same degree of change when they get married. A couple who have lived together for some time and then get married have already made the practical social and emotional adjustments of being an intimate pair: for them getting married does not represent a

► **Taking pleasure in your partner's achievements** *boosts their self-esteem as well as your own. Feeling their triumphs and disappointments as though they were your own helps to bind the relationship.*

◄ **Balancing what they share and what they do not,** *the actress Sophia Loren and film director Carlo Ponti are both known for their individual achievements as well as their long and stable marriage. The most important task for modern couples is to create a balance* *between their need to be recognized as separate individuals and their desire for intimacy and a shared identity.*

BETROTHAL AND ENGAGEMENT

■ *In ancient times betrothal was a formal ceremony that preceded marriage. Sometimes the period of betrothal was short but in some cultures infants were betrothed – India even permitted infant marriage. The betrothal ceremony still exists in some cultures and usually consists of exchanging rings, a kiss or joining hands in front of witnesses.*

In the 17th century, betrothal was the recognized rite of transition from being friends to being lovers and it conferred on the couple the right to sexual as well as to social intimacy. Although betrothal was an agreement, it was possible to break the arrangement if both parties consented. Dissolution was carried out publicly before either a priest or other witness and involved returning gifts. Sometimes a new suitor would pay off the marriage contract so that the woman was free to marry him. After betrothal there was a short but special period during which the young couple would act as a couple. It marked their separation from their peers and a time of seclusion while they considered the duties of marriage and gathered together necessary material resources.

Couples today usually announce their intention to get married and then spend several months as an engaged couple during which time they save up for a home and household equipment. We still mark the change of status with a ring – this is usually bought by the man for his fiancée but can sometimes be a family heirloom that is given by his mother.

Betrothal and engagement serve the same basic function – that of allowing not only the two people, but also their family and friends, time to adjust to the idea of their new, married status as an adult couple.

major change of identity. But even people who have lived together can experience a change in the expectations of their partner now they are a wife or husband and not just a companion. One woman who married someone she had been living with for some time reported that since getting married she felt she had lost her financial independence, even though she still had her own bank account and earned her own living. Other women find that their husbands display a surprisingly traditional attitude to their going out to work. A third of married men would prefer their partner to give up work, while only one in 10 single men shares that point of view. This may reflect an unconscious belief that was actively suppressed until the status of marriage was acquired.

Maintaining the balance

The most important thing that we have to do when we become one half of a married couple is to create a balance between our desire to be recognized and appreciated as a unique and separate individual and our desire to be dependent and part of a shared identity. This balance must be mutually satisfying to each partner. A commitment to either extreme can be disastrous. If one partner takes too much care of their own identity there may be insufficient commitment to the relationship and the couple can simply become two individuals sharing the same home and passing in the hall. It is just as bad if the partners devote themselves totally to the marriage. This can lead to a complete loss of personal identity and a paralyzing dependence on each other. Such a marriage may be held together strongly but it has little room for growth and it could ultimately be very unhappy as individual needs are sacrificed for the "good of the marriage." A successful marriage must have a flexible and adaptable movement between "I" and "we." **MDN TC**

◄ **A major turning-point**, *marriage affects almost every part of our lives. It changes our roles and responsibilities and often our social and financial status as well. Adjusting to these changes – whether they are what we hoped for or not – requires flexibility, honesty and openness. For people from different backgrounds, such as this mixed-race South African couple, or people of different nationalities or religions, it is an even greater transition.*

WEDDING CUSTOMS

■ Marriage ceremonies and weddings abound with rituals and symbols. Most of these date from earlier days and relate to fertility or warding off an evil spirit. A magician or elder conducted the ceremony before two or more witnesses. This practice persists to this day, with a minister or justice of the peace taking the place of the magician.

The white wedding The big wedding originated in the 19th century among the upper classes. Prior to that, women married in their best dress but with the coming of Victorian morality, white was seen as being a symbol of the bride's purity.

The banns Many countries require banns, or public notices, of the proposed marriage to be announced a few weeks before the wedding. The purpose of the banns is to give other people the chance to object to the marriage if they have a good reason.

Attendants The bride and groom usually choose several close friends or members of their family to participate in the wedding ceremony. This symbolizes their transition from a world of friends and relations of the same sex to the new relationship with a member of the opposite sex. The bride may have several bridesmaids, a maid-of-honor and a flower girl to accompany her while the groom chooses ushers, a best man and sometimes a ring-bearer to assist him. The custom of the best man probably goes back to the days when the groom took a friend with him to help him "capture" the bride.

Rings Nowadays the vows are marked by an exchange of rings, but in previous centuries other gifts such as gloves or coins were also accepted. The engagement ring represents the old custom of giving a gift to a girl desired in marriage. The diamond ring originated in Italy where diamonds were called the "flame of life."

In Egyptian hieroglyphics, the ring was a symbol of eternity. The ancient Egyptians are thought to have been the first to use rings in marriage. The ring may symbolize the captive bride whose hands were tied to prevent her from escaping. It may also symbolize the capture of the heart – the ring finger was thought by the Romans to have a direct link to the heart.

The ring was a powerful symbol of union in the 18th and 19th centuries, and church officials were known to pay for the bride's ring to induce couples to marry officially. It was considered unlucky to drop, break or even remove the ring and in some places a wife could free herself from a relationship simply by returning it to her husband.

The cake The wedding cake also stems from ancient Rome when it was made of salt, water and flour. Today's wedding cakes are a much more elaborate affair, often decorated with white icing and usually with more than one layer. It is sometimes the custom for the top layer to be kept for use as a christening cake for the couple's first child. Other people keep it to be eaten on the couple's first wedding anniversary for continued good luck in their marriage.

The garter and the bouquet The garter was a favorite love gift in the 17th and 18th centuries in the north of England. It was stitched with the initials of the man and given to her sweetheart as a pledge of their faithfulness. The garter was worn on the girl's left leg just above the knee and the bridegroom was not supposed to see it as only virgins were allowed to wear a garter. In France the bride threw her garter to the crowd after the ceremony and the girl who caught it was believed to be the

The cake

Something old, something new ■ *Today's marriage customs all have their origins in past rituals* ■ *They are part of the serious rite of passage into adulthood, symbolic of the couple's changing status.*

Throwing confetti

Attendant

Gifts

The garter

next bride. A similar custom is connected with the bridal bouquet today.

Gifts and the dowry A part of the courtship ritual in the past involved suitors visiting their chosen bride with a gift. Some gifts were believed to have magic powers: people thought that if you delivered a lock of hair or articles of clothing you would be in the other person's possession. Acceptance of the gifts showed that the courtship was serious.

For many centuries the bride and her family provided a dowry to the husband on the marriage. The family may have saved and collected for many years to assemble the dowry, which was considered essential to attract a suitor. This custom still persists in some countries where the dowry may consist of food and animals such as cattle, goats and sheep. It might also contain household goods, jewels and

other valuables. The dowry is not now usually a part of the wedding ritual in Western countries but engaged couples do receive a great many presents from friends and relatives.

Tin cans and old shoes Pranks have become a standard part of sending off the couple after the wedding. Throwing old shoes or tying them to the car goes back to ancient Egypt when the father handed the bride's sandal to the groom as a symbol of the transfer of authority.

Throwing confetti or rice Throwing rice carries the wish that the wedded couple will be blessed with children. Until Indian rice became a part of the Victorian upper-class diet it had never been associated with weddings. Then it became a substitute for the custom of throwing clods of earth. Today we have substitutes for rice such as confetti and bird seed. **MDN TC**

How Couples Have Changed

THE RADICAL transformation in the roles of men and women in recent decades has had an important effect on the way we interact as couples. Prior to the 20th century, marriage was much more a social institution than a personal relationship. The success of the marriage was judged not by how well the two partners got along but by how well they lived up to their responsibilities and the expectations of their roles.

When we talk about a couple we usually mean a married couple. For earlier generations this was the only accepted definition. Each partner had a clearly defined role with the husband traditionally being responsible for economic support and the wife for housekeeping, children and emotional support. The image of a perfect couple was a successful, hard-working husband, a domestic, supportive wife and several happy children. Boys were prepared for a future of achievement outside the home and girls were encouraged to think of marriage, motherhood and their home.

Becoming adult

People got married to acquire their own home, to gain adult status and to enjoy a sexual relationship. Girls were encouraged from an early age to think about marrying and marriage was enormously important to them. It provided their only escape from being a dependent daughter and their only path to any sort of personal fulfillment. Although they were supposed to be highly romantic in their love affairs, women were more often extremely practical. They realized that their future status and security depended entirely on their choice of husband and were less likely to be blinded by affection than attracted by the ability to provide a comfortable home.

Historically, men, too, gained adult status through marriage but by the end of the 19th century marriage was becoming less important to them as a way to adulthood. They were now able to acquire status through their career and earning potential. Women, by contrast, did not yet enjoy that option. Even when it became possible for them to work outside the home and receive further education, their achievements did *not* count as much as being married – they were still considered inferior, a failure and not true women unless they were "Mrs." The implication behind this is, of course, sexual. Sex outside marriage was not acceptable and the assumption that all unmarried women were virgins persisted well into the 20th century.

▲ **The 1950s** *was an era when marriage rates shot up, the average age at marriage fell briefly, and the baby-boom generation was born. Men and women still had distinct roles: the husband was responsible for economic support, and the wife for emotional support and for managing the home.*

◄ **Victorian values.** *Marriage in the 19th century was a mainstay in the social order, a public commitment to family responsibilities and to a well-defined role in the local community.*

Being married – how different are the implications of this today? ■ *New options have altered the status of marriage* ■ *How easy has it been for these options to become part of accepted social behavior?*

Even as recently as 1947, for example, over 80 percent of British men and women felt that it was unacceptable for unmarried people to live together. Marriage was seen by both sexes as the only way to meet their material, social and sexual needs and the only way to be a legitimate couple.

Staying young at heart

In the past, couples expected their lives to change after marriage. Marriage signaled the end of romance and the start of a new, responsible adult phase in their life in which they took on the burdens of raising children and looking after the family fortunes. One generation handed over to the next in a continuous cycle. Couples today seem to be

rejecting the adult role conferred by marriage – they no longer need the institution of marriage to give them freedom and independence. They want the romance and excitement of their courtship to continue into marriage and see no need to change their behavior or attitudes. We see less and less distinction between married and unmarried couples and even between couples of different generations.

Couples are taking less notice of traditional roles and responsibilities and are starting to use marriage as a source of personal fulfillment. We are coming to expect more and more of our partners in terms of emotional benefits. The quality of our relationship is the most important thing and far outweighs outside factors such as duty, religious beliefs and even children. If our needs are not met within marriage we have little hesitation in breaking up the partnership to look for satisfaction elsewhere (see *Ch 13*).

LIVING TOGETHER

■ *Not all couples are married couples. One of the most significant ways couples have changed is that more and more of them are deciding to live together without getting married. In 1981 there were about 1.8 million unmarried couples in the United States – approximately 4 percent of all*

couples. In Sweden, the cohabitation rate is as high as 12 percent. Living together no longer attracts the social disapproval it once did and unmarried couples are less likely to suffer discrimination at work than in the past. "Living in sin" is becoming an outmoded concept.

Many people want the companionship of a married relationship but do not want to compromise their need for independence. Cohabitation allows them to retain their legal status as a single parent while at the same time enjoying the shared intimacy and partnership of living with someone as a couple. Such couples want to protect the equality of their relationship without being forced into the traditional roles expected of a married couple.

CHILDREN AND COMMITMENT

Most cohabiting couples do not have children – 72 percent of unmarried American couples in 1981 were childless. If they do consider having children they usually get married eventually, often after the birth of the child. Long-term commitment is also uncharacteristic of cohabiting couples. One study found that while there were many couples who had been together for between five and eight years, fewer than 2 percent had lived together for ten years. This could be because cohabitation is a relatively recent form of couple relationship or because most couples eventually either marry or break up.

COHABITEES' CHECKLIST

Cohabiting partners may be disadvantaged by the lack of legal protection which marriage provides. Here are some suggestions for alternative provisions.

Draw up a legal contract setting out your financial arrangements so that if you split up you know who is entitled to what.
● Make sure the house is owned or leased in both your names.
● Make a will – otherwise if you die your property goes to your next of kin.
● Check out your pension and life insurance. Your partner must be named as the dependent – some policies only pay out automatically to spouses.
● Protect your children's rights to inheritance, and yours to child benefits.

71

◄ **Resisters of convention.** *Spencer Tracy and Katherine Hepburn lived together without marrying, in spite of social conventions. The relationship did not damage the success of their careers, but others were not so lucky.*

Many of our needs for intimacy, companionship, love and security used to be met in other ways by friends and families. But with increased mobility and the tendency of couples to isolate themselves from other people we no longer belong to the same community for any length of time. When we move we can only rely on those relationships we take with us. Responsibility for satisfying all our emotional needs now falls on the relationship itself. This can place considerable strain on the couple. On the one hand, we are free from social interference and having to seek approval from our neighbors and peers, but on the other, we are deprived of much-needed social support that could relieve a lot of the pressure on individuals to be so dependent on each other. Social psychologists emphasize the importance

Shock waves of change within the social order ■ *Couples have had to cope with both independence and isolation as the extended family fragments under the impact of increased mobility and newfound sexual freedom.*

of social support contacts and suggest that couples would benefit from integrating themselves more into community life (see *Ch27*).

A quest for passion and equality

The 1960s saw a real revolution in the way people looked at their relationships. Young people wanted no part in the kind of marriage their parents had where self-sacrifice and a lack of intimacy were accepted as the price of security and other institutional benefits of being married. Young couples wanted to be equal and to retain passion in their marriages.

72

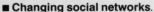

■ **Changing social networks**. *In many societies cultural traditions and economic necessities encourage an extended household of several generations living and working together. This British family TOP, working as hop pickers in the summer of 1949, shared a stable sense of community offering companionship and security. Forces of social change have made this type of group increasingly rare in the West. TOP RIGHT A couple is now more likely to live away from their parental home and to travel some distance to work every day. In this situation they*

may become entirely dependent on each other for social support, and the relationship has to bear the emotional strain which this entails. Often nuclear families form new social networks RIGHT to provide a substitute for some of the elements of life in an extended family. In particular these networks offer companionship, emotional support and help with child care.

They saw equality as the way to avoid the frustrations they had observed in their parents' relationships and they were beginning to feel less inhibited about their sexuality.

It is, however, easier to desire equality than to achieve it. The old inequalities can resurface when a couple become married, home-owning parents and have to divide the labor and responsibilities these bring. Earlier conventions still influence the way society is organized, and it is hard to break free from the traditional view of the high-status, wage-earning husband and the low-status, childrearing wife.

Even equality, however, cannot guarantee enduring passion in a relationship. It is, anyway, questionable whether a constant high level of passion is a good thing in a marriage given that it leads the couple to exclude other people and

▲ **The swinging sixties** were an era of radical change in the social and sexual roles of men and women. Unisex dressing and long hair and makeup for men blurred the traditional visual difference between the sexes, and were pointers to more significant shifts in gender stereotyping.

THE END OF THE TRADITIONAL FAMILY?

■ *In a recent report, the American sociologist Pepper Schwartz claims that the family is no longer the basic unit of society. The driving force behind everyday life is no longer group welfare but individual well-being. The modern family is less firmly held together by duty and responsibility and has become a loose grouping of individuals, each having limited power over the others. It is easier for partners to leave the family if they feel unhappy or deprived; children can find support elsewhere if the family breaks up; and parents are less willing to sacrifice their own plans for the sake of their children. The image of the nuclear family based on love, loyalty and a lifetime commitment is still desirable in our culture, but not so easily attained.*

Single parent families. *In poor and economically unstable groups, marriage becomes a way of increasing financial stability. However, families are likely to consist of women and children only in countries where government child benefits combine with poor financial incentives for low-earning men to marry.*

Blended families. *These are the middle-class, double-income couples where individuals marry because neither partner alone earns enough to provide for the desired lifestyle. These families will be combined, broken and recombined as couples divorce and remarry in search of "the good life."*

Executive families. *These are couples where the husband is a high-earner. His wife may decide that she does not need to work even if she has a career. If they remain a dual-career couple their income will allow them to decide how much each will contribute to the home and the family. Their high level of economic independence leaves them free to regularly reassess the value for money they are getting from their partnership. Divorce will be inevitable in many cases if the marriage does not come up to expectations.*

73

INDUSTRIALIZATION AND THE COUPLE

■ *During the 1790s, about 94 percent of the people in the United States lived on farms. With the turn of the century, industrialization began and, by the latter part of the 19th century, new forms of technology were increasingly drawing men away from the farms and into the cities and factories, leaving their wives and children at home. The independent farm couple began to disappear. This ultimately led to the isolation of American women, as well as to a decline in their position as equal partners with men. Marriage expressed men's rights over women, including their sexual and childbearing capacities.* **MDN TC**

neglect other interests, both of which could be beneficial to their well-being in the long-term.

Evidence that men and women are becoming more equal could come from the trend toward concern with health and body image. Body awareness has always been considered a feminine characteristic but now men too will visit beauty salons and fashionable clothes stores, and worry about their diet and appearance. This increasing concern with image on the part of men may also be the result of women exercising a greater degree of choice in whether or not they enter into a relationship and with whom.

New roles for women, new kinds of couples

The social revolution of the past 25 years has brought great changes to the way we interact as couples. The two-parent, nuclear family is no longer the only possibility and couples have much more choice in how they organize their relationship.

The feminist movement has given women a heightened awareness of their own potential that has caused them to review their role in society. This is having a dramatic effect on couples. Many women no longer want to be subordinates in a traditional marriage or be restricted to being a wife and mother. They want to develop their education and their career first and, as a result, often postpone marriage and children to later in life. The availability of safe birth control for women has freed them from being forced into motherhood and they can now choose when and if they have children. Women are at last able to acquire adult status, just like men, through their personal achievements, without having to depend on marriage.

Men need to change

Women who are involved in their own careers and education will have less time to spare for the traditional role of supporting other people. In fact, as they respond to the

EVENTS THAT HAVE CHANGED COUPLES

Women's Suffrage
Gave women the potential for political influence. In many countries this was granted at the end of World War I, though often with limitations.

World War II
Women's roles expanded to include significant activity outside the home while men were at war.

Increased geographic mobility
Encouraged partners to be more mutually supportive in the absence of nearby relatives.

Increased affluence
Provided many couples with domestic luxuries and more freedom of choice in lifestyle, especially during the post-war boom.

Effective birth control
Allowed couples more control over limiting the size of their families and choosing when to have children; gave women the opportunity to express their sexuality without fear of pregnancy; separated sexual involvement from the traditional pattern of marriage and childrearing.

Legalized abortion
In many countries provided psychological freedom of knowing that a medically safe alternative to an unwanted pregnancy was available.

Sexual revolution
Loosened traditional restraint of morality and religion on nonmarital sexual intimacy.

▲ Events that have changed couples. *Significant factors of social change are woven into the developing pattern of male and female relationships. Votes for women and the tendency for women to work outside the home are closely linked with the impact on women's lives of two world wars. The temporary absence of men from the family and the labor force meant that women drew on strength and abilities which had been dormant before. The return of the men from the front led to a temporary revival of traditional family values in the 1950s before the sexual revolution of the sixties altered the pattern again.* TOP RIGHT *Women assembling a barrage balloon during World War II.*

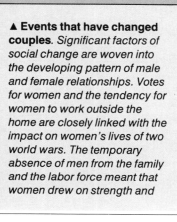

◄ Germaine Greer, *leading feminist writer and teacher, best known for "The Female Eunuch," her influential study of women's behavior and motivation.*

Women's expectations are changing, and men need to change too ■ *Wars, birth control and feminism have completely altered traditional stereotypes* ■ *Men are learning to respond with a new expressiveness and sensitivity.*

greater demands on them outside the home, women are coming to need the same degree of emotional support which they have given to others in the past. This is particularly marked when the traditional male role as breadwinner is undermined by the woman's own earning power. These changes in women's needs and in their ability to look after others mean that men are being expected to adjust to the situation by taking on previously "female" roles (see *Ch 18*). They are being encouraged to be more expressive and open in their relationships. Many men find this difficult and

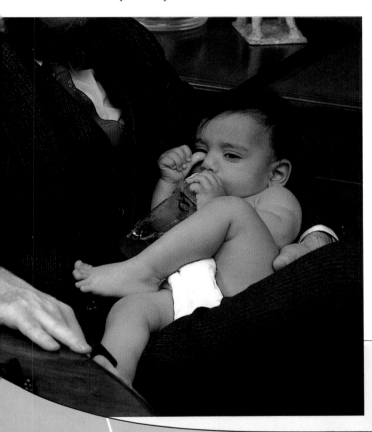

although they are generally more aware of the need to take on these new supportive roles, they have not yet become as expressive as women. Because they have not adapted as rapidly as women to the new roles, there is still an imbalance in many relationships. This can often disrupt the smooth running of the marriage because they are not fulfilling the expectations of their partner to provide this support. It could cause the wife to become dissatisfied with the marriage and eventually leave the relationship.

In the United States, over 80 percent of adult married women of childbearing age are employed in the workforce. The implication for couples is that men and women should now share the responsibilities of marriage and no longer divide roles in the old, traditional way (see *Ch 23*). But couples who have equal status outside the home are very often far from equal on the domestic front. Research over the past ten years shows that, even when their partner has a full-time job outside the home, men spend relatively little extra time on housework and child care. It is no longer unheard of for a man to look after the children while his wife pursues her career.

Commuter couples

When both partners work, there is often a problem about *where* they work. Few cities offer the same career possibilities for both partners so decisions have to be made that may cause a real dilemma. In traditional marriages with one wage earner, it did not really matter if the couple had to move to another area when that partner was promoted or wanted to further their experience. But now, such a move for one partner could cause trauma and resentment for the other partner. Some couples resolve this by becoming commuter couples, each living and working in a different place and meeting up at weekends (see *Ch 6*). **MDN TC**

◄ **Executive fathers**. *Although the balance of responsibilities within the home is still tipped toward the female, increasing numbers of men are sharing* child care and parenting. *Particularly when both parents work, many men realize the importance of spending time with their children (see Ch 28).*

tended adolescence
layed marriage; expanded length of time young people re financially dependent on rents; promoted premarital ationship alternatives.

Feminist movement
Created the ideal of an egalitarian relationship, and increased the power and opportunities of women.

Escalating divorce rate
Granted social permission to leave an unhappy marital relationship. Fostered a cautious and tentative attitude toward marriage.

Changing sex roles
Increased potential roles and opportunities for men and women and changed traditional division of labor.

Development of dual-career marriages
Undermined the assumed priority of husband's work over other family concerns.

Emphasis on personal autonomy
Shifted focus from giving up individual wishes for the good of the relationship to personal well-being.

AIDS
Encouraged greater restraint in sexual expression outside of committed relationships; reduced number of sexual partners.

Making Love

LOVEMAKING means trying to please a partner, to enhance the value of their sexuality – not just in bed but hour by hour and day by day. Sex takes up a mere fraction of the time partners spend together relating to each other. They also show affection for each other in small ways in the daily round of work and recreation – even when physically separated. Acts of mutual consideration – including things as general as looking after the children or earning the family's living – are consciously treated by some couples as love offerings; not just as affirmations of commitment to the partnership, but almost as a kind of foreplay, giving extra meaning to sex whenever it occurs. In such relationships, closely bonded by affection, the sex act acquires a depth of meaning which can be overlooked by those whose lovemaking is limited to genital stimulation.

High expectations in lovemaking can place burdens on a relationship. Studies suggest that three-quarters of all people have had a significant sex problem at some stage in their lives. However, surveys of happily married couples show that this does not spell disaster – no couple's sex life stands still, and overcoming sex problems can be one of the shared experiences that help to strengthen a relationship.

The sex drive

Different stages in life for men and women are associated with highest sex drive. For men, interest is at its most intense and persistent during late adolescence and their twenties, whereas women are thought to reach a peak of sexual interest during their late thirties and forties. Individual variations in this pattern, though, are less significant

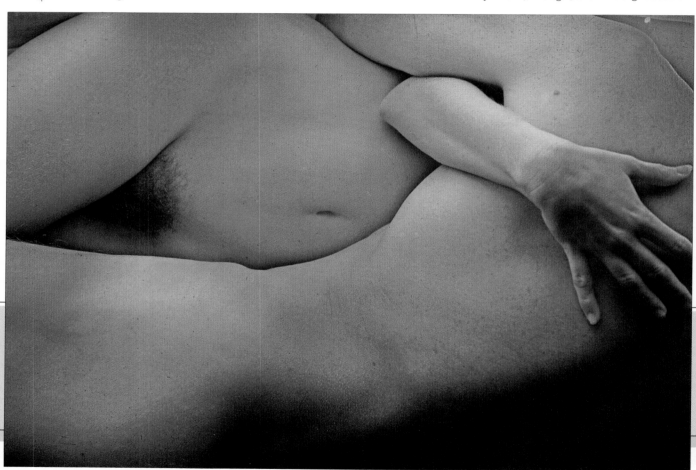

76

IT IS THE SPIRIT IN WHICH YOU MAKE LOVE THAT IS IMPORTANT

■ *A couple's sex life can gain from a varied, experimental approach, both in bed and out. Yet just doing new things does not necessarily make sex any more pleasurable or rewarding in terms of a one-to-one emotional relationship. Sexual gymnastics themselves can be a sign of inhibition if you get more involved with these than with your partner.*

To achieve the greatest satisfaction you should

concentrate less on what you do than on how you do it. Since lovemaking is about giving and receiving pleasure, and is the main way of showing passionate love, the emotional side of sex outweighs any other. Even among highly satisfied couples most make love in only a few positions all their lives. Partners should make love how and when they enjoy it, rather than work their way mechanically through a sex manual. AS

Lovemaking involves much more than the act of sexual intercourse ■ *Within a loving sexual relationship almost everything you do for each other can take on the significance of foreplay* ■ *Your partner may have a stronger sex drive than you suppose* ■ *When making love, what you do is less important than how you do it.*

than the constancy of sexual interest that spans adult life.

Compared with animals, human beings are extremely sexual. Sexual desire in humans is not simply dependent on times of the month or release of arousing body scents. Women's monthly cycles can have some effect in both these respects, but the potential for either partner to be aroused can also depend on clothes, words, movements, glances, smells, touch and, not least, thoughts.

How often couples physically make love varies greatly. Even some happily united couples have intercourse far less often than the average 2.5 times per week suggested by surveys. One explanation lies in varying expressions of the sex drive. Almost everyone has a sex drive, but some people reveal a stronger drive than others. Most of us know some

people who seem to show a surprising lack of interest in sex. But in fact what varies from person to person usually proves to be less the amount of drive than the amount expressed.

Sex therapists see many clients who claim total lack of interest in sex, and only seek help because of pressure from a sexually frustrated partner. Yet once therapy has overcome their inhibitions these "sexless" men and women can quickly become not only interested in but often enthusiastic about sex – a transformation so rapid that it would have been impossible if they were naturally low-sexed.

Evidence suggests that the amount of sexual expression we allow ourselves depends less on any inherited tendency than on how life has conditioned us. Early upbringing, past sexual experiences, present relationships, our work situation – these and other factors can affect the level of our sex drive, or libido. In some people this has always been depressed; in others loss of libido follows life crises such as bereavement or redundancy. At such times the loss is usually only temporary. **AS**

RELIVING YOUR EMOTIONAL PAST

■ *During lovemaking we unconsciously work through the stages of emotional and sexual development that we passed through as babies, children and adolescents. As we start with kissing, cuddling and caressing we hark back to the days of infancy when our mothers made us feel loved and valued for ourselves; their expressions of affection helped build our self-esteem and capacity for demonstrating love. As we move on from cuddling to genital stimulation we add an ingredient we discovered after experiencing the joy*

of childhood's nonsexual embraces.

Most of us take for granted an ability to show love in such ways. Yet these acts of love do not come easily to those who missed out on crucial learning stages. As children, some individuals lacked mother love, felt insecure and so never learned to trust, were punished as they started showing an interest in their genitals, or never grew away from their parent of the opposite sex. We need to negotiate all these steps successfully sooner or later if we are to make good lovers. **AS**

THE ROOTS OF SEXUAL DESIRE

■ *The need for another person physically and emotionally is there from the beginning of life. According to Sigmund Freud and his followers, the first sexual stirrings are in infancy, and the object of associated desire is our opposite-sex parent.*

When Freud first expounded this theory, it met with outrage. Some of the theoretical elaborations did not help to make the notion of child sexuality any more believable. For instance, it was suggested that girls are demoralized and envious when

they discover that boys have a penis. Another suggestion, which stretches credulity when it is summarized, is that a small boy's desire for his mother arouses murderous impulses toward the rival, his father. And the shame of these secret desires can be followed by considerable feelings of guilt.

Freudian theories can have a mythical ring to them, and can seem heavily biased toward a society long gone and quite unlike our own. This does not mean that their underlying claims are invalid. Taking what

Freud said about infant sexuality, there are in fact physiological indications that infants do experience genital arousal and do derive pleasure from touching themselves in these areas. And it is true that such inclinations are prohibited or limited by the civilizing process of growing up.

However, Freud thought that sexuality was dormant between infancy and puberty, and here there is evidence to the contrary. Infant schoolchildren may be observed mimicking adult sexual mannerisms and rituals,

such as pretending to flirt or be seductive. Becoming socially mature brings self-consciousness plus awareness of what is appropriate behavior, together with the knowledge that a sex life is reserved for "grown-ups." Although children's sexual feelings are not exactly dormant, as was at one time believed, sexual maturity awaits physiological changes in adolescence. **RB**

Considerate lovers are familiar with the phases of sexual arousal ■ *If they climax first, they ensure that a partner who still anticipates orgasm is not disappointed* ■ *They welcome but do not make a fetish of simultaneous orgasm.*

The phases of lovemaking

Lovemaking begins with sexual arousal, which leads on to four successive phases commonly labeled "excitement," "plateau," "orgasmic," and "resolution." These phases stiffen the penis, make the vagina receptive to the penis, and lead to sperm release when the penis is best placed to fertilize an egg. During resolution the sex organs return to normal.

Men and women alike pass through these stages, though women tend to be more emotional than men, take longer to respond to lovemaking, need more foreplay, and during sex enjoy romantic remarks whispered in their ears. If men ignore these needs they may not arouse their partner enough for penetration. These last remarks, however, are soft generalizations. They do not apply to all women – or necessarily to any one woman at all times. They may also reflect the influence of men's expectations of women. Some women respond as rapidly as their male partner, and many prefer, for example, an earthy rather than a romantic approach to lovemaking.

The *arousal phase* is associated with the physical changes that prepare men and women for intercourse. Arousal can be triggered by something seen, heard, smelt or felt. It often follows blowing on, kissing, stroking, or touching nerve-rich areas of the skin, especially the genitals, belly, thighs and buttocks. The breasts, eyes, nipples, nose and tongue are also highly sensitive. Stimulating all or some of these may cause erection of the clitoris or penis – ultimately the most responsive areas of all.

The *excitement phase* can last minutes or hours according to the methods of arousal used and the presence or absence of such negative factors as fear or noise. During this stage in both sexes the heart rate rises, breathing grows faster and perhaps more irregular, and there may be sweating, restlessness and trembling or muscle tension. As blood vessels dilate, blood starts engorging and enlarging the sexual organs.

In most women the nipples now grow erect, breasts swell and veins in the breasts become more conspicuous. A sex flush may spread a rash over throat, breasts and belly. The vagina's inner lips darken and pout a little, slightly widening the vaginal opening. The vaginal walls secrete a fluid lubricant. The clitoris grows erect.

In men blood pumps up the penis into a stiff, elongated phallus, the scrotum grows tense and thick, and the testes rise and enlarge. Pelvic muscles start contracting. Most men do not get a sex flush.

The *plateau phase* is short and intense, with penile penetration and thrusting. In both sexes breathing gets faster and louder, and pulse rate and blood pressure rise.

In women the vagina's inner two-thirds may continue ballooning until its walls have grown considerably in length and width. The clitoris rises but its shaft length decreases as it draws back under a hood. Stronger stimulation is preferred.

In men the penis may grow still larger and more erect, and a few drops of lubricant may leak from its tip. This may

FERTILIZATION

■ *In the man, spermatozoa pass from the testes, where they are constantly produced, to the seminal vesicles. In the woman, an egg shed by an ovary at "ovulation," about midway through the menstrual cycle, passes into a fallopian tube on its way to the uterus, or womb. When contraceptives are not used during intercourse and the man ejaculates, fluid containing spermatozoa (semen, or sperm) is deposited near the cervix, or entrance to the womb. Spermatozoa then swim through the womb, and the first to meet and penetrate a live egg in the fallopian tube fertilizes it. (See also Ch 26.)*

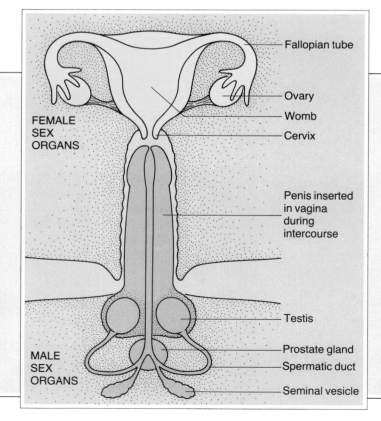

FEMALE SEX ORGANS

Fallopian tube
Ovary
Womb
Cervix

Penis inserted in vagina during intercourse

Testis
Prostate gland
Spermatic duct
Seminal vesicle

MALE SEX ORGANS

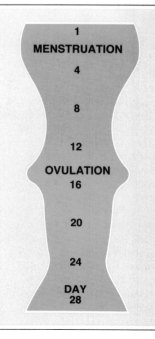

1
MENSTRUATION
4

8

12

OVULATION
16

20

24

DAY
28

contain sperm so should not come in contact with a woman's vagina unless she is contraceptive safe or the couple are wanting a baby. The testes rise higher still, and may reach half again as much as their normal size. There can be involuntary grimacing, clawing and toe curling.

The *orgasmic phase* lasts just a few seconds. In both sexes, blood pressure, pulse rate and respiration all peak as an intense sensation of pleasure floods from the genital area right through the body.

In women the sex flush is now at its strongest. Waves of contraction pass through the womb and orgasmic platform

(the vagina's outer third), and rhythmic spasms envelop the whole body. The face tenses, and many women cry out. Some women may experience more than one such orgasm before their partner ejaculates.

In men orgasm arrives in two phases. In the assembly phase liquids enter the urethra, giving intimations of orgasm – a feeling described as "inevitability." Then comes the delivery phase, as muscular contractions of prostate gland and urethra expel the semen. The body may jerk during the ejaculation, the most ecstatic part of male orgasm. Men, too, may cry out.

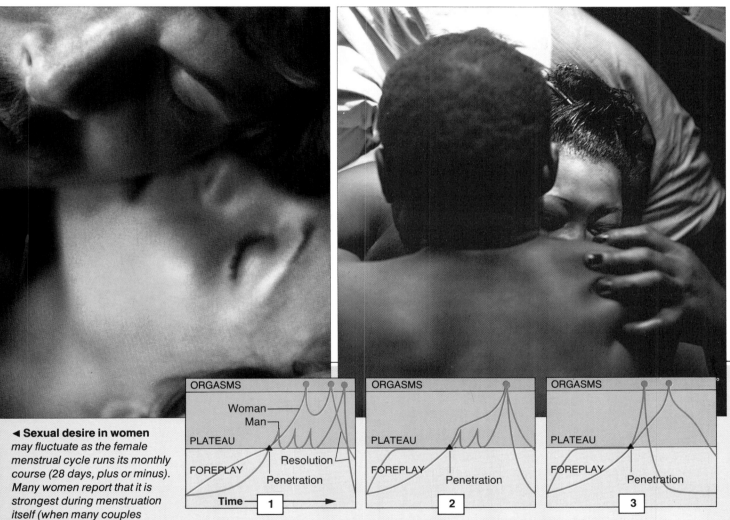

◄ **Sexual desire in women** may fluctuate as the female menstrual cycle runs its monthly course (28 days, plus or minus). Many women report that it is strongest during menstruation itself (when many couples unnecessarily avoid intercourse) and also strong at the time of ovulation. Other women report little noticeable fluctuation. Premenstrual tension, period pain, "mittelschmerz" (pain sometimes accompanying ovulation) and the contraceptive pill are sometimes associated with depressed desire.

MUTUALLY SATISFYING PATTERNS OF SEXUAL INTERCOURSE

■ Couples who say they enjoy making love generally find that the most satisfying patterns of intercourse are those in which both partners experience orgasm. In pattern **1**, the man ensures that his partner is able to experience at least one orgasm (several, if she is prac-

ticed) before he ejaculates. He does this by concentrating mainly on her arousal, and, after penetration, successively breaking off his ascents to climax. In pattern **2**, he similarly delays ejaculation until he is aware (or she tells him) that her orgasm is imminent and then

attempts to coincide his orgasm with hers – and sometimes he may succeed. In pattern **3**, intense arousal leads to early ejaculation – but he helps her manually to achieve her orgasm, before he recovers his erection.

79

After orgasm comes the *resolution phase*. Sexual excitement dies down and its bodily changes reverse. Tensed muscles relax, pulse rate, breathing rate and blood pressure fall and genitals resume normal size. Excitement and urgency give way to calm contentment, and often sleep follows, although some couples may seek to repeat the cycle after a short rest. **PG**

Common worries and complaints

The way that sex is often presented in magazines stories and novels may make us feel that it should come easily and automatically to us all. Yet countless couples suffer problems that interfere with intercourse. These difficulties can take different forms in men and women.

Men may find they cannot manage an erection, or sustain one long enough for making love. Then there are those who cannot readily achieve a climax: these are said to suffer from delayed ejaculation. For a third group the problem is the opposite: they ejaculate too soon, perhaps even before penetrating.

Women may complain that they feel no sexual excitement, and their vagina fails to lubricate. For such women penetration feels uncomfortable, or even painful. Many fail to reach a climax with their partner. This phenomenon – anorgasmia – is matched by problems of delayed ejaculation in men.

Both men and women may complain that they do not feel like making love, even though they love their partner.

▲ **After orgasm, resolution and withdrawal**, *considerate partners do not immediately turn over and go to sleep but* *continue to show affection, acknowledging their emotional closeness, until the afterglow of lovemaking subsides. Some* *couples like to talk about their feelings at this stage; others prefer to lie quietly in each other's arms.*

Most of the problems associated with love-making that disappoints can be solved

■ *Learning more about your partner's sexual anatomy, likes and dislikes can often help*

■ *But professional advice may be useful.*

Some of these sexual problems show up at the start of a relationship; others may develop later and make one partner lose interest in sex. Either way, problems can arise from any of a number of physical, emotional or other causes.

Physical causes include disabilities such as a small penis or a torn foreskin, and operations that make sex temporarily painful. Persistent medical conditions like arthritis, diabetes, anemia and backache can reduce desire or sexual capability. Stress, worry, tiredness and depression have similar effects. So do some medications such as sleeping tablets, steroids and certain drugs used for treating angina

or high blood pressure. Some women claim that certain brands of contraceptive pill affect their interest in sex. Similar problems can be caused by the social drugs alcohol and tobacco, and by cannabis, cocaine and heroin. Alcohol, for instance, releases inhibitions, but even a little reduces performance in both sexes.

Often, though, an emotional difficulty underlies inability to have or enjoy intercourse. People brought up to think of sex as wrong or dirty may find difficulty "letting go." So may adults who suffered sexual abuse as children, or harbor homosexual thoughts, or have fallen out of love. Anxiety can be inhibiting. A man may fear hurting a woman; a woman may fear being hurt by a man. Men and women may feel equally anxious about whether their partner really

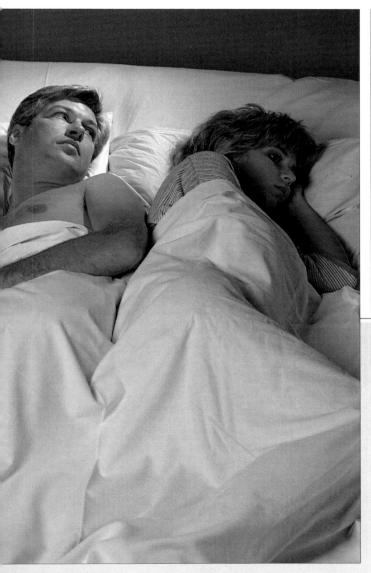

▲ **Disappointment after love-making**, if not caused by inconsiderateness, is best left unexpressed. Disappointed partners should question the realism of their expectations and discuss their problems as constructively as they can.

SOLVING SEXUAL PROBLEMS

■ *Self-help methods are appropriate for some sex problems: others need professional therapy (see Chs 25, 26). Here are just a few examples of recommended approaches. Nonsexual massage, preceding foreplay, can relax partners suffering from sexual tension that prevents them achieving sexual excitement or orgasm. Learning to relax can also help overcome the anxiety that is often responsible for premature ejaculation. Thinking about a favorite sexual fantasy or allowing themselves a rest pause may help men with occasional erection problems. Frequent erectile failure needs deeper relaxation and self-stimulation or mutual masturbation where the man deliberately loses an erection several times. Lovemaking education, and relaxation and massage with the partner can help non-orgasmic women who fail to reach the excitement stage of intercourse. Those who can pass on to the plateau stage but never manage orgasm with their partner may benefit from self-stimulation involving an exaggeration of movements that previously brought on anxiety.* **PG**

81

PERFORMANCE ANXIETY

■ *For intercourse to happen a man must first obtain and then maintain an erection. This can be less automatic than people generally think, for the penis is in fact a fragile organ, easily discouraged. On the other hand, women can have sex even if unwilling. Performance pressure therefore falls more heavily on males than females.*

That said, though, performance pressure increasingly applies to women, too. Because our culture lays growing stress upon the masculine components of their personalities, many women strive for sexual arousal and release as much as men. They are also as eager to be pleasing lovers. **AS**

Sexual myths often give rise to false expectations about lovemaking ■ *The idea that women are, or should be, sexually passive and the idea that masturbation is intrinsically harmful are two good examples.*

wants them, or how well they perform in bed. Someone may feel anxious about contracting sexually transmitted diseases or starting an unwanted pregnancy. Then, too, one partner angered by the other might deny sex as a punishment. Intercourse may even peter out from boredom in relationships that have gone stale.

Some problems have both physical and emotional roots. Adding a baby to the family may cause the mother to go off sex for a while. A new baby can change a couple's perceptions of each other, so that the father unconsciously equates his partner with his mother. (Conversely, some women unconsciously think of their lover as a father, or identify with their own mother whom they see as sexless.) Aging can impair sexual activity. Men's sex drive does fall with age, yet many couples give up sex because they wrongly feel that it is only for the young. Even the place where sex occurs can cause difficulties if intercourse is hurried because a couple fears discovery – by family, friends or public. **AS**

Sexual myths

Myths and taboos born of ignorance distort popular views on the rights and wrongs of different kinds of sexual impulse and behavior and this can undermine confidence, creating sexual problems and a sense of guilt that persist through life. Distortion occurs because many parents and teachers feel too embarrassed to teach children more than the basics of sex education. Sex manuals and some late-night radio and television programs present a more rounded picture of sexuality, but children still often pick up the details largely from their school friends. Many of the "facts" they glean are fallacies.

Myth 1. "Sex is tiring." Athletes commonly abstain from sex before events, mistakenly convinced that sexual activity drains vital energy. The opposite appears more likely to be true. Sex researchers Masters and Johnson found that sexual intercourse absorbs no more energy than a 50-yard run, though it does release sexual tension that, if unrelieved, can cause fatigue. Of course, some people are tired before they even start sexual activity. Anyone who is run down, overweight or unfit should let their partner do most of the work, adjusting position accordingly.

Myth 2. "Intercourse is essential to satisfactory sex." On the contrary, inexperienced couples may find going all the way stressfully unenjoyable, though many are too embarrassed to admit it. They would be better starting with foreplay and moving on to penetration later. (Women often need more foreplay than men anyway.) The partners might prefer sexual activities such as massage, masturbation or even oral sex. These alternatives reduce performance anxiety yet still provide sexual pleasure and relief.

Myth 3. "Oral sex is dirty." There are still strong moral objections to oral sex. Yet Kinsey's famous surveys found that half the men and women studied had experienced at least one or both versions: cunnilingus, where the man kisses and orally stimulates the woman's genitals; or fellatio, where the woman takes his penis in her mouth. Fastidious people object on grounds of hygiene, and some women fear swallowing or choking on semen. But research shows that natural genital odors and tastes can enhance excitement; and that healthy, AIDS-free couples who practice sensible hygiene have little to worry about. And although semen itself is perfectly clean and harmless, there is really no need for a man to ejaculate in his partner's mouth if she prefers him not to.

Myth 4 "Women are sexually passive." Most cultures

83

◄ **By taking the initiative** *in lovemaking, from time to time, while her partner plays a passive role, a woman can bring stimulating variety and a mutually welcome new dimension to a couple's sexual relationship. Against the traditional view, fewer and fewer couples nowadays believe that it should always be the man who plays the active role and is the dominant partner.*

SELF-STIMULATION AND FOREPLAY

■ *Guilt and anxiety once widely accompanied sexual self-stimulation. In the last century people thought masturbation led to blindness or caused brain damage. Doctors have shown this to be nonsense. They see masturbation as a harmless practice serving to relieve sexual tension and even menstrual cramps.*

Sex surveys reveal that more than 90 percent of people have masturbated at some time. The activity marks part of normal sexual development: self-explora-

tion before sharing sexual activity with a partner. Some people permanently opt for solo sex.

Foreplay has been described as mutual masturbation without climaxing. This helps each partner to discover what the other wants, and so increases their pleasure. Some couples prefer to climax at this stage instead of during intercourse. Oral sex is often part of foreplay, and many couples consider that kissing each other's genitals enhances lovemaking. **PG**

foster some such belief. Yet American researchers have found that women are especially aroused by listening to stories in which women initiate sex play. Such tales strongly arouse men, too. Plainly, sex should be a shared activity. Women increasingly recognize this, and many now let their partner know when and how they want sex.

Myth 5. "Men are always willing and able to have sex." The reason for this myth is that men are less likely than women to admit sometimes not wanting sex, or failing to achieve an erection. Popular fiction tends to reinforce the stereotype of male sexual prowess.

Myth 6. "A large penis is the key to good sex." There is no truth in the idea that a large penis provides a woman with better physical stimulation: only the outer third of the vagina has the sensitive nerves associated with orgasm. Some women receive more pleasure from a man's finger than from his penis. Then, too, a man capable of a huge erection will not necessarily have the sensitivity to his partner's needs to make sex a truly enjoyable experience for her.

Myth 7. "Women should be stimulated to orgasm by the penis alone." One study found that less than one-third of the women surveyed achieved orgasm this way. Many women seem to need extra manual stimulation of the clitoris. **PG**

The changing sexual climate

Intercourse gives instant physical gratification. It can also bring emotional reassurance. By helping partners to get to know each other intimately sex may help to forge a pair-bond – a stable basis for the procreation needed to keep our species going.

Attitudes to lovemaking are influenced by the changing social climate ■ *Contraception and greater economic independence have widely altered women's expectations of sex and men's expectations of women.*

For millions of years sex and procreation seemed inseparable. Now, though, most Western couples regard sex primarily as an expression of love and bonding and as a form of recreation. This change has happened largely in this century. Before effective contraception the price of sexual enjoyment was often high: the average woman of childbearing age was almost always pregnant or breastfeeding. Women paid for sexual pleasure with a chain of babies whose needs prematurely aged poorer mothers and drained their families' resources. Also, before women's sexual needs were understood, countless women probably endured sex rather than enjoyed it.

Birth control has largely removed fears of unwanted pregnancy from sex, and couples can now enjoy sex just for pleasure. Despite these changes, old religious views and taboos still influence millions of people's sexual attitudes or behavior.

The switch from old beliefs in the sinfulness of pleasurable sex to the attitude that sex is fun owed much to social change – especially to the growing influence of women as they won the vote, entered the professions and exercised greater sexual independence. By the 1920s, 19th-century prudery and sexual repression were already giving way to a new permissiveness. This gained fresh impetus after World War II. Permissiveness probably peaked with the much publicized open marriages and wife-swapping of the 1960s. By the 1980s unmarried couples were cohabiting on a scale

▲ **The new image of women,** *as reflected in two icons of the age. The postwar years have seen the emergence of a grow-* *ing body of women for whom the idea of passive submission to male power and dominance is anathema. These are women* *who expect to live their own lives, seek their own pleasure, and share their futures with men as not less than equal partners.*

undreamed of a generation earlier. But, as the shadow of AIDS lengthens – people are increasingly questioning promiscuity, and social attitudes to sex are swinging back toward restraint.

Couples probably attach more importance to successful intercourse now than ever in the past. There are at least four reasons for this. First, partners living in a small nuclear family (father, mother, children) usually come to depend emotionally on one another more than couples did in the days of large, extended families. Second, because most modern couples need no longer worry much about securing basic needs, they lay more stress on emotional fulfillment. Third, as life expectancy increases, growing numbers of partners face the prospect of sharing half a century together. Fourth, the threat of AIDS that goes with promiscuity lends new weight to old values placed upon monogamy. All these factors underlie the rising tide of interest in the quest for perfect sex with one life partner. **AS**

CONTRACEPTION

■ *People are often confused about the roles, risks and value of various forms of contraception.*

There are seven main reversible forms in use. Which are they and how do they work? The pill, taken orally, prevents ovulation. IUDs (intrauterine devices) seem to prevent any fertilized egg from implanting in the womb. The cervical cap, the cervical diaphragm and the condom mechanically block the passage of sperm. Withdrawing the penis before ejaculation (coitus interruptus) may stop sperm entering the vagina. With natural birth-control couples avoid sex on a woman's predicted fertile days.

Of all these methods the most effective are the pill and IUD, but both carry associated health risks, which may or may not be significant in the individual case. Cap, diaphragm and condom are also highly reliable if unperforated and used with unfailing care – and especially if used in conjunction with spermicides. The natural method requires painstaking measurements and record-keeping and can still be upset by unpredictable physiological events; and because the penis can discharge sperm before conscious ejaculation, the withdrawal method is notoriously unreliable.

Sterilization is normally fail-safe but irreversible. In women, tubal ligation stops eggs reaching the uterus. In men, vasectomy stops sperm leaving the testes.

Abortion ends unwanted pregnancy by killing the embryo or fetus, but may arouse moral objections.

Abortion, sterilization, the cap, pill, and IUD all require medical supervision.

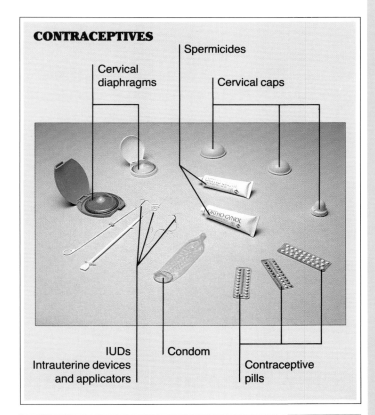

CONTRACEPTIVES

- Cervical diaphragms
- Spermicides
- Cervical caps
- IUDs Intrauterine devices and applicators
- Condom
- Contraceptive pills

▶ **AIDS** *(Acquired-Immune Deficiency Syndrome), an as yet incurable sex-related disease, which is not restricted to homosexuals, is having the social effect of directing interest away from promiscuous sex toward safer, lasting relationships. Men and women who* *previously equated sexual variety with a variety of sexual partners, and acted accordingly, are now beginning to endorse claims that the range of sexual satisfactions achievable within just one loving, imaginative long-term partnership is unrivaled.*

AIDS DON'T DIE OF IGNORANCE

GAY OR STRAIGHT, MALE OR FEMALE, ANYONE CAN GET AIDS FROM SEXUAL INTERCOURSE. SO THE MORE PARTNERS, THE GREATER THE RISK. PROTECT YOURSELF, USE A CONDOM.

MORE O'FERRALL P.L.C.

Thinking of Parenthood

THE MAJORITY of couples become parents. In North America, for example, only 5 to 7 percent of marriages in recent decades have remained voluntarily childless. A slightly higher percentage, perhaps 8 to 10 percent, are childless because the couple is biologically unable to bear children.

Among those who do have children, it is probable that some did not plan to. Those who did plan to may be motivated by a sense of religious or social duty. In the first book of the Bible, God exhorts his people to "be fruitful, and multiply, and replenish the earth." However, pregnancy and childbearing are more a matter of *personal* choice than ever before. Why do people choose to have children, and how does this choice affect their relationship?

The reasons parents give

Contemporary parents in Western societies say that they have children chiefly for emotional reasons. This is in contrast to many Asian and African cultures and also in contrast to earlier times in history when childbearing was a family duty and children were both an economic asset and a means of security in old age. Parents today expect that having children will bring them love, joy, companionship and fun. After the decision to have a child has been made, it is common for new parents to describe a unique, entirely new dimension of love that comes from being trusted unquestioningly and uncritically by a totally dependent human being, and being able to love spontaneously in return.

New parents sometimes also find that the experience of having children forges a stronger emotional bond between them. Some say that even though they were already very close, they feel that their child is a strong uniting force between them. Sometimes children also strengthen relation-

ships between adult generations and bring about a greater appreciation by new parents for their own parents. New parents, for example, often ask their own parents such questions as "Did I do that when I was little?" or "Why is she crying?" And only when they have their own children do many people appreciate the emotional and physical effort that went into their upbringing.

One of the most universally enjoyed aspects of having children comes through observing and identifying with them as they grow.

As children develop they provide a link to the parents' past, enabling them to relive some of their own childhood

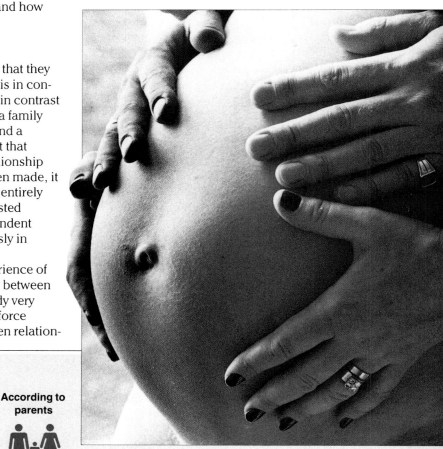

▲ **A new life in your hands**. What impact will it have on your own life and on your relationship with your partner?

◄ **More value than expected**. What do nonparents think they would like about having chil-

dren, and what do parents actually appreciate? In this American survey, the percentage of parents who notice most of the commonly mentioned advantages is greater than the percentage of nonparents anticipating them. More nonparents than parents, however, consider that children are useful and that they give parents a sense of creative achievement.

BENEFITS OF HAVING CHILDREN

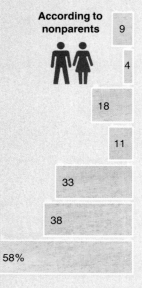

According to nonparents			According to parents
9	**Usefulness** - financial and practical help	7	
4	**Morality** - feeling a better person, becoming less selfish	7	
18	**Creative achievement** - a feeling of competence	10	
11	**Maturity** - feeling useful and grown up	22	
33	**Self-development and fulfillment**	34	
38	**Stimulation and fun** - pleasure derived from watching children grow	58	
58%	**Family love** - companionship and affection	63%	

About 90 percent of parents would do it all again ■ *Babies and adolescents, especially, may strain their parents' relationship, but couples enjoy their children's love and companionship, and a strengthened sense of identity.*

experiences. Having children can forge a sense of continuance between the past and the future. Many parents find themselves probing their own background for the first time and asking, for example, what great Aunt Anna used to wear, or where Grandfather lived.

A sense of maturity...

Another positive reason for becoming a parent is the personal growth that comes with being viewed as an adult, becoming more mature and responsible, and thinking and planning for the future. Parents are forced to look outward beyond themselves and consider the new child. Undergoing the important experience of having to put someone else first brings maturity. Caring for a child demands unselfishness

and responsibility. Parents frequently feel that they have done something wonderful by having a baby and they speak of feeling more complete and fulfilled. Also, because parenthood is still expected of most people as they mature, parents may see having children as a rite of passage into the adult world.

...or a result of immaturity

Reasons behind the decision to have children may be entirely positive. On the other hand, some people want children because they need someone to love them, or they are immature but want to feel grown-up. As a young woman reaches adulthood and it becomes necessary to prove she can do something, she may well choose the easily available occupation of motherhood, especially if she has not been encouraged to pursue a career. Childbearing may result from the lack of an alternative to provide the sense of iden-

IS THERE A RIGHT TIME?

■ *Nowadays we choose when we wish to start or increase our families. We are likely to live longer than we would have done a century ago, and, knowing that survival rates are so much higher today, we have fewer children. A woman who stops working to raise a family can still have a valuable working life either before or after childbearing and rearing.*

So is there an advantage to having children at a particular age? Researchers who have studied parents between the ages of 30 and 50 compared the effects of having first children at 20, 30 and 40. While they found that there were many differences, there did not appear to be one age better than another for rising to the demands of parenthood. Whatever their age, most parents felt that they themselves had developed through the experience of having children.

OLDER PARENTS

In the last decade there has been a noticeable change in birth rates with an increase in the number of women having their first babies after 30. The rise in the average age of mothers is understandable at a time when there is greater opportunity for women in higher education and they are less likely to want to leave interesting jobs.

Studies indicate that parents who have children later in life feel both advantages and disadvantages. Professional women, trained to be organized and competent, often prepare themselves well for the coming of a child but may find it difficult to cope with the impact. Used to a busy career, they may find it hard to relax and just be with the baby. The baby's apparent disregard for routine and order conflicts with their training and requires an unaccustomed degree of flexibility and

▲ **Genetic counseling** *has reassured a pair of prospective parents. The counselor holds a karyotype (a chromosome chart) based on an examination of a single cell of the baby the woman is carrying. It shows that the baby does not have Down's Syndrome, for there is* *a normal 21st chromosome pair (rather than a trio at the 21st point on the chart). The risk of Down's Syndrome increases with the mother's age. At 30 it is about one chance in 1,000, at 40 about one chance in 100.*

patience. Nevertheless, most "late" parents feel they were more appreciative of their parenting experiences than they might have been, had they been younger. Many say that they were less obsessed with themselves or their partners than they were at a younger age and were better able to enjoy their new roles.

PARENTHOOD IN THE BALANCE

■ For all parents, raising children is costly in psychological, marital, social and financial demands as well as missed opportunities. The extent to which these negative effects bother parents varies greatly. For some parents who have additional problems to cope with, such as handicapped or difficult children or the prospect of raising children alone or with meager resources, the stresses of parenthood are intensified.

Yet, in a recent study carried out in the United States approximately 90 percent of parents say that they would choose to have children if they were living life over. The love and affection between parents and children and between the parents themselves, the unique opportunity to create, influence and participate intensely in another person's growth and the personal development that may be experienced by fulfilling this natural but demanding role: for most couples, these are the rewards that make parenthood desirable.

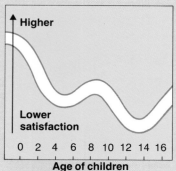

▲ **How marital satisfaction changes** *across the lifespan. This W-shaped graph results from several studies. Other studies produce a simpler U-shaped graph, without the increase in satisfaction shown here during the preadolescent years. All agree that satisfaction increases as children leave home (see Ch15).*

HOW MEN AND WOMEN VALUE CHILDREN

% MEN			% WOMEN	
Without children	With children		Without children	With children

Usefulness - financial and practical help

Morality - feeling a better person, becoming less selfish

Creative achievement - a feeling of competence

Maturity - feeling useful and grown up

Self-development and fulfillment

Stimulation and fun - pleasure derived from watching children grow

Family love - companionship and affection

▲ **Two become three** *and Sunday mornings in bed take on a new character. The preferred number of children is falling: in 1973 1 percent, in 1986 5 percent, of Americans thought one child ideal. The percentage preferring two rose from 46 to 59.*

◄ **Men disagree more than women** *about the value of children. This comparison of the attitudes of men and women with and without children is based on the same survey as the graph on page 86.*

THE POSITIVE SIDE OF PARENTING

"I have a special kind of love for my baby that I never knew existed. I would have been a lesser person without her. It's like seeing a part of yourself that you never saw before."

"My child has made me more mature in the sense that caring for him has made me less selfish and more able to take on responsibilities."

"I would look with disbelief at this fragile wonder."

"The pregnancy and birth has made me feel so much closer to my wife. This has been a time of learning and discovery for me. I just love watching our baby grow and do new things."

THE NEGATIVE SIDE OF PARENTING

"I felt torn by raging emotions over his safety – unwilling to leave him alone, listening to his breathing through the night and yet equally longing to be free again from the suffocating burden of motherhood."

"The most disruptive aspect of her birth is the change we have had to make in our thinking and planning for both of our careers. Where we could previously measure decisions affecting our careers in terms of an ideal of equality for both of us, now the equation is much more complicated."

Is there anything wrong with having no children or only one? ■ *Only children are not disadvantaged* ■ *Only children, elder children and children from small families receive more parental attention; they achieve more and they are better adjusted* ■ *Couples without children or with only one have more time for each other.*

tity she needs. Quite commonly, women become pregnant and find themselves with children, without ever having made a deliberate decision.

Why couples choose to limit childbearing

There are understandable reasons why people limit childbearing or choose not to have children at all. Raising children is demanding and difficult. Hardly anyone claims that parenting is easy and, even under the best of circumstances, most say that parenting is stressful at least part of the time. Many studies have shown that parenthood is at first a combination of fulfillment and stress, and that conditions may not improve later. In the early months and years of parenthood, there can be enormous physical demands on time and energy. New parents talk about loss of sleep, constant fatigue, extra work around the house, and drains on both emotional and physical strength. They may feel mentally

and physically exhausted. A mother will say: "He takes so much of my time that I find myself going in circles." Usually parents can cope with this during the day, but find it difficult to be objective at night. These physical demands of caring for a baby do subside over time as infants develop routines and require less constant attention, but active tasks such as feeding, diapering and cleaning continue to require substantial parental time and commitment over the early years.

I've never felt so helpless

A potentially longer-lasting negative effect of having children is emotional stress. The sense of your baby's absolute dependence on you can be overwhelming, especially when parents consider the number of years that this responsibility will last. They may also have a feeling of uncertainty about

▲ **Pulled between parenthood and freedom.** *Being a parent competes for time and money with other activities that are important to adults – social life, travel and entertainment. Having a baby, in particular, is associated with feeling "tied down" and a rather dramatic loss of freedom to do some things that were formerly enjoyed. New parents frequently comment that they stay at home more and are less able to do things spontaneously. Because both mothers and fathers are increasingly likely to have careers, parents today may need to make alternative child-care arrangements or adjust their work schedules to fit in with their parental responsibilities. Women, especially, are likely to feel some strain about how to divide their time between commitments to work and children. They are caught between their natural desire to care for their child and their wish to continue an interesting career. Mothers who are employed are sometimes criticized by people who believe that they should be with their young children. Conversely, women who remain at home to care for their children are sometimes regarded as not living up to their full potential (see also Ch 28).*

89

their competence to care for and raise a child. Mature women, for example, often complain after the birth of their first child that they have never felt so helpless. Having the responsibility for someone else's life may produce self-doubt, a feeling of inadequacy, and a feeling that you have lost control of your life. Parents may question their capacity to meet the challenge. At a workshop attended by new mothers, the women spoke of devastation, interruption, crisis, turmoil, rage, lack of privacy and deprivation when asked to describe their experiences. But they all agreed that they would not have missed the experience and talked of its almost mystical quality. Most parents have mixed feelings at times, but the low points are usually temporary.

For some parents, though, emotional strains are so constant and heavy that depression, frustration or resentment seriously interfere with their lives. Such parents find themselves worrying constantly about where their children are, if they are safe, and how they are doing compared to their peers. Also, because parents are viewed as being responsible for their children, life can be particularly stressful when the children get into trouble or do not measure up to parental standards or community expectations.

While children can enhance a marriage that is already strong, the stresses of parenting can also erode marital relations. Most research studies suggest that marital quality declines at least modestly during early parenthood and rises significantly after young adult children leave home. Graphs plotting marital quality commonly show a U-shaped pattern over the life cycle, with the low points when childrearing demands are greatest. Part of this negative effect of parent-

hood on marriage is simply competition for time and attention. The tendency for any two people to interact less when a third person is present is especially exaggerated when the third party is an infant or young child. Couples accompanied by a child in public places are seen to touch less, and talk and smile less at each other.

In the early years of parenting especially, marital strains

▲ **The empty cradle.** *Up to 10 percent of marriages are childless by no choice of the couple and in spite of medical efforts to identify and correct the cause of their infertility. In about 30 percent of cases, infertility results from factors in both partners. The remaining 70 percent are divided equally between those in which only the man is infertile and those in which only the woman is.*

WHAT CAUSES INFERTILITY?

■ *By far the largest reason for impaired fertility in women is the scarring of the Fallopian tubes that sometimes follows pelvic inflammatory disease (PID). The primary causes of PID are sexually transmitted infections such as gonorrhea and chlamydia.*

Other blockages of the Fallopian tubes, failure to ovulate (because of hormone irregularities) and high acidity in the female genital tract are also reasons for difficulty in conceiving. Some forms of contraception have been blamed, along with badly done abortions and many women's decisions to delay childbearing. Male infertility problems are most often due to low sperm production or sperm abnormalities, including low motility (ability to swim) and defective quality.

An increase in environmental and industrial toxic products has also been accused of affecting both male and female reproductive systems.

FERTILITY AND AGE

There is increasing interest in the relationship between age and the ability to conceive, because many women are choosing to have their children later in life. The concern that women who delay childbearing might run out their fertility clock appears to have been overplayed, because female fertility declines only moderately from the mid-twenties until the late thirties.

After that, though, there is a sharp upturn in infertility and sterility. The risk of failing to bear children, for women who rely on the fertility of one male partner, increases from about 5 to 6 percent, at ages 20 to 24, to 14 or 16 percent by the mid-to-late thirties, and very sharply after that. Men's ability to impregnate declines more slowly: between the ages of 50 and 54 it is still approximately three-quarters what it is in their early twenties.

Between 15 and 20 percent of couples have difficulty conceiving a child ■ *The resulting disappointment and loss of self-esteem may strain marital relations* ■ *About 45 percent can conceive with medical help.*

can arise from spending less time together as a couple, having sex less frequently and the general belief that the needs of the child are more important than the needs of the partners. Once a child arrives, most parents take on specific roles, dividing their activities and specializing in what they do in the marriage more than they did before.

Couples who cannot conceive

Whenever something really important cannot be achieved there is likely to be disappointment. When that goal is parenthood the situation can be devastating. Infertility can be very damaging to a person's self-image and this may affect their relationships. For the couple themselves, there will be strong tensions. Each may react in different ways. A woman may feel distraught, a man distressed by what he perceives as a threat to his masculinity. Women may worry that in trying too hard for a child they put their relationship at risk. Sexual relationships can suffer greatly at this time. Previously sex may have been a loving and exciting experience. Once medical tests are started, partners sometimes become tense, and sex can become mechanical, something to be completed as soon as possible or to be avoided.

When only one partner is infertile, he or she may feel guilty and worthless and may also be the object of the other's anger and accusations. They may even fear that their partner will leave. Men are less likely to display their feelings and this can give rise to misunderstanding.

Other relationships can also be affected. The workplace may make you unhappy if colleagues talk about their families, and a pregnant friend may evoke feelings of jealousy and resentment. While some friends will be supportive, others are sometimes embarrassed by the couple's distress and will leave them out of their social circle. Parents, even when sympathetic, may feel their own sense of loss at not having grandchildren. All these tensions will, in turn, affect the relationship between the couple.

Couples frequently question why it has happened to them. If they are religious, they may think they are being punished by God. If they have had extramarital affairs they may wonder if this has made them infertile. They tend to isolate themselves from situations where there are children, or even from society generally. They are likely to get on each other's nerves. The partner with the problem may have an affair to prove their desirability, especially since sex at home is probably not at its best. They often feel anger at doctors, parents, friends, other people's children, their partner and particularly themselves. They may even resent it if their partner takes an understanding attitude.

Between 15 and 20 percent of couples in the United States have difficulty conceiving a child. Male factors account for 35 percent of the total, female factors for 35 percent, and in the remaining 30 percent combined factors are to blame. Medical problems are found in 90 percent of infertile couples and half of these can be successfully treated. Medical treatments include carefully matching ovulation and intercourse to give the greatest chance of conception; collecting and concentrating the man's semen for artificial insemination; opening blocked Fallopian tubes and neutralizing acidity in the woman's vaginal tract. Other ways of treating infertility include in vitro fertilization ("test tube babies"), surrogate mothers, and semen-donor fathers.

Couples who cannot overcome infertility usually redefine their life goals not to include parenting or make arrangements to foster or adopt a child. **BCM**

TREATMENT OF INFERTILITY

THERAPY

● Sex therapists help clients to find the best methods and times to have intercourse. Pioneers Masters and Johnson claimed a success rate of 20 percent. In 5 percent of cases infertility rights itself without medical or any other treatment.

MEDICAL TREATMENT

MEN

● Some problems respond to the use of hormones.

● Surgery may remove obstacles to free movement of sperm.

● Sperm can be inseminated artificially into the woman.

● Antibiotics may attack obstacles to free movement of sperm.

WOMEN

● Hormones and drugs can be used to correct hormonal imbalances, help induce ovulation and correct body-chemistry problems after ovulation.

● Surgery can remove obstacles to fertilization and implantation.

● Special douches can be given to correct acidity.

▲ **Overabundant fertility** *was a side effect of early fertility drugs. Multiple births are now less likely, as hormone treatments use more precise doses.*

PARENTHOOD BY ADOPTION

■ *If you and your partner are unable to have children of your own, or want to expand your family, you may decide to adopt. By adopting, you can experience the rewards of parenthood, as well as giving a needy child the chance to enjoy family life. But how easy is it to adopt? What special tasks will you face and how well can you expect the adoption to work out?*

WHO CAN ADOPT?

In many countries adopters have to be over the age of 21 (no upper age limit is set). Couples who have been married for several years are in the best position. Unmarried couples or single people may find it difficult, though agencies are sometimes more willing to consider them if they want to adopt special-needs children – for example, an older child with physical or mental disabilities or two or more siblings who want to stay together. It is becoming increasingly acceptable for couples where the partners have been married before to adopt.

Many adoption agencies have moved away from vetting and inquisitorial procedures and toward the use of both individual and group counseling as preparation for adoptive parenthood. Couples wishing to adopt have the chance to talk to parents who have already adopted or to people who are adopted themselves.

Workers assess the extent to which an infertile couple has resolved any negative feelings about their inability to have children. Though the evidence is not conclusive, experts believe that couples who have not come to terms with their infertility will find it difficult to acknowledge the differences between having an adopted child and having a child who is biologically their own.

ADOPTING A SPECIAL-NEEDS CHILD

As the number of babies available for adoption decreases, agencies and prospective parents, especially in the United States and Britain, have turned their attention to children in public care who have special needs and whose parents are unable or unwilling to look after them. For example, a new adoption agency was set up in London in the mid-1970s to concen-

ADOPTING A BABY

■ *From the late 1960s onward there has been a steady decline in the number of babies relinquished by unmarried mothers for adoption. This is mainly because being an unmarried mother has become more socially acceptable, but also because of improved social conditions and better services for single parents. In addition the use of contraceptives and abortion has meant that fewer unwanted babies are being born.*

As a consequence the number of adoptions by non-relatives is falling. For example, in Britain they fell from a peak of 16,010 in 1968 to 4,157 in 1984. A similar pattern developed in North America, in other western European countries, in Australia and in New Zealand.

If you want to adopt a baby, the main way open to you is to go on the waiting list of a public or voluntary adoption agency. (In the United States and some European countries, it is also legal for would-be adopters to try to secure a child through a third person, such as a doctor.) However, many voluntary agencies have gone out of existence because of the diminishing number of infants available for adoption.

Finding a baby can take time: you might be on a list waiting for an infant for anything between three and eight years, depending on where you live. Your turn might never even come.

Faced with such realities, and as they see themselves growing older, many couples begin to modify their preferences and are more prepared to consider an older or a handicapped child. Agencies claim that they have few difficulties in placing children under five unless they are severely handicapped. Placing children between five and ten is more difficult but can be achieved provided the children are not too problematic. More complexities arise with children aged about ten and over, and considerable preparatory work is required for adolescents wanting adoption.

trate exclusively on the placement of Down's syndrome children.

A number of new studies have helped to encourage special-needs adoptions by showing that adverse psychological experience and separations in early childhood can be overcome in a loving and caring environment.

If you adopt such a child, you may also need other help such as the support of a group of similar adoptive parents, special counseling, or respite care which allows you a break from your responsibilities

Adoptive parenthood is for couples who are genuinely reconciled to their infertility ■ *An adopted child will have its best chance of feeling secure in your home, and finding a strong sense of identity, if you are open about its origins.*

▲ Different races, same parents. *In transracial adoptions it is vital that the parents recognize the child's cultural background and prevent identity confusion by encouraging links with the child's community. At school, some adoptees may encounter racial prejudice, which can be as painful for the parents as the child. They should avoid being overprotective. The parents' own ability to cope will set their child a constructive example for successful adjustment. Sympathetic relatives and friends can give parents invaluable support.*

while someone else looks after your adopted child.

Intercountry adoptions, mostly children from the Third World, have also become an important option. For example, all but 200 of 1,550 children adopted in Sweden in 1985 were children from overseas.

TELLING CHILDREN THEIR ORIGINS

Besides having to perform all the normal duties associated with parenthood, adoptive parents are encouraged to undertake two additional tasks. First, you should tell the child about its origins and the circumstances of the adoption, giving as much information as the child is able to understand. Second, you need to help the child adjust to the idea of two sets of parents.

Numerous studies have demonstrated how important it is for children to learn the truth about their origins, and in a way that does not give rise to any sense of shame or stigma. They need to be able to place themselves in relation to their past and to society in general. Children can usually accept and be comfortable with the idea

that they have separate biological and psychological parents; confusion occurs only when the adults themselves are confused or secretive. In Britain, Israel, Finland and Sweden, adopted people who have reached adulthood now have the right of access to information from birth and agency records.

An increasing number of adopted people also try to contact one or both of the parents who relinquished them, most often the mother. As many adoptive parents may at the best of times feel that their parenting is always under scrutiny, it is difficult for them not to feel threatened by their child's search. They will feel vulnerable and may even wonder if they have done something wrong. However, in most cases their child's interest in its origins does not reflect inadequate parenting and need not worry adoptive parents. Research shows that adopted people generally continue to regard those who cared for them and brought them up as their true parents, rather than those who gave birth to them.

DO MOST ADOPTIONS TURN OUT WELL?

Numerous studies carried out over the last 40 years suggest that about seven out of ten adopted people who were placed either as infants or as old as nine years are doing well or very well, and there is mutual satisfaction between them and their adoptive parents. About 15 percent are doing moderately well. The rest are less successfully integrated with their families or in society. When it comes to children of ten and over, failures range from 20 to 40 percent.

Overall, adoptive parents are not very different from the rest of parents. Some are overprotective and some have very high expectations, but only a tiny minority are rejecting and uncaring. Evidence suggests that problems are by no means inevitable in adoption, and that adopted people do not always experience identity or personality problems. Surveys examining the experiences of adoptive parents have found that the majority express a sense of fulfillment at being parents and emphasize the joy that their adopted children have brought them. **JT**

93

Extramarital Affairs

MONOGAMOUS, long-term love relationships are a characteristic of Western society. When two people make a commitment to each other, they implicitly agree to be faithful – never to have sexual relations with others. However, remaining true to the same person for a long time may in some cases lead to monotony, boredom and disenchantment with the relationship, and for some, the response is to have an affair. This can, in turn, bring additional problems of deception and jealousy, and may threaten the relationship itself. For a minority, though, an extramarital affair can bring a renewed appreciation of their partners.

What we think of extramarital affairs

In general, extramarital sexual relations are perceived as a violation of one of the basic assumptions about marriage and other long-term relationships – that they should be sex-

AFFAIRS: A SIGN OF A LESS MORAL SOCIETY?

■ *Many have pointed to extramarital affairs as an indication of society's growing moral decline. The lack of sexual inhibition in the 1960s and the development of the "me" generation have been blamed for undermining the institution of marriage.*

However, historical evidence shows that extramarital affairs have existed wherever marriages have. This is not surprising when it is realized that marriage itself has only recently come to be considered a love relationship. In Europe's not-too-distant past, marriage was more of an economic arrangement in which love and intimacy were not so much preconditions for success but fortunate side-effects if they occurred. (This is still the case in marriages in many nonwestern societies.) Liaisons outside marriage were frequently used as a means to fulfill people's needs for intimacy and sexual expression.

In medieval England, for example, adultery between masters and servants was widespread, partly because separate sleeping arrangements were unknown and bedrooms, when they existed at all, were overcrowded. Among the nobility of Europe, where arranged marriages were
common, men often expressed their longings for sex, love and romance within relationships with mistresses.

According to the historian Lawrence Stone, 17th-century England during the reign of Charles II saw a dramatic upsurge in extramarital liaisons among members of the court aristocracy, a trend that eventually spread to the lower orders of society. As sexual promiscuity became a hallmark of fashion at court and in high political circles, the crude word "adultery" was replaced with the more attractive "gallantry."

▼ **The sexual revolution of the 1960s**, *as portrayed by Elliot Gould, Natalie Wood, Robert Culp and Dianne Cannon in the film "Bob and Carol and Ted and Alice." At the height of experimentation in the early 1970s, a survey indicated that only 3.5 percent of couples in the United States had been swingers as often as once or twice, and only 1 percent had been swingers more often.*

VIEWS OF EXTRAMARITAL AFFAIRS

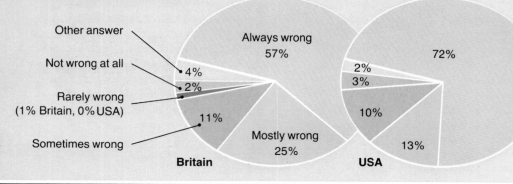

Other answer
Not wrong at all — 4%
Rarely wrong (1% Britain, 0% USA) — 2%
Sometimes wrong — 11%

Always wrong 57%
Mostly wrong 25%
Britain

72%
2%
3%
10%
13%
USA

◄ **Disapproval of extramarital affairs** *was already high in these early 1980s findings. Since the mid-1980s, an increasing consciousness of the AIDS virus has sharpened the trend.*

What impact would an extramarital affair have on your marriage? ■ *Most affairs are secret* ■ *For a minority, they can contribute to a revitalization of the marriage* ■ *Many involve fear, anxiety, confusion, guilt and conflict* ■ *Although not the most frequent one, affairs are a common reason for breakup.*

ually exclusive. Sex is seen as the most private and intimate behavior that can take place between two people, and sex with someone outside the relationship destroys the meaning of that behavior. Even if those involved are swept along by the romance, excitement and novelty of the experience, they are still liable to feel guilt, shame and disgust.

During the sexual revolution of the 1960s some people became more tolerant of extramarital relationships and viewed them more as alternative routes to intimacy rather than as the betrayal of the other partner. For instance, in a study of Dutch women, 8 percent in 1960 considered extramarital sex to be acceptable in certain circumstances; by 1971 this had risen to 17 percent. However, studies show that, in the United States and Britain, as well as in the Netherlands, tolerance of infidelity hardly increased over the next fifteen years. Since the late 1980s, with AIDS spreading among the heterosexual populations of Western nations, tolerance is on the decline again. In addition, what tolerance there is seems to be toward people in general, not toward one's own intimates – an attitude characterized by the view that "If others do it, it's up to them, but it's not for me and my partner had better not do it."

In many nonwestern societies, sex outside marriage is viewed more positively, although it is always restricted in one way or another. For example, in some cultures, it is only allowed among brothers- and sisters-in-law, while in others,

men are granted sexual access to the wives of other men but only on special occasions. In the West, there are differences, too: Europeans are, on the whole, more tolerant of infidelity than Americans.

Men are generally more at ease with the subject of adultery than women, but that is by no means the end of the story. In almost all cultures around the world, a double standard exists that makes a man's unfaithfulness more acceptable than a woman's. This can have historical roots: in medieval England, the sexual behavior of the women of the ruling classes was limited in every possible way, both before and after marriage, so that there would be no doubts about the legitimacy of offspring and, therefore, the legitimacy of inheritance. A man's infidelity was condoned because it was seen as simply the consequence of his polygamous nature. Although the Christian Church eventually demanded that both partners in a marriage swear to be faithful to each other, the double standard persisted.

There are signs that these gender differences are beginning to decline in the United States and Britain. For example, studies in Britain have revealed that about 20 percent of both men and women consider extramarital sex to be acceptable in all or at least some circumstances, and this percentage applies to all age groups. Moreover, even though men may find the idea of adultery less distasteful than women, this does not necessarily mean that they are any more tolerant when their own partner is straying.

How often affairs occur

Given all the disapproval that infidelity engenders in Western society, it is surprising how many people actually have affairs. However, because of the taboo nature of the

▶ **Affairs involve high emotional stakes** *for all parties. If the lovers become committed to each other, both they and their original partners face a serious emotional upheaval.*

subject, reliable information on the incidence of extra-marital affairs is hard to come by. The most trusted figures apply to the United States only.

In the well-known Kinsey studies of the 1950s, about 40 percent of all men and 26 percent of all women were estimated to have experienced sex outside marriage by the time they reached the age of 40. Later studies have, in general, slightly increased these percentages, although the figures of Shere Hite (of the Hite Report) and others, who have claimed that a large majority of people have engaged in affairs, should be treated with caution. The best estimate available at the moment is that nearly half of all marriages are affected by extramarital involvements in one way or another.

It is also not clear to what extent having affairs is a recurrent and stable pattern within relationships, rather than an incidental and unstable one. However, it seems that the large majority of adulterous men and women do not have

more than a few affairs in their lifetimes. It is certainly rare to find people who engage in them for most of the duration of their marriages.

Secret affairs and open affairs

The arrangements that people make to have sex outside marriage (or outside any other long-term relationship) can take many forms. One partner may occasionally "stray" in secret, or there may be an agreement between the two partners that sexual relations can take place outside the

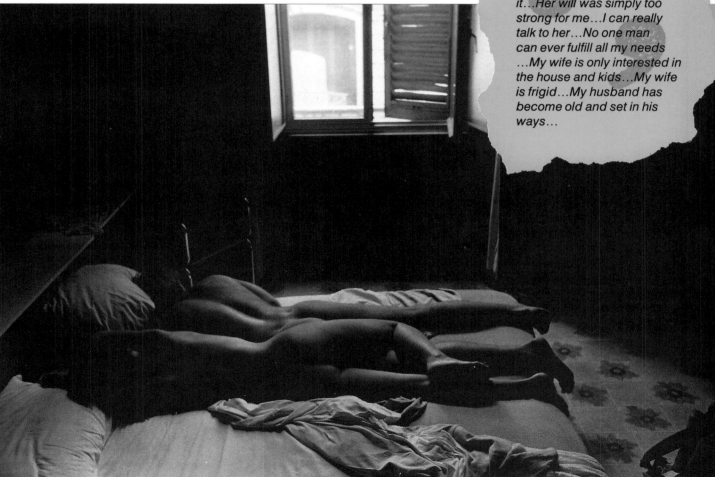

THE REASONS THEY GIVE

My wife doesn't understand me…What she doesn't know won't hurt her…If she can do it, so can I…I couldn't help it…Her will was simply too strong for me…I can really talk to her…No one man can ever fulfill all my needs …My wife is only interested in the house and kids…My wife is frigid…My husband has become old and set in his ways…

■ **The reasons people give** *for having affairs often focus on dissatisfaction with their primary relationships. Some say* they are seeking a sense of intimacy or of sexual satisfaction that they believe their partner cannot give them, others that they are acting out of revenge for their partner's unfaithfulness. Apart from people in open marriages, those who do not give dissatisfaction as a reason tend to see themselves as helpless objects of seduction.

Who has extramarital affairs? ■ *Probably more than half of married men and more than a quarter of married women* ■ *The great majority of adulterous men and women have no more than a few affairs in a lifetime.*

marriage under certain circumstances. The reasons why people have affairs also vary: for some it seems to be a conscious act, while for others it is just something that "happens."

The most common kinds of affairs are the secretive ones, when one partner has a sexual liaison with someone else and tries to keep this from the other partner. In these cases, disclosure of the affair can often result in a crisis within the marriage.

However, not all extramarital affairs are hidden from the other partner. In an "open marriage," both partners tend to look positively on them and to give each other the freedom to pursue them.

This fits their philosophy of life in which values such as autonomy and independence play a central role. At its best, the open marriage is an expression of realistic expectations, equality, respect for personal privacy, trust, honesty and open communication. However, not all open marriages achieve this ideal.

Yet another distinctive pattern of nonexclusive relationships can be seen in the modern institution of highly organized "swinging" or "mate-swapping." In this, as in open marriages, extramarital sex is approved, but in swinging this occurs only when both partners engage in it at the same time and usually in the same place. Swinging couples meet through personal contacts, advertisements and public or private "swinging clubs." Characteristically, swinging is very regulated, and independent affairs and emotional involvement are discouraged.

How affairs start, and why

For some people, such as swinging couples and, to a lesser extent, those in open marriages, extramarital involvement is a conscious act. For others, however, it happens unexpectedly, when the situation allows for it.

Flirting has traditionally been branded as a cause of marital infidelity. It is true that some people use it as a signal of interest or availability, and it can be the first step toward an intimate contact. However, flirting by itself does

▲ **When one partner becomes obsessed with work** *or otherwise loses interest in the relationship, the other may feel motivated to look outside marriage for intimacy. The desire for emotional closeness is a stronger influence on most people involved in extramarital affairs than is the desire for sexual satisfaction.*

▲ **Opportunity** *– for example, to become involved with someone at work – will not by itself bring about an affair. Most marriage partners, during most of their married life, are not interested. Long-distance commuters and people who travel in their work do not have significantly more affairs.*

WHO GETS INVOLVED IN AFFAIRS?

■ *What kinds of people are more likely to get involved in extramarital relationships? Studies have revealed that they are apt to be young, male, highly educated, not religious, politically progressive, positive toward nontraditional sexual behavior and dissatisfied with their marriages. There is also evidence to show that those who have affairs tend to suffer more from psychological problems. It is not uncommon for such people to feel alienated, to have sought marital therapy in the past and to experience emotional difficulties. These problems are especially likely where partners fail to communicate and engage in secret affairs.*

not necessarily lead to an affair. In fact, more than half of those who are married indicate that they have flirted during the previous year, but very few of them have actually had affairs during that time.

There are a number of factors that can influence whether or not a person will have an affair. For instance, receiving invitations from the opposite sex, knowing someone who has had an affair, discussing the matter with others and thinking about getting involved will all increase the chances that a person will decide to have an affair. Opportunity is not a major factor: it simply makes it easier for those who have already persuaded themselves to get involved with some-one. For example, commuters would seem to have greater opportunity to have secret affairs than those who work close to their home and partner. However, most commuters never have affairs.

The explanations that people give for having an affair are quite varied, but they all come down to the same few things. Dissatisfaction with their primary relationship is a common reason given for affairs: some people feel that there is a lack of real intimacy or that their sexual needs are not being met.

Sometimes one partner will have an affair as an act of revenge on the other's unfaithfulness. The fact that the partner has been or is involved with someone else, or simply the belief that this is true, is sufficient reason for some to look for sex outside their marriages.

Others claim that the affair they are engaged in is not something over which they have any control – they have been seduced by the other person. This is a convenient way of denying all responsibility and placing blame onto the third party. Alternatively, those in open marriages or who indulge in mate-swapping deny that there is anyone or anything to blame, saying that we must be open to all the possibilities of new relationships.

The novelty, variety and excitement that are part of any new sexual relationship are particularly important to those with open marriages and to mate-swappers, but they are also an essential feature of secret affairs. For some, the discovery of previously unknown aspects of their personalities, as well as sexual exploration (which is especially desired by men) and opportunities for having new experiences, can counter the boredom they may feel with their usual partner.

RULES FOR AN OPEN MARRIAGE

■ *To prevent their own relationship from being damaged, those who agree to have an open marriage usually institute informal or formal ground rules. In a study of some 50 open marriages, it was shown that honesty and consideration were the two most common ground rules. It was important to these couples that any relationship outside the marriage would not be kept secret, and that the marriage itself would always be put first, with the other partner being given enough time and attention. A substantial minority of couples established more specific rules – for instance, the "primary partner" had to know the "outside partner" (32 percent), the extramarital relationship was not to become too intense (35 percent), it had to be agreed in advance (22 percent) and it had to be terminated if the primary partner asked for this (29 percent). Openness was clearly less important to some: 15 percent did not want the primary partner to know more about an affair than absolutely necessary, and a few (8 percent) did not want him or her to know anything at all.*

◀ **Newly involved people** *take a special interest in each other, and a lover, at least in the short term, may offer a higher quality of communication than an established marriage partner can. Some people report a sense of self-discovery through talking with a lover, giving them an enhanced self-esteem that* *allows them in the end to appreciate their marriage partners better – in a revitalized relationship. However, these represent a minority of straying partners – in most cases, the affair puts a strain on the marriage.*

> *Attachment to the extramarital partner is an often unforeseen complication* ■ *You may feel painfully torn between your marriage partner and your lover* ■ *Resolving this conflict will mean sacrificing one of them.*

This loss of interest is sometimes blamed for the so-called "seven-year itch."

Finally, love and friendship are important motivations for becoming involved with someone else. As friendship and intimacy develop between two people, a decision has to be made as to how far the friendship is allowed to go. In a minority of friendships between people of the opposite sex, love-making becomes part of the relationship.

The benefits of having an affair

Extramarital relationships can have the potential for being highly rewarding, and most people report that having an affair can be a positive experience in some respects. The majority consider the sexual aspects of their new relationships to be superior to what they had with their partners. "Swingers," in particular, mention the shedding of sexual inhibitions, relief from sexual monotony and an improvement in their sexual performance. For them, having sex with another person can increase their sexual interest in their partner.

The higher quality of communication that is possible with a lover is also an important plus for some people. Without a long history of disagreement, and given the interest that newly involved people take in each other, it is hardly surprising that communication will be enhanced, at least in the short term. This can lead people who are having an affair to discover new aspects of their personalities and thus to personal growth, which in turn can lead to greater self-esteem. A consequence of this can be, perhaps surprisingly, revitalization of the marriage and a renewed appreciation for their partner.

The costs of having an affair

Even among people who consider their affairs to be justified, there are various problems that have to be faced. First, there are the practical difficulties, especially for those who conduct secret affairs. An out-of-the-way place to meet is an absolute necessity – one where the two people will not encounter any friends or acquaintances and especially not their primary partner. Finding the time to be with the other person can also be problematical, and care must be taken when telephoning and writing. All these difficulties can eventually kill the excitement of an affair, although for a few, they may enhance it.

Those in open marriages and those who indulge in swinging are also not immune to problems of logistics. Lack of time, trouble in finding babysitters and difficulties in scheduling sleeping arrangements and housekeeping agreements are experienced by the majority of couples.

However, the most costly negative aspects of having an affair are the emotional ones. Almost everyone who has affairs has been brought up to believe in marital monogamy. As a result, fear, anxiety, confusion, guilt, ambivalence and conflict are commonly experienced. This can increase the possibility of destructive, even violent, conflicts with the partner and threaten the marriage, the family and all the positive elements associated with both.

It is not uncommon for married couples to have an unwritten rule that, if either partner had an affair, that would mean the end of the marriage. When one partner "strays" and the "faithful" partner finds out, some marriages do end: in studies of divorced persons, extramarital affairs are constantly mentioned as a frequent (although never the most frequent) reason for the breakup.

The marriage comes under even more threat if a significant emotional attachment develops from an affair, even if

▼ The discovery that your partner *is having an affair is bound to be painful. Knowing what kinds of feeling and* problems they may be experiencing could help you to cope with the situation.

THE POSITIVE SIDE OF HAVING AN AFFAIR

Fun and excitement A sense of freedom and the shedding of sexual inhibitions may even lead to an increase in sexual interest in your marriage partner.

Self-esteem Rediscovering aspects of your personality brings self-confidence and can result in a greater appreciation of your partner and your marriage.

THE NEGATIVE SIDE

Practical The need for secrecy and complicated planning, and the conflicting demands on your time, can be very stressful.

Emotional Fear, anxiety, guilt and confusion may lead to conflict with your partner and even to breakup.

Health hazards The increased risk of sexually transmitted diseases, such as AIDS, may strain both relationships.

THE AIDS FACTOR

■ *Sexually transmitted disease (STD) has been a problem throughout history. Today we have drugs that can eliminate most of the common STDs such as syphilis and gonorrhea. However, there is still no cure for, and no tested and reliable immunization against, the viral infection that can lead to AIDS. Although fewer than 5 percent of the people in the West who are now living with AIDS contracted the disease in heterosexual contact, there are indications that, as has already happened in Africa, this percentage will increase, with appalling consequences for*

those involved and possibly for their partners and unborn children. Of all the negative aspects of extramarital affairs, this is the most serious.

this was never intended. The partner who is having the affair may find that he or she is painfully torn between partner and lover, and resolving this will involve sacrificing one or the other.

However, in most cases, the partners manage to salvage their relationship. Marriage is generally perceived as being too valuable to give up, especially if there are children. The injured partner may eventually feel that he or she will be even more injured by the pain, grief and financial disadvantages of a breakup than by having to live with the fact that their partner has been involved with someone else.

How long do affairs last?

Continued involvement with another person depends a great deal on how those involved rate the positive and negative aspects of their affair. People tend to be aware of both of these, and it is the rule rather than the exception to feel ambivalent.

However, being involved in an affair is not the best circumstance in which to evaluate rationally all the pros and cons of a situation. Emotional and irrational considerations can sometimes become all-encompassing, making it difficult to gain a clear understanding of what is actually

▲ **Passionate woman, jealous man.** *Men's jealousy is more likely than women's to be expressed as angry, and even violent, possessiveness. Women are more likely to blame themselves for their partners' transgressions. The French opera "Carmen," by Georges Bizet (1838-75), based on a story by Prosper Mérimée (1803-70) leaves the straying Carmen (played here by Julia Migenes Johnson in the Francesco Rosi film) dead at the hands of her outraged lover Don José (played by Placido Domingo).*

100

happening and how it is affecting those close to us. To do this requires a great deal of bravery in terms of opening up to our partners and lovers and being willing to ask and answer questions about what affects us most deeply. Sharing our feelings (especially with our partners) and commit-

THE ETERNAL TRIANGLE

■ *"Robert and I have been married for 15 years, and for most of that time, I guess we were fairly happy. However, when the children were old enough to go to school and I got a job, I suddenly found that I had a life of my own again. Then I met David, and for the first time since Robert and I married all those years ago, I decided not to hide my feelings but to show David just how attracted I was to him. I suppose part of the reason was that my experience of sex was totally limited to Robert – we'd married when I was quite young – and I was very curious about what sex would be like with another man. Anyway, one thing led to another, and David and I started having an affair.*

After all the time I had devoted to raising the children and maintaining a home for them and Robert, I really felt that now it was my turn – I have a right to my own life and my own friends. That's not to say that Robert and the children don't come first; they do. I'm really committed to my family, and because of this, I'm not afraid of what my new way of life will do to my marriage.

Besides, I know only too well that my relationship with David is quite limited. For one thing, we only ever see each other when we are at our best. That might sound like bliss, but it does mean that I'm always wondering what must be wrong with him! We also never seem to have enough time to spend with each other – for example, I've never stayed with David for an entire night. All this means that our relationship is really quite superficial, and I suppose that it is bound to stay that way.

I've always been very open and honest with both Robert and David. Right from the beginning, I told Robert how I felt about David and that I wanted to sleep with him. After the initial shock, Robert learned to put up with how I'm living my life now, but he still can't accept the fact that I'm sleeping with someone else. The fact that I'm not always around when he wants me bothers him even more, and sometimes when I am, he's been cold and distant. He had a short affair himself, but I think it was more a reaction to our new situation than anything else.

As for David, he's known from the start that my family has to come first. He usually copes with this quite well, but there are times when he becomes quite irritated by the fact that his needs can never be the most important to me."

Is one affair a sign of many more to come?

■ *Affairs become less likely as your main relationship matures, and even open marriages settle into a monogamous one-to-one pattern after five to ten years.*

ment are two other elements that are necessary if we are to come to grips with our predicament.

Fortunately, most marriages that have had to cope with affairs eventually evolve into happy, monogamous relationships. Almost all the studies that have been carried out on this subject have shown that extramarital affairs become less likely as a marriage matures, and even open marriages settle into one-to-one relationships after some five or ten years of outside experimentation. It seems that, in the end, most couples agree to enjoy the intimacy and satisfaction that being with one person for a long time can bring.

A partner's jealousy

Extramarital affairs are frequently the cause of one of the most powerful of all emotions – jealousy – which combines feelings of bruised pride and fear of "trespass" rather than sentiments of love and affection. It is not only felt by those who suddenly discover that an affair has been going on between their partner and another person. In fact, several studies show that, even in sexually open marriages, 80 percent of those involved are bothered by jealousy to some extent.

Some people are more likely to become jealous than others. Anthropologists have observed that jealousy is more common in societies that value partners as possessions or that emphasize sexual exclusivity.

There are also, according to psychologists, gender differences. When men feel that a relationship is threatened, they deny that they are jealous, express anger toward the alleged rival and concentrate on restoring their own self-esteem. Women are more likely to admit feeling jealous, become depressed, blame themselves, cling possessively to their partners and work to strengthen the relationship against future threats.

Most researchers agree that there is a link between jealousy and low self-esteem: partners who are secure in themselves and in their relationships are less prone to become jealous or possessive.

In sexually open marriages, women tend to be more jealous and to blame themselves for this; men blame their partners or their lovers for their own feelings of jealousy. However, in mate-swapping situations, it is the men who tend to be more jealous. This occurs when they have difficulty in freeing themselves from the traditional double standard – that is, it is all right for men to sleep around but not women – and when they believe that "women have the best time." It has also been found that jealousy is the main reason why couples stop "swinging."

One old belief, that "once a jealous person, always a jealous person," can be laid to rest. The results of a study of sexually open marriages, in which couples were interviewed twice, five years apart, indicate that jealousy is generally not a constant characteristic of a person's personality. Most of those who were initially quite jealous were not five years later, and those who were not jealous could very well have become so by the second interview.

A decrease in jealousy was more likely in those who had learned not to be so dependent on their partners and had come to trust them more. **BB BvD**

► **Accounts and apologies**. *Confronted with jealousy, some straying partners respond with an "account" – an explanation that attempts to make the jealousy seem misplaced – a claim of innocence, for example, or of entitlement to small indulgences. Other partners apologize and promise that they will not be unfaithful again. Research has found that trying to justify an affair is less likely to succeed than apologizing, if you want to save the marriage.*

Falling Out

CONFLICT can take up a great deal of time and energy, leaving partners feeling depressed and angry. We might hope that in an ideal relationship there will be no serious problems. Realistically, we need to recognize that there are bound to be some in any relationship, and then look for ways of dealing with them. One possible way is to use conflict to explore values, make compromises and strengthen the commitment to our partner and to the relationship. When this fails, a relationship can stagnate, and go through predictable stages of decay.

Constructive and destructive conflict

Conflict often arises when partners become aware of incompatibility between their own and the other's actions or goals. For a relationship to work, certain joint decisions must be made about how to divide work loads or share resources (see *Ch 23*) and conflicts can develop when the couple disagrees on strategies. In an intimate relationship, some resources, like money and time, are limited. One partner may feel "If they get more, I'm left with less." Unlike other valuable resources, such as love, there is only so much to go round.

Conflict can be either destructive or constructive. *Destructive* conflict is the result of incompatibility in matters of basic principles and has a negative effect on personal relationships. This kind of conflict comes about because partners expect or want opposing things from the relationship. For example, you might want to get married but your partner just wants to cohabit. Conflict can also be destructive when partners lack the communication skills for negotiating. In

this case, trivial disagreements can escalate into major ones. But conflict can be *constructive* if both partners share the same basic principles and values and, despite occasional differences, are able to discuss them openly, honestly and caringly – in other words, if they can negotiate with mutual acceptance and respect. Positive conflicts look at roles and tasks in a new light, renegotiating who does what, in a way that is acceptable to both partners. These kinds of conflicts are really ways of working out the problems in a relationship: they help to keep it healthy by providing solutions that satisfy both partners (see also *Ch 4*).

Perils of intimacy

Coping with conflict is not often just a matter of avoiding touchy subjects or persuading your partner to "see it your way." Whether they recognize it or not, partners in a close relationship are mutually dependent and this interdependence will grow as the relationship develops. As we become closer, we increasingly come to expect certain behavior in each other and we rely on each other to take responsibility for mutually important tasks. This interdependence means that the relationship is vulnerable in many areas and so the chances are that conflicts will increase and escalate in intensity as the partners become closer.

Among the risks of interdependence is the danger inherent in intimacy itself. We assume that in a close relationship, partners can be themselves with each other and share very personal and sensitive information without fear of ridicule, rejection or breach of confidence. Ironically, the better we know each other, the higher the price of misplaced

► **Before and after the honeymoon.** *English engravings from 1805 testify that disillusionment with marriage is nothing new. Between 30 and 40 percent of all marital breakdown occurs in the first five years. Romantic love declines and the partners make unpleasant discoveries about habits and quirks of personality that earlier escaped their attention. Issues that the couple thought they had previously settled – about money, sex, in-laws, friends, religion, children and how to spend time together – tend to re-emerge.*

Intimacy can be perilous to the stability of a relationship ■ *As we draw closer, expectations increase* ■ *We feel free to be more open with our demands and criticisms* ■ *The resulting conflicts can lead to breakdown.*

confidence and broken loyalty. Betrayal by someone you love is far more devastating and damaging than neglect or indiscretion by a friend. So partners have good reason to be cautious in revealing themselves to each other. There may also be conflict when partners open up to each other at different rates, because one may be more willing to take risks and make commitments than the other. Moving too slowly may frustrate one partner; moving too quickly may seem stifling and stressful to the other. These timing or pacing conflicts are most obvious in the area of sexual intimacy.

Couples who argue about sexual behavior should bear in mind that there is no objective standard to measure what is *right* in terms of kinds, time or frequency of sexual activity between adult partners. What is crucial is that the partners communicate to each other what their preferences and

ESCALATING LEVELS OF CONFLICT

■ *Even a couple's minor squabbles can easily develop into hostility. Here is an example.*

"You left wet towels on the bathroom floor this morning. I had to pick them up after you before I could go to work!"

"Well, it's your job to do the cleaning around here, not mine."

I'll clean up, but I won't be your slave! Why are you so sloppy and inconsiderate?"

"Talk about inconsiderate! I was in a good mood until you started nagging and yelling at me!"

What started out as a specific criticism about a small task, becomes an argument about roles and then moves on to an attack on personality. The argument has become much more complex and far-reaching. Anyone can pick up a towel: reorganizing roles takes longer, and changing personality might seem impossible.

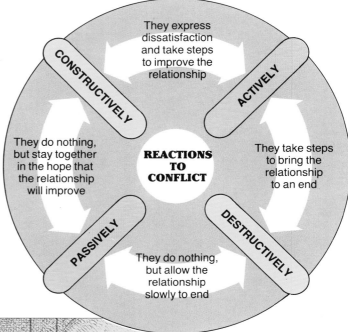

REACTIONS TO CONFLICT

CONSTRUCTIVELY — They express dissatisfaction and take steps to improve the relationship

ACTIVELY — They take steps to bring the relationship to an end

PASSIVELY — They do nothing, but stay together in the hope that the relationship will improve

DESTRUCTIVELY — They do nothing, but allow the relationship slowly to end

▲ **Four ways of reacting to dips** *that inevitably occur in all relationships. The four possibilities reflect your answer to two key questions. Shall I do something about the problem (shall I be active or passive)? Is this relationship one worth saving (should my response be constructive or destructive)?*

intentions are and what they feel is right for them (see *Ch 9*). But conflicts that are ostensibly about sex often have a hidden agenda – not about sexual behavior, but about power. Couples are usually happier when both partners have an equal right to initiate or refuse sex. But when the traditional roles are reversed and the woman has more initiation power or the man more refusal power, the couple is likely to be unhappy about it.

How will we spend the money?

One of the main areas for potential conflict is a couple's attitude to money. One partner may, for example, be an anxious saver and penny-pincher, the other a spendthrift who loves shopping and cannot resist a good buy. Money conflicts can also be about who earns it or who has more. However, a large-scale survey of American couples found that the single most important factor in couple conflict was the amount of money a couple has.

Money is a powerful symbol of status and success. Having it makes people feel worthwhile; not having it makes them feel worthless. This is particularly true of men, who are more likely than women to feel the need to control spending decisions. Money is not just a symbol of success. It is also the economic unit of exchange and the yardstick for measuring material well-being. The less money a couple has, the more conflict they seem to experience. In practice, however, when partners are actually arguing over money they tend to focus more on *how* it is spent than on how *much* there is to spend; and even then, the *amount* of money seems to be significant to them in terms of long-term financial security rather than immediate spending power. A

▲ **"How much did you say that cost?"** *Most of a couple's money comes from earned income. What seem to be conflicts about money are often conflicts about who earns it and how. If a woman works outside the home, her earnings can have either of two very different effects on the stability of the relationship. On the one hand, her contribution increases the total income in the family and this may stabilize the union and strengthen the relationship. On the other hand, her income may make her financially independent of her partner, freeing her to leave the relationship if she becomes dissatisfied.*

> **The single most common factor in marital conflict is money** ■ *We argue about how to spend it, but our underlying conflict is often a more general dissatisfaction with the amount or the reliability of the family income.*

modest but dependable source of income gives a couple a greater sense of stability than a larger but less reliable source of funds. Overall, the key to resolving conflict in money matters is for both partners to agree on making spending decisions jointly (see *Ch 23*).

Conflict over who does what

Strangely enough, partners often seem to be split apart not by the big issues like goals and values but by little things like "bad" habits and the division of labor in their day-to-day

lives. The complaint that my partner "doesn't squeeze the toothpaste tube right" or "never cleans the toilet" may seem trivial, but they usually mask a deeper kind of conflict. Arguments about things like this are really about the partners' *roles*. As the relationship develops, each partner will be expected to live up to a set of standards. In a traditional marriage, for example, the wife may keep house and care for the children; in return, the husband acts as breadwinner and head of the household. Conflict can arise when this pattern is broken. But even these traditional gender-based roles, although they have been accepted for hundreds of years, are *learned* rather than biological. This means that allocating roles to partners in a marriage on the basis of gender is mainly a matter of tradition: such roles, like others, can successfully be reassigned.

In any relationship, at least one partner ideally acts as the "advocate" in times of conflict – trying to re-establish the peace and sort things out. This role helps to promote the well-being of the relationship. When both partners work full-time, neither has as much time or energy to devote to smoothing things over. For example, when the wife has a job outside the home, the couple fight more about raising the children than they would if she were at home and this can have an adverse effect on the couple's relationship. In a perfect world, it would not be necessary to compromise either our job or our relationship. In the real world, we often have to.

Fair shares

Despite the popular belief that "true love is unselfish" research confirms that the best kind of relationship is one in which both partners feel they are getting a fair share of what is available. Getting more out of the relationship than you put in may be pleasant and pampering for a while, but in the

105

◄ **The little problems that matter** *can include disagreements about who should be in charge of this task or that. But not every couple has this kind of dispute. Research identifies three approaches to being a couple (also discussed in Ch 22): "traditional," "independent" and "separate."*

■ *Traditional couples try to settle judiciously and with restraint only those issues that appear momentous and crucial, ignoring problems that seem trivial and transitory. Traditional partners are highly interdependent and apt to be very dedicated to the preservation of their marriage.*

Independent couples relish

confrontation and like to bring every issue out into the open for discussion.

Separate couples try to minimize or avoid differences and arguments. Often they find that they have better things to do.

■ *In a minority of couples, the partners do not share the same approach, and this can create a strain. An independent who is matched with a traditional may offend the traditional's expectations that the harmony of the relationship will be of paramount importance. An independent matched with a separate may meet constant frustration because the separate cannot see the point of expressing small grievances.*

long run leaves you feeling guilty. Getting less out than you put in leaves you feeling cheated and resentful. When one partner feels that the relationship is unfair they are likely to change what they put into the relationship or what they expect from it. Alternatively, they might leave their partner. It may be unromantic to view relationships as exchange transactions, but an emphasis on fairness in allocating chores and obligations may be the best strategy for minimizing conflict.

Everything that partners do together may be a form of communication between them, whether they are talking, making love or sitting in silence. Even moods can communicate themselves – in fact they can be quite contagious. For instance, when one partner is sad for any reason, the other may fall into a similar state without knowing why. You and your partner can become so wrapped up in what is happening between you that it becomes difficult to separate your feelings from your partner's. Research with married couples in the United States has shown that dissatisfied couples match each other frown for frown and criticism for criticism, forming a vicious circle of conflict from which neither can break free. Satisfied couples, on the other hand, seem to break the pattern when one or the other responds positively. They are both then free to continue their interaction in a more constructive direction.

Unresolved conflicts

Dissatisfaction in a long-standing relationship can usually be traced to elements that were there at the start. The problems may not have been recognized at the time or not thought serious enough to do anything about. Often, full-blown conflict flares up much later, when the relationship has been going for some time and is integrated into both partners' lives. As two people become closer, they also become more important to and more dependent on each other. Ironically, each is also more likely to see the other as the cause of their problems and to blame each other when things go wrong.

Established couples with a history of unresolved conflict often give up. They simply put less time and effort into problem-solving than newer couples do . A background of continual conflict can eat away at the love and affection that partners once felt for each other, wearing down their will and ability to cope, and leaving them emotionally drained. Over time, bouts of conflict may be few and far between, but they are all the more painful when they happen.

People react to conflict in a number of different ways. Some decide not to let the relationship expand, and pull back. Others put very clear-cut limits on the relationship. Some pull out altogether and break it off. Alternatively, when faced with a potentially contentious situation, many couples have an unspoken agreement to avoid it by steering clear of touchy subjects and taboo areas.

If partners want to deal constructively with their problems, they can explore and develop methods of resolving conflict, such as turn-taking, openness, testing new ways of behaving or simply setting up new goals and standards for themselves (see *Chs 19, 24*).

All relationships experience conflict at some stage, yet most conflict is *not* terminal. What is the difference between relationships that break up and those that do not? It seems that there is no difference in the kinds of conflict experi-

FOUR RELATIONSHIPS THAT BREAK DOWN

▶ *Most conflict does not lead to breakdown, but research has found four types of relationship in which it often does.*

■ **A common thread** *that links the sudden-death category* BOTTOM *with the other three is that at least one partner cannot accept something that the other is unable or unwilling to change.*

Often, in the case of partners who do not like each other's personalities, one has hidden ambitions for making the other into a new person. When they realize that this is impossible, they may leave.

When relationships are badly

The relationship conducted badly, uncommunicative or inequitably

The relationship is doomed from the start by a serious difference in values or personality

Over time the partners grow apart, eg a wife's work achievements undermine her partner

The relationship dies suddenly when one partner discovers something they cannot accept about the other

The most serious problems in a relationship are usually there from the start ■ *They may not have been recognized at the time or thought important enough to do anything about* ■ *After time brings home the reality of them, and effort fails to resolve them, they may eat away the couple's love and affection.*

enced, but there is a very great difference in the partners' responses to their problems.

Research carried out in Britain and North America by Professor Steve Duck has shown four common patterns that increase the likelihood of breakdown. First, there are those relationships that are doomed from the start by a serious difference in values or personalities. For example, a couple may have married very young, in the face of parental opposition, and then found themselves unable to cope with the emotional pressure of feeling isolated and rejected. One partner in a relationship may be a secret alcoholic, or be acting out a hidden agenda for radically changing the other.

A second reason why relationships often deteriorate is because of the way they are conducted. There may be failures in communication or because one partner feels a strong sense of injustice. Most people can tell stories of neighborhood mothers with several young children, whose partners not only do not help significantly with child care and housework, but also spend most of their evenings out drinking with their friends. Many men, too, feel a deep sense of hurt and injustice with partners who withhold sex as a means of getting even for not getting their own way.

Sometimes the disintegration of the relationship is a result of the way partners develop over time. For instance, one may feel stifled. A capable professional woman who gives up her job when she marries because her partner prefers her not to work may at some future stage ask herself what his motivation really was. Was it simply that he wanted

her to be available to look after children and entertain company executives, or was he so insecure that he could not cope with the idea of a wife who could look after herself? Whatever the reason, when either partner feels that their potential is unfulfilled or their skills are undervalued, the relationship is likely to be abandoned as a result of "too little, too late."

Finally, there are relationships that die a sudden death. This usually happens when either partner discovers something new or shocking about the other. A husband who finds out that his wife is having an affair or a wife who discovers that her husband has committed a crime may want to opt out of the marriage. Even the kinds of thing that an outsider might see as minor deceptions or betrayals can be enough to bring the relationship to a sudden end.

How do relationships break up?

In real life the disintegration of a relationship is likely to be messy, uncontrolled and fragmented. It is an uncertain process, in which individuals respond in a variety of ways. Some people express their feelings openly or decide to end the relationship. Others are more passive and either neglect the deteriorating relationship or wait in silent loyalty for the other to do something about it.

In most cases, disengagement is not mutual. It tends to be indicated – directly or indirectly – by one partner. A partner is likely to take the *direct* approach to ending the relationship if, for instance, intimacy has recently been relatively intense and a less direct approach would be confusing. Partners tend to take the *indirect* approach if there is dis-

conducted, someone who needs communication may feel unable to continue with an uncommunicative partner; or the problem may be a sense of injustice: one partner considers that the other is demanding too much, or not contributing.

Change over time is often good for a relationship. Partners often develop in complementary ways that enhance their satisfaction with each other. Cruelly, however, the bride who goes to work to put her young husband through university may discover that he finds her too unsophisticated once he has his education.

■ **Do you speak the same language?** Men and women may speak different "languages" of love. Research suggests that women prefer statements about feelings, like "I love you," or nonverbal gestures like touches and embraces. Men, on the other hand, prefer to express love by doing things like chores or favors. Conflict develops when partners cannot speak or understand each other's language. If we want to resolve our conflicts we must begin by listening to each other, and accepting these differences in expression. '

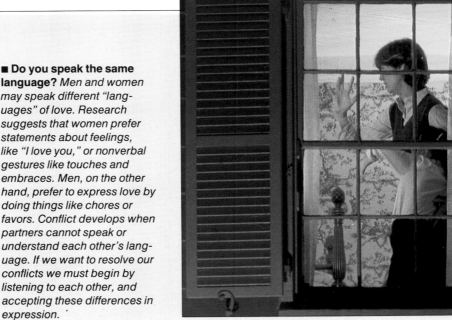

tance between them, or if they have less power or fear losing face. Regardless of who left whom, most people save face by claiming *they* ended the relationship. **ALW**

The final stages

For most couples, the end of a relationship is signaled when the partners make it public in one way or another. But the run-up to the end is usually a slow and agonizing process. However we cope with it on the surface, underneath each of us experiences discontent, anger, self-doubt, alienation, depression, blame and guilt.

Long before the end, one or both of us may have had an inkling that something was badly wrong with the relationship. We begin to think critically of each other and seize on and intensify every negative aspect of the other's personality. Instead of focusing on the positive characteristics or simply recognizing that we do not appreciate aspects of the other's behavior, we start to attack their whole personality – we see them as uncaring, insensitive, egocentric and unfair. The result usually is interminable arguments and deeply hurt feelings.

With a lot of effort, and possibly professional help, the relationship can still be salvaged at this stage if we are able to adapt in order to meet each other's needs (see *Ch 25*). Without that effort or help, the relationship tends to deteriorate still further. Previously unvoiced hurt and anger surface and we express them openly. We each lose respect for the other. This shows in the way we interact – showing no interest for the other's conversation, standing physically distant from each other at parties, putting down each other's friends and family, and so on. Sex, too, becomes part of a power game rather than a confirmation of intimacy. Real commitment has gone. Obviously, living on a daily basis with such high levels of stress becomes intolerable.

108

The typical pattern of breakdown is slow and agonizing ■ *Long before the end, one or both partners will have an inkling that something is badly wrong* ■ *Attacks on each other's personality create an accumulation of hurt feelings* ■ *Exploding hurt and anger are followed by silent withdrawal.*

THE STAGES OF BREAKDOWN

■ *BOTTOM In the first three stages of breakdown, a relationship can still be retrieved, and most relationships do move back and forth between higher and lower levels of contentment and commitment. TOP If stage three results in a decision to end the relationship, the decision is very often not mutual. If disintegration has occurred quickly, the partner who wants to leave is likely to say so in a very direct way. When intimacy has recently been high, subtle or gentle signals of departure are not easy to understand.*

1
Problems lead to disillusionment and dissatisfaction with the relationship, but discontent is not yet openly expressed

2
One or both partners reflect on the other's flaws and consider whether these justify withdrawing from the relationship

3
Dissatisfaction is now openly expressed. They both decide to repair the relationship or to end it

If conflict during a relationship is stressful and preoccupying, the end of a relationship – even if it is in some ways a relief – is usually traumatic. Regardless of why partners break up or who leaves whom, the loss of a partner causes intense emotional pain and distress. People in the final stages of breakup may suffer psychological reactions such as depression, anger, bitter hatred and feelings of worthlessness and panic, as well as numerous physical symptoms, including insomnia, ulcers, migraine headaches, impotence and heart attacks. The end, when it comes, often leaves us feeling confused, emotionally lonely and perhaps socially isolated (see *Ch13*). **SJP**

Getting over it

When a relationship has been integrated into our lives, it becomes part of our identity. The loss of that relationship is in many ways a loss of self. Many people describe it as "feeling as if I were half of a pair of scissors." The sense of loss is usually accompanied by an obsessive review of the breakup. At this stage, our constant preoccupation with the lost relationship can find no conclusion, and we go over and over the "if onlys" and "what ifs." We keep reviewing the events of the past, trying to find out what went wrong. Throughout this period, we feel stuck in continual, distorted reminiscence. This is a normal reaction: it seems that what had previously been curiosity about why our partner behaved in certain ways becomes a pressing need to understand and then to close the door on the relationship.

Since our partner is no longer there to confirm or deny the explanations we give ourselves, we are not constrained by facts or fairness. Whether the stories we tell ourselves are true or not, once we feel we have identified the causes for the breakup, we can emotionally move on. Each time we tell our story, it may vary a little according to our audience and the occasion. We highlight the different themes and motives that seem important to us at the time. Ultimately, a complete (if biased) account of our past relationship will help us to understand and accept our loss, to redefine our own separate identity and to make a healthy transition to life without that relationship. **ALW**

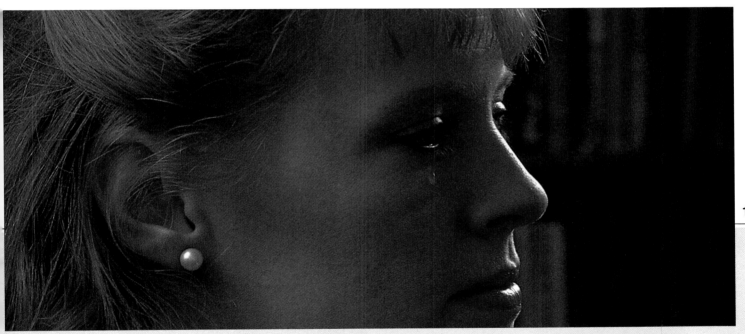

109

4
If the partners have decided to end the relationship, they begin to admit it publicly. Each partner tries to enlist the loyalty and support of their friends and relatives

5
The ex-partners go through a stage of interpreting the experience, each developing their own story of the relationship. They grieve about and come to terms with the breakup

■ **Getting over a breakup** *involves managing your mood. Make a conscious effort not to think of what you liked about your ex-partner – think of other people and times that have been rewarding. But allow yourself to remember that your ex-partner was imperfect – only human, and replaceable. You should also congratulate yourself on what you have gained in experience: the rewards and the lessons of the relationship.*

Contemplating Divorce

DIVORCE is the second most stressful life experience after the death of a loved one. It is also one of the most common: for example, in the United States close to 50 percent of marriages end in divorce; in Britain and France around 30 percent. Although the rates of divorce seem to have stabilized in recent years, the percentage is still very high. Why is this, and why do couples continue to go through this personally traumatic and socially disruptive experience?

How does society view divorce?

Nowadays, divorce is increasingly recognized as a major life crisis that has many complex causes. We no longer automatically brand the people involved as failures. Our approval or disapproval is more likely to depend on the circumstances of each particular situation. Nevertheless, some divorced people continue to suffer from the social stigma attached to being divorced. Most people still consider the two-parent nuclear family to be the norm and some have little sympathy for those who find themselves in an unconventional family grouping. Despite a generally more understanding public reaction to divorce, it is still viewed with a certain amount of distaste.

Fatal attractions

Rapid increases in divorce rates reflect recent changes that have made divorce easier than it used to be. These changes include increased educational and employment opportunities for women, fewer children per family, higher family income, the availability of inexpensive or free legal aid and the relaxing of the divorce laws in most countries. Increases in divorce rates probably do not reflect a significant rise in the number of people who feel discontented with their relationship.

Couples do not divorce because of unhappiness alone,

and marriages that survive can be deeply fulfilling or a misery to both partners. The question of happiness is just one of many factors contributing to marital stability or instability. What are the others? What points are people likely to weigh up when considering the attractions of remaining married and the alternative attractions of leaving?

Besides the level of personal happiness resulting from their marriage, attractions that make people want to stay married include the degree of interdependence of the two partners (do you enjoy a sense of mutual reliance?); the sense of having things in common (do you appreciate the fact that your partner shares your tastes, opinions and sense

"THEY WERE THE PERFECT COUPLE"

■ *"We had been friends for so very long...so many neighborhood parties, working together on innumerable civic concerns, car pooling for the kids and their activities and now this. Everyone thought they were the perfect couple...a caring family concerned about each other and their friends and community. Divorce? It couldn't be. That was something that happened on TV, was reported in the newspapers or was the tantalizing lead article in one of the "pulps"...it was not something that happened to your best friends! And yet, the closer I got to the house, the more the cold reality settled in...our closest friends and the godparents of our children were breaking up. What was I going to say when I got home? How was I going to explain this to our kids? Why was this happening? Worse yet, how could I be sure the same thing wasn't about to happen to us?"*

▲ **The formalities completed,** a father looks on sadly as his wife and daughter leave the court building together. All three will now have major readjustments to make to their lives and their relationships with each other.

Divorce hurts, but this does not prevent people from going through with it ■ *It is no longer something that only happens to other people – in countries that allow them to, 30 to 50 percent of couples end their marriages.*

of humor?); and the quality of the couple's sex life. It is also true that the possibility of achieving a progressively better lifestyle makes staying married an attractive option (will you miss out on better times if you leave?). Other things that are regarded as good anchors for marriage are higher levels of education and income (partners feel attracted to the lifestyle that has been attained and shared), and the two partners sharing similar social characteristics such as age and religion (they feel comfortable together).

If a person is dissatisfied with any of these elements in their marriage, they may look for contentment outside it. If they think they will have a more satisfying social life, or see the clear probability of a more meaningful relationship or more chance for personal growth, they are more likely to contemplate leaving the marriage.

Having enough money and the necessary skills to secure a sufficient income will also be a factor. Among older people this is more likely to apply to men than to women. As men get older, their income usually increases and they become more financially able to sustain an independent life. They become more desirable as mates because of their

QUESTIONS TO ASK

■ *When contemplating separation, there are many decisions that should be made. Some of the questions the couple needs to discuss are:*

1 *Where is each partner going to live? Who stays in their present home, and where does the other partner go?*

2 *What is the family's financial situation? Is the family income sufficient to provide for two households? Should the standard of living be reduced for one partner or for both? If one partner is unemployed, is this person to seek employment?*

3 *Who is responsible for expenses such as utilities, food, clothing, child care, household maintenance, transport, medical and dental care, insurance, and so on?*

4 *If the couple has only one car, is a second car needed? Who is going to select it? Who will care for it? How is it going to be paid for?*

5 *How and when are children, extended family and friends to be told about the separation? Are these to be told by one or both partners? Will you agree on an account of why you are separating or does each partner tell their own story?*

6 *Where will the children live? What criteria are to be used for this decision and should the children's own views be taken into consideration?*

7 *What are each parent's rights and responsibilities in relation to the children? When will the children see each parent? Who will take the children to school and to other activities? Who will provide financial support for the children? How much say are the children to have in these decisions?*

8 *Who is responsible for decisions related to the children's daily lives? Who is to make major decisions about the children? How is an emergency to be handled?*

9 *How are differences of opinion about the children to be handled? What will be the role of grandparents during separation? How often will the children see their grandparents?*

10 *Is there a specific length of time for the separation period when the couple will decide whether to pursue a divorce or reconciliation? If so, how long will this be and how will the final decision come about?*

111

Attractions of staying married	Barriers to divorce	Attractions of divorce
Quality of relationship Companionship Esteem for partner Sexual partnership Better lifestyle Feeling akin to partner	Family pressure Social stigma Young children Divorce laws Obligations of marriage Lack of money Religious beliefs	New relationship Sexual freedom Independent single life Economic freedom Employment opportunities Personal growth

success and resources. This is less so for married women, who have often neglected their job skills during the marriage while bringing up children and, therefore, find it harder to be economically independent after divorce.

Even if they are able to support themselves financially, older women are more restricted in their choice of potential partners. It is socially acceptable for a man to have a relationship with a younger *or* older partner; women are mostly restricted to relationships with men of a similar age or older (but see *Ch3*). Consequently they have less chance of establishing a satisfying social life and eventually remarrying.

Weighing the obstacles to divorce

Even when someone has decided that the alternative attractions to marriage are worth considering, there remain obstacles to going so far as divorce. These barriers may keep people in a marriage regardless of how unhappy they are or how inviting the alternative attractions are. One of the strongest barriers is religion. Many religions disapprove of divorce – the Jewish and Christian faiths are particularly resistant to it.

However, the fact that a religious organization disapproves does not mean that it can prevent its members from becoming divorced. Evidence suggests that Protestants, for example, get divorced at generally the same rate as the rest of the community. There is, however, a slightly lower divorce rate among Catholics, although this is not evidence of less frequent marital breakdown. The failure of a Catholic

▲ **The love that cost him his crown**. *In 1936 this man was Edward VIII, King of England. When he fell in love with Wallis Simpson, an American divorcee, he encountered unshakable religious, social and constitutional objections to marrying her and making her Queen. The marriage of the monarch – and nominal head of the Church of England – to a divorced woman was unaccept-* *able, since national institutions were expected to reinforce the family by preventing divorce. In the face of opposition to his marriage, Edward chose to renounce the throne rather than give up the woman he loved. He lived the rest of his life abroad.*

In the 1930s divorce in Britain, as in most countries that then allowed it, was granted only on grounds of infidelity. *Under today's more flexible rules, marriage breakdown is the most usual ground, and divorce is much more common. In the 1980s divorcees were still not allowed to marry in the Church of England but could have a church service of blessing after a registry-office wedding.*

RELIGIOUS OBSTACLES TO DIVORCE

■ *Family bonds that create obstacles to divorce are reinforced by strong religious and cultural traditions that place great value on family unity.* TOP *A Jewish family gathers round the table for Friday night prayers.* BOTTOM *Argentinians attend a mass demonstration in 1986, organized by the Catholic Church, in the Plaza de Mayo in Buenos Aires. They are protesting against government proposals to legalize divorce.*

> **If you want to be apart nothing will stop you**
> ■ *It does not matter whether a couple's religion is against divorce, or whether they have children – the chances of their marriage ending are about the same as anyone else's.*

marriage may tend to involve a desertion or a separation rather than a divorce.

Other barriers to divorce involve cultural resistance. Parents may raise their children to view divorce as an inappropriate response to marital difficulties. In close-knit communities, social disapproval may prove too strong for couples to end their marriage. Young children may place a responsibility on the parents that outweighs any desire of their own to abandon the marriage.

Money – or the lack of it – is a very powerful barrier to divorce, particularly for women. Women who have few financial resources or little employment potential may feel that, on balance, they are better off in the marriage. Men who see themselves faced with a long-term responsibility for maintaining two households after divorce may also feel divorce is not worthwhile.

The law itself can be a deterrent. The prospect of a lengthy and expensive legal process is, for some, too daunting to be contemplated.

But although these barriers to divorce still exist, their power has considerably weakened since the 1960s and couples are almost as likely to get divorced regardless of religious affiliation, the presence or absence of children, income level or family background. They place more and more importance on personal growth and compatibility.

LET NO MAN PUT ASUNDER

■ *"I'm a Catholic – we don't believe in divorce – so for years I've put up with the situation. But now I have to get out. I've got three children and it isn't fair on them to live like this."*

Many Christian denominations have strict rules about divorce and although these do not necessarily prevent their believers from going through with divorce, it does present such people with two special issues. The first is guilt. Most people divorcing their partners, whatever the circumstances, feel some guilt about the effect on children and parents and about their own part in the breakdown. Christians often suffer extra guilt, which is religious in nature, as well as alienation from the support of their faith and the Church community.

A great deal is being done by the Christian churches to ease the guilt of its divorced members and the Christian community as a whole is becoming much less severe. Divorced Christians are now encouraged not to isolate themselves from their church and many priests and ministers will urge people in this position to continue to attend their church services, participate in the sacraments and derive as much strength from their faith as possible.

The second issue is remarriage. Many Christians will wish to marry again after divorce and even remarry in church. Catholics in this situation must obtain a decree of nullity that considers the first marriage as null and void. These decrees used to be hard to obtain but are now granted more easily. Other denominations are a great deal less strict and will often agree to remarry divorced people who have a strong faith. The important point to appreciate is that, while Christianity upholds a high moral code regarding marital stability, in practice it is understanding toward people whose marriages have broken down. **JD**

113

The pain of separation

The breakdown of the relationship may start with a series of crises that the partners fail to resolve. These crises or arguments may lead to a variety of events – affairs, drinking problems or violence. Whatever the reason, one partner usually decides first that the marriage is over or that they would like to live with someone else. Their decision may well be quite unexpected for the other partner.

No matter how it was brought about, separation is a very traumatic stage of the divorce process. It is not an easy decision to make because it is a public action. Irrespective of why partners break up or who leaves whom, the loss of a partner causes intense emotional distress.

When the separation finally becomes a reality, both partners may experience extreme stress. Their feelings will range from rejection, abandonment, depression, anger and low self-esteem to guilt and a sense of failure. They may have symptoms of insomnia and anxiety. Neither partner is likely to feel relief at first. The newly separated can also expect to suffer deep emotional loneliness due to the loss of their intimate partner, as well as isolation as a result of the change in relationship, status and identity. Separation means getting used to changes in daily routines, dealing with legal authorities and organizing personal and family finances. It will also involve confrontations with children, relatives and friends, and the public admission that the marriage has serious problems.

Making the final break

The decision to separate is not always made at the same time by both partners. One partner may decide, quietly and without any discussion, that the alternative attractions of being single are very high and that any barriers can be surmounted. This partner, though likely to feel guilty, is often

INITIAL PAIN AND LONG-TERM LONELINESS

■ The shock of suddenly being single is accompanied by anxiety and a sense of isolation. TOP A young woman who no longer has a partner to confide in and share with may feel trapped in an emotional void. BOTTOM Many divorced people, especially older ones, have to face the prospect of living alone for many years. They may feel that life has nothing to offer and that it is too late to start again.

Women who get divorced are increasingly less likely to re-marry the older they are (see Ch14). Losing a partner late in life can have a serious effect on health and men are particularly at risk of developing stress-related illnesses. Even the companionship of a dog and familiar, cherished surroundings can help the older person cope with life on their own.

Who is better off after divorce – the husband or the wife? ■ *Divorced men and women are in an equally difficult position, and men cope less well with it* ■ *Men have fewer domestic skills and when on their own do not take as good care of themselves* ■ *With fewer skills of emotional expression, they do not handle tension as easily.*

better able to work through the process of separation and the possible eventuality of divorce. In contrast, the partner who has been left often feels rejected, abandoned and inadequate. They have lost control of their life and find themselves having to react to rather than initiate events.

Research has shown that it is easier for people to cope with divorce when they have benefited from a lapse of time that allows them slowly to prepare themselves for the final break and to become more detached from their partner. A sudden separation followed by divorce is likely to leave at least one partner in a state of shock. In many cases, however, the decision to separate and the announcement of the divorce is merely the culmination of what has been a long process of deterioration in the relationship (see *Ch12*).

Picking up the pieces

Mourning is as important in divorce as it is in death, although it can be less easy because society does not expect a public display of grief in such circumstances. The divorced person has lost the central focus of their life as surely as the bereaved person. The process for mourning will take many forms depending on the circumstances of the divorce. It will reflect anger, intense hurt, resentment, bitterness and loneliness. Some people experience severe depression. But these are all part of the vital healing process

that will eventually lead to recovery. Gradually, divorced people come to terms with themselves and others and are able to look at their former partner and life more objectively. They are able to focus on the positive elements rather than dwelling on the negative, unhappy aspects. Their regained sense of integrity can also provide an opportunity for personal growth through new experiences of travel, hobbies, education, friends and even the development of new relationships.

At first the divorced person may pursue these new activities with vigorous desperation. On the one hand, they feel a need to prove themselves, while on the other they derive comfort from being totally involved. It is easier to push feelings such as loneliness into the background if you are constantly doing something. It takes a long time to find a new direction and to stop feeling hurt. Many divorced people have a very strong need for simple affection and they are likely to cling to anyone who shows a sign of warmth during this period.

Fortunately, most divorced people eventually do achieve some degree of wholeness and control but it is not easy. It will take from two to ten years for this to develop and for the feelings of disorientation to fade. At this point people may be ready for a new relationship (see *Ch14*).

Coping after a divorce

People often want to determine who "has it better" after divorce – the husband or the wife? It might be better to ask, "How do men and women react to divorce?" It is generally accepted that they do react differently. These differences, however, may be the result of the different sex roles men

TELLING THE CHILDREN

■ *For many children divorce brings a sense of loss, feelings of failure and unsettling changes. They are often plunged into a new lifestyle that may include changing schools, neighborhoods and friends. The news that their parents are getting divorced is usually distressing and shocking for children and their reaction will depend to a large extent on how their parents break the news to them. This is such a difficult task that some parents do not tell the children until one or both parents move out of the house. This is the worst thing they could do. It is important for parents to tell their children as clearly and rationally as possible what is happening. They should try to get across the idea that the decision has been carefully considered and that it will bring happiness to at least one parent.*

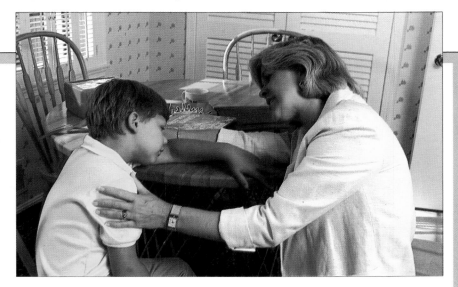

They must make a strong point of saying that the divorce does not mean they do not love the children. Finally, the children should be given as much time as possible to ask questions and to express their own feelings.

▲ **Breaking the news to her son.** *A mother tells her child about the divorce, making an effort to smile and reassure him with gentle physical contact.*

and women are socially conditioned to adopt. As sex roles become less rigid, our reactions to stressful events may eventually be more similar.

Many aspects of divorce are, in fact, the same for men and women. For both it is a public event that is almost always painful and stressful. During the process of divorce, men and women alike have to deal with the disintegration of their marriage and make major adjustments in their personal lives and their relationships with children, friends and family. In addition, both will probably have to deal with day-to-day problems like home repair and maintenance, work, household organization and money. In time, the stress felt as a result of these major adjustments will lessen. Most people – men and women – are able to move on to a more positive life. There is, however, some evidence that an emotional divorce is more stressful for men than for women. This could be because men find it more difficult to express their feelings or because many do not have the domestic skills for living on their own. Most men will suffer the loss of daily contact with their children as well as losing the familiar surroundings of the family home.

Men cope less well than women

Divorce may result in serious emotional stress. As a consequence, the health problems of both divorced men and divorced women are greater than for married people, but even greater for men. Divorced men are at greater risk of contracting numerous illnesses including cancer, heart disease and diabetes. They are more often hospitalized, they visit doctors more often and miss more days off work because of illness. They are also more likely to have drinking problems, car accidents, commit suicide or be a victim of homicide.

While women may experience fewer health problems, they suffer from other painful consequences of divorce. Financial problems make it more difficult to adjust after divorce, and even if a women continues to receive financial help from a former partner, these problems may not be alleviated. Every time she receives an alimony check she is reminded not only of their former marriage but of her lingering dependent status.

In addition, most divorced women have to cope with looking after the children and running the home on their own. As a result, they may experience feelings of being overburdened and they will have little time left over for social life. Because of this, women with children are more likely to feel isolated after divorce and to suffer more from loneliness.

Nevertheless, in spite of the feelings of being burdened, being isolated and lonely, divorce may offer, particularly to women, the opportunity to realize their potential for personal growth and competence. These opportunities may never have been available to them during their marriage. In fact, simply overcoming the problems of divorce may result in higher self-esteem (see *Ch 14*).

Living in the world of the not-married

During the period of the separation and divorce people seek out the help and support of those closest to them. Women are perhaps more likely than men to ask for emotional and material support but in the initial stages both sexes appear to reach out to friends and family. In general, these people are supportive and provide many services. One

ENDING ON AN UNSENTIMENTAL NOTE

■ *Weeding out her old wedding photographs is part of the process by which this woman is coming to terms with the end of her marriage. Statistics on stress-related illness in divorced people suggest that women are more able to look back calmly on the past, and they deal more effectively with the practical difficulties of being alone. Both divorced men and divorced women have poorer health than married people, but the men are on average less healthy than the women.*

FEELING THE STRAIN OF SEPARATION

■ *A man breaks down under the emotional strain of divorce. Men find it harder to cope with stress than women and usually have more difficulty expressing their feelings. By seeking comfort more readily from people who are close to them they could relieve the tension of bottled up emotions. Former partners can give each other valuable emotional support even after their relationship has formally ended.*

Most children get over a divorce but they seldom cope easily ■ *Young, dependent children may feel threatened and frightened* ■ *Adolescents may experience conflicts of loyalty* ■ *Boys may become aggressive and disobedient.*

of the most important things they can do is just listen to the story of the divorce. Their companionship is also very valuable during the lonely, and often frightening, early days. However, this support tends to be short-lived and divorced people often report feeling forgotten two to three months after the divorce.

These feelings, coupled with changes in lifestyles, mobility and interests often lead the divorced person to mix more and more with divorced, separated or single friends. Many people who have been away from this world of the not-married during the years of their marriage find it a very strange world. They have to relearn how to act when out on a date and how to meet new people. They may also have to adjust to new attitudes toward sex. Although the threat of AIDS has probably caused a decrease in random sexual activity among divorced people, dating is still valued as a way back into a serious relationship.

Dividing the spoils – who gets what?

According to popular mythology women are out to bankrupt their husbands during the process of divorce. There is a cliché of divorced men living in poverty while their former wives enjoy a lavish and luxurious lifestyle. These myths have been perpetuated because the true economics of divorce have received little attention: in fact, divorced women and their children are often in a poverty trap. Arrangements

for the division of property differ from country to country, but the result is seldom satisfactory for either partner and can be particularly difficult for women. Most couples do not have significant assets – in the United States less than half of divorcing couples own their own house. Even when a couple does own a home, this will probably have to be sold if assets have to be divided equally, and the funds received are unlikely to be sufficient for either partner to buy an equally comfortable new home. This can be a serious problem, particularly for a custodial mother. In cases where the man retains the car and business and the woman the home and furnishings, she may lose out on medical insurance and retirement or pensions benefits from her husband's employment.

In some countries, such as France, it is customary for many marriages to include a formal marriage contract that provides the basis for dividing assets in the event of divorce or separation.

Alimony and child support

Benefits such as alimony are awarded to redress the balance between women and men, but alimony is not awarded automatically. In the United States only about 15 percent of

THE POVERTY TRAP

■ *Kimmie Jo Larimore at 30 earning a few dollars an hour working as a waitress in a café – on her own and with four children to support. For women like Kimmie Jo, and for their children, marriage breakdown is a road to economic hardship. Although 80 percent of div-* *orced mothers in the United States are awarded child support, there is no guarantee that it will be paid, and their buying* *power can be reduced by as much as three-quarters after divorce. If they have neglected their job skills during marriage,* *they will probably only be able to get badly paid work.*

all divorced women will receive alimony. There has been an assumption that women can, and should, be self-sufficient within two years of the divorce, but it is increasingly recognized that this seldom holds true. Even if someone is qualified for particular work, the disorientation and depression caused by the divorce can destroy their ability to cope

with a demanding job. This is especially so if they have not been working during the years of the marriage. The expectation is even more unrealistic for the woman who has devoted her life to her husband and children rather than acquiring marketable job skills. Although child support is awarded to 80 percent of divorced mothers in the United States the arrangement may fall far short of requirements.

Studies of the financial status of divorced men and women indicate that men fare better than women after divorce. One American finding is that the man's financial position is 42 percent better after divorce, while the woman's is 73 percent worse. As a result, many divorced women take whatever job they can get, often doing two jobs and suffering from "overload" in an exhausting struggle to try to make ends meet.

How children react

Regardless of how children first learn about the impending divorce, they are seldom able to cope easily with the news. Their reaction will probably differ according to their sex and age. Younger children may exhibit more severe social and emotional problems. These children rely heavily on the security and dependability of family life; they see their parents' divorce as a threat and they are frightened.

Adolescents may feel depressed or guilty and experience serious conflicts of loyalty. They are also more likely to express their anger to the parent they feel is most responsible for the decision.

Boys are often more aggressive and less compliant than girls and they cause more discipline problems. Some mothers put their son in the role of their ex-husband as the "man of the house." The boy is expected to act as an adult while still coming to terms with the upheaval caused by the family breakup. **SJP PCM JS**

119

CHILDREN'S REACTIONS TO DIVORCE

Denial. *During the denial stage, children choose not to accept reality, but instead perceive the world as they would like it to be. For example, they may withdraw from others into a fantasy world of images of the happy family life prior to divorce.*

Anger. *During the anger stage, children frequently attempt to strike out at anyone they are involved with in the hope that negative attention will engage both parents and bring about a reconciliation. For example, they may direct emotional outbursts toward those who take the place of parents, such as school personnel.*

Bargaining. *When denial and anger prove to be unproductive, children enter the bargaining stage. They "make a deal" with themselves to overcome the loss. For example, a child may imagine that by improving its behavior it can bring about a reconciliation.*

Depression. *In time, mourning over the loss of their previous family lifestyle begins. When children discover that they cannot control or have an impact on their environment, they become depressed. For example, they may regret past "bad" behavior with a parent and blame themselves for the divorce.*

Acceptance. *A stage comes when children learn that reality exists, whether or not they like it. For example, they may realize that their father will not always be available as often as they would like, but that a satisfactory relationship will continue to exist with him in a different form.*

HELPING CHILDREN COPE

■ *The way a child adjusts to its parents' divorce will depend a great deal on the quality of parenting during the period of separation and divorce. Unfortunately, parents themselves are under extreme stress at this time and may be less consistent with discipline, less caring and less communicative. Some parents experience so much stress that they lose any capacity to comfort or attend to their children. They may even expect their children to look after them and act as comforters in turn. This can put a great deal of strain on children, particularly on adolescents, who are going through a major transitional period in their own development.*

Because parents are less able to look after their children during divorce, it is important that the children *have access to other support systems – siblings, friends, neighbors and extended family members. Many schools now offer programs for children who are experiencing divorce. These programs appear to be very successful and, because the school is a permanent feature in their lives, it provides a stable structure that serves as a refuge from family problems.*

Research shows that in spite of the stress produced by divorce many children eventually come through the experience well. There is evidence to suggest that children whose parents get divorced may be better adjusted than children whose parents remain in an unhappy marriage. It is often the problems that existed in the family before the divorce, rather than the divorce itself, that create difficulties for children.

Starting Again

HOW DO YOU reconstruct your life after the breakup of an intimate relationship? Society offers a wide variety of special rituals that help couples to make the psychological and social adjustments they face in marrying, but no such rituals exist to help them through divorce. Starting again after a broken relationship has to be done alone and the post-divorce period can be a difficult time. How do separated and divorced people adjust to their new life? What kind of relationship do ex-partners usually maintain after divorce? What are the problems and the benefits of remarriage and stepparenting?

Coping after separation

The period of separation and divorce is intensely stressful even for those people who *want* to leave their marriage (see *Ch 13*). However, once the partners are

10 POINTS FOR MAKING A NEW START

■ *Ending any intimate relationship entails loneliness, regret, grief, endlessly wondering "what went wrong" and a difficult restructuring of your life. How you get over a breakup will depend a great deal on the nature of your relationship and at what stage the breakup happened. When nonmarital relationships come to an end, they are unlikely to involve complex legal problems. The breakup of a marriage, however, will probably attract more sympathy and support from family and friends. Therapists recommend several tried-and-true ways of getting through this time.*

PROBLEMS OF STARTING AGAIN

■ *ABOVE Loss of emotional security and of a shared routine often leaves ex-partners disoriented. They may rely more on comfort-giving drugs, such as nicotine, and their sense of isolation may make them more susceptible to stress-related illnesses.*

■ *RIGHT Noncustodial parents often need to learn new practical skills as well as adjusting emotionally to reduced contact with their children. Those wishing to remarry may find their choice of partner restricted: new partners may react unfavorably to the idea of a readymade family.*

1	2	3	4	5
Be kind to yourself. Eat well. Allow yourself treats.	Avoid thinking too much about your ex-partner.	Devise new independent ways to challenge and reward yourself.	Be honest about your relationship and why it failed.	Set objectives to he you develop as a stronger person.

After a divorce, how do the ex-partners fare? ■ *Childless couples and those who are financially independent of each other make the easiest adjustment* ■ *Supportive friends and family are vital to a successful new start.*

divorced it does not automatically mean that their problems are over. The experience of being alone after having been married can be a frightening one and many couples discover that although they found life with their partner impossible, life without them brings its own difficulties.

The problems facing the ex-partners differ somewhat for men and women. Whereas women have more practical problems to contend with, men seem to suffer from more emotional problems and are less able to cope psychologically (see *Ch 13*).

What is the best way to adjust to divorce?

How you come to terms with the emotional crisis of divorce or separation may well depend on how much you are in control of events and how much you are prepared for what you will experience. The people who are most likely to adapt successfully after divorce are those whose marriage was brief, who had no children, who are not financially dependent on their ex-partner and who have friends of their own. This is not to underestimate their emotional hurt, but in practical terms they are in a positive position. Older people, especially women, who have no regular employment, and are left with a network of friends shared with their ex-partner or with custody of young children, face the greatest problems of adjustment.

Where young children are involved the ex-partners may have to cooperate in parenting. It is helpful to both partners if they can be as mutually supportive as possible. Where

there are no children, or where the children are now adult and no longer dependent, partners do not need to cooperate with each other at all and do not have enforced ties with each other.

People who have close relationships with family and friends also find it easier to cope – they are less likely to feel isolated after the breakup. It is particularly helpful to talk to someone who has gone through a similar crisis. Keeping healthy is another obvious way to improve your ability to cope.

The importance of financial self-sufficiency

In any intimate relationship it is a great advantage for both partners to be financially independent. Following a divorce where children are involved, a woman's financial self-sufficiency may be a key factor in allowing for a more satisfactory parental role. She will be more likely to have a sense of self-esteem and will be able to run her own life without constantly having to turn to her ex-partner for help. Both partners are, therefore, able to concentrate on their role as parent, and with fewer sources of conflict they can cooperate more effectively.

Unfortunately, this ideal situation does not always exist. In many cases women lose around 70 percent of their income after divorce and only one-third to one-half of fathers contribute financially to their children's upbringing (see *Ch 13*).

Women who remain in the labor force after marriage and even after they have children have an advantage over those who do not. Because the divorce rate is so high, becoming a housewife is a risky business. There is no evidence to show

▲ **The companionship of friends** *can ease the pain of separation. Research finds that those with little support from friends and family experience* *more post-divorce stress than those who have close family ties and a good social network.*

6	7	8	9	10
Take comfort from familiar habits and routines.	Do not be afraid to seek professional help.	Give yourself time and do not expect an instant recovery.	Call on old friends for support.	Make new friends and try new activities.

that working wives and mothers are any more likely to get divorced but in the event of this happening, they are better able to cope and adjust.

The second marriage

In the United States, three-quarters of divorced men and two-thirds of divorced women eventually remarry. In France in 1977 63.7 percent of divorced men and 57.3 percent of divorced women had remarried. By 1984, however, the figures were only 46.4 percent for men and 42.1 percent for women. An undetermined number of divorced people enter into permanent, unmarried relationships.

Men tend to remarry sooner than women and not necessarily a divorced woman. Divorced women, on the other hand, are more likely to remarry divorced men. Older divorced women are more likely than younger women to remarry a widower.

Some studies have shown that there tends to be a wider age difference between the partners in a second marriage than in first marriages. Where such an age gap does exist it will lead to a proportion of married couples who are at different stages in their life cycles. This can cause problems. Research indicates that women married to men more than eight years older than themselves are likely to be less happy than women whose husbands are closer to them in age.

Does second marriage mean second divorce?

American statistics indicate that second marriages are somewhat more vulnerable to divorce than first marriages. In fact, although the divorce rates are higher for second marriages, most people who marry again actually stay married. They are not disillusioned with the institution of marriage and despite an unsuccessful first marriage they are determined to try to avoid making the same mistakes. Nevertheless, some will fail. All marriages have problems and the

122

WOMEN AND REMARRIAGE

■ "I'd like to get (re)married but that seems an impossible dream...My daughter's future marriage is more important to me than my own. I'll love being a grandmother."

The older the woman, the less the possibility of her remarrying after divorce. After she reaches 40, the likelihood of a woman remarrying falls to only 31 percent. Why is there such a dramatic decline after 40? After this age there are new elements to consider. A woman may not wish to remarry; she may value her freedom and the opportunity to continue her career.

Statistics show that the higher the income of a divorced woman, the less likely she is to choose to remarry and a woman over 40 with a career is likely to be financially self-sufficient. There is the "double standard" of aging – "women get wrinkles and men become distinguished." There are also fewer available men as potential partners. **AA SJP**

▶ **Aging and remarriage in women**. As a woman's age increases, the likelihood of her remarrying decreases.

◀ **The rewards of sharing** are a major attraction of remarriage for older people. Having spent most of their lives with someone else, many find living alone difficult. Remarriage provides not only the companionship of a partner but also of their friends, children or grandchildren. However, older couples also report other reasons for remarrying, such as a wish to be looked after, financial security, love and sexual satisfaction.

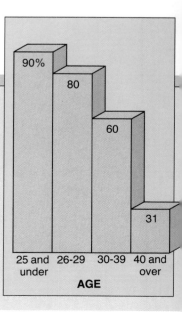

90%	80	60	31
25 and under	26-29	30-39	40 and over

AGE

Do divorced people find it difficult to form new relationships? ■ *Second marriages, especially of partners who are close in age, have a good chance of success* ■ *Remarried people whose ex-partners have also remarried experience fewer divided loyalties between their old and their new relationships.*

problems of second marriages seem to be different and potentially more serious than those of first marriages.

The presence of ex-partners can complicate the new relationship. Because many divorced people are contributing financially to the ex-partner's and children's support as well as to their new family, there can be considerable economic pressure on both families. The situation may be particularly difficult when only one partner remarries, especially if that partner is the ex-husband. The new marriage may bring about a renewal of conflict with his first wife if she and the new wife are competing for the same financial resources. Many men are relieved when their ex-wives remarry since they no longer have to contribute to their support.

Couples without children from their previous marriages have the best chance of making a fresh start. They are able to concentrate on each other and on making their relationship work without having to cope with the pressure of divided loyalties and financial responsibilities.

Other people whose marriages have a good chance of being successful are those couples, especially elderly couples, who choose to remarry for companionship and

perhaps also in order to extend their family circle by including new grandchildren or adult stepchildren. Such marriages are generally very rewarding. Similarly, those couples who are able to cooperate over the arrangements for their children or whose new partners are of a similar age to themselves, are likely to experience remarriage as an exciting fresh start giving life renewed purpose.

Keeping in touch with your former partner

Divorced men and women must come to terms with what has happened to their relationship with their ex-partner. Contrary to popular belief, the emotional death of the relationship does not always spell the end of all contact with the former partner. Divorced people often remain bound to each other by children, love, financial dependence, business or friendship and some people are surprised by the strength of the attachment.

To begin with this may cause confusion. On the one hand, each person has begun to establish an independent life and identity. On the other hand, each still retains the memory of themselves as a couple or a member of a family unit. Former partners may feel compelled to re-establish contact even if a new relationship has been formed.

The best way to approach the situation is to recognize that the relationship with the former partner and family is not dissolved but is reorganized. A new relationship has to be built around each partner's new identity.

123

◀ **Marriage second time round** *was unsuccessful for Richard Burton and Elizabeth Taylor. The couple first met in 1962 when playing opposite each other in the film version of "Cleopatra" and married two years later, after divorcing previous partners. A stormy relationship led to divorce in 1974, though they continued to attract each other. A cancer scare for Taylor brought them together again, and they remarried in 1975. Only months afterward, in 1976, this second marriage ended. Few marriages after divorce are to a previous partner, and most do not lead to another divorce.*

Children are a major factor in determining whether ex-partners keep in touch after they have split up. Ex-partners who have married briefly and who have no children rarely keep in touch but those who share children usually do. For many the contact is kept to the bare minimum as they wish to distance themselves from their past. They feel tied down to their ex-partner because of the children.

The way in which the marriage is terminated also influences later relationships between the former partners. For instance, where the divorce is caused by an affair that in turn becomes a second marriage, particularly where an older woman is left for a much younger one, the ex-partners are unlikely to have a fruitful continuing relationship. This situation is often emotionally damaging for the former wife.

Keeping in touch for the sake of the children

In a study carried out over six years it was found that ex-partners tended to see less and less of each other as time went by and as their children grew up. Only one-half of those who had dependent children saw each other or even talked to each other on the phone except very occasionally. Moreover, only 31 percent of the ex-couples had a truly supportive relationship and shared parenting. The couples who were most likely to have a cordial relationship were those where both ex-partners were financially independent of each other. Most of the other parents who were still in touch tended to do "parallel parenting," that is, each partner had responsibility for the children separately and at different times during the year, with little joint planning. However, ex-partners who were supportive of each other did not necessarily see each other more often than those who were still embattled six years after separation.

Adjusting to the new family unit

Because approximately 60 percent of divorced couples have children, when either partner remarries the question of stepparenting will be a serious issue. Remarriage is some-

124

WEEKEND PARENTING

■ *ABOVE A little girl is reluctant to visit a father she rarely sees. Less than half of the children with divorced parents visit their noncustodial parent regularly. Keeping in contact with both parents can benefit the child, though continuing conflict between ex-partners and long distances between their new* *homes may restrict visiting. RIGHT Binuclear families bring both problems and rewards. Young children generally adapt better than adolescents. They find it easier to accept stepparents. Children of any age may benefit from acquiring new siblings and friends within the family.*

Ex-partners with children have a special need to cooperate ■ *They should support and encourage each other's efforts to continue parenting the children* ■ *They should allow each other to give time and care to stepparenting.*

times problematic for their children. Adolescents, in particular, find the adjustment difficult, although research indicates that young children suffer more from the actual divorce (see *Ch13*). Adolescents, who are already less dependent on their parents may adjust more easily to divorce. When it comes to remarriage, however, the adolescent may resent interference from a stepparent in their newly developing freedom. It is usually easier for the stepparent to be with a young child who is more willing to establish an affectionate, dependent relationship and will, therefore, fit more easily into the reconstituted family.

Remarriage and stepparenting is not always problematic. Many couples and their children find the reorganization of their families both enjoyable and stimulating. Children may acquire new siblings and new friends within the family; parents are once again able to share the responsibilities of child care with a partner.

Children will feel more comfortable if the stepparent, especially the stepmother, does not attempt to replace the real parent and does not criticize that parent. Both children and adults need a good deal of time to get to know each other and to get used to the new situation, and stepparents should be prepared to work hard at adjusting to this new stage in their lives. Many studies clearly show that this period of readjustment often results in a close family unit based on mutual respect and openness. **AA**

THE "WICKED" STEPMOTHER

■ *Studies have found that the role of stepmother is more difficult than that of stepfather. Children seem to accept stepfathers more easily than stepmothers. One explanation for this could be that the role of mother is more important to the child than the role of father. Children usually spend more time with their mother, especially in their early years. They would consequently resist a relationship with a stepmother more than one with a stepfather. Moreover, the children's biological mother may feel threatened by her ex-husband's new wife and may fear that she will lose her children's loyalty. This fear, or even jealousy, may be passed on to the children who in turn react negatively toward the stepmother.*

Another reason why the stepmother role is often less rewarding than that of the stepfather rests in the traditional division of labor by sex. Where the stepchildren live at home it is usually the stepmother, and not the children's father, who is responsible for childcare and household duties. If the stepchildren just visit, the stepmother will tend to inherit additional chores while her husband spends time with his children. Remarried women who have their own children and who combine both roles of mother and stepmother have a particularly difficult task.

HELPING YOUR STEPCHILD COPE

Acquiring a new parent can be very stressful for a child. You can help by putting time into building up the relationship and by showing sensitivity:
- *Be patient with a child who resents you.*
- *Respect an adolescent's desire for freedom.*
- *Maintain a young child's familiar routine.*
- *Avoid criticism of the real parent.*
- *Encourage access to the real parent.*

The Mature Years

AS WE GROW OLDER, does our love for our partners change? If so, in what way? Does it become more or less, or is it of a different kind? Early studies of sexual behavior supported the common opinion that our sex drive, and along with it our capacity to love passionately, declines rapidly with age. This can make it seem that the onus is entirely on companionship and mutual respect to sustain a happy, loving relationship when, one day, youthful passion burns itself out. In fact, however, for most mature couples, love and sexuality have stood the test of time well. Moreover, men and women who enjoy such fulfilling relationships are more likely to remain mentally and physically healthy in old age.

How long does love last?

Broadly, we experience two distinct forms of love – a passionate love and a companionate one (see *Ch 5*). Love is passionate when emotionally intense and focused on sensual excitement. Companionate love is less intense. It describes the affection people feel for those with whom their lives are deeply entwined. Can love of either kind last for life or will it inevitably wither and die?

While many marriages end in failure, as the high divorce rates show, for those couples who do stay together love can,

on the evidence of recent surveys, be unexpectedly robust. Research data and common experience concur in showing that couples start out loving their partners intensely. In a series of studies in the United States, over 1,000 dating couples, 100 newlyweds and 400 long-married women were asked how they felt about their partners. Steady daters and newlyweds in their early twenties reported feeling "a great deal" of passionate love and "a great deal" to "a tremendous amount" of companionate love for each other. However, even after 30 years or more of marriage, women aged 50 and upward still said they felt "some" passionate love and "a great deal" of companionate love for their partners.

Asked whether they had feelings of resentment or hostility toward their partners, newlywed couples replied "none" or "very little," while the responses of older married women differed only slightly, from "very little" to "some." Interestingly, these two groups gave the same replies, but the other way round, when asked how much depression they experienced in their relationships: newlywed couples said they experienced "very little" to "some" depression; older married women "none" or "very little."

EBBS AND FLOWS OF LIVING AND LOVING

■ *In an interview he gave before his 70th birthday, the Swedish film director Ingmar Bergman spoke for many people of mature years when giving his views on life and mortality. As the river of life approached the falls beyond it, he said, it held no fears for him, only fascination and beauty.*

To the young the prospect of growing old can appear terrifying – thinning hair, unromantic sagging bodies, people who, alone once their children have left home, and with their friends and relatives becoming ill and dying around them, have little to look forward to in the way of either love or life.

To those who have reached maturity this picture is as far from the truth as is the romanticized view of youth. As shy, pimply adolescents, our first experiences of love and sex were often marred by fear and ignorance. Unrealistic expectations of our relationships distressed us, made us behave stupidly, and in some cases this resulted in disastrous marriages.

Many years later we are much wiser. Having learned by our mistakes, we know how easily love can go wrong. Many of us have learned to live alone if necessary and to supplement our lives with a rich mix of friends. We have grown more tolerant of ourselves and others and are happier for it. We know what it is reasonable to expect from a partner and what it is not. Now, we can enjoy all-round richer relationships and have learned to bounce back from the inevitable surprises and disasters of life.

MARITAL SATISFACTION IN LATER YEARS

■ *Ups and downs of family life influence the amount of satisfaction couples feel at different stages of their life together. The years after children leave home are among the most contented. Only a minority of couples are saddened by a sense of an "empty nest," and then only temporarily. In most cases, more time for shared leisure activities allows partners to begin very quickly to rediscover* each other and become closer. The contrasts in satisfaction shown here are relative: they do not mean that most couples are dissatisfied with mid-marriage, only that they are more satisfied in earlier and later years (see also Ch 10).

In the mature years is passion only a memory? ■ *Happy couples go on loving one another, sexually and as companions, far into their later years* ■ *Older women report less depression about relationships than newlyweds.*

While both passionate and companionate love may decline from the time of courtship and the first year of marriage, the decline is far less drastic, and relationships are potentially far more durable, than you might suppose. All partners experience some negative feelings, but these are frequently too weak to destroy a close relationship or marriage. Indeed sociologists have found that events within the family cycle have a much greater effect than aging on satisfaction with married life. For instance, couples are least happy and under the greatest strain when there are children in the home, especially teenagers. Despite such problems, prospects are good for couples who stay deeply in love throughout their lives.

127

MARITAL SATISFACTION INCREASES AFTER THE MID-MARRIAGE YEARS

Married without children

Empty nest

Teenage children (oldest 12–16)

Higher

Ups and downs of the child-rearing years

Children leaving home

Lower satisfaction

The myth of sex and aging

"Put a bean in a jar on your wedding night every time you make love and go on adding beans in a similar way for the first year of marriage. Then start *subtracting* a bean every time you make love. There will still be some beans left in the jar when you die." This old adage typifies conventional wisdom on the decline of sexual activity with age. Pioneer studies of sexual behavior in the late 1940s and early fifties such as the Kinsey Report supported this view, which went unchallenged until the late 1970s.

According to Kinsey, nearly all men and women up to the age of 40 regularly had intercourse with their partners, but after that the frequency fell away sharply. Couples in their thirties reported making love twice as often as couples in their fifties. Six percent of men aged 60 and as many as 20 percent of women of similar age claimed that they no longer had any sexual relations.

Later researchers found that, by the age of 70, nearly a quarter of all men and a half of all women were sexually inactive. The differences in sexual activity between men and women of the same age were largely attributed to the fact that husbands tended to be older than their wives and that it was generally the male partner who determined the frequency of sexual relations.

Setting the record straight

Experts have since criticized Kinsey for using small, unrepresentative samples (including elderly people who were clinic patients) that quite possibly led him to false conclusions. For instance, his findings on levels of sexual activity among 80-year-olds, as compared with 40-year-olds, made no allowance for the fact that there were proportionally far more 80-year-old widows and widowers with no available partners. Kinsey also failed to take into account

128

Age is no barrier to happiness or an active sex life ■ *Research suggests that there may be more snuggling, cuddling and petting among older couples than among younger ones* ■ *Comparisons of the same mature couples at different times in their marriages find little decline in sexual activity.*

the different attitudes of different generations toward sex. People interviewed in the 1950s at the age of 20 would be unlikely to share the same values or have the same sexual habits at the age of 60 as men and women born in the Victorian era who were 60 at the time of being interviewed. Likewise, people brought up in the more liberal 1960s and 1970s might be more sexually active throughout their lives.

To arrive at a truer picture of contemporary sexual behavior, and to reflect the fact that our attitudes change

DOES SEXUAL ACTIVITY DECREASE?

■ *American researchers interviewed married men and women ranging in age from 46 to 71 about their sexual activity. Six years later they interviewed* *them again. The results suggest that for most middle-aged and older couples, passing years do not affect sexual activity.*

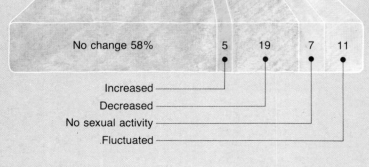

No change 58%   5   19   7   11

Increased ——————————
Decreased ——————————
No sexual activity ——————————
Fluctuated ——————————

■ **Awkward uncertainty** *often dampens early encounters with the opposite sex* ABOVE. *Our relationship skills grow as we come to terms with our sexuality, and* RIGHT *interactions with the opposite sex become more spontaneous. And despite myths of dying passion, studies* *have found sex to be a vital part of many older couples' relationships. Earlier reports of sharply declining sexual activity in later years have been criticized for relying on inaccurate research methods.*

with time, the most recent studies have followed the same couples over a fixed term. One group of respondents made up of 140 couples aged between the mid-forties and early seventies recorded little change in their levels of sexual activity over a six-year period. The results of another study, carried out on 800 men and women aged between 60 and 91, showed that they retained their interest in sex, often desired it and enjoyed sexual relations on average 1.4 times a week – the same frequency as reported by Kinsey's 40-year-olds. Generally, it seems that, except for reasons such as loss of partner or ill health, our sexual activity does not decline substantially with age, as Kinsey believed. Some researchers have suggested that snuggling, cuddling and petting may be more frequent among older couples than they are among the young.

Do our expectations change?

Interviews with a wide cross section of couples in the United States showed that, whatever their age or sex, they expected very similar things from their partners and from their relationships.

The most desirable personal qualities listed were social grace, intelligence and good appearance. Emotional rewards included liking and loving, showing understanding and concern, acceptance and appreciation of each other, physical expressions of affection and sexual fulfillment, faithfulness, a feeling of security and the confidence to plan ahead.

Other rewards arose simply from the day-to-day business of living together. These included someone to share the responsibilities for finances, for running the house and for

making decisions, and having a constant companion who is sociable, good with friends and relatives and can help with such things as remembering special occasions.

Benefits of a healthy relationship

Love and intimacy are basic human needs, and probably essential to our physical and mental well-being (see *Ch1*). In particular, loving relationships can be critical for older couples, offering stability and a degree of self-protection. In the first place, it is better to have than not have a partner in old age. Those without are more likely to suffer from stress-related illnesses or behavior that will hasten their own

Relationships can be crucially important to older couples ■ *In the first six months of bereavement, widowers have more heart attacks* ■ *Older women who are happy with their partners have better health.*

death, such as heavy smoking or drug or alcohol abuse. Researchers have found that, during the first six months of bereavement, the death rate among widowers aged 55 or more was 40 percent higher than for the age group as a whole. After six months, the rates gradually fell back to normal. Since the increase in death rate among recent widowers is mainly in the form of heart disease, it is often called the "broken heart syndrome."

Almost as important as the presence or absence of an

ADVICE FROM GOLDEN ANNIVERSARY COUPLES

■ *When couples celebrating their Golden Anniversaries were asked their secrets of success and what they had learned in 50 years, they gave answers like these:*

● *I started out expecting marriage to be like something out of a romantic novel — he would be like a Mr Rochester, strong and protective, and I would always be gentle and yielding like Jane Eyre. Finally, I learned that just wouldn't work. When he tried to push me around and I let him, he lost all respect for me. Give-and-take includes making a stand sometimes. That way, you keep your respect for each other.*

● *I learned how different two people can really be. For the first dozen years of marriage, I made myself miserable. I thought that if she really loved me, she would like to sit by the fire and spend her day planning long romantic trips. When she didn't, I couldn't believe it! How could she not want to be with me when all I wanted was to be with her? Now I realize she is just different — she is wired up to be on the go. When she's not tidying up, she wants to spend time alone, reading. I've just had to learn to love her for what she is, not for what I was convinced my wife should be.*

● *Actually we don't have too much in common. Before my husband retired, we led separate lives: mine was at home, his was at the office. I did everything I could to save him any trouble. I told the children "Don't bother your father." That was a big mistake because he never really got close to*

them. When they left home, we had nothing. Luckily, we have a second chance now — we've got grandchildren who we spend a lot of time with, going for walks or to the movies.

● *I couldn't stand to see her suffer. I'd withdraw right away if I thought what I had to say would make her cry. Now I realize people don't really grow up if they never suffer. You know the old saying "Without a hurt, the heart is hollow." It's often better to say your piece than to bottle things up because you're afraid of hurting the other person. Now I'm less worried about her or the children, we can get a lot closer. I've also learned how to listen without trying to control or fix things all the time.*

▲ **Long life and good fortune**. *Celebrating their parents' 60 years together, a French family sing a traditional song, sprinkle the couple with champagne through a piece of linen, in a traditional good luck ritual, and wish them long life. Research confirms that sharing old age with a partner improves our chances of remaining physically and mentally healthy. The more satisfying the relationship, the more likely it is to have this beneficial effect.*

intimate partner in your maturity is the quality of that relationship. Interviews with some 240 American women aged between 50 and 82 showed that love, sex and general satisfaction with the relationship greatly affected the women's health. The happier and more contented they were with

their partners, the fewer symptoms of self-consciousness, depression and anxiety they showed. A loving, satisfying relationship not only makes for greater happiness in later years, but also improves your chances of enjoying good health, remaining in sound mind and living longer. **RLR EH**

A TIME FOR REFLECTION

■ *ABOVE Bound together by shared experiences, an elderly couple enjoy peaceful companionship as they watch the tide. Discussing old times with a partner is one way of fulfilling the need most elderly people feel to reflect on their lives. Putting past events into perspective helps us to make sense of our lives, and this is a key to contentment in old age. We reflect on what we have contributed to the world or how we will be remembered. LEFT For this woman facing her last years*

without a partner, a photograph album provides the stimulus to reflection on the life she shared with her husband. Memories of the relationship they had help to sustain her sense of worth and her sense of having something important to say about family history.

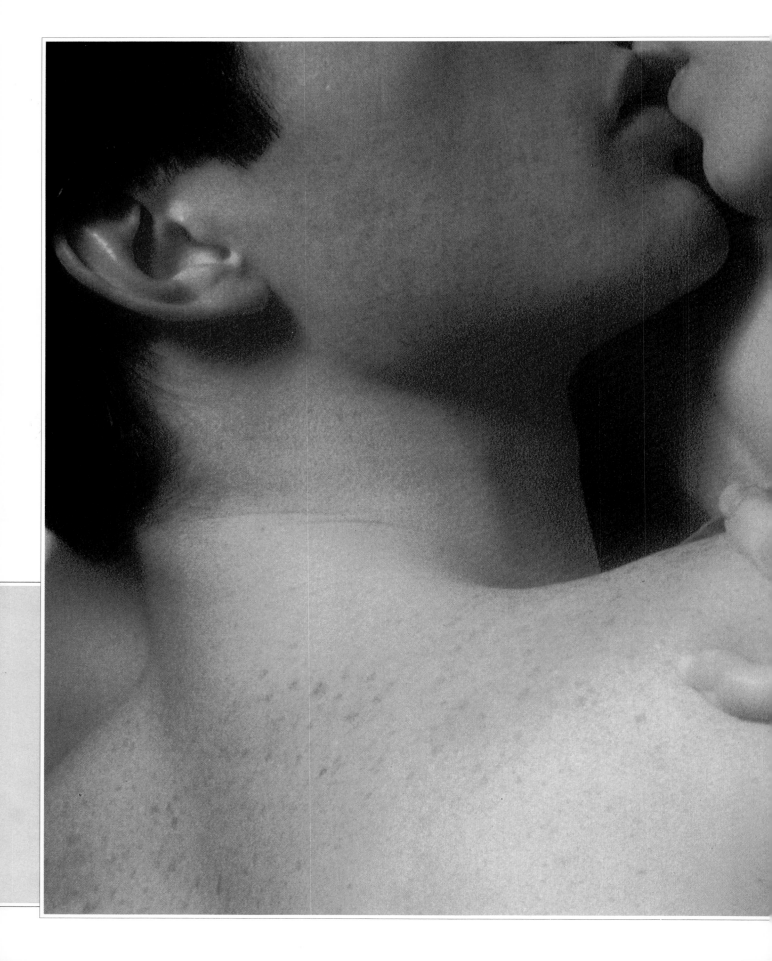

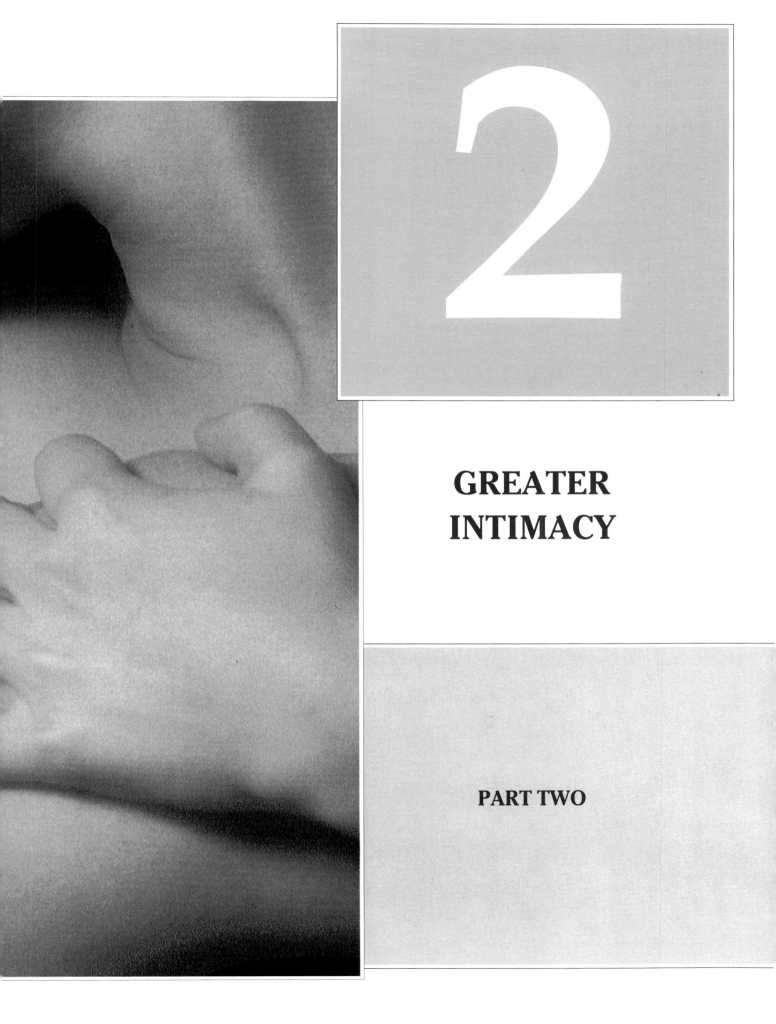

2

GREATER
INTIMACY

PART TWO

A Sense of Intimacy

IN BECOMING a couple, you and your partner have probably become each other's most intimate associate – you are closer to each other and each share more of your private world with the other than with anyone else. In the excitement of forming your partnership, there may well have been little time to think clearly about what this means. What exactly is the intimacy that you have developed together and what are its implications? What are the skills that enable a couple to prevent the sense of intimacy they enjoy from declining, or becoming unattractive, when they begin to take each other for granted – as will happen to some extent in any secure relationship?

Why we limit intimacy

Two of our major preoccupations are to avoid and to achieve intimacy. As we move along a crowded street, we take care not to touch people we do not know or catch their eye too often or for too long. We even stare at the ceiling or

▲ **What brings you close?** *To gain a better insight into what helps you and your partner to feel more intimate, each of you could write a short list under these headings:*
● *Situations when you feel closest to your partner.*
● *What you do to express love for your partner.*
● *How you would like your partner to express their love for you.*
Exchange and discuss your answers. You may be surprised to discover that some of your intended expressions of love went unrecognized. Or you may learn that your partner was expressing love when you thought they were not even thinking about you. You may even find that situations that made you feel close to your partner do not even figure in their notes at all.

Do not be too surprised or dismayed if you learn new things about your partner. They can be a source of excitement and growth within your relationship. **LKA**

What makes you feel close? ■ *When you are ready for intimacy, it is essential to draw close physically, exchange eye contact, touch, feel the warmth of each other's body, and – above all – express what you could not say to another.*

the floor and keep our faces expressionless in a packed elevator – we are standing too close for comfort, and no one must form the impression that we are signaling, with a glance and a smile or a frown, an invitation to use this physical closeness to become involved with us. Meanwhile, among the advertising images that appealingly catch our attention in subway stations and on billboards are pictures of people touching, embracing, smiling with pleasure at each other and at us.

We all need the privacy we gain by excluding other people from our lives. Without it we would overload ourselves with the stimulation of socializing, especially the high stimulation of interacting with people we are getting to know for the first time – people with whom it is exciting to be involved because we do not know how they will react to us as they get to know us, nor what we will discover about them.

Physical intimacy and emotional intimacy

Because physical intimacy is so much a part of emotional intimacy it is easy to observe from people's behavior whom they have chosen to be close to and whom they have not chosen. Why they have so chosen is usually more private – a more intimate matter.

When you are with a mere acquaintance you will probably stand more than a meter (3.3 ft) apart and might touch only by reaching out to shake hands. Since you are acquaintances, it is no longer an invasion of privacy to look at each

other – so long as you look mainly at each other's faces and show, by exchanging conversation, that the looking is polite attention. Since you are no more than acquaintances, there is much that you do not talk about. Experiments have found that people form a better first impression of someone who discloses a small amount of personal information – for example, about where they work – than someone who makes purely impersonal remarks – for example, about the weather. But those who give less guarded insights into their personal life – for example, mentioning how they feel about another person – make an equally poor impression.

In more personal relationships, we move closer – to as near as 45cm (18in). The advantage is partly that we can speak more privately, but the main importance of accepting each other's physical closeness is that it signals a special acceptance of each other's personalities and outlooks. We have judged that investing in a higher level of involvement will be rewarding, and we now accept a more personal range of self-disclosures, because we expect to feel a sense of rapport with each other's more private opinions and tastes. The boost that this moderate sense of intimacy gives to self-esteem is one of the main rewards of friendship.

Close friends, close relatives and romantic partners can step inside the 45cm that separate more distant friends. They do so especially when greeting – men might reach an embracing arm across the shoulders at the same time as shaking hands, and women might hug and kiss. Romantic partners kiss, touch and hug each other in public statements of their closeness. This intimate space is shared as well when giving emotional comfort.

We also like to share this intimate space when exchanging

DO YOU WANT INTIMACY?

■ You may desire more intimacy than your partner. Psychologist Dan McAdams has shown that people vary in their level of intimacy motivation. For a quick self-assessment, think up a story to fit this scene RIGHT.

SCORING

Give yourself 5 points for each of the following:
● You wrote a story in which interaction between the characters led to good feelings (eg closeness, love).
● Your characters communicated with each other simply for the sake of communicating.

Give yourself 1 point for each of the following:
● As a result of their interaction at least one of your characters became better adjusted or developed their personality or character.
● At least one of your characters showed commitment and concern.
● In your story, there is an enduring relationship.
● Your story involves a reunion or a reconciliation.
● Your characters are in harmony.

● One character relinquishes control over another.
● At least one of your characters is seeking intimacy.
● Your characters have a sense of belonging in society.

If you score high you are probably warm, loving, natural, appreciative and sincere. You favor closeness and communication and spend time thinking about people and relationships. You probably engage in conversations and write letters, expressing good feelings. You are probably not a highly dominant, outspoken or self-centered person.

intimate views, not just to avoid being overheard but to reaffirm to each other that we are close enough emotionally to be talking in this way. There may be private thoughts that you would not reveal to this or that close friend or to your partner in particular, and there may be secrets you would never share with anyone, but the overwhelming feeling within a close relationship is that we accept each other at a much deeper level of mutual acquaintance – with a much deeper knowledge of each other's character and personality – than we have experienced with almost anyone else. It is because they know us so well and accept us that we can turn to someone close for comfort, confiding worries, disappointments and weaknesses.

Also within the 45cm closest to us, we experience sensuality. Visual sensual intimacy may occur at a greater distance – the excitement of seeing your lover's body revealed is only possible when you are farther away than this. But the sensual intimacies that do most to draw lovers close emotionally are usually in the most intimate zone: sexual intercourse itself, but also intense unbroken eye contact as you hold your faces near; touching and holding, and speaking

in soft, seductive voices that make it impossible for anyone to overhear. We speak in soft, intimate tones even when no one else is there to hear, thus emphasizing that the words exchanged are special, for the listener alone. The words exchanged, of course, are intensely personal. At this distance we are also aroused by pheromones – body scents that affect us without our consciously detecting them.

Intimacy problems for couples

Sexual intimacy is a special part of the couple relationship. It is not usually the most important part of the intimacy that partners share, but finding mutual acceptance and emotional satisfaction in this most private of spheres is a powerful motivation for treating each other as special. If you

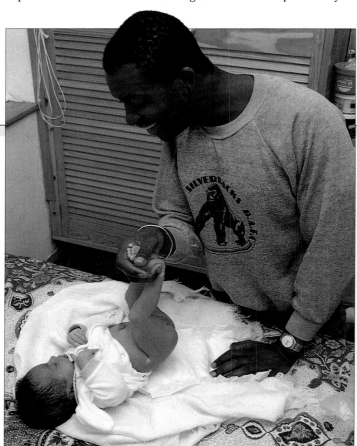

THE INTIMACIES OF FAMILY LIFE

■ *Within the family, we experience little privacy. A baby begins with none at all. If you are lucky, the family into which you are born uses their free access to you to provide the human contact you need. The baby is held and touched in ways that comfort it. The gazes it receives are long and loving ones. Parents and other members of the family talk to the baby and play with it in stimulating ways. As it becomes more aware of individual identities, it recognizes its caregivers and takes its first steps toward controlling intimacy by allowing only these people who are emotionally close to it to draw close physically – at about eight months it becomes shy of strangers, crying and turning away from them and toward someone familiar.*

Soon, however, and culminating in adolescence, there is a gradual retreat from intimacy with parents, as separateness becomes increasingly important to the development of an individual identity. Boys especially are allowed and encouraged to assert their independence and maleness by refusing to be kissed. Children learn to develop personal tastes and opinions and to express them. They also learn how to have secrets. By late adolescence most are committed to finding most of the intimacy they need outside the home they grew up in, and many look for a better quality of intimacy.

There is no guarantee that simply by sharing the physical intimacy of the home, the people who live in it will be emotionally intimate. Many children who have difficulty making friends describe their families as cold, disagreeable and distant. They spend less time with

their parents than more sociable children do. Family intimacy can also be abusive. The absence of barriers puts children at the mercy of their parents. Even in the most healthy of family settings, the implications of living intimately are not all positive ones. We have to put up with the constantly intruding needs and preferences of other family members. We have to accept the way the household is managed, and the people who live in it are always the same people – there may be little sense of adventure in family intimacy.

Why tolerate all the mundane, day-to-day intimacies of a shared life? ■ *Our partners leave us little privacy* ■ *People can be more exciting and interesting to become involved with when you do not know them* ■ *But in the long run only someone who knows you well for a long time can give you a lasting sense of acceptance.*

are concerned that a disappointing sex life is undermining your relationship, you should turn to Chapter 26.

What couples need is to feel that they know and value each other in a special way. The sense of closeness that gives them this confidence depends mainly on what they say to each other and how they say it, as well as on subtle looks, touches and tones of voice that speak in their own way. There is no guarantee, however, that a couple will use to the best effect the opportunities their closeness creates for intense communication. Rather than the gratification of knowing that at least one person in the world understands you, you may find yourself bitterly resenting your partner's failure to see or bring out the real you. To learn about better communication and mutual understanding, turn to Chapters 20, 21 and 25.

A couple likes to feel that the life they share intimately is intimate living as it *should* be. They are apt to measure their relationship against conventional ideals and standards, and this form of self-criticism can be inappropriate (see *Chs 17, 18*). However, even without such prompting, every couple will at some point find themselves taking each other, and their relationship, more for granted than they originally bargained for. Intimacy, once established, becomes famili-

arity. We find ourselves making less effort to please. Courtesies that we reserve for strangers and for friends may not seem worth the trouble when you are dealing with someone who seems certain to carry on with the relationship no matter what. Strategies for keeping intimacy rewarding are described in Chapter 19.

Sharing life as intimately as couples do includes being affected by the rest of each other's private life. Friends and relatives, when visiting your partner at home, are entering *your* private territory if you live together, and sharing attentions and time to which you have a claim. Making room in your life for these other people is the topic of Chapter 27. For most couples, the *mundane* intimacies of occupying a shared home day to day also have to be coped with. They are unromantic, because you might have to negotiate many of the same kinds of problems with an acquaintance you became involved with only because you advertised for someone to share the rent, but the problems of managing together have to be faced (see *Ch 23*), especially when you have children to care for (see *Ch 28*).

Sometimes, in the more revealing intimacy of an established relationship, people discover that they have a partner who is positively difficult. Chapter 24 discusses when and if you should put up with the worst side of your partner's personality and behavior.

Very commonly, the worst that intimacy teaches us about ourselves is that we are capable of boring each other, if we do not make a special effort. Chapter 29 explains how that effort might be mounted.

◄ **A chance to be alone.** *The exclusiveness of the couple relationship means seeking privacy for intimate moments, especially for an intimate discussion of matters that trouble us. When they are with other people, lovers hold hands, stand close and exchange other positive displays of attachment. This is communication not only with each other but with the people around them – it helps them to establish their identity as a couple. But, for a majority, such mild intimacy is the most intense communication with each other in which they will ever feel comfortable about involving others.*

Ideals and Realities

THE REALITIES of life together take many couples by surprise – those who start out believing themselves to be the perfect match may quickly find themselves disillusioned and in difficulty. However, it is not as though anyone is kept in the dark before they commit themselves to a relationship. We grow up in less than perfect families and watch television programs about domestic life. The statistics on marriage breakdown are widely publicized, and marital dissatisfaction is the bread and butter of soap operas.

Why do we think *we* are different? We naturally want to be different, and it is encouraging, to say the least, that so many couples seem to have a rewarding relationship. Even if faced with mainly negative examples, the healthy response is surely to try to do better.

Ideals help to motivate us to invest ourselves in a relationship. However, to avoid ideals becoming in themselves a strain on the resulting partnership – by acting as standards that cannot be met – it is crucial to be constantly open to change: change in what your relationship is really like from one year to the next and change, in the light of experience, in what you consider is reasonable to expect.

Images of partnership

We have become increasingly interested in the quality of relationships and we are constantly exposed to information on the subject. Couples that we know, especially our parents, provide us with models of how things should be, or, if they are unhappy, of how things can go wrong. Media coverage of relationships is extensive. Even those popular television serials and dramas ostensibly about life in hospitals or crime detection concern the personal relationships of the main characters as much as their occupation. Alongside the images of glorious royal marriages and the celebration of love in romantic films, we are shown many of the negative aspects of relationships. Trauma and heartbreak are the preferred material of the scriptwriter because they have more dramatic potential. Husbands deserted by their wives go mad with grief, while wives deserted by their husbands battle with depression. In real life, apart from the numerous newspaper accounts of famous people changing partners, we all actually know at least one couple whose relationship has come unstuck.

In recent years more popular television programs deliberately portray characters which viewers recognize as "just like us." These may be more misleading than those which unmistakably depart from real life. They are sufficiently lifelike for closer self-comparison to be made, and for discrepancies to be worrying; yet, despite their naturalness, there is always a degree of exaggeration or fantasy. There may well be subtle influences about what is normal and proper and implications about consequences for anyone who does not conform.

Is it wrong to want an ideal relationship?

■ *Without ideals, there is nothing positive to aim at in a partnership, but they should be formulated realistically, and it is as well to be ready for a less-than-perfect achievement.*

Such influences may be regarded as harmful but can be to the good. Dramatic treatment of issues in relationships (divorce, affairs, child-care) can give insight into why people do what they do – so that viewers might become more tolerant of similar behavior in their own relationships. "Soaps" may comfort us with the knowledge that we are not alone with problems, and the debate which surrounds events may make us examine our prejudices and points of view. Soap opera fans have time to develop an affinity with characters so that they can understand motives and reasons in greater depth. And watching lots of situation comedies, where couples laugh at themselves and their predicaments,

LOOKING FOR AN IDEAL MODEL

■ *Public images of marriage, far from being helpful as models, are simply confusing because there are so many of them. Looking around us we see both negative and (especially in the media) unbelievably positive pictures of what to expect of a life shared with another person. We are familiar with typical images such as the old-fashioned relationship with stark male and female sex-role divisions, or the romantic and simplified one. We may read about typical stages in the development of marital relationships. But most people will probably find it hard in the end to identify their own experience of marriage with any of the common stereotypes.*

persuades us that relationships can be fun and that it helps to keep a sense of humor.

Of course, viewers do not simply sit and soak up programs like sponges. They bring their own assumptions, argue back or interpret something so that it fits with what they know already. What appears on the screen is not just a matter of what writers and producers want to communicate. Viewers too, simply by choosing what to turn on, play a part in deciding how lifelike or fantastic television relationships should be.

Adjusting your role expectations

Whether or not it is reflected in the programs you watch, research has found that many of our expectations of marriage have to do with the roles we think we will or should play. Marriage today is far more symmetrical than it used to be and most couples now expect to share the responsibilities as equally as possible while still retaining, to some extent, the traditional distinctions of their sex roles (see *Chs 19, 23*). An ideal strongly expressed in women's magazines and the women's pages of newspapers is that the modern marriage will make ample room for women to develop talents and careers. In reality, in a marriage where

Which of our ideals are most commonly compromised? ■ *Leaving a husband's career unaffected while allowing full scope for a wife's may be harder than you think* ■ *Women find it difficult to burden their husbands with an equal share of the housework* ■ *Husbands may find married life disappointingly unromantic.*

both husband and wife go out to work both usually regard the man's job as more important. Looking after the home is still generally seen as the woman's job. Keeping some traditional divisions makes good practical sense for married couples who plan to have children, although cohabiting couples tend to be more flexible in sharing status and roles.

▲ A kiss of condescension? *A tender image such as this can make us feel uneasy. It offers a positive vision of ideal love, but may at the same time offend an ideal of equality. When kissing is not mouth-to-mouth, one person gives this token of affection and the other receives it. Giving a kiss, unless you bow low to kiss a bishop's ring or the hem of an oriental lord's garment, is associated with being older, more mature, more powerful.*

▲ A vision of the ideal home-maker *is a persistent standard for women, both when judged by men and when judging themselves. Most men and* *women have relinquished the belief that the man of the house exclusively should be the family's provider, but the husbands of women who go out to* *work continue to expect priority consideration for the demands of their own careers and they continue to regard themselves as domestically unskilled.*

An ideal mix of traditional sex-role activities and equal sharing of responsibilities is very difficult to achieve. Conscientious involvement in both the domestic and employment scene can be a juggling act, as demonstrated by the case of the British footballer who was dismissed from his team because he missed a league match in order to attend the birth of his first child.

Adjusting expectations of intimacy

Becoming a couple is an adventure that both partners embark on in a glow of euphoria. At the same time, they are probably vaguely aware that, over the years, this glow will fade. The moments of passion and drama that dominate romantic fiction occupy a much smaller proportion of our time in a real-life relationship.

After a heady start with lots of sex and tenderness, both partners turn their attention to the practicalities of home and raising a family. The initial excitement is replaced by a sense of security, a deepening understanding of each other and a shared routine.

Within this general framework, all couples are bound to have their ups and downs. Arguments may occur or the partners may simply fail to agree without having an argument. The good times are mixed with difficult phases when

UNREALISTIC ASSUMPTIONS

■ *Unrealistic ideals are not the only unrealistic expectations that can undermine a relationship. An imaginary domestic situation illustrates this point. Ann believes all husbands like some private, quiet time after the evening meal; he does not realize her belief stemmed from watching how her mother and father interact. Every evening after supper, then, Ann and her husband John sit in separate rooms. She reads; he watches television. She would like to talk but thinks he prefers his own company. Because Ann is always running off to another room after their meal, John comes to believe she wants no conversation.*

This pattern grows fixed for several reasons. First, Ann assumes she know John's preferences. Second

she behaves as though she prefers being alone after dinner. Third, she has never told John she wants his company. Fourth, John accepts Ann's behavior without telling her he would rather be with her.

Each thinks they know what the other wants, yet neither tells the other their preference. Accordingly, both wind up trapped in a frustrating routine. Resentful that their needs are not being met, the pair may drift emotionally apart.

This need not happen if Ann realized she was confusing John with an image of her parents, asked what he wanted, and took his answer at face value. The ability to interpret our partner's needs and express our own, is crucial to a happy relationship. **LKA**

141

◄ **The excitement of starting a new relationship** *helps to create an ideal sense of intimacy that long-term familiarity cannot match up to. It is much more of an adventure to draw close to your partner and make them the focus of your attention when they are still an intriguing, undiscovered reality. Long established couples derive profound satisfactions from their relationship which may not be available to beginners – however, a sense of boredom can accelerate into emotional distance if they do not from time to time rediscover each other to maintain and revitalize their relationship (see Chs 19, 29).*

the partnership gets out of synchrony or is defeated by particularly trying circumstances.

Women frequently complain that there is not enough talking in the relationship, particularly about feelings and problems. Since a woman is ready to concede so much to her partner, giving his work priority at the expense of her own and taking on the bulk of the housework, she likes to feel that her efforts are appreciated.

If the man is critical of her and does not acknowledge the difficulties of her role, she may become resentful, but it is the lack of openings he gives her to discuss her position with him and foster his interest in it that is the real source of her frustration.

Men, on the other hand, frequently complain that there is not as much sex in the relationship as they would like, or that they have to take all of the initiatives in sex (something they did not mind during courtship but now want to progress beyond).

The fact that men and women tend to interpret events and concepts in different ways does nothing to help. British sociologists have found that men understand the term "confiding in each other" as meaning a purposeful discussion of specific problems.

Women, on the other hand, take it to mean giving vent to feelings and sharing detailed accounts of the day. This being the case, women who complain to their partners that they do not talk things over much are likely to be met with blank looks and denials. In the early stages of your life together, you do not assume that your problems and concerns are your partner's. As your commitment grows with time, however, you may start feeling unloved if your worries do not keep your partner awake at night too.

Intimacy is never a once-and-for-all achievement: it comes and goes, depending on new developments and the way you interact as a couple.

People change too

As time goes on, change is inevitable, not only in the emotional quality of the relationship but also in the man and woman themselves – as individuals. Their patterns of activity alter as they grow older. As they become used to each other's ways and to "having" each other, they are

---

READJUSTING THE RELATIONSHIP

■ *With the complex changes now being experienced by most men and women, it is not surprising to find that they must periodically readjust their relationships. Research being conducted at the Center for Developmental Studies in San Francisco suggests that most modern couples go through at least one major readjustment in their lives together, when they will take apart their relationship and put it back together again in some new pattern, with new roles being played by each member. Sometimes this "remarriage" means an actual physical separation of the two people from each other; usually, it at least involves an emotional separation.*

Whatever kind of separation takes place it involves a real possibility that the two partners will never be able to rebuild their relationship. Yet couples who refuse to take the risk of a major rethinking of their marriage will often either become committed to someone else (have an affair, get divorced and remarry, or devote most of their attention to their children), or become "married" to their job or to a hobby. Even if they remain together, the couple will typically settle into a sterile relationship that meets the needs of neither member.

Men and women typically come with different needs to the remarriage that most contemporary couples experience. Wives will demand that their husbands become more actively involved in housework after their children leave home. Husbands will ask their wives to become more emotionally accessible in response to their own emerging mid-life interest in relationships. A woman who has lived outside of marriage with a man

for ten years may expect him to become increasingly supportive of her own career plans, including moving to another city so that she can accept a major promotion. A long-term lover will expect a new level of commitment from the significant woman in his life as a result of his own confrontation with the isolated aspects of his life as a male.

The "seven year itch" that was made popular in a Marilyn Monroe movie of the 1950s may actually exist. A couple typically encounters problems after a relationship has existed for five to ten years. The initial idealized phase of the relationship has faded away, as each member comes to see his or her partner in more realistic terms. Partners in mid-life who have known each other for better or worse for many years will acknowledge and in some manner accept the weaknesses as well as strengths of their mate. At some point, however, one or both members of the couple will demand that at least some of these weaknesses be corrected, especially those associated with gender-related traits (such as male aloofness or violence, or female emotionality or passivity).

CHANGE AND RENEWAL

Couples should be willing to accept and work with the conflicts and tensions of their lives, periodically renegotiating and restructuring their roles and expectations. Otherwise, they could experience a big emotional earthquake that may shatter the very foundation of their relationship and make reconciliation impossible.

Be prepared in your married life for at least one major readjustment ■ *It may involve at least a temporary emotional – if not a physical – separation* ■ *Without risking this adjustment, you may settle into a sterile relationship.*

bound to take the relationship for granted to some extent. On the other hand, because neither partner has to devote so much effort to making it work, they can channel their energies in other directions. The relationship becomes a means rather than an end. Instead of living face to face with your partner, you start to share life and its challenges side by side.

We also develop as individuals in relation to other aspects of our lives – for example, promotion to a managerial position may bring out latent facets of your personality; these changes will, in turn, affect the relationship. We are usually aware of changes in our partner but may be oblivious of the possibility that our own personalities are also developing in ways that are affecting the relationship. An awareness of this personal and mutual growth is important in coming to terms with reality in the most constructive way.

Interpreting reality

Real-life relationships, as opposed to ideal ones, are highly complicated and influenced by some factors over which we have little or no control. Feelings are all-important and it is the continually shifting kaleidoscope of emotional interaction between the partners that forms the basis of the relationship. The actual incidents that give rise to our moods and changes of attitude are of far less importance than the way we react to them.

FACING UP TO THOSE REALITIES

What are the realities you must adjust to if your relationship is to work?

● Your relationship is constantly shifting.

● Feelings change all the time.

● People develop and this affects their relationships.

● You are not in charge (nor is your partner).

● You and your partner may interpret events in different ways.

● In the early stages, you may not see your partner in a realistic light.

● Your view of your life together so far may be distorted.

● You cannot predict the future.

At critical turning-points, men and women must "remarry," adopting a new set of rules and expectations. Such a challenge to their old style of marriage carries a risk. Their relationship may not survive intact. If they are willing to live with conflict and tension and to commit a substantial amount of time to the marriage during this difficult period, even though the relationship offers little immediate gratification of personal needs, they may be rewarded by a happier marriage.

Provided they are not financially or physically infirm, many couples can make this adjustment at any time: it is never too late. Men and women who have lived together for many years often seem to have learned much from each other and have, as a result, become more alike than when they were younger.

Gender-related issues seem to fade into the background as the older husband and wife learn to place their long-crafted relationship at the heart of their lives. With the demands of earning a living and child-rearing behind them, they begin to focus inwardly, more fully developing their spiritual or expressive side. Frequently, their partner becomes their guide for this internal journey. **WHB**

143

We can never be completely in command of what is happening in our relationships. Two people are involved, and although you may be sure of your own aims and intentions, you will not be able to succeed without the cooperation of your partner. What you do and say depends on what your partner does and says and neither of you can anticipate what will happen in the future. In a romantic novel, the author has worked out a plot for the characters in advance but we cannot be the authors of our own relationships. They have no plot but evolve independently of us and build up as we go along.

We cannot give an accurate account of the way our relationship has developed up to the present because it is still in the process of developing. We cannot even safely give an account of it as it is *now* because something may happen tomorrow that changes it. The bond that joins a couple together may be strong but it is, at the same time, infinitely flexible.

▲ **What does your partner really think?** *Making joint judgments and decisions is especially complex when we try to accommodate each other's views before revealing our own. If both partners do this, they have access only to disguised and guarded revelations of the wishes they are trying to take into account.*

REALITY IS WHAT YOU MAKE OF IT

■ *Much of what goes on between a couple has implications beyond the obvious. The same event can be interpreted in different ways by each partner. Usually the variations are slight and of little importance, but psychologists exploring this question have found that divergences in couples' views can be quite striking. In the long term, this may lead to them not seeing eye-to-eye.*

To take an example – Mary rushes out of the house without saying goodbye. James, *her husband, believes she is cross with him because he has not mended the toaster as she asked him to. Tim, their son, thinks it was a good thing that she did not come in and interrupt the football match they were watching on television. Daughter Emma knows that a neighbor had called round earlier and made her mother so late that she would never have got to her meeting in time if she had said goodbye to everyone. When she comes*

Do you understand the past realities of your relationship and can you anticipate its future? ■ *Unlike the author of a romantic novel you cannot work out in advance how the relationship you are creating will develop in the end, but like an author you may find yourself rewriting what has gone before.*

As a couple look back on previous stages of their relationship, they may delude themselves as to the exact nature of what was happening at a particular time. In order to make sense of past events, they unconsciously use information from later events – things they could not possibly have known at the time.

Suppose two people meet for the first time, feel strongly attracted emotionally and physically and shortly afterward go to bed together. This event could then develop in two alternative ways. Either they could become more romantically involved and commit themselves to a future together, or one of them could meet someone else and end the relationship. In the first case, both partners could look back on their first night together and say they loved each other from the start. In the second, the abandoned partner may decide that the other had just been using them without intending anything further to develop.

However, at the time of their first sexual encounter, neither of these explanations is sound because the couple had not then clarified their feelings for each other. Both are trying to be wise after the event.

Love creates illusions

We should also be aware of the fact that love can create illusions that make it hard for us to see what is really happening both to ourselves and in our relationship. Couples may believe they know and love each other just as they are, but the truth is that most people start out with an ideal conception of the kind of person they could love. When they meet someone suitable, each goes through a process of responding and adapting to the other's expectations. Far from accepting partners as they stand, we mould them into the shape of our ideal. By making them aware of what we most wish to see in them, we show them how to please us. It is the person they will become that we fall in love with.

In the meantime, our own personality is itself being subtly adapted by our partner to fit *their* ideal.

Public images of what relationships are or should be are conflicting and confusing and ideals built on such images are bound to be as well. But while the reality of our own lives can be disappointing it can also be exciting, especially if we learn to interpret events and moods accurately and to adjust to the inevitable changes in ourselves and our relationships. **RB**

▶ **Playing a romantic role.** *Do you really know and love each other just as you are? Is it possible that at least one of you has fallen in love with a character that the other is interpreting in a kind of amateur theatrical performance? It is important to look beyond the self that your partner creates in order to please you.*

back, she is likely to get a very different reception from her husband, on the one hand, and her children, on the other.

Although our interpretation of behavior is based on what we know about the events leading up to it, we can also adopt a particular interpretation because it suits us. If your partner falls asleep during lovemaking, it is less wounding to conclude that the cause is a tiring day than that it demonstrates a lack of enthusiasm for you.

145

CHASING A DREAM

■ In choosing a partner, people tend to look for someone who seems, as far as possible, to fit an ideal. Whether this image of the ideal partner is conscious or unconscious, it will affect your interpretation of your real relationship.

Trying to analyze honestly just what ideal person you are looking for in your partner can be a step toward re-evaluating the relationship. The reality may be disillusioning but it can also prove surprisingly better than the image.

Other halves Many of us will choose a partner who has leanings and limitations that match our own, so we feel comfortable with them and can continue to believe in ourselves without feeling threatened. Everyone has been left with some imbalance by their childhood: the failure to master some skill, the over-strict control of emotions or, simply, odd habits. Partners who match and compliment each other can get on in life without their blind spots mattering. Unresolved conflicts from childhood are bound to reemerge – in times of stress, for instance, and adversely affect the relationship. However, a complementary partnership can cope, with each person stabilizing the other. But more idealized images of the perfect partner are more dangerous, based as they are on romantic stereotypes which, in the light of reality, are bound to disappoint.

Me Tarzan, you Jane Some couples consist of a strong, active man and a vulnerable, helpless woman. If childhood experiences have reinforced gender roles ("be a man"; "act like a lady"), finding a partner who conforms to the stereotype of the opposite sex might be an attractive option. Living "happily ever after" depends on each acting their part without ever departing from type – "me dominant, you dependent," "me hunt, you cook," and so on. Their needs must never reverse and there must be no jealousy.

Knight and maiden The knight and the maiden consists of an inexpressive man and a highly emotional woman. She has had a traumatic time until he came along and rescued her. Her need is for continual understanding, affection and reassurance

Knight and maiden

but these do not come readily from a partner whose speciality is repressing emotion. She likes him being her guardian and provider but his remoteness frustrates her, just as her woes and complaints cause him to withdraw.

Prince Charming Others pursue a fantasy lover (who, if ever found, might prove far from ideal to live with). Some women – even in this era of feminism – have an unconscious tendency to choose men who best fit their romantic ideals of the "perfect man" who will sweep them off their feet, change their life, make them feel different. He has a combination of exciting qualities – charm, mystery, aloofness, style – not present in more suitable partners, whose own valuable qualities are concealed by superficial ordinariness and lack of shine. **RB**

When you look at your partner, do you see the person who is really there? ■ *Take this idealized person off their pedestal, rise up from your knees and start getting to know each other as you actually are.*

APART MEANS CLOSER TOGETHER

■ *Ironically, growing closer to someone calls for mentally separating ourselves from them. Too often we see our partner not as they are but how we think they are or would like them to be. We get involved in a relationship with an image we have created – often more an extension of ourselves than someone with their own identity. To escape from that illusion we must first grow more aware of our own personality. Only then will we be able to separate our own wishes, attitudes, and problems from our partner's.*

A common fault is doing something for our partner that we would really like our partner to do for us. Assuming they must like anything that we do is not the best basis for doing what would truly please them most. **LKA**

DANGERS OF IDEALIZING YOUR PARTNER

■ *If you place your partner on a pedestal, you are likely to set yourself in a lower position, and go along with everything they say and do. You deny your own needs for theirs, and your partner never gets to know you properly because you fail to express yourself. Eventually your illusion will crumble, and then you may take an equally unrealistic negative view.*

Normally, partners gradually learn to know each other, seeing themselves as well as each other for what they are, including things they like and things they do not. Provided you accept that neither is a paragon you will be able to deal with each other in an honest, non-defensive manner. Meanwhile, of course, never forget to love your partner for those things that you loved about them in the first place. **LKA**

Me Tarzan, you Jane

147

Expectations of the Opposite Sex

IN ALL COUNTRIES surveyed, researchers find that a majority of couples believe that it is better for their relationship if the man is definitely masculine and the woman is definitely feminine. We like a partner to fulfill our expectations about the opposite sex. However, most couples also want intimacy, and a majority (75 percent in the United States) consider equality important.

These ideals can easily come into conflict, for while the traditional image of femininity allows women to be very expressive of feelings and very sensitive to their own and other people's, it is considered more natural for men to have difficulty expressing and understanding emotions, and to find it hard to be intimate. Another traditional view is that it is very masculine to be a rational, systematic thinker, more

feminine to depend on another's judgment. Thus a woman may see herself as losing some of her femininity if she shares equal responsibility with her partner for decisions.

Partners in almost every relationship feel at least in some degree the tension of this conflict between old and new ideals of the surrounding society. By considering more closely what is involved in the conflict, you may find it possible to decide with more confidence what the standards for your own relationship should be. You may conclude that you really are a feminine and masculine pair and that this is the right character for your partnership. This may mean that you accept a lower level of male than of female emotional investment in your relationship and accept that the man and the woman will contribute to decisions in distinctively dif-

148

▲ **Contrasting expectations.** In a French railway station, dress announces individual decisions about how to inter-

pret the male and the female roles. Couples use personal appearance to send messages about their identity to each

other and to the world. Those who wish to identify themselves less strongly with traditional sex roles will tend to mix traditional

signals – a woman may wear a tie and a man a brightly colored and patterned shirt.

How opposite do you and your partner need to be? ■ *Most couples want to be masculine-feminine pairs* ■ *However, differences in masculine and feminine emotional style are a deep-rooted obstacle to intimacy* ■ *Strong distinctions between male and female ways of knowing undermine equality.*

ferent ways. You may conclude instead that you and your partner are androgynous – you combine masculine and feminine traits in the same personalities.

Are women more expressive?

A trait that we typically expect of women, and that researchers agree they really have as a group, is their emotional expressiveness. Women are expert at expressing their feelings in an open and articulate way. Studies have also found that most women are easily able to monitor and recall their thoughts and emotions. Men very often do not know what to say when asked to state what they feel or have just been feeling, and it is not as common for them to try to talk to someone about their feelings.

Society accepts women's ways of expressing feelings and increasingly sets its standards by them. The ability to articulate emotions is highly valued and respected as a sign of maturity, of sensitivity in interpersonal relationships and even of mental health. Emotional accessibility and openness are useful not only in marriage and the family, but we are becoming increasingly conscious of their importance in business and community life.

Men tend to be more inarticulate, expressing their feelings through actions and decisions rather than words. A man who feels love may express it through a gift, a specially prepared meal, or financial support for a project that the other person values. Similarly, anger is expressed by means of a loud voice, withdrawal of a favor, of financial support or

149

MALE AND FEMALE EMOTIONAL STYLES

■ *Socially defined male and female roles tend to exaggerate these differences between men and women.*

Women are more expert at responding to other people's needs and emotions, and they easily show their own feelings.

Men are more isolated in their emotions, showing them less easily, expecting less emotional support and giving emotional support more silently.

WOMEN

MEN

▲ *TOP A veteran pays private tribute to his dead comrades at a Vietnam memorial. Though research has not established whether men or women actually feel more emotion, women tend to show it more readily. Male strategies for coping with crises rarely involve open or shared displays of distress.*

BOTTOM A mother reassures her son with a loving look and comforting touch. Women's caring role associates them more than men with positive emotional expressions like concern and tenderness. Women tend to be better at sharing emotions and feeling empathy.

of approval. It can also lead to physical abuse. In our more remote past, men often expressed feelings through dance, rhythmic pounding of drums, or ritualistic enactment. These forms of expression are usually not available to men in contemporary industrial countries. The "wild man" (see box) who is only partially tamed by women in many nonindustrial societies seems to have been more totally tamed in ours, and both women and men sense a loss of male spontaneity. Sometimes, however, the "wild man" surfaces in violent and self-destructive actions.

One of the few remnants of this predominantly male way of expressing feelings is the sporting event. At a football game men can shout, pound their feet and release emotion ritualistically. Wives often complain that their husbands show more emotions during a sporting event than they do while making love or caring for their children. While there is some truth in this observation, it is more accurate to say that men find a more natural way of showing their feelings through watching and playing sports than they do in most contemporary family settings. They do not necessarily have more feelings during the game, they only know how to express them more freely.

Are men less responsive?

A typically feminine way of experiencing feelings is the sharing of emotions. Apart from ritualized expressions, men, by contrast, tend to experience their feelings in isolation. Typically, they focus inward on them, rather than risk being distracted by talking with or receiving the empathy of another person. Men and women may also show different ways of giving comfort to someone in trouble or distress. Many men tend to take a nonverbal approach – walking or sitting next to the other person but saying very little; they remain on the sidelines as silent witnesses. Most women, on the other hand, take a more active, helping approach, talking to the person about feelings and problems.

The male style is often criticized, for men frequently become isolated from people who are important to them, unable to enjoy the support and rewards of an intimate relationship. They also tend to be much less supportive than the women in their lives need them to be. A man's own experience of dealing with his emotions privately may mislead him into assuming that his partner's should not be intruded upon, or he may simply feel incompetent to help, because his silent-witness style seems inadequate. Only a minority of wives report that they receive as much emotional reinforcement from their husbands as they do from other women.

What gives men their emotional style?

There is no generally accepted explanation of the origin of masculine and feminine styles of dealing with emotion. Emphasizing biological evolution, some writers speculate about an inherited tendency among child-rearing, camp-

150

THE EMOTIONAL WORLD OF MEN

■ *LEFT Triumphant American gymnasts give their feelings free rein. Whether spectating or participating, men tend to express emotion more freely during sporting events than in family life. Emotional constraint may leave a man's wife and children unaware of the strong, genuine feelings he has for them.* RIGHT *The relaxed, open camaraderie of these young Moroccans would be out of place in many other cultures. The ideal of male detachment, and anxiety about being thought homosexual, make many men uneasy about displaying affection toward their*

own sex. Women are much more likely to show their attachment to female friends or their relatives through physical contact.

Can we change our emotional styles to suit our relationships? ■ *Differences in emotional expressiveness and responsiveness may be partly inherited* ■ *Upbringing and social standards strongly accentuate male-female differences* ■ *Yet your own sense of individuality can allow you to interpret your sex role as you please.*

tending women to respond to human needs, and to highly expressive face-to-face communication at close quarters. Men, it is suggested, inherit a greater tendency to concentrate on planned, coordinated activities.

In hunting, for example, they would communicate with each other mainly about their activity, and often at a distance from each other. Their acceptance within the male group would depend on their *not* showing emotion when this would undermine the other's confidence in their ability to perform unflinchingly.

It is likely, however, that for hundreds of thousands of years, men have had an advantage in reproduction when they formed emotional attachments to their women, identified particular children as their own and helped to protect and care for them.

This would create a modifying evolutionary pressure, and like all inherited traits, a tendency toward inexpressiveness would vary in its inherited strength from individual to individual. Many men are in fact very spontaneous and achieve emotional closeness easily.

Variability would also occur because any inherited trait can be heavily influenced by the environment in which it develops. The environmental fact that, almost universally, a woman is the primary caregiver of any child, has been suggested as being virtually enough in itself to create a sex difference in emotional style: little girls becoming aware of

THE POWER OF A WOMAN TO TAME A WILD MAN

■ *A theme in many fairy tales, myths, novels and even contemporary movies is the "wild man" who first appears to be very powerful and destructive, then is tamed by one woman or all of the women in the village or city. Typically, the women are ambivalent about taming the wild man for as he becomes more domestic he loses much of his power and may become instead a sad and docile lap dog. The wild man is central in fairy tales such as "Beauty and the Beast," in novels such as "The Hunchback of Notre Dame" and "Wuthering Heights" and in films such as "King Kong."*

In almost all of these stories, the feelings of the wild man are considered inappropriate to the civilized world in which he lives. Often he is captured and brought into society against his will. He is spontaneous and acts upon his feelings, but only in a domestic setting do these feelings and actions become destructive. The wild man finds himself attracted by a beautiful and/or

cunning woman who seeks to bring some order to the chaotic and frightening behavior she sees. In some stories, once she succeeds in taming him, he is killed by a mob that does not understand him, or does not realize that he has been tamed. In some, she loses interest and leaves him dying of a broken heart.

What folk wisdom do these stories express about male feelings? First, the feelings of men are frightening and out of control. Second, women must allow and even encourage men to express their feelings, or these feelings will be transformed into violence toward others or violence toward the self (usually in the form of depression or self-doubt). Third, men must find an appropriate vehicle for the expression of their feelings. They must allow themselves to be partially "tamed," for women often understand better than they do the impact of emotional expression on relationships.

151

▶ **"Beauty and the Beast"** – *an illustration by the English artist Walter Crane (1845-1915). In the well-known fairy tale a beautiful girl saves her father's life by agreeing to live with the Beast. Beauty's love eventually civilizes the Beast – really a prince – freeing him from his wild nature. Numerous fairy tales and stories are about women of great emotional maturity who tame wild men.*

their own sex are aware of being the same sex as this first important person in their lives; a little boy's first relationship, however, is marked by his being different from the other person. The little girl goes on to develop her own identity through accepting the woman as her model. The little boy defines his identity as unique and separate from the woman's. Eventually, he models himself on his father, but he finds it difficult to become emotionally close to this man, who is usually absent. It has been predicted that today's increasing participation by fathers in child care will help future generations of men to have a less isolated emotional life (see *Ch 28*).

Some experts warn of the "wounded father" who is the main adult model for many boys – a father who, when he is at home, is distracted and discouraged by and uncommunicative about the problems he has to deal with outside the home. Because he has been deprived of opportunities to express his feelings, his children see him as remote, exhausted and preoccupied. Such fathers create an overly strong impression on their sons that men are naturally distant. Their daughters may come to expect the future men in their lives to be naturally inaccessible.

Can men change their style?

Between them, do heredity and/or early environment fix a man's emotional style for life? The evidence of continuing development suggests not – the social expectation that a man will be a strong and silent type is an ongoing reinforcing influence, and at different times of life men tend to

respond to this influence in different ways. In their teens both sexes show a stronger conformity to sex stereotypes than they do before or after this time. In their late teens, young men hold themselves aloof from serious relationships until they have resolved an identity crisis. They do not answer the question "Who am I?" by saying who their friends and intimate partner are. They seek a set of more

FIVE WAYS OF KNOWING

FEMININE			MASCULINE
Researchers have identified three styles of thinking and knowing, adopted by men too but often	regarded as distinctively feminine. Two are submissive to the authority of male opinion. A	subjective way of knowing that rejects the special authority of objective principles also occurs.	Men, and career women who adopt male strategies, tend to have a fourth way of knowing.
1 **Silence** – some women are reluctant to form or express opinions, feeling that because they are female they are mindless and voiceless and subject to authority.	**2** **Received knowledge** – some women feel that, although they are capable of knowing, because they are female, they can only know what people in authority have found out.	**3** **Subjective knowledge** – truth is seen as personal, private and subjectively intuited, something that emerges from a sensitivity to human needs.	**4** **Objective knowledge** – knowledge is seen as objective and dependent on procedures for finding it out and communicating it clearly.

ANDROGYNOUS

Recent generations of androgynous men and women look for ways of combining the subjective and objective approaches. Researchers who have studied the five attitudes to knowledge and decision-making believe that this constructed style offers men and women their best opportunity to be effective joint managers of their relationships and their marriages.

5
Constructed knowledge – truth is seen as reflecting both subjective and objective insights and the particular circumstances and individual needs of participants in each situation.

Can we change our thinking styles to suit our relationships? ■ *Women's greater sensitivity makes them seem more subjective and less systematic* ■ *However, both men and women can combine sensitivity with logic.*

abstract and general categories for themselves ("I am career-oriented," "I am a liberal") before they develop a stable sense of self and have enough confidence in their masculinity to move from merely transient and superficial relationships toward genuinely intimate ones. A young woman of 20 to 25 years of age, by contrast, accepts emotional closeness as a central part of the feminine experience, and she will answer the question "Who am I?" in part by defining her relationships with other women and with men.

Exaggerated displays of manhood are more common in adolescents than in adult men, but a young man anxious to be accepted in a career will also find motives for accentuating his masculinity. This may include learning not to disclose too much about himself and learning how to display a tough resistance to emotional pressures. When a man has reached 40 or 50 years of age, however, there is often a belated move to become closer to his family. The father from whom he has always been distant is retired and now has time for relationships.

The son himself might by now have made his mark on the world or at least come to terms with his not having accomplished what he dreamed of in his early twenties. He too has more attention for relationships and may have less care for things typically masculine.

Changing cultural patterns also point to a male ability to choose how masculine to be. Before the 1970s there were no measures of androgyny such as the one on page 154, but researchers agree in interpreting the proportion of American students who turned out to be androgynous in the 1970s and 1980s (about 25 percent) as reflecting in part an interest in personal flexibility that did not exist in the 1950s.

Do men and women think differently?

Research shows that men's way of thinking fits with our general view of what it means to be a rational and thinking person. When we consider usual and acceptable ways of thinking, we expect people to be coherent and systematic, arriving at conclusions through a step-by-step process. We want their decisions to be based on a clearly articulated, generally applicable set of principles that will stand up to criticism and scrutiny.

Although research finds no inherent overall difference in male and female intelligence to support an expectation that men would think more systematically, slight differences in mental organization have been studied. Men tend to have verbal processing concentrated in the left side of the brain, and spatial processing in the right. In women, both types of processing are more spread out and some researchers believe that there are more connections between the right and left sides of most women's brains. On average, women score slightly higher in tests of verbal skills (which may help to account for their being emotionally more articulate). Men score slightly higher in tests of spatial and mathematical skills. However, there are wide overlaps – one quarter of women and girls, for example, have more mathematical aptitude than the average male. With each passing decade, moreover, the measured differences between boys' and girls' abilities become smaller. This seems to reflect the fact that parents and teachers tend increasingly to have more equal expectations of girls and boys.

Are men more rule-governed?

The way men and women make moral decisions has also been studied, with men described as more rule-governed than women. When researchers ask people to imagine that their partner is dying and can only be saved if someone

WHAT PEOPLE SAY ABOUT HOW THEIR PARTNERS THINK

■ *Women often become irritated because their partners seem to be overestimating the power and usefulness of rational thinking:*

● *"He comes home and lectures me about how we have to think out better ways of managing the household and the children, so that I won't always get into a frenzy when I get home from work. I don't need a lecture on management – I need help with the vacuuming and someone to test Shirley on her spellings while I'm giving George his bath."*

Men are often frustrated by what they see as too much responsiveness to children's whims:

● *"Because she goes out to work she feels guilty about not spending more time with the children and so she*

lets them stay up late. She says she agrees in principle that we'd all be happier if they had a regular bedtime, but it seems there's always a special reason for letting them stay up."

Wives sometimes feel that their husbands are pouring mental energy into questions that have no immediate effect on the family:

● *"My husband makes all the important decisions in our house – he decides what this country should do about the international trade imbalance and how we should solve the problem of social injustice in the world. I make all the small decisions – where we will live, where the children go to school, and how we spend our money."*

steals medicines for them, men and women tend to have different ways of deciding what they would do.

Men tend to apply general, abstract moral principles. They decide to steal the drug because the life of a human being is more important than the profit a drug company should obtain from its product.

Alternatively, they decide that stealing is never right, and therefore they should not take the drug but, instead, somehow find more money.

Women tend to respond by asking more questions: "What is the condition of my dying husband?" "Why is the druggist behaving as he is?" "Do I have dependent children to care for as well?" Women want a fuller context before making a decision. "If my husband and I have children, then who will care for them if I am sent to prison for stealing drugs?" "How have I alienated the druggist so much that he acts in this irresponsible manner?" "Can't I do anything to convince the druggist that I can be trusted to pay him back or that he has more to gain from his drug than just money?"

Women generally show a greater sensitivity to the situation and the context, whereas men generally show a greater sensitivity to rules, procedures and precedence. Women tend to take into account more of the particulars of a situation. Men seek to make decisions based on an impartial sense of right and wrong. Women like to find a solution that at least partially meets the needs of everyone.

Does this sex difference mean that women are less capable of working with systems of rules than men are?

Some writers suggest that men might be at an advantage in working with rules, because, as boys, they grew up playing competitive team games with intricate rules and learned to insist that the rules be applied fairly. In their isolation from the particular needs and emotions of others, men may be likely to pay more attention to rules – feel more at home with them – because, to them, rules are what constitute naturally isolated individuals into teams and social units. Women, meanwhile, if their play as girls was traditional, are more likely to have been practicing their relationship skills and verbal skills by talking to dolls and soft toys or serving each other play meals; these styles of play did not give them an experience of applying principles.

Research, however, shows that when men and women of equivalent educational and occupational background are compared, women are just as likely as men to think about abstract principles of right and wrong. For example, among schoolteachers, both men and women tend to be concerned about making sure that children learn to follow rules and apply abstract principles, and both tend to be concerned about the individual problems and needs of children.

In a relationship, we contribute to decisions in the same way if we see our responsibilities as equivalent. If there is a division of labor, we may contribute in different ways. Masculine men more often see it as their role to manage the family's relations with the abstract, rule-governed world at large. Feminine women more often have the role of being alert to the specific needs and emotions of particular family

HOW MUCH MASCULINITY AND FEMININITY DO YOU HAVE?

■ *Complete this questionnaire to see whether you are masculine, feminine or both (androgynous).*

1 *I feel particularly complimented when someone tells me that I am:*
   a *gentle and/or cheerful.*
   b *self-reliant and/or ambitious.*
2 *When I disagree with another person, it is particularly important for me to be:*
   a *sympathetic and eager to soothe hurt feelings.*
   b *forceful and willing to take a stand.*
3 *When someone else seems to be experiencing problems I am most likely to be:*
   a *independent and/or assertive.*
   b *understanding and/or compassionate.*
4 *I would feel particularly offended or hurt if someone said that I was:*
   a *aggressive or defensive of my own beliefs.*
   b *gullible or childlike.*
5 *Other people are most likely to be annoyed with me because I am:*
   a *too dominant or competitive.*
   b *too shy or yielding.*
6 *I would most like to be known as a person who is:*
   a *affectionate and sensitive to the needs of others.*
   b *a leader who is willing to take risks.*

SCORING

If you find considerable difficulty in choosing between (a) and (b) for all or many of these six statements, you do not need to calculate a score: you are androgynous. Men are masculine and women are androgynous if they choose five or six of the "masculine" answers: 1b, 2b, 3a, 4b, 5a, 6b. Women are feminine and men are androgynous if they choose 5 or more of the "feminine" answers: 1a, 2a, 3b, 4a, 5b, 6a. You are androgynous if you score 4 or fewer on one list and 2 or more on the other list.

Should you be masculine, feminine or both?
■ *Traditionally, men, unlike women, have felt free to pursue their own personal goals and satisfactions. Today, women are free to do the same* ■ *Traditionally, women have found fulfillment in caring for others. This is now a role that men too can freely share.*

members. Since many family decisions affect both its relations with the outside world, however, and the welfare of its individual members, the decision-making process is usually tuned to reflect both kinds of input.

Can masculine and feminine styles merge?

Many differences between the sexes are not fixed. Men and women change over time, and they learn from each other about how to be more androgynous. This can happen at any time in life, but in particular as women who have mainly been caregivers to their children and husbands enter their thirties and forties, many become frustrated with the selflessness of this role. They seek opportunities to express themselves in more independent, more traditionally masculine ways by developing their opinions and by seeking to make a mark on the world beyond the home.

As men become less career-oriented in their mid-forties, by contrast, and their interests turn toward the home and their family relationships, this shift in the woman's interests can lead to disappointment: the homeward looking husband's new expectation may be for undivided attention from a wife he has for years not had time for. However, the change often results in the husband taking pleasure in giving his wife support through more involvement in looking after the house, and thus helping her ambitions.

Young couples increasingly combine ways of knowing and feeling that cross the traditional boundaries between male and female. Many men are committed to raising their children. Some are "house husbands," some single parents or fathers who actively participate with their wives in rearing their children. They do not necessarily forsake their career, but balance it against more "feminine" concerns. Young women cross boundaries with their strong commitment not only to home but also to career, and by holding their own clearly defined views while also showing concern for others in their decision-making.

Women can include in their ethic of care the care for self that has traditionally made men unashamed of pursuing their own goals and their own self-expression. Men can include in a male ethic the care for others that has traditionally helped women to make the family and the couple relationship possible. Studies have found that women who score high in androgyny tests, by displaying a more masculine assertiveness and independence than purely feminine women do, have more self-esteem and better mental health. Men who score high lose none of the higher self-esteem and mental health that men as a general group enjoy, but they show more flexibility and freedom from convention. In both sexes, androgynous people are more likely to score high in creativity tests. **WHB**

155

ANDROGYNOUS STYLES

■ *LEFT A female executive's appearance borrows from traditionally male styles. In her work she may balance "masculine" ways of thinking with a sympathetic approach to others. RIGHT Though house husbands like this one are still uncommon, men are increasingly taking on traditionally female tasks. Looking after his children allows a man to develop "feminine" skills of nurturing and concern. Androgynous people are more versatile in their behavior and score higher in creativity tests than strongly sex-typed men and women.*

Sustaining Your Relationship

IF WE become seriously ill, we usually consult a specialist physician who prescribes some form of emergency treatment or therapy. But our day-to-day health depends on less dramatic maintenance measures such as eating a balanced diet, getting sufficient rest and avoiding harmful elements in our environment. Similarly, when a relationship is in crisis, the partners may consult a professional counselor or enter a special therapy program (see *Ch 25*). But the continuing well-being of the relationship depends on simple yet very important maintenance strategies. It has been estimated that as few as 10 percent of married couples maintain their relationship well enough to enjoy its full potential.

One of the keys to getting the most from any aspect of life is to decide on the positives and the negatives, and then to take appropriate action to increase or maintain the rewards and reduce the costs. It is not easy to give general guidelines about how to apply this principle to relationships, because people are so different: what seems rewarding to one may seem like a cost to another. In addition, people are always changing. However, research has established what *most* people find rewarding in their relationships.

Why it matters to keep up your appearance

We know intuitively that personal appearance is an important factor in the early stages of attraction. This is borne out by studies of preferences in dating partners, which have found that good looks are more important than good character or personality. As people grow older and more experienced in their ways of relating, they learn that continuing attraction is built on a deeper, more stable foun-

AFFECTION DOES NOT JUST HAPPEN

■ *Few couples continue to experience the intense passion that marks the early stages of romantic relationships. New relationships are exciting: we are doing things for the first time and we are not sure what our partner will do next. But part of getting to know someone is learning to predict their actions and reactions. This is why continuing relationships tend not to be as exciting as new ones.*

Research has shown, however, that by using "affinity maintenance" strategies such as those below, a couple in an established relationship can sustain and even deepen their affection.

● Be faithful – do not have extramarital affairs	● Be honest – avoid lying, cheating and "bending the truth"	● Include your partner in your social plans and activities	● Be physically affectionate – give kisses and hugs; sit close
● Be physically attractive – in appearance, dress and hygiene	● Show the relationship is close – use flattering pet names	● Be verbally affectionate – say "I love you" and "I care"	● Be sensitive – be warm, caring and sympathetic

EVERYDAY MAINTENANCE

■ *RIGHT A couple adopt a team approach to fitness. Through health consciousness, they make exercise a daily routine. Whether consciously or not, by sharing this routine they are also working together to sustain the vitality of their relationship. LEFT Some men care about keeping their relationship at a high level of mutual satisfaction. If your partner says there is no need to spend money on gestures like buying her flowers, it may be wiser to trust your own judgment.*

How can you maximize the benefits and minimize the costs of staying together?
■ *Most people neglect simple strategies that could greatly increase the value that their relationship has for their partner.*

dation than looks alone. However, appearance still matters in an established relationship. Studies indicate that the more evenly matched partners are in their attractiveness, the more likely they are to stay together. Apparently, people feel rewarded just knowing that their partner contributes equally to the couple's visual impact and appeal.

In some relationships, what one partner lacks in physical beauty may be made up for by other assets. A study involving 6,200 people found that those not as good-looking as their partners tend to be unusually loving, self-sacrificing or rich. Such relationships can be mutually fulfilling. However, this effect can work in reverse as well, so that one partner begins to neglect their appearance. Contributing more in the way of caring, self-sacrifice or financial support may foster the belief that looking good is not as necessary as it was before. The housewife who spends a major part of her day tending to children and chores may feel she has earned the right to stop tending to make-up and hairstyles. The husband who spends long hours at the office to make a good living for his family may feel more at liberty to ignore his beginning-to-bulge waistline.

157

Inattention to appearance can have an adverse effect on the relationship. Couples participating in one research project pointed to "having a good-looking mate" as one of the vital characteristics of a good relationship, along with other concerns such as being liked and loved and having a mate who is faithful. Looking after our own appearance seems generally to be a relationship plus.

Being there for each other

The main reason why two people remain a couple is to ensure a source of support in their daily lives. They count on each other to be there, ready to give advice in a crisis, to lend a helping hand or perhaps just to give a sympathetic smile – supportive actions that can determine whether your partner achieves a life goal, or is able to accept disappointments, setbacks and to find pleasure in living. So "being there" for a partner is another source of relationship rewards (see *Ch1*).

We can give our partner emotional support by showing that we love and care for them. You may express affection directly by saying "I love you," but there are also many more subtle ways to show you care: a squeeze of the arm, touching the cheek, a kiss, a warm glance, standing close, giving a gift or doing a favor.

It is important to realize that people may differ in the ways they express their affection: one may like to talk about their feelings, another may be more comfortable with less direct expressions of affection, like doing favors. In general, women and men differ in how they typically signal affection.

▲ **Fun to be with.** *We all need friends to share the activities and ideas that stimulate us. Making your partner one of the most important of your friends is typical of relationships with a high sense of satisfaction.*

▶ **Affirming the relationship.** *By means of conventional gestures signifying that we belong together we remind the world – and ourselves – that our relationship matters.*

Do you know what your partner needs?
■ *We often fail to recognize how different our partner's needs are from our own* ■ *In most relationships, there is not enough listening, asking for advice, giving sympathy or paying compliments* ■ *Partners easily miss opportunities to lend each other support.*

Women tend to express feelings of intimacy more overtly by telling their partner how much they care or giving relatively direct nonverbal signals like a hug or a pat. Men are more likely to view practical assistance or simply being together as expressions of affection (see *Ch 18*).

Additionally, men are more likely than women to view sex as a way of showing emotional support. Many women needing support just want a cuddle or some other form of nonsexual physical contact. Misunderstandings arise when their partner interprets affectionateness as sexuality. He gets aroused, she backs off, thinking (or saying), "That's all you ever think about!" They both retreat from the encounter feeling frustrated, misunderstood and rejected.

Showing that you respect and value your partner confirms their sense of self-worth and encourages your partner to feel good about himself or herself. This sort of psychological support can be given by listening attentively and acknowledging the opinions of your partner, asking for advice, paying compliments, and expressing sympathy, understanding or reassurance. In a broad survey of marriage and family counselors these ways of giving support were ranked among the most important for healthy relationships.

Support can also take more practical forms, such as giving your time, effort, expertise or material resources to help your partner meet a challenge or accomplish a goal. The task you perform need not be critical nor the support overwhelming. Sometimes it is the little things that count. Helping a partner prepare a dinner, choose a new jacket, plant a garden or practice a presentation for work are all ways of giving support.

Maintaining the ties that bind

The term "couple" does not just refer to the two people in a relationship; it includes the way those people relate to each other. Being a couple means being bonded together in such a way that what happens to one partner affects the other. This strong sense of togetherness is what satisfied couples value. They tend to share time, activities, interests, beliefs and values. They enjoy each other's company and feel that they are compatible and that they are working toward the same goals (see *Ch 2*).

Partners develop this kind of bond partly by being together, talking about their experiences and sharing their feelings. In the early stages of their relationship, couples

FLIRTING WITH YOUR MATE

■ *Most of us think of flirting as a way of starting a romantic relationship. But flirting can communicate a much deeper, more stable form of attraction as well, and research shows that flirting is a particularly good way for established couples to communicate their affection to each other. Except in a crisis or on special occasions, many partners avoid direct talk about their relationship and their feelings (see Ch21). Apparently they feel that declaring their attraction explicitly could be embarrassing to the other person or to anyone who might overhear. The subtlety of flirting can make it an effective alternative – a way of expressing things that need not or cannot be said.*

▶ **Taking liberties**. *Pretending that they are discovering each other for the first time helps a couple keep alive a sense of pleasure and excitement in having a relationship.*

159

seem to do these things almost instinctively. Later on, they may need to make a conscious effort to set aside time to be together. They need to remember that it is not just the quantity of time together that matters, but the quality as well.

Celebrating the relationship

Another way of stressing togetherness is to celebrate being a couple. We are all familiar with the ceremonies and celebrations that mark the beginning of romantic relationships – engagement parties, weddings and honeymoons. These events formalize the relationship by making its existence public. They also heighten a couple's sense of togetherness.

Commemorations do the same for established relationships. Couples often celebrate the anniversary, not only of their wedding, but of other important events in their lives

Celebrate the fact that you are a couple
■ *It keeps a relationship special when partners commemorate not just their wedding day, but all the important events in the life they have shared – such as the day they met.*

together, such as their first meeting or the day they bought their house. Some couples formally renew their marriage vows in a special ceremony. Small things like photographs of themselves as a couple, or objects engraved with their names all help to honor the couple's togetherness and reinforce their sense of themselves as one unit.

Couples can celebrate their relationship privately as well. Taking a second (or a third, fourth or fifth) honeymoon, or regularly getting away for weekend trips provide partners with opportunities to renew the more intimate bonds between them.

Some couples develop regular rituals. They may have a special way of making up after a fight or a comfortable evening routine for catching up on each other's day. Sunday mornings may mean one of them goes for pastry and the newspapers while the other fixes coffee before they settle down for a few private hours of reading and relaxing together. Whatever the nature of the ritual or celebration, its function is to highlight the couple's existence as a couple and deepen their sense of togetherness.

All couples have problems

What can we do to prevent small difficulties from escalating into huge ones? How should we approach the large problems so that effective solutions can be found? And how can we avoid our relationship being damaged by the conflict, stress and dissatisfaction that often accompany interpersonal problems?

Family therapists, counselors and communication experts can offer some answers to these questions but there is a lot that you can do without help. First, you both need to

▲ **Memories of shared times** *reinforce a couple's sense of togetherness. The present is enriched when we preserve objects that have meaning for the relationship, return to places where we shared some of our best times, and talk to each other about them.*

▶ **Special occasions** – *when we were courting we created them and sought them out, in order to make the relationship special. Now that the relationships is established, there is no need to stop celebrating.*

160

do some thorough detective work to understand just what the problem is. Describe your perceptions and concerns freely and openly to each other, ask questions and listen carefully to the answers.

Second, you should treat problem-solving as negotiation, involving the full and equal participation of both partners in working toward a mutually beneficial solution. Give-and-take is important: too much of one or the other is likely to create future problems. Couples also need to realize that rarely is one partner the sole cause of a problem and rarely will one partner be the sole solver of a problem. Problem-solving requires the commitment and willing participation from both partners if it is to prove effective. The third strategy is to think creatively by considering as many options as possible. A good imagination is sometimes better for problem-solving than a strictly factual attitude. Problems become problems because the usual approaches and strategies fail to work in the new set of circumstances.

Fourth, when you think that, together, you have found a good solution you should implement it, analyze and evaluate the results, and sometimes modify it.

Finally, throughout negotiation, you need to communicate with each other in an honest, caring, compassionate and positive way (see *Ch20*). **BMM**

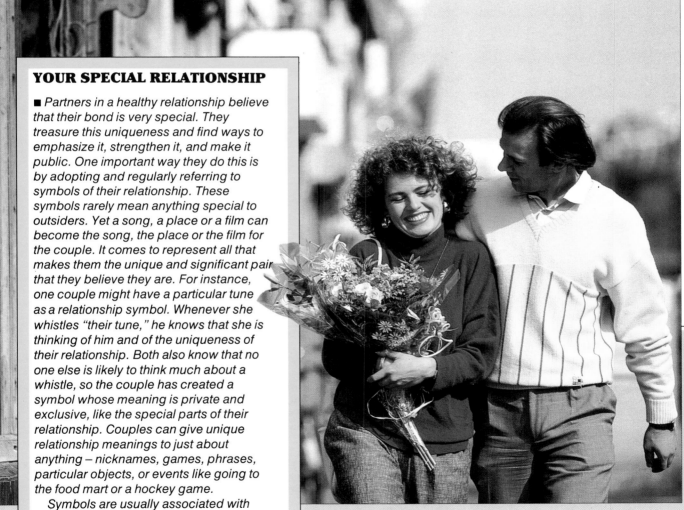

YOUR SPECIAL RELATIONSHIP

■ *Partners in a healthy relationship believe that their bond is very special. They treasure this uniqueness and find ways to emphasize it, strengthen it, and make it public. One important way they do this is by adopting and regularly referring to symbols of their relationship. These symbols rarely mean anything special to outsiders. Yet a song, a place or a film can become the song, the place or the film for the couple. It comes to represent all that makes them the unique and significant pair that they believe they are. For instance, one couple might have a particular tune as a relationship symbol. Whenever she whistles "their tune," he knows that she is thinking of him and of the uniqueness of their relationship. Both also know that no one else is likely to think much about a whistle, so the couple has created a symbol whose meaning is private and exclusive, like the special parts of their relationship. Couples can give unique relationship meanings to just about anything – nicknames, games, phrases, particular objects, or events like going to the food mart or a hockey game.*

Symbols are usually associated with happy or romantic moments in the couple's history, and so their use evokes some of those good feelings. They are also signs of closeness, trust and affection and can increase the couple's sense of exclusivity. Sometimes symbols are just plain fun and offset the boredom of the extreme seriousness that can develop in a close relationship.

▲ **Setting your relationship apart** from ordinary social encounters requires awareness of your partner's particular likes and preferences. Knowing which flowers she prefers or which is her favorite color contributes to the unique bond between you. Romantic gestures that use your knowledge of each other not only prove that you care but also heighten your sense of forming an exclusive partnership. Preferences you share are particularly important.

161

HONESTY IS THE BEST POLICY – OR IS IT?

■ *Lisa greets her husband, Ted, at the door of their apartment saying, "Surprise! I got my hair cut at the salon today and I'm crazy about it! Don't you just love it?" Unfortunately, Ted does not. In fact, he thinks it looks childish and not at all attractive. But how should Ted answer her question? If he tells her the truth, he will hurt her feelings. If he tells her that he likes it, he is being dishonest.*

Ted's dilemma arises out of a conflict between the desire to be sensitive and the desire to be honest.

Both of these characteristics are highly valued by partners in close relationships and both have been identified as key tactics for maintaining the high quality of mature relationships. But under some circumstances, like the situation Ted is in, the two seem to be incompatible. To be honest is to be insensitive, and to be sensitive is to be dishonest.

The conflict between honesty and sensitivity is even more complicated when deal-

FACED WITH A DILEMMA

OPTION 2
Ted should lie and say that he likes Lisa's new hairstyle because:
● while honesty is vitally important in central relationship issues, preference about hairstyles is a minor relationship matter
● telling the truth is likely to hurt Lisa's feelings
● telling the truth cannot change the situation: Lisa's hair will still be short
● telling the truth could start an argument about a relatively trivial matter

OPTION 1 Ted should tell the truth and say that he does not like Lisa's new hairstyle because:
● one lie is rarely enough: additional lies usually follow in support of the first one
● Ted may resent having to lie and begin to act in an irritated or less affectionate way toward Lisa
● it is difficult to decide what it is all right to lie about and what demands the truth
● lying shows disrespect and violates the bond of trust between partners
● in the long run Lisa will appreciate being able to count on Ted's honesty

162

What do you say when you do not like your partner's new hairstyle? ■ *Being honest with your partner and being sensitive to their feelings are both valuable to the relationship – however, they are not always compatible.*

TRYING TO SAY THE RIGHT THING

■ *LEFT Noncommittal facial expressions disguise opinions as a couple examine expensive jewelry. Even in the closest relationships, our reluctance to disappoint or anger the other person sometimes causes us to suppress our true feelings in matters of personal taste.*

RIGHT A couple find that they are of like mind. How open you are with your partner may be influenced by the seriousness or informality of the situation in which you find yourselves.

ing with serious relationship issues: Should Peter tell Beth that he lost half his paycheck in a poker game? Should Mimi tell Robert that she had a one-night fling while away at a convention? Should Michelle tell Jack that she does not love him as much as he thinks she should? The answers to these questions are not easy. There is no research evidence that consistently supports one choice over another. Everyone has to grapple with the problem within the context of their own relationship values, desires and goals.

However, experts are able to offer some advice that may help as you make your own choices:

● The dilemma must be considered in relation to the issue at hand. There is no simple rule like "Just tell the truth" that will make partners happy.

● Honesty does not mean telling every thought you have; rather, it means selectively sharing relevant thoughts.

● The thoughts most important to share are those that may make your needs, feelings or intentions more obvious to your partner.

● Usually, simple information must be shared before complex information: being honest may require withholding some information until your partner has a good grasp of the preliminaries needed to understand it.

● Your actions should be as honest as your words. You express your feelings as much by what you do as by what you say.

● It is sometimes good to be honest about why you have been dishonest! Sharing the reasons why you chose at some time in the past to withhold or distort information can open the doors to new levels of understanding.

● Sometimes we do not know what we are feeling or thinking. Questions like "Do you like my new hairstyle?" and "Do you love me?" may not have clear, simple "Yes" or "No" answers. Sharing our inability to answer is being honest too.

● Temporary dishonesty may be justified if your partner is in a state of extreme depression or insecurity that will not allow them to understand the information you have to share.

● Being sensitive does not mean coddling your partner. Overprotecting a partner shows a disrespect for their rights in the relationship.

● Dishonesty should not necessarily be used as a tactic to avoid conflict. Conflict, while momentarily distressful, tends to increase understanding between partners and help them grow together as a couple.

● A fear of rejection is usually not a good reason for choosing to be dishonest. Hidden feelings or thoughts usually do not remain completely hidden; they emerge in snide remarks or subtle avoidance behavior. Sometimes they are saved up until you explode with a tirade of grievances. The end result is a kind of rejection too. **BMM**

Better Communication

COMMUNICATION is a vital part of all relationships, yet we often seem to be talking at cross-purposes or missing the point. Why is this? Where do we go wrong? Are there any guidelines to help us get it right?

Most of us wish we communicated better with our partner. We would like to have fewer arguments, experience fewer misunderstandings and have our feelings hurt less often. We would like our conversations to go more smoothly and be more interesting. But much as we would like these things to happen, most of us find it difficult to bring them about. There are, unfortunately, no easy answers to the problems of communication – no foolproof rules that will guarantee success. What works for some people does not work for others. Our relationships and circumstances are all different and each couple has to work out their own system of effective communication.

While it is not possible to prescribe an exact formula for improving communication for every couple, it *is* possible to offer some general principles that will help develop good communication techniques. It is up to each individual to do a personal assessment in which they adapt and apply these suggestions to their own unique situation.

Actions can speak louder than words

It is important to be sensitive to both verbal and non-verbal communication. We are *verbal* when we speak or write, *nonverbal* when we make gestures, assume different body postures, display facial expressions, vary our tone of voice or dress in a certain way. These actions can either reinforce our verbal messages or contradict them – for example, when someone says they are not angry in a loud, sharp voice and with a scowl on their face.

Studies show that adults usually take more notice of nonverbal than of verbal communication. This is especially so when the purpose of the message is to convey feelings, but, in fact, between 60 and 80 percent of the meaning of *most* messages is received via nonverbal communication, particularly when the verbal and nonverbal messages contradict each other. We tend to take more notice of *how* someone says something than *what* they say.

Different styles of communication

When we decode the meaning of a message we do not only consider verbal and nonverbal communication, we also evaluate our partner's overall manner or style of com-

■ **Feeling distant, feeling close**. *Happy communication depends partly on having something positive to talk about and feeling free to openly dis-* *play positive feelings* RIGHT. *The negative topics that couples have to discuss* LEFT *do less to drive them apart, and may draw them closer together, when* *they give each other a sense of jointly controlling a conversation about topics they jointly acknowledge to be at issue.*

> *Three signs of good communication are positiveness, openness and coordination*
> ■ *Happy couples smile more and display more humor* ■ *Happy couples speak openly, but they know when and where to be open and in what ways* ■ *Happy couples listen to each other, and they coordinate their conversations.*

municating. Some people are consistently "animated" while others might be consistently "relaxed." Whatever their style, it is an important part of their personal identity. Because we have observed a particular quality in their behavior in the past, we expect the same behavior from them in the future. This does not mean that they will never change the way they communicate: most people are quite flexible and adapt

their styles to different people and different circumstances. Nevertheless, we will recognize a similar manner – a common behavioral thread – that characterizes most of their conversation. This common thread is their communication habits. Each person has a unique and complex style made up of a combination of many different communication habits. No one style should be considered a model for everyone to follow, but some combinations are more successful than others (see box).

Better communication depends not only on how you and your partner communicate as individuals, but also on how you communicate as a pair – how your styles fit together to set the tone of your exchanges. Three important signs of

WHAT IS YOUR COMMUNICATION STYLE?

■ *To work out your personal style of communication, read the descriptions below, based on work by the American psychologist Robert Norton.*

● *You have a highly dominant style if you:*
speak very frequently in most social situations.
tend to be forceful in most social situations.
tend to dominate informal conversations with other people.
try to take charge of things when you are with others.

● *You have a highly dramatic style if you:*
speak in a very colorful way.
frequently exaggerate to emphasize a point.
often act out what you want to communicate.
regularly tell jokes, anecdotes and stories when you communicate.

● *You have a highly argumentative style if you:*
have a hard time stopping yourself once you get wound up in a heated discussion.
are bothered if you have to drop an argument that is not resolved.
argue frequently and intensely with others.

● *You have a highly animated style if you:*
actively use facial expressions when you communicate.
tend to gesture when you communicate.
communicate your emotional state even if you say nothing about it.

● *You have a style that leaves an impression if:*
you tend to be remembered by others.
people tend to remember things you have said.
you make a notable first impression that people react to.
you communicate in an unusual way.

● *You have a highly friendly style if you:*
are very encouraging to people most of the time.
readily express admiration for others.
habitually acknowledge others' contributions.

● *You have a highly attentive style if you:*
can repeat back to a person exactly what was said.
indicate that you empathize with people.
like to listen very carefully to people.
deliberately react so that people know that you are listening to them.

● *You have a highly open style if you:*
readily reveal personal things about yourself to others.
tell people quite a bit about yourself before you get to know them well.
openly express your feelings and emotions.
can talk about any intimate subject with most people.

● *You have a highly relaxed style if:*
you are not conscious of nervous mannerisms in your speech.
you are very calm and collected when you talk.
the rhythm or flow of your speech is very smooth.
you communicate well under pressure.

● *You have a highly precise style if you:*
like to be strictly accurate when you communicate.
insist on very precise definitions of terms in a discussion.
very often insist that others present some kind of proof for what they are arguing.
typically are precise in your messages, consciously trying to say exactly what you mean.

INTERPRETING YOUR STYLE

American researchers have found that in general, women's styles tend to be more animated than men's and men's styles tend to be more precise than women's. Both men and women who are seen as good communicators have a style that is highly dominant, friendly, relaxed and open and leaves a strong impression. Happily married couples describe their own and their partners' styles as highly open, dominant, friendly and attentive.

165

good communication are positiveness, openness and control. These patterns seem to be beneficial for most couples although they may be achieved in different ways.

Creating a positive exchange

As children we learn a variety of rules for being polite to others. We are taught to smile, pay compliments, be attentive and do favors. It seems that many of the adults in unhappy relationships would benefit from a refresher course in how to apply these rules. Researchers have consistently found that partners in unhappy relationships communicate in a more negative way than partners in happy relationships. They are more likely to disagree with each other and express their disagreements through negative actions like frowns, smirks, glares, rude and angry gestures or sarcastic and cold tones of voice.

Studies of how couples complain have shown how disruptive this negative nonverbal behavior can be. Almost all partners find fault with each other from time to time and, interestingly, happy couples and unhappy couples tend to air their complaints at about the same rate. However, happy couples tend to complain about specific actions that their partner did or did not do, such as not cooking dinner or overdrawing on the bank account. Unhappy couples, on the other hand, will complain about each other's personalities and basic natures; they are more likely to engage in name-calling such as labeling a partner a "snob." Happy couples are considerably more positive, often using humor or a

Positive communication begins with the rules for being pleasant that we learned as children ■ *Smile and pay compliments, be attentive, do favors* ■ *Avoid unnecessary frowns, smirks, glares and other gestures.*

smile to soften their messages. Unhappy couples are more cruel, negative and harsh in their delivery styles. Their facial expressions, gestures and voices give very negative overtones to their complaints. Finally, while happy couples' complaints usually meet with acceptance and apology, unhappy couples' complaints more often meet with counter-complaints that may well develop into an escalating spiral of mutual criticism.

How openness helps couples to be intimate

Most of us value a feeling of closeness with our partner. We strive for a relationship in which we know and understand each other. This search for intimacy in our personal relationships seems to have intensified over the recent decades and shows no signs of becoming less important in the future. Intimacy is the goal of this search, and communication is the way the goal is attained.

We become intimate by sharing, disclosing, revealing and expressing ourselves to each other (see *Ch22*). This is the real "communication" of relationships as opposed to mere "talk." Indeed, there is a clear link between the expression of thoughts, feelings and beliefs between partners and how happy and satisfied they are with their relationship. However, there are some ways you should not be open (see p170).

GOOD AND BAD FIGHTING

■ *A good argument settles an issue without unsettling a relationship. A bad argument rarely settles any issue and always unsettles the relationship between the arguers. One of the key ingredients that makes an argument good or bad is the way the partners communicate.*

FIGHTING WITH WORDS

Unhappy couples make many more antagonistic comments during conflicts about important issues. They are much more likely to criticize ("You get too angry with the children"), reject ("Leave me alone"), threaten ("If you don't quit, I'm leaving") and blame ("All of this is your fault").

In contrast, happier couples make the sort of constructive comments that focus on problem-solving and supporting each other.

They are more likely to present a balanced description of the problem ("Our work schedules just don't seem to coincide"). They are more likely to disclose thoughts, feelings and intentions that their partners could not otherwise know ("I've never been so frustrated at work"). They are more likely to ask questions about the other's thoughts or feelings ("Doesn't it bother you when I'm out with my friends?") and be supportive ("I can see why you would be upset").

FIGHTING WITH BODY LANGUAGE

Even more important than what couples say is how they say it. Happy couples are much more positive and consequently much less negative in their nonverbal behavior during an argument than are unhappy couples. These differences become even more pronounced if the issue being argued is an important one to the couple. Then unhappier couples are even more likely to exchange unfriendly looks, smirks, harsh tones, shouts, sarcasm and the like.

WHY POSITIVE COMMUNICATION WORKS

Research suggests that constructive verbal remarks and positive nonverbal behavior produce two responses in arguing partners: a sense of satisfaction with the way the argument is progressing and an appreciation of the partner's good communication style. These feelings, in turn, contribute to the more general feelings of being able to manage difficult situations together, of trust in the partner and of happiness in the relationship. Confrontational and negative behavior, on the other hand, produces the opposite effect, often more directly and with more intensity. This suggests that trying to avoid negative behavior is even more important to a relationship than trying to be more positive.

The art of synchronized communication

Good relationships are not the product of luck, chance or coincidence. In other words, they do not happen by accident. Good relationships result from the efforts and abilities of both partners to control and direct their lives. One way that partners can actively exercise their control is by successfully managing their communication. In a good relationship the two partners control their communication rather than letting the communication control them.

One sign of this control is their ability to have coherent conversations in which comments are clear, topics are introduced smoothly and developed appropriately and statements and questions follow each other logically. In short, both partners cooperate to construct an orderly verbal exchange. Partners in unhappy relationships do not demonstrate this basic ability to direct their communication and, as a result, their conversations are often out of control.

Having a conversation is like dancing. To do either well, the two people involved must coordinate their actions, each constantly adjusting to the movements of the other. In fact, a sizable portion of the pleasure associated with dancing and talking is simply knowing that you and another person have together produced a unique event that neither could have done on their own. This kind of pleasure is experienced quite frequently by satisfied couples when they talk. Unsatisfied couples, on the other hand, are more likely to

HOW HAPPY AND UNHAPPY COUPLES COMPLAIN

Happy couples complain about specific actions

Happy couples use body language to soften their complaints

Happy couples accept each other's complaints

Unhappy couples use body language to make their complaints more harsh

Unhappy couples complain about each other's personalities

Unhappy couples complain in return

167

▲ **Using humor to soften a disagreement**. *For almost all couples, disagreements are a part of life. In fact, research finds that happy couples complain to each other at about the same rate as unhappy couples. However, they are more likely to soften their complaints with a smile and to complain only about specific problems that can be corrected.*

◄ **The urge to retaliate.** *Couples who lack a positive style of communication are more likely to have complaints about each other's basic traits of personality, often expressed through name-calling. Their body language (especially facial expressions) and their tone of voice carry very negative overtones. Rather than accepting complaints and apologizing for something that could have been done better, a partner is likely to hit back with a complaint of his or her own.*

A CHECKLIST OF CONVERSATIONAL HABITS TO AVOID

■ Satisfying conversations are coordinated achievements in communication. Partners feel a sense of shared control and they feel that they are cooperating with each other in bringing about a result. The American psychologist John Gottman and his colleagues have identified several habits that disrupt this sense of cooperation.

Kitchen-sinking. People who introduce one topic after another into a conversation are often said to have "dragged in everything but the kitchen sink." When intimate partners do this, they become overwhelmed. A discussion that started on one issue must suddenly address many issues. Rarely do partners have the time or the energy to deal effectively with all of them.

Cross-complaining. This happens when partners respond to a complaint with a complaint of their own. The result is likely to be a conversation in which each keeps repeating his or her own grievance without listening or responding to the other's.

Yes-butting. The person who responds to a partner's statement with "Yes – but..." may only be trying to introduce more information or to clarify a point. However, the partner is most likely to see yes-butting as a rejection of their own viewpoint.

Talking about talk. People can become preoccupied with communication about communication. It might sound like: "I'm trying to tell you how sorry I am," or "What you seem to be telling me is..." Usually, some of this kind of talk is good for a relationship, because it is a way of clarifying interpretations of messages. However, unhappy couples often become trapped in cycles of talk about talk, with each partner repeating some alternative interpretation of a message: "What you seem to be saying is..." "What I meant to say was..." "No, I heard you say that..." "Well, what I really meant was..." Too much of this blocks conversational progress.

Mindreading. Partners in intimate relationships often assume that they can know what the other is thinking or feeling without having to ask. For example, a man might say, "Sam offered us some tickets to a concert Saturday night, but I declined because I know you don't like classical music." His wife responds, "That's not so; the real reason you said no was because you hate going into the city at the weekend."

Making our conversation work requires coordination ■ *Show that you can concentrate on the issues that matter most to your partner* ■ *Partners listen better when they feel they can be confident of being heard in their turn.*

GOOD COMMUNICATION WORKS FOR YOU

■ It is generally a good thing for the partners in an intimate relationship to emphasize and practice being positive, open and keeping their conversations in control. These strategies seem to be beneficial for most couples. But partners do have the ability to generate unique patterns of their own that they count as good communication.

They can develop these patterns through a process very much like a friendly negotiation in which one partner makes a suggestion about what their communication should be like and the other partner either agrees or makes a counter-suggestion. These suggestions can be exchanged explicitly ("I think we need to argue more and – when we do – to argue more fairly!") or implicitly in the way one partner acts toward the other and the way the other responds – eg, one partner choosing to treat a statement like "You're not cooking meatloaf again tonight, are you?" as a tease instead of an insult.

In this way couples establish what counts within the confines of their relationship. They decide which patterns of communication are acceptable and unacceptable, rewarding and costly, satisfying and unsatisfying. They may decide to count arguing as caring, rejection as teaching, lying as saving face for the other or putdowns as attentiveness. In short, they set their own standards for determining what is good communication in their relationship.

FIVE HABITS TO AVOID

Trying to raise too many issues at once ("Kitchen sinking")

Interrupting with too many clarifications ("Yes-butting")

Answering complaint with complaint ("Cross-complaining")

Too much interpretation of what you are saying ("Talking about talk")

Assuming too much about the other's thoughts and feelings ("Mind-reading")

Both of these partners are mindreading. However, since it is impossible to know what the other person is actually thinking or feeling at any particular moment, they both stand a good chance of being wrong in their assumptions and, as a result, of irritating their partner.

▲ **Habits that prevent conversations from coming to a focus** leave couples feeling frustrated and misunderstood.

experience frustration and anger in their conversations. One reason for this is conversation mismanagement. A common habit of couples who mismanage their conversations is to introduce a succession of different topics into the conversation in a very short space of time. This makes it impossible to deal with any single issue effectively. Other couples lock into a cycle of "cross-complaining" where the conversation degenerates into two monologues – each partner repeating their own grievance. Another potentially disruptive habit is responding to your partner's remarks with "Yes, but..." Some couples end up just talking about talk – "What you seem to be saying is..." "No, what I meant was..." And partners often only *think* they know what the other is thinking or feeling. This can lead to irritation.

Adjusting to your partner

Another way we control our exchanges is by coordinating our nonverbal behavior. Partners need to adjust to the way the other uses speech rate, pause length, eye contact, body orientation and physical distance to pace their conversation. When coordinated, these nonverbal traits help conversations start smoothly (each moves to decrease the physical distance between them and increase their direct eye contact), and keep conversations going (not letting volume trail off, keeping eye contact, turning the body toward their partner). This coordination also helps in the repeated transfer of talking and listening roles (dropping vocal pitch to signal that you are finished talking). This adjustment is often more unconscious than conscious, but it does take place. In well-managed exchanges, partners' nonverbal communication helps to produce a smooth conversational flow with few interruptions, talk-overs or long-drawn-out silences.

Finally, partners in control of their communication usually interpret messages in a similar way. Shared meanings may, of course, come about because the partners come from similar backgrounds or because they have had common experiences since being together. Unhappy couples, though, do not draw on these resources as much as happy couples. They experience a greater degree of misunderstanding between the message one person attempts to send and the message the other person receives. Moreover, they tend to interpret messages that were intended to be either neutral or positive in a negative way. What is even more disturbing is that distressed partners are more likely to assume that their misinterpretations are correct. In other words, they expect their partner to send negative messages and this expectation colors their interpretation. So, not only do unhappy partners misinterpret each other more often, but they do not even realize that they do.

Ultimately, couples themselves decide what is good communication for them. This chapter provides guidelines, but apply them as seems best to you. **BMM**

▲ **Finding it hard to get through**. *Sometimes when the person you are trying to speak to is distracted, no amount of gesturing can help. Here food and impressions of a musical performance fight for attention during the interval of a concert in the English countryside.*

▶ **Synchronized conversation** *is marked by facial expressions, and especially a use of the eyes, to signal interest and attention.*

TO TELL OR NOT TO TELL

■ *Since the mid-1960s relationship professionals writing in magazines and books have been encouraging couples to be open and expressive. That encouragement, though, takes a different form today than it did in the 1960s and early 1970s. Then partners were advised that in order to have a peak relationship experience they must share themselves totally and completely. They were instructed to "Open up," "Be yourself," "Tell it like it is."*

Today, however, few relationship experts condone such indiscriminate openness. Study after study has shown that this extreme form of expressiveness is simply not healthy for a relationship.

WHAT TO BE OPEN ABOUT

Evidence suggests that couples should be selective about what they discuss openly. For instance, it is usually better not to be open about:

Negative personality traits. *Telling your partner that you think he or she is conceited or overdemanding, even if you honestly think the label fits well, is not likely to contribute to a happy emotional atmosphere. A better alternative would be to describe specific actions that your partner does and how you feel about them. Saying, for instance, that when he does not ask about your day at the office you feel unimportant, is more productive than telling him he is self-centered. This is because (a) most people think that it is easier to change their actions than their personalities; (b) describing actions – ie, what a person does – is less personally threatening than describing personality – ie, what a person is; and, (c) your own feelings are as much at issue as your partner's behavior and should be part of the discussion.*

Insults. *Calling your partner a name or attaching a label to them such as "loser" is unconstructive. In response, your partner is most likely to become defensively closed or, worse yet, launch a counterattack. It would be better to state specifically what your partner does and how it upsets you: "When you didn't ask your boss for that promotion, I had this sinking feeling that we would always be counting our pennies." It is easier to discuss the issue of speaking up than it is to discuss why one partner is or is not a loser.*

Things that cannot be helped. *Telling your partner that you wish she was taller or that he did not have children from a previous marriage may be honest disclosures, but they lack sensitivity. There is no way you can change these kinds of circumstances, and voicing your feelings can seriously bruise your partner's self-image and wound their feelings.*

Your partner's old offenses. *Storing up grievances until they come spilling out all at once at some later date does not help your relationship. It is important that complaints are dealt with as soon as possible after the offending event has taken place. There are several reasons why this makes sense. Details are then fresh in both persons' minds and time has not distorted memories and feelings. The conversation can focus on one specific event, which is more productive than dividing your attention among a number of issues.*

Your own old offenses. *Partners often reveal past indiscretions because they feel guilty about them. Perhaps she had a brief affair for which she is sincerely sorry and would like to ask her partner's forgiveness. He may have lied, when they first met, about a past involvement with a mutual acquaintance and now feels some remorse. While it is true that such disclosures may reduce the burden of secrecy for the teller, it is equally true that they frequently increase the burden for the listener. If that burden is likely to be fraught with self-doubt or self-recriminations, it is probably more responsible to keep quiet.*

As a general rule partners should avoid sharing thoughts and feelings in the form of personal attacks, foregone inevitabilities, or guilt-reducing confessions about events that are no longer relevant to their relationship.

Open exchanges should always lead to constructive action and feelings. When they lead in the opposite direction, they are detrimental to a relationship.

WHEN TO BE OPEN

Besides being selective in what you express, you should also be selective in when you express your feelings and ideas. It is generally not a good idea to attempt openness when you have just come home from a bad day at work, or are in the midst

FIVE WAYS IN WHICH OPENNESS DOES HARM

Criticizing your partner's personality

Insulting your partner

Criticizing things your partner cannot help

Complaining about old offenses

Revealing your own past offenses

Being open with your partner can greatly enhance intimacy but this advice needs qualification ■ *Choose the right time and place* ■ *Avoid raising issues out of the past* ■ *Be silent about things that cannot be helped.*

▲ **In a private and relaxing setting** *a couple takes the opportunity to talk over in a calm and unhurried way some of the more difficult issues that they have to face together.*

more private the surroundings, the better. Openness, whether in the form of a complaint or a compliment, is highly intimate. It reveals thoughts and feelings in much the same way that removing clothes reveals a body. When you are open you become vulnerable. You may well also increase the vulnerability of your listener. This kind of risk-taking, done in an atmosphere of protectiveness, sensitivity and forbearance, can enhance intimacy.

WHAT TO EXPECT

Research has produced some further qualifications yet to the old advice that open communication is what we need for happy relationships. First, nonverbal openness is more effective than verbal openness. Partners are usually more attuned to each other's facial expressions, tones of voice and eye contact than they are to exactly what is being said. This may be because partners view nonverbal behavior as more spontaneous and, therefore, more honest than verbal behavior.

Second, openness develops as the relationship develops. Partners become increasingly more and more expressive as they get to know each other better and develop trust in each other. Too much openness at the beginning of a relationship is usually thought to be socially inappropriate, threatening and, therefore, damaging (see Ch 21).

Third, even after partners get to know each other quite well, they may experience stages of being less open. It is quite natural in healthy relationships for partners to alternate between being open and emotionally accessible and being closed and emotionally inaccessible. These cycles help to meet the needs for both privacy and sharing, for both separateness and togetherness. Intimate partners should not expect to be open and expressive with each other all the time.

Fourth, being responsive to a partner's openness is as important as the openness itself. People in happier relationships behave in ways that let their partners know they are listening and thinking about what is being said. They are careful to address the same topic as the partner when they speak and to make eye contact, smile, nod and give encouraging feedback. **BMM**

of an overheated argument with your partner or are expecting your dinner guests to arrive in the next ten minutes. It is much better to postpone a highly open conversation until both you and your partner can give it the level of attention it deserves.

WHERE TO BE OPEN

It is very important where open exchanges take place. As a general rule the

171

Understanding Each Other

TO FEEL that your partner holds you in high regard is unsatisfying if you also feel that he or she does not really understand you – does not appreciate your real strengths and weaknesses or is insensitive to your needs and goals. The sort of understanding required can be elusive. It depends on mutual cooperation, it is complex, and it changes with time. And because it demands loving attention and constant updating by both partners, it can all too easily become an illusion of understanding – which is why for many couples there comes a time in their relationship when they suddenly seem not to understand each other as well as they thought. It could be during an argument or as a result of too little recent communication. Perhaps the problem has been brewing for a while but until now has been shrugged off. Or perhaps something occurs – a telling remark, a confession, a discovery – that jolts them into acknowledging the distance between them. If you find yourself in this position, or simply recognize a need to understand your partner better, what can you do about it?

Being loved for what you are

You could begin by reminding yourself of one of the key features and greatest joys of a genuinely close relationship: not *having* to put on a good show. When two people spend much time together, they can learn to see past the appearances and begin to understand and accept each other's underlying motives and intentions. Intimate partners can become sufficiently well known to each other to be able to drop the social masks they wear for less intimate friends and acquaintances – and to do so without fear of ridicule or reproof or loss of esteem in the other's eyes. Private inner experiences can be shared in a mutually rewarding way –

UNDERSTANDING AS A SHIELD

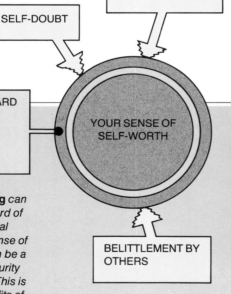

SELF-DOUBT

YOUR "FAILURES"

THE LOVE AND REGARD OF YOUR PARTNER IN AN ATMOSPHERE OF MUTUAL UNDERSTANDING

YOUR SENSE OF SELF-WORTH

BELITTLEMENT BY OTHERS

172

▲ **Mutual understanding** *can endow the love and regard of your partner with a special power to protect your sense of self-worth. The result can be a deep, inner sense of security that is difficult to shake. This is one of the greatest benefits of seeking to understand your partner more fully.*

▲ **Sharing an experience** *involves understanding another's reactions – the better we know each other, the more intensely we can share. A conscious decision to take a greater interest in each other can help. Here a couple experiences together what is more usually the pleasure of one. Although both are* thinking mainly about someone distant, they reinforce each other's enjoyment of this, and the woman achieves her entire sense of contact with the caller through interpreting the responses of her husband.

> *Make mutual understanding your conscious goal* ■ *Recognize the importance of understanding in your relationship* ■ *Keep alive – or make an effort to revive – your original curiosity to know more about your partner* ■ *Care enough to work at understanding whatever puzzles you about them.*

and, as understanding grows, it becomes easier to anticipate each other's true feelings. Within such a relationship a strong sense of togetherness develops and you gain the priceless assurance that you are worth loving despite your shortcomings. If, however, there is a distinct lack of understanding in your relationship, you are likely instead to feel lonely and alienated.

Why understanding takes time

The deeper understanding vital to our closest relationship does not come quickly. For as long as the association lasts there will be more to learn about our partner – not only because there is so much to learn but because we are all constantly changing in one way or another.

We also need to remember that our knowledge of our partner had to begin somewhere – and that our early, more stereotyped, less accurate impressions can often color our later impressions more than they should. It takes sustained care and attention, and time for a relationship to develop, before these early stereotypes can begin to be replaced by real understanding.

Progress also depends on the active cooperation of both partners. Mutual self-disclosure, for example, is probably the richest channel of information available to us. But there is a limit to how much can be told or asked at any one time, and there may also be a current limit to what we are prepared to divulge. Transforming a potentially close relationship into one that is fully realized tends to be a cautious, turn-taking business, with each partner gradually discovering and revealing more. Patience is required.

"I DIDN'T KNOW THERE WAS ANYTHING WRONG"

■ *Arthur came home from work one evening to find that Lucy had packed a suitcase and gone. There was no note, and at first he just assumed she was late returning from a shopping trip. It was mid-evening before he became concerned and began telephoning people she knew. Eventually he located her at the house of a friend and was stunned to learn that she had walked out on him. At 29, Lucy was not someone who had ever complained much. Though she was frequently quiet and withdrawn, Arthur accepted this as part of her nature. He was puzzled therefore, to discover that she had been despairingly unhappy for some time.*

The crisis shocked him into asking himself questions about their relationship that he had never asked before – and this led to insights he was able to act on. He and Lucy had never lost faith in each other, but Lucy had suppressed her ambitions and deferred to Arthur's preferences – never revealing her own wishes – to a point where she felt stifled and dominated. She had really colluded in a pattern of inequality that ultimately oppressed her, and Arthur simply had not noticed. Understanding this altered the pattern of their relationship and revitalized it, allowing them to reconcile.

In this case, crisis provoked a constructive response. Not every couple is as fortunate. And all too often couples reach a stage of being fairly comfortable together through familiarity, and settle for this indefinitely, even though they continue to find aspects of each other perplexing or hard to appreciate. Greater happiness eludes them.

HOW MISUNDERSTANDING CAN TURN FICTION INTO FACT

FICTION
A, not understanding B, misinterprets B's innocent flirtation as evidence of an affair.

A withholds affection and rebuffs B's advances – making an affair more likely.

FACT
What might have remained an innocent flirtation turns into a real affair.

173

◄ **Individual tastes** *continue to matter even after two have become "one." Understanding involves sympathetic tolerance of the fact that your partner (even when alone with you) needs emotional space to pursue his or her own interests. Here it happens that a little body-contact and an occasional remark makes a shared experience of the otherwise solitary pursuit of reading.*

Common barriers to understanding

Desirable as mutual understanding is, to some extent most couples hinder progress by putting up unnecessary walls between them, often without realizing it. Perhaps they are overconcerned about the risks of self-disclosure or have persuaded themselves that special initiatives are likely to be ineffectual.

For some couples the state of their relationship is a taboo subject. All talk about it is avoided. In one American study several reasons for this were offered by some of the partners questioned. For example, it was felt that such discussion might actually wreck the relationship because it could force acknowledgment of difficulties that it might be impossible to resolve. Another reason was that people thought they would too easily lay themselves open to emotional hurt. Others who were questioned said that discussion was pointless because relationships will take their natural course regardless. Also, some partners claimed that talk was not needed – understanding is achieved through non-verbal cues.

Simply learning to suspend the habit of keeping up a public front – the publicly displayed, edited version of our underlying personality – can itself present a problem. Our normal social behavior is designed to win the approval and

174

Are you creating unnecessary barriers to mutual understanding? ■ *Are you taking your partner too much for granted?* ■ *Do you ever discuss your relationship?* ■ *Could you express your true feelings more openly?*

cooperation of others. So we choose to show some of our qualities and conceal others – and we may come to feel, mistakenly, that the well-being of all our relationships depends on how successfully we do this.

Fear of being found out or of discovering and having to face something unwelcome about oneself are common inhibitions within couple relationships. One or both partners may have sides to their personalities that they would prefer to keep to themselves. For example, it may be important to a highly insecure person always to seem relaxed and confident, important to someone who is ruthlessly competitive always to display pleasure when others are successful. This secretiveness is usually not deliberate, however, for we often hide truths of this sort even from ourselves.

Of course, mutual self-disclosure is not a simple panacea. Even at the best of times, not everyone welcomes the idea of another person tuning in to their private thoughts and feelings. And for most of us there are right and wrong moments for personal communing. Moreover, although the word "understanding" has a sympathetic ring, to understand somebody is not necessarily to be in sympathy with them. It could indeed be one partner's growing realization of the other's imperfections that brings the relationship to an end. As a movie character remarks after an astute observation

by his ex-wife: "You are so bloody perceptive, no wonder our marriage failed."

When we lower our guard and reveal intimate information we make ourselves vulnerable – and this may matter on a future occasion if our partner ever becomes hostile. If this is a concern, it is important that the pace of self-disclosure is related to the growth of mutual trust. But we should also bear in mind that a timid or ungenerous reluctance to take risks in seeking to further a relationship can itself be a barrier to understanding.

Another barrier to understanding arises when one or both partners begin to take the health of the relationship too much for granted. Allowing themselves to be distracted by daily cares and preoccupations – household chores, careers, children – they fail to notice significant changes in each other's feelings and attitudes. No relationship, however important to us, can always be center-stage in our lives; but if we bother to stop and think about the relationship only when prompted by an unexpected crisis, we could be asking for trouble.

It is of course true that much of our understanding of our partner is unspoken – especially when the relationship is well established. However, as counselors constantly discover, partners who rely almost exclusively on intuition and indirect communication all too easily lose track of each other's concerns. Talking about how we see the relationship may be the best way to forestall misunderstanding.

◄ **Drifting apart.** *As personalities and careers develop, partners may outgrow activities and concerns that were once shared, and so lose part of the basis for their relationship. With less of mutual interest to talk about, they may find themselves with few opportunities to develop their understanding of the changes in each other. The resulting sense of distance can make self-disclosure difficult and unrewarding, a trend which may be accelerated if there is a reluctance to discuss the state of the relationship.*

A counselor's insights can sometimes open the way to renewed understanding in a relationship that has lost its vitality.

"THEY HAD SET UP BARRIERS"

■ *Ellen and Bruce – both in their early thirties – had been threatening each other with divorce almost since the day they married, nine years before. Although they had continued to live under the same roof, they reached the stage of avoiding being in the same room together, and they took turns to be with their two sons. When the children (their agreed reason for staying together) began to show adverse effects, they both worried and turned to marriage guidance in desperation. Ellen was bitterly angry, claiming that Bruce regularly ignored her needs and treated her unfairly. Bruce described Ellen as lazy, unwilling to please him, and embittered without good reason. Both complained that the other was not the person they had married and did not understand them any more.*

But of course, any understanding between them was practically impossible. Gradually they had set up barriers – an impenetrable wall behind which they con-

cealed themselves. First, they stopped telling each other things, and so each was in the dark about the other. Second, they could not relax together and so never expressed themselves freely. They had also become emotionally closed to each other, disregarding anything creditable the other did, because this did not support the overall negative view they now had. Being under mutual attack, they only put up more defenses. Because each was so miserable, they had no reserves of caring and sympathy and they became mentally blinkered against each other's more attractive characteristics. Ellen and Bruce had lost the openness and cooperation necessary for understanding.

Counseling made them realize that to rebuild trust the artificial barriers would have to be identified and dismantled – a lengthy and uncertain task, but not a hopeless one.

Does understanding require any ability?

How easy is it to understand your partner? Do some of us have more aptitude for the task than others? We might suppose that understanding occurs naturally in the course of a developing relationship, given time spent together and sufficient honesty and openness. We might also suppose that our understanding would be based on years of previous observation and experience of interpersonal relationships? And we would be right...up to a point.

We are bound to learn quite a lot about relationships simply by being part of them – but the range of situations we encounter and what we learn from them is often just a matter of chance. It would be a mistake to suppose that everyone grows up adequately equipped to understand close emotional partnerships. The process of understanding is complex and involves a wide range of abilities – and in most of us these abilities are unevenly developed.

Some people seem to be unusually perceptive – almost as if their skill were an inherited personality trait or specially nurtured from birth. Such individuals seem to have a talent for grasping what is of concern to others – even if they are

How easily are you able to see things from your partner's point of view? ■ *Use empathy and imagination to gain more insight into their feelings and attitudes* ■ *Be sensitive to their nonverbal cues* ■ *Try to anticipate their needs.*

only very briefly acquainted with them. (Merely talking to someone with this talent is likely to teach us something new about ourselves.) By contrast, there are other people who can seem particularly obtuse and insensitive in personal interaction – despite the benefit of role models who do show understanding.

Such individual differences suggest that there may be inherited factors that facilitate greater or less understanding of other people. At the same time, however, in-depth understanding of a relationship cannot be a property of just one person. Your partner is also involved – helping to make themselves known to you, choosing what to reveal, deciding how to go about this on the basis of what they know about you. The level of understanding that animates a relationship is a joint creation – as much the outcome of cooperative effort as it is of the natural ability of either partner.

The perspectives of men and women

There is also something else that needs to be taken into account. Research into personal relationships points to a sex difference in attitudes toward relationships. Some people are more relationship-centered than they are work-centered, and they tend to be women. Men, on the other hand, are generally more work-centered. Relationship-

---

SHOULD IT ALL BE LEFT TO FATE?

■ *Edward and Laura (he a lawyer, she an actress) met in a parkade elevator. There was instant attraction. They got out at the same level, introduced themselves, and in the first conversation fell in love. They viewed their coming together very much in terms of fate and chemistry – something they were powerless to resist. But the great passion they felt at the beginning gradually faded, and now, after 14 months of marriage, it had disappeared completely. Again, they see a certain inevitability in this, with divorce as the obvious next step.*

Although both are young people, they resist the suggestion that they have a lot to learn about relationships. Nor do they see any point in attempting to identify problems and striving to become close again, because they believe that they have no control over what happens between them: their relationship just worked for a while and then their feelings changed.

Yet, alongside this passive approach to their personal life, these two people take completely the opposite line in their professional lives. Edward and Laura are both high-fliers in their careers. They would resent any suggestion that they might just have been lucky. They studied hard, planned ahead, used their initiative and generally applied themselves to making the best of their career opportunities. It was while talking to a counselor that the inconsistency of their attitudes toward building a relationship and building a career first dawned on them.

LEARNING TO ACKNOWLEDGE PROBLEMS

■ *Nothing was drastically wrong, but Alan and Maria were becoming increasingly discontented and, for both, this was their second marriage. Apart from their disappointment, they dreaded having to face friends and relatives with yet another "failure." Alan was particularly unhappy about the sexual side of their relationship but decided that to make an issue of it would only aggravate the problem. Maria felt that Alan had become emotionally remote, and she doubted his affection for her. They were often strained and irritable with each other. Despite this, in some ways they were still shy together and had not ever talked much about their feelings or the kind of relationship they wanted. They had both grown up in families where emotions were guarded and never discussed.*

Alan heard about an evening class on personal relationships intended for the general public, and persuaded Maria that it might be interesting for them to attend. Maria agreed: certainly it might be less embarrassing than going to a counselor. They were able to extract from the general information on the course a better understanding of their own situation and gradually began to specify what the problems were for them, and to communicate what they wanted from each other.

centered partners are motivated to seek and expect greater intimacy in a relationship; they are more likely to take note of what is happening and make appropriate adjustments. Work-centered partners are less likely to monitor their relationships; they are likely to roll along as if expecting things always to be the same. Women are generally more analytical about relationships than men are; they have more to say about them, and are more likely to regard thinking and talking about them as useful. Men, by contrast, are likely to see such activity as pointless or even silly. Taking close rela-

tionships for granted after the early stages – something we all do – appears to be more characteristic of men. Men are more likely to be caught napping when the relationship is heading toward disaster. It is women's greater attentiveness to such matters that enables them, on the whole, to be more understanding of their male partners than vice versa. Against the old plaint "My wife doesn't understand me," women could perhaps argue with rather more justification that it is they who are not as well understood by their spouses as they could be.

THE DIFFERENCE – IN PERSPECTIVE

■ *Women seem to be more relationship-centered than men, men more work-centered. Why? Part of the explanation is linked to cultural expectations. Being concerned about relationships is traditionally a feminine activity. But there may also be a biological basis for this. An evolutionary perspective suggests differences for men and women in the value of such concern. The opportunities for any one woman to pass on her genes are restricted by the lengthy process of childbearing and child-rearing. Her chances of success in seeing this process through are improved if she engages the support of a long-term mate – it is biologically in her interests to concentrate on keeping him happy. The male human too gains a biological advantage from a long-term reproductive relationship. By monopolizing a woman and providing for her children he has a better chance of perpetuating his genes than he would in open promiscuous competition with other men. But opportunistic extra matings may result in more offspring for him, so there may be an evolutionary pressure on men to be less intensely committed to just one relationship. Polygyny, the marriage of one man to more than one wife, institutionalizes this sex difference for millions of people in Africa and Asia.*

However, even if deep within our genetic make-up there is something that motivates women to be more concerned about relationships and motivates men more to activity and work, the social circumstances that accentuate this difference are being removed. Relationships are becoming more widely recognized as worthy of discussion and thought – by men as well as by women. It is difficult to pin down the precise origins of this change. In part, it reflects the increased power of women, whose views and values are now

more influential. Partly, too, it is because expectations for emotional fulfillment are higher, and this has led to a gain in importance for relationships themselves. Another change hails from the world of formal education. Only quite recently have academics turned to personal relationships as a subject to be studied and taught. Giving academic status to the subject of relationships reflects and fuels a more thoughtful approach to them in everyday life. The greater value now being placed on relationships, along with the new knowledge that results, is enlarging the subject for the rest of us.

▲ **Your relationship or your work?** *It is possible that men are biologically more prone to become work-centered than women are. In circumstances that promote this tendency, men will often devote themselves to their work at the expense of their personal relationships.*

The knowledge required for understanding

What do you need to know in order to understand your partner well? Several layers of knowledge are involved. There is knowledge about people in general and knowledge about relationships in general. Then there is particular knowledge – of the society in which you find yourselves, of your relationship and of your partner as an individual. But before all this comes self-knowledge. Understanding yourself, many therapists argue, is the key to understanding your relationships.

We learn about ourselves by looking back over events in our past, particularly those in childhood. Psychoanalysis, for example, is based on this kind of retrospective exploration, and also on reliving in thought particularly emotional or traumatic events.

We also learn about ourselves through interacting with

Make a conscious study of your relationship
■ *Watch how you interact with your partner – and learn more about yourself* ■ *Keep your knowledge of your partner up to date* ■ *Learn more about relationships through reading or attending a course* ■ *Consult your feelings and learn to understand them.*

---

other people, especially when we are prompted to talk intimately about ourselves. Your partner might ask a probing question that leads to a sudden moment of self-discovery as you look for the answer.

Figuring out another person involves self-knowledge because we use ourselves as a standard. ("He is very assertive about things I hold back on"; "She is as bored with this film as I am.") We can turn this self-knowledge around to better understand our partner ("I know I've been unresponsive recently, so I guess she's feeling disappointed, and that's why she has gone quiet on me.")

General knowledge about people is important, and reading about psychology and relationships can also help a couple understand each other better. But there is no substitute for spending time together with your partner. Understanding involves learning about each other's past, each other's values and plans and typical reactions. It means exchanging ideas and knowledge, and also continually noticing each other's needs and reactions.

The role of feelings

Feeling, intuition, knowledge and reason all have a place in making sense of relationships. In the past, most psychological research concentrated on knowledge, reasoning and

---

IMPROVING MUTUAL UNDERSTANDING

■ *Your partner may be an expert on one or more subjects, but is he or she an expert on you? Experts spend time finding out about their chosen field. They collect information. They talk and read about their subject. At times, they become absorbed in it as an interest. Being an expert on just one person is not something you would expect to take a trained mind or academic study. Spending time with that person, talking with them, observing what they do and learning about their background all seem much more relevant. No one is in a better position to do this than the person chosen to share their life. However, just spending time together is not always sufficient: thinking about the relationship can easily become stultified; couples can become like strangers after spending years in each other's company. An external spur is often helpful.*

Can you and your partner be taught to understand each other better? Studying can never replace concerned attention and talking to one another, but books and courses can make caring and communicating more informed and effectual.

Much of our understanding is based on intuitions – and such knowledge can be difficult to articulate. This can be because what is meaningful to us, in many instances, has to do with our emotional responses and cannot easily be unraveled.

But sometimes we find ourselves with vague intuitions only because we do not know enough about relationships to be able to explain – even ourselves – what we mean. We may protest that we "just know instinctively." Or perhaps, after thinking the idea through, we find some sort of explanation but it seems feeble. Learning about relationships enables us to manage our ideas about them more effectively and to make our insights more intelligible to others.

UNDERSTANDING
REQUIRES
KNOWLEDGE OF...

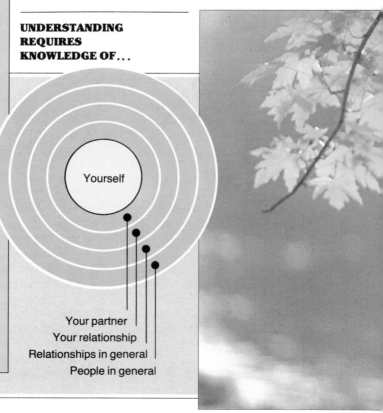

Yourself

Your partner
Your relationship
Relationships in general
People in general

various psychological capacities while neglecting the role of emotions. Emotions and feelings were generally treated as intrusive. More recent research, however, shows not just that emotional responses and feelings are important keys to our thoughts and actions, but that our feelings are probably more significant than our reasonings.

In a series of experimental studies in England, for example, married couples were found to identify each other more easily and accurately from descriptions of their emotional patterns and behavior than from biographical facts. Another study showed that it was their knowledge of each other's emotions rather than each other's history that influenced their decisions about their relationships.

Emotions aid our understanding in two different senses. Understanding what is important to partners (what they like, fear, hope for) helps us to account for their actions and motives. For this we make use of our own capacity to share and identify with the other's feelings. For example, if a partner seems indifferent and uncooperative following an episode in life which has left them feeling dejected, we can ask ourselves how *we* would react. It might then occur to us that our own reaction would be quite similar. Using empathy in this way is particularly helpful in making sense of any change in a partner's manner.

Asking yourself how you *feel* about something or someone, rather than simply asking yourself what you think, know or believe, is an important way of gaining self-knowledge. It is a matter of noticing and interpreting your feelings in order to gain personal insights. It is also worth remembering that how *you* feel at any particular time can produce

temporary shifts in what you regard as significant. It is important, for example, to recognize when it is your own mood of irritation, not any change in your partner, that is making their faults difficult to tolerate; and to recognize that it is often within your power, by putting yourself into the right mood, to bring out the best in others. **RB**

■ **Experts on each other's feelings,** *couples who communicate well know each other's emotional responses and moods. This helps them to judge when to be intense* LEFT *and when light-hearted* ABOVE. *Experiments show that couples know each other's emotional patterns better than they know biographical details. When researchers write stories including a character whose times and places of birth, graduation and marriage match* our partner's, and whose career choices, interests and so on correspond, we recognize who the character is less readily than we do in stories focusing on their typical moods and responses. Our own feelings are part of understanding our partners because it is only by experiencing emotions that we can empathize with those of another. In addition, we learn to manage our own moods in ways that help our partners to manage theirs.

A Sound and Happy Marriage

ONLY A THIRD to a half of our marriages will last until one partner dies. For a marriage to fall apart, at least one person is likely to have been unhappy. But is the reverse true? Are all enduring marriages happy? And is happiness a matter of chance or are there things we can do that will help a marriage to be both long-lasting and successful?

What makes a marriage stable?

Research has shown that there are factors that increase the likelihood of a marriage enduring. Some of the most important of these are linked to the background of the

couple. Partners in stable marriages usually come from similar cultures and from families with the same level of income. They have probably had the same sort of educational experiences – such as both going to university or both not going to university. Surveys show that stable couples are usually of the same religion and tend to vote the same way in elections – or at least to agree on the importance or unimportance of particular political issues.

Your age and the circumstances in which you marry can influence the stability of your relationship. For example, you are more likely to have a stable marriage if you did not

GIVING YOURSELVES THE BEST CHANCE

■ *If you are about to choose a partner for an enduring and happy marriage, then you should of course choose someone you like a lot. Your partner should, if possible, come from the same social and educational background as you and have similar interests to your own.*

Marry someone whose friends you like and who likes your friends. When you are married, organize your time together so

that the chores are spread in a way that makes both of you comfortable, and structure time so that you spend a lot of your leisure together but significant amounts of it apart with other people. Be sexually faithful, share secrets, handle arguments in a way that respects the other person's point of view, and be prepared to make significant compromises. If you get all that right then you have at least a chance!

▲ **Why are they so happy?**
Our everyday experience and what we see on television tell us more about what makes couples unhappy. Part of the reason for this is that when both partners are content, there is little incentive to examine or to explain to other people why they feel that way. Having set their course on an automatic pilot, they have no cause to return to manual unless a problem arises.

Can you influence your chances of being happy together? ■ *One of the best guarantees is to choose a suitable partner in the first place* ■ *Stability is enhanced when partners are equally involved in creating a shared home and treat their commitment as binding* ■ *Happiness is deeply affected by the way we communicate.*

marry before the age of 21, neither you nor your partner was over 30 when you were first married and there is no marked difference between your ages. If a couple married after a pregnancy then the marriage is more likely to be unstable than if they married before pregnancy. Partners who did not have a large number of sexual contacts before marriage are also more likely to stay together.

Staying together through thick and thin

Awareness of the factors that promote marital stability may be useful to people who are contemplating marriage and wish to avoid major pitfalls. However, some partners discover too late that they have made a mistake in choosing to marry. This does not necessarily mean that their marriage will not last. Unhappy couples often stay together simply because they feel the ties that bind them are too strong for separation or divorce to be a viable option. They may stay together for a variety of "negative" reasons: for the sake of the children; or because of fear of what their neighbors, family or friends might think if they split up; or because they think they cannot afford to break up; or they are afraid to

change their lifestyle and face the practical and emotional adjustments that inevitably accompany the dissolution of a marriage.

Some experts claim that it is not so much that love and attraction pull a couple together, as that what they have invested deters them from parting. Money can make a difference to the longevity of a marriage: low income is associated with unhappy marriages. Similarly, joint home ownership and other possessions can help to bind a couple together. The work, care and effort that each partner has contributed to a shared life are crucial to its chances of survival. Partners buy each other presents, spend a lot of time together, share secrets, pool resources, and may feel that they have simply come too far to just let go.

On the more positive side, some couples stay together because from the start they treat marriage as a binding com-

A SENSE OF UNITY

■ *Friendship and commitment are among the factors that keep couples together. Yet surveys and explanations may fail to capture a further element that is essential to couples' experience. Whether or not a couple remains in love and sexually active, after all they have shared they can come to feel as united as kin. They may also feel connected in a spiritual sense. There may be a religious dimension to this, but individuals without religious beliefs might equally recognize a depth of feeling for the other and sense of their special significance. For them, even the estrangement of rows, declining attraction, or changing values does not eradicate the connection.* **RB**

181

◄ **Someone to hold on to.** *Stability is an essential part of marital happiness. The emotional bond between well-established marital partners runs very deep, and the mere thought of breaking the bond can cause sorrow. Stability alone, however, is not enough for happiness. Partners who do not maintain a sufficient sense of shared emotional intimacy will allow their relationship to slide into distant formality.*

mitment. Long-term marrieds tend to believe that once you marry you stay together for life. Whether you are happy or not, it seems that stability is partly a matter of believing that marriage is for keeps.

Is love the answer?

Background factors that promote stability are often indicators of future happiness in a marriage. But, if stability as such does not necessarily ensure happiness in marriage, what does? Are there key ingredients? Part of the answer lies with our expectations. What is common sense about marriage may be different at different periods in history. Your grandparents' attitudes and expectations may vary greatly from your parents' and even more so from yours.

Today most of us believe that we will not be happy unless we love our partner and express that love openly. If one partner suspects that the other does not love them, that in itself may be seen as a reason to regard the marriage as in trouble. Yet 200 years ago this ingredient was not universally regarded as either important or necessary. It would not have mattered as long as the marriage was fertile and financially stable. Indeed many cultures today still enjoy arranged marriages and, incidentally, such cultures have divorce rates of as little as 1 percent. Even in Western society, parental approval for a marriage is very desirable, so merely loving your partner is not all that counts in entering a successful marriage.

We also assume today that partners will be faithful to each other in an exclusive sexual partnership, although some recent surveys have suggested that people nowadays do not rate sexual fidelity as highly as they rate emotional

closeness. Indeed in one survey in Holland (carried out before AIDS was in the public mind), it was found that some people did not object to their partner having other sexual partners as long as the spouse did not become emotionally attached to those partners.

Is there a magic ingredient?

Love and fidelity are only part of the answer. What else is necessary for our marriages to be happy? Happiness is a complex emotion: we are not all made happy by the same things and in the same way. Nevertheless research has found certain common factors in many of the marriages which couples claim are happy.

Being open about our feelings, emotions and inner experiences (see *Ch 19, 20*) is an important factor in marital success. Men reveal themselves less than women (see *Ch 18*) – and therefore expect to do it less and expect others to do it less – but almost everyone would expect that marriage partners will talk to each other about their secret fears and concerns. Giving emotional support is another form of openness and is also important. This is more than being prepared to help your partner through difficult emotional times. It also goes to the root of the reasons for being in relationships at all. We appreciate relationships precisely because they help us to test our emotional reactions and to have other people tell us if we are acting or reacting in an acceptable way. Did I do the right thing? Should I be feeling the way I do about all this? Am I overreacting? These are all

▶ **Do you have to be in love?** *Happily married couples love each other, but this does not necessarily mean feeling a sustained sense of excitement.*

◀ **Does frequent sex mean happy marriage?** *After the honeymoon excitement, sexual frequency drops off. Researchers have not established whether couples have sex often because they are happy or whether happiness results from frequent sex, but 89 percent of American husbands who have sex three times a week are happy with their marriage. The percentage of those with lower frequencies who are happy has not been established.*

important questions and we expect our marriage partner to know us better than anyone else does and to tell us if we are handling things as well as we can.

Your partner's self-esteem

Although there are many styles of marriage, experts have been able to make broad comparisons between happy and unhappy couples. Their general finding is that happy couples will, directly and indirectly, bolster each other's self-esteem, while unhappy couples will mutually undermine confidence.

Happy couples express their agreement with their partners when they feel it and support each other in discussions. They respect the points made even if they do not agree with them personally. When arguments or problems arise, they will try to focus on the agreements more than on the disagreements. They show their approval of the other person's opinions and disagree in ways that do not put the

THE IMPORTANCE OF SELF-DISCLOSURE

■ *Getting to know each other in a way that strengthens the positive bonds of marriage involves what researchers call reciprocal self-disclosure – telling each other about the kind of person you are, and freely talking about your feelings, desires, needs and hopes. This can be risky but usually, if the relationship is basically good, personal knowledge contributes to reciprocal feelings of emotional closeness. In turn, that closeness makes you feel safe to reveal more of the vulnerable side of your nature without getting hurt. And once you and your partner fully accept each other, both can overcome further fears that haunt growing intimacy – fear of abandonment, fear of loss of individuality, and fear of being emotionally smothered.*

AVOIDING FALSE ASSUMPTIONS

Building a sense of intimacy becomes easier if you can remember to avoid making unwarranted assumptions about each other. For example, if Paul finds out

that Mary loves the Beatles, beer and pretzels – some of his own favorites – he must not assume she shares everything else he enjoys. Making such assumptions would help to distort his image of Mary and undermine his own sense of individuality. Paul should discover Mary's other likes and dislikes bit by bit as both get to know each other better. He can ask questions like, "Do you like Monty Python, too?" But he must encourage and accept truthful answers.

Discovering differences between partners helps preserve individuality at the same time as it strengthens the mutual bond they are forging. Even when intimacy seems well established, open communication remains vital if the relationship is to go on growing. Partners who know each other well today might know each other less well in a year's time. We all change in subtle ways – for instance in attitudes or ambitions – and we should try to let each other know as changes occur. LKA

▲ **Disclosing the real you.**
Even if your partner tries to cajole you into saying it is not true, you should let him know about at least some of the ways in which you are different from what he assumed — he should understand that even though you have much in common and love each other, you do not have exactly the same tastes and opinions. Sharing information about themselves honestly and openly makes a couple feel close and more secure.

183

other person down. Unhappy couples seem concerned to emphasize the disagreements and tend to disregard agreement or take it for granted rather than remarking on it. They will often make each other look foolish. Happy couples try harder to avoid conflict or at least to reinterpret that conflict in a positive, respectful light, by seeing it as an issue where they agree to differ and respecting each other's rights to different opinions. After an argument or a rough patch in a relationship, unhappy couples are more likely to do such antisocial things as avoiding the other person or refusing to make up; being cold and unrelenting; refusing to talk about how they feel or to share their emotions; neglecting to do the other person any favors; and generally to imply that the relationship is of little value and has an uncertain future.

Happy couples, by contrast, are likely to talk over their problems and to reassure each other that the storm was temporary and is now passed. Each partner will make it quite clear that what really matters to them is the relationship rather than the temporary winning of a point over the other person.

Happy couples give each other both verbal and nonverbal support. They smile or nod when their partner is talking or expressing an opinion. They say clearly how much the other person's opinions matter and how much they value them. Happy couples will make explicit statements of worth such as: "My life would mean nothing without you." By contrast, unhappy couples seem to make a point of denigrating each other both explicitly and nonverbally. They may show this by looking bored when their partner is talking, frequently interrupting, or challenging every opinion, or refusing to be amused by their partner's jokes.

Happy couples bolster each other's self-esteem ■ *When they agree with each other they say so* ■ *They support each other in discussions* ■ *They show respect for what they do not agree with in each other's outlook.*

KEEPING TO THE RULES

■ *Do most of us follow the same rules for marriage? Social psychologists Michael Argyle and Monika Henderson explored the rules that apply generally to relationships, and specifically to marriage, by recording the responses of some 1,000 people of different ages and from different cultures and found attitudes common to all. They found four particular rules that people felt were important in all relationships: respecting privacy; making eye contact; keeping confidences; and not criticizing each other in public.*

As far as married couples were concerned they found 25 general rules. At the top of the list were: showing emotional support; sharing news of success; being faithful; and creating a harmonious atmosphere. It seems, too, that it is important to address your partner by name, and to give gifts. Having sex and being loyal were rated high, along with openness. Tolerance was valued and couples said they enjoyed touching, public affection and joking. These rules were common to both sexes. But Argyle and Henderson also found a few rules that applied mainly to men and women separately. Men should show interest and involvement in domestic matters, and women should express their anger but should not nag.

▶ **Happy couples understand each other's meaning.** *The one knows what the other is trying to say and they can read moods and preferences with accuracy. They often have a semi-private language of gestures and expressions of their own.*

When they are in a group and one partner is talking, the other will listen attentively and show interest. Happy couples also laugh at each other's jokes!

Paying attention to each other

Happy couples tend to be better at reading each other's moods. They care enough to understand the other person's behavior and to be aware of subtle changes. If you are paying attention to your partner you are far better able to predict and react appropriately to his or her moods and feelings. Your partner feels understood and appreciated and enjoys that. This enhances your relationship and your satisfaction with it. Couples who are happy often develop a private language so that they can tell each other that they feel loving or want to have sex or are bored without actually saying so. For instance, a woman may say to her husband: "Let's go for some tennis" when they are in company; what she is really saying is: "Let's go home to have sex." Unhappy couples are unlikely to have signaling systems that make the relationship special and private.

One big difference between happy and unhappy couples is the ability of a husband to read his wife's nonverbal behavior correctly and to know when she disagrees with him, is angry, or is reacting negatively to what he is doing or saying. Husbands in unhappy marriages tend to be poor at knowing what their wives are feeling. Paradoxically, they are much more likely than husbands in happy marriages to think that they *are* very good at reading their wives.

Being aware of each other's needs and preferences and taking them into account when making decisions is crucial. Happy couples are more willing to compromise. They may choose a middle course between two opposed desires, so that each of them gives up something but also gains something. For instance, Mary wants to spend a two-week holiday by the sea and Jake wants to climb mountains. They may spend one week in each, instead of two weeks in one of them. Or, they compromise by trying to work out what their respective objectives are and then reconcile those objectives. So, instead of making a choice between going to the coast or going to the mountains on holiday, Mary and Jake look at what they really want. Mary wants to be near water where the swimming is good and Jake wants to be in high forests with good walking areas. They can satisfy both needs by spending the whole holiday somewhere that has both woods and water.

Time off together

The way couples organize their time – especially how they cope with daily chores and leisure appears to be much more important to successful marriage than we realize (see *Ch 23*). Many of the arguments that occur during courtship are about who does what and who spends how much time with whom. The way in which courting couples sort out the necessary changes to their leisure and chore time is vital to the progress of the marriage (see *Ch 4*). As two people become more involved with each other, so we would expect them to be able to spend less time with their old friends. As they begin to do more things together, so it will become more important that they spend their joint leisure time in a way that satisfies both. Couples also have a greater chance of a stable and happy marriage if they build each other into their respective networks of friends. While it is more likely that the wife will take on her husband's friends, studies show that the couples that do this equally have a better defense against future troubles than those that keep their separate groups of friends.

185

◄ **Happy couples give each other attention.** *This makes them far better able to predict and react appropriately to each other's moods. In unhappy couples, it is especially the husband who is likely to be unskilled at interpreting what the wife is feeling, but these husbands are much more likely than husbands in happy marriages to think that they are good at understanding their wives.*

Defining the perfect marriage

Happy marriages are not only unlikely to break up; they also satisfy both partners very deeply. However, our assessment of whether our own marriage is happy is decided not only by our personal emotional reactions to our partner but also by other equally important influences. The current views of what we should expect in a marriage influence our judgment of whether our marriage is a good one and these ideas are subject to fashion and social change.

We get our impression of what a perfect marriage ought to be like from the media, from friends, from relatives and from collected folk wisdom (see *Ch17*). Magazines and popular novels give us some idea of the sorts of things we should expect from our relationships, and so do popular TV programs. When a leading character in a popular English soap opera attempted to take an overdose of pills as a result of a relationship problem, hospitals reported a 25 percent increase in overdoses caused by so-called relationship problems during the next week. The standards for judging whether our marriage is a good one can thus change as society changes.

A marriage of like minds

Each of you can do things to enrich your marriage and make it happier (see *Chs19, 29*). But studies have found that for a marriage to be successful both partners will also need

No one shared approach to marriage need be better than any other ■ *Partners who present a common front to the world may be no more or less happy than those who discuss their similarities and differences before others* ■ *Partners who do not feel comfortable with the same approach are likely to be unhappy.*

to have similar views about the relationship as such. Researchers have identified three main approaches to marriage. The style that suits one couple is likely to be different from the style satisfying another. But you and your partner are more likely to be happy if you have broadly similar beliefs about your relationship.

Traditional people have conventional views about marriage and believe that they should do things as a couple. They believe in confronting rather than avoiding conflicts and feel they should communicate their emotions in certain ways – such as in private rather than in public. They have a strong belief in the value of sharing and of doing things together. They say "we" and "us" and "our" in conversation, talking about themselves as a couple.

Independent people are very expressive of their feelings about each other and prefer to be open and frank about everything. They face up to conflict assertively, unrestrained by traditional feelings such as when and where it is appropriate to talk about their feelings. They believe strongly in disclosing their opinions and feelings and will say outright what they feel each has put into solving any problems they have. They are more likely than traditional couples to see themselves as two individual people in a single relationship and thus will emphasize their independence and separate identities by talking about "my husband and I" or "my partner and I" rather than "we."

IT HELPS TO BE REALISTIC

■ *Within marriages, difficulties are sometimes wrongly interpreted as an indication of failure. Low tolerance level or the extreme view taken can incline some to "ditch" a partner who might ultimately have been suitable. Others take a positive view despite unpromising events, and strive to strengthen rather than destroy the bond. If a couple starts out expecting that they will always be blissfully happy, they may be all the quicker to despair when something goes wrong, and faster in ending their relationship. A more realistic couple will not be daunted by the same problems or disagreements. They may even come through setbacks with strengthened affection and confidence in each other. Thus, one couple's failed relationship can be another couple's successful one. It is common experience to find some aspect of a relationship unsatisfying at times and to wish for some changes. All couples experience irritations and disappointment mixed between the highs and periods of contentment. How the less pleasing parts are interpreted and which kind of response is made to difficulties can make the difference between whether couples regard themselves as failing or succeeding in their relationship.* **RB**

186

ONE SITUATION: THREE RESPONSES

On your way to a dinner party your car runs out of fuel — you forgot to refill it. Your response may depend on the kind of couple you are.

Traditional couple
Ann and John agree to make some lame excuse about the fuel gauge not working and to present a united front although Ann is obviously furious. On the way home after the dinner they argue about the problem in a way that they were not prepared to in front of hosts.

Independent couple
Brett and Maisie go into their friends' house, arms flailing. They argue openly and explain their feelings to each other. By the dessert they have forgotten the incident and will be recounting their individual reactions to their teenage daughter's outrageous new hairstyle.

Separate people are not very expressive about their feelings and behave in ways that do not seem closely linked with their partners. They will avoid conflicts rather than confront them. They will keep an emotional distance, and live in largely separate worlds within the marital household. Separate people propose adjustments to their relationship by asking questions rather than expressing emotions directly. They generally see themselves as being in a satisfactory relationship because of the particular contribution made by each partner – viewing themselves as essentially complementary or opposite to their partner rather than similar. Their language reflects their separation, showing a strong tendency not to communicate couplehood at all, but rather to talk about what each person in the partnership does or thinks separately.

Some 60 percent of couples are partners who have the same beliefs about marriage. This is not to say that successful couples must be in the same group. Quite satisfactory relationships are possible in mixed types of partnership. It seems most likely, however, that couples will be happiest when they share beliefs about the best way to conduct a marriage, particularly when they need to deal with conflict. Obviously, if one partner likes to confront problems and one likes to avoid them, then each person will be dissatisfied with the way the conflict is handled, whatever they actually do to handle it. **SD**

187

Separate couple
oxanne and Ted have probably ach made their own way to the nner party. Roxanne has come n her own car. Ted explains to her as well as to the company resent how he came to run out f fuel. Roxanne does not find it necessary to apologize on Ted's behalf.

■ **What kind of a couple are you?** *Traditionals ABOVE LEFT present a common front to the world. Independents TOP have a strong sense of mutual in-* *volvement but discuss differences openly and in detail. Separates ABOVE treat life as two quite different canvasses which each fills in without* *involving the other. Couples can be happy with any of these approaches, so long as both partners feel free to express themselves.*

Managing Together

THE FAMILIAR newspaper photograph of a couple celebrating their golden wedding anniversary may remind newlyweds that with today's life expectancy they face the possibility of spending the next 50 or more years together. Such a future is almost impossible to contemplate when you are in love, but all too soon that dreamy romantic relationship will also have to become a practical, economic partnership requiring negotiation and hard work. "All you need is love" is a fine sentiment for a song but the reality is that you need to agree a way of dividing up all your tasks, which you both feel to be efficient and fair; you need an income from employment to meet your joint expenses; you need to decide how to plan your leisure and work time; and even minor daily chores need to be allocated.

The choices you face today are certainly ones that your grandparents, and possibly your parents, never had to consider. In the past the duties of each marriage partner were clearly understood: husband was breadwinner, wife caregiver. Now these roles are less defined and can be undertaken by either sex: who does what is legitimately open to negotiation.

The economics of living together

Money is involved in almost every aspect of living with someone. How much money is coming in? How will the day-to-day management of financial matters work? Who will be in charge of the books? How will major financial decisions be made? Will earnings be shared or kept personal? A number of surveys have found that money relates to marital satisfaction and that it frequently leads to serious problems in relationships: it is difficult to be happy when budgets are

tight and the bank balance causes anxiety (see *Ch 12*). However, money has an even wider significance than this. In many societies having money symbolizes success and achievement; lack of it fosters a sense of failure in a couple. Your discussions about money may well be a barometer for the state of your relationship or you may be engaged in a power struggle, since the balance of power tends to be with the partner who is the major pay-check earner.

In the early stages of the relationship we may find it difficult to discuss the somewhat unromantic subject of money, although a British opinion poll did find that most established couples were willing to work out together how to arrange their spending, with 89 percent of men and 82 percent of women feeling that they agreed on most monetary matters. And most people told their partners how much they earned. The same poll revealed that 86 percent of men trusted women in money matters, although only 75 percent of women trusted men.

If you and your partner are both working outside the

▲ **The haze of romance** *usually belongs to the early days of marriage when partners enjoy the excitement of a new status and lifestyle. It may fade as* *practical concerns take over, though careful monitoring of the relationship can help keep alive the excitement of being a couple (see Ch 29).*

MANAGING YOUR MONEY

■ *Interviews reveal the variety there is in the ways couples manage their money. One young couple, recently married, both feel that the wife is better than the husband at managing, so she arranges the payment of the mortgage and keeps the accounts. He says, "If it was up to me our marriage would have serious problems and everything would be a mess." They have no children yet and are lucky in that they both earn good salaries.*

Not so lucky is an unemployed couple with two children. They say they do not argue about money because there is no money to argue over. However, they are an obvious support to each other: each of them cuts out personal indulgences; they shop together on Saturdays, buying only basic foods; and they share where they can with equally hard-up neighbors.

One well-to-do executive couple, on the other hand, has investment accounts and each uses credit cards. They have always had joint accounts but only one checkbook for each account to keep their records simple. They discuss major items of expenditure but he will spend the equivalent of half a day's pay on the garden without thinking to mention it. They try to shop together – one an impulse buyer, the other sticking to her list. They employ professional help to look after their house and their three children.

One professional couple without children have separate accounts. The man, by nature more of a free spender, pays the mortgage and insurance; the woman, better at keeping an eye on things, pays for the food. When the rest of the bills come in they pay them from whichever account can afford it. They both disapprove of debt and they try to keep their credit card expenditure down.

How equally do you and your partner share responsibilities? ■ *If you both work, are you each doing your fair share in the home?* ■ *Agree on a policy for managing your money and balancing decision-making power.*

home you will need to decide as soon as you marry or cohabit whether to pool your finances or keep them separate. In a pooled system you both put all your income into joint bank accounts upon which either of you can draw. All your money becomes collective, none individual. In a separate system you will keep at least some money in individual bank accounts although you may also have a joint account for common expenses such as mortgage payments and electricity. In a separate system you need to work out your basic expenses and each contribute a set amount to cover them. When the husband is the sole wage earner in a household, he usually takes it for granted that his earnings will be available to his partner. But many women who work are unwilling to pool their earnings. Most women have lower incomes than their husband's, so this feeling of having

some authority may be important to them. Many couples who have chosen separate accounting systems will tell you that neither partner should have authority over the other's savings. Separate means equal. Conflict is avoided. But there is more to the issue than finance. Decisions about income involve choices between interdependence and independence: sharing and trust versus autonomy and self-reliance. Underlying the actual pooling of financial resources is the gesture of commitment. Joint accounts indicate clearly that you are expecting a long-term relationship. So the way you look upon your finances can indicate and indeed shape your future life together.

Should women work?

Until fairly recently paid employment was an exclusively male territory, while women ran the household. Although many couples still abide by traditional values, the number of two-income families is increasing rapidly, not least

189

▲ **Practicalities of married life** *include managing the money. Learning to make joint decisions about finances can be difficult but some couples who agree to pool financial resources do so to express their mutual commitment to the relationship.*

▶ **How you handle money matters** *as a couple is likely to affect the quality of your relationship. Asking yourselves these key questions may help you to decide how satisfactory your present financial arrangements are.*

Do you tell your partner what you earn?

Who takes care of day-to-day expenses?

How much of your earnings do you pool?

Who keeps the accounts?

Do you share the big decisions?

because the financial strains of modern living make it virtually impossible for young couples today to survive on one income. So despite continuing job discrimination, women are entering the work force in large numbers. By 1986, over half of American women over 16 worked and 60 percent of them were married, many of them with young children.

Not everyone approves of the move toward two paychecks and there is much public concern over the effect of working mothers on the family. Critics have been quick to blame the rising divorce rate, problems of childhood and adolescence and other family difficulties on the increase of women in the work force. The debate about the rights of women is also carried on at national level. And while many of the legal barriers against women have been removed, some of these changes have only been made recently and with difficulty. For example, the Swiss law giving women equal rights in marriage and making it illegal for a husband to prevent his wife from working and from opening a bank account without his approval was only passed in 1985 and

by a very narrow margin. The critics say the new law is anti-family and anti-marriage, turning marriage into a business-like partnership.

The dilemma of the two-income family

The obvious major benefits when both partners work is that the couple can enjoy a higher standard of living and they can be less dependent on the success of one career. For both partners there is the self-esteem associated with working for a living and a feeling of equality. And yet these benefits invariably come at a price.

When both partners work full-time they must perform a balancing act between work and family obligations. This often creates what sociologists call role strain – the result of a conflict between the demands of work and the demands of family. Picture a typical day: dropping the children off at daycare; rushing to work; meeting deadlines; picking up the children; doing grocery shopping; preparing dinner; bathing the children, putting them to bed; doing the laundry; making

190

HAPPY AT WORK, HAPPY AT HOME

■ Our home and our work lives are inextricably bound up, each being influenced by the other. For example, when you are praised at work this boost to your self-esteem is likely to make you more responsive toward your family, just as criticism might cause you to withdraw into yourself so much that your partner finds it difficult to make contact with you. Or if your partner is fired, he or she may vent frustration and anger on you and the children. Conversely,

an argument at home could engross you at work when you should be concentrating on other things and your performance could be affected. It is hardly surprising, then, that evidence proves that the happier people are with their jobs, the happier they are with their marriages. Women, particularly, say that their relationships flourish when they or their partners are doing well at work. If you have problems at work, it is wise to avoid bringing them home.

■ **On duty at work and at home.** ABOVE LEFT *More career opportunities for women mean more dual-income couples. Vagueness about who does what in the home can place undue strain on partners. You can reduce conflicts between your professional and domestic commitments by examining what you expect from each other, establishing priorities and considering possible short-cuts.* ABOVE RIGHT *Willingness to share traditional roles allows for a fairer balance of responsibilities.*

Is it a good idea to be a two-income family?
■ *Benefits include better living standards, greater security and high self-esteem* ■ *The hazards include role strain: conflicting obligations to work and family* ■ *Remember that your relationship needs as much time and attention as your job.*

time to be with your partner: there are simply not enough hours in the day to do all that needs to be done. If you feel you are in this position, what can you do about it? There are some useful questions you can ask yourself. Are you and your partner sharing as much as possible? Are you sure you are not being reluctant to give up any of your roles? Are there any chores your children could do regularly? If you are both earning, could you not afford to pay someone to shop and do the laundry? List your priorities and see whether there are tasks that could be dropped altogether or whether there are shortcuts you could take. As the British author Shirley Conran said: "Life is too short to stuff a mushroom."

There are emotional strains, too, which involve a choice between work and family roles. You may have a crucial meeting with a very important client at the same time as your child is performing in his school play. For your child it is very important for you to be in the audience, even if he has only one word to say. Or, a crucial meeting may be on the same night as your wedding anniversary. Do you choose your career or your family? While your partner may understand the importance of work obligations their feelings may still be hurt.

Problems are not helped when, at the end of the day the couple is too tired, too short of time, too lacking in awareness to discuss their growing tensions. If you are both working you may be just too busy to devote your time or interest to your partner's career, or more dangerously, to the relationship itself.

You cannot expect your relationship to take care of itself. It needs the same input as a career – time, energy, thought and involvement. Successful couples seem to have worked it out. Despite the demands of two careers, the majority of two-income couples have at least one partner who takes on the responsibility of nursemaiding the relationship in addition to his or her career. Usually it is the woman who performs this role. Women are more likely than men to think deeply about how their relationships are doing, make an effort to spend time with their partners and begin to talk about problems when they sense tension.

Open to negotiation

For some couples "doing what comes naturally" precludes direct negotiation about who does what. Roles, decision-making and chores are mutually acceptable because of custom, tradition or chance.

WILL YOU BOTH WORK?

POINTS IN FAVOR	POINTS AGAINST
Your standard of living is likely to be much higher. You are less dependent on one career.	*Sex roles are called into question as some men feel undermined if their partner works.*
Even if you know, logically, that staying at home is valuable work, it is good for self-esteem to be earning. Earning a salary may give you more say in running family affairs and greater equality in the home.	*There is a constant balancing act between work and family – the physical and emotional demands can be just too great. Emotional demands can pull in two directions at the same time – the interstate conference or your son's bar mitzvah.*
There may be better communication between two people working outside the home – you share a common language. Your daily rhythms are similar and you are more likely to agree on how to spend your evenings – going out or collapsing in front of the television.	*There is no one to listen to the problems you have in your career – your partner has their own work problems. You are both too busy to look after your relationship – your paths may be diverging without you being aware of it.*

LEARNING TO MAKE THE RIGHT DECISION

■ *Decisions between partners do not have to be made on a 50/50 basis. The important thing is to try to agree a balance that will allow you both to feel that you are contributing whatever decision-making skills you have.*

Who makes decisions and how you make them does not have to conform to any norm. Make changes by mutual agreement. If you are rivals in all decisions, or if neither of you wishes to make any, you need to work out practically what you will each accept.

Accept that your partner's perspective can add to your decision-making power. If you are at home minding the baby you are more likely to notice that you need a new washing machine. If you are the wage earner you are more likely to know whether you can afford it. Together you can work out the desirability and the feasibility of an important purchase.

Who actually makes decisions about different issues? It can be helpful to discuss this: see if you agree and if you are content with what you discover. Who decides: whether to move house; where the children will be educated; how to spend extra money; how much to give to charity; how to deal with difficult neighbors? Your conclusions will help to understand what your partner sees as important.

Do not cherish your authority for its own sake. It is the issue that is important – not your right to decide it, irrespective of the facts.

If one of you has more expertise than the other in a matter it is sensible to put that expertise to good use when making a decision.

MARITAL POWER

■ *In all relationships — between man and woman, mother and child, employer and employee — part of managing together has to do with the ability to influence others. If you feel that your partner is always the one to make decisions but you do not like it that way, or alternatively your partner never makes decisions but leaves everything to you (another kind of power), then an understanding of what produces power may help you to accept or change the situation.*

Powerful people are those who can get others to do what they want when they want, and in most satisfactory relationships there is a balance, perhaps unspoken, with power being split according to the situation. What gives someone power? If that person has something you want, then they have power. This can be something concrete like money, or abstract like love, companionship, emotional support, sex, knowledge or respect. But you have to value it or it is useless as a source of power to the other person. For example, if Steven loves Mary, Mary loves Sam, Sam loves Jessica and Jessica loves Steven, not one of them has power because the resource is not needed by the right person. If Fred is the sole wage earner in the family, he ultimately has control over the money: when Jane, his partner, wants to buy a new lawn mower and does not have access to any other money, Fred is in a position of power. If he is manipulative he may use this power in an attempt to get Jane to do something he wants; if Jane will not his resource is not powerful enough. The exercise of power may not always be so deliberate but the example illustrates why husbands traditionally had power and why, when wives work outside the home, men may feel threatened. The woman who does not earn has no financial power, although she may have power in other areas.

GETTING YOUR OWN WAY

In the best relationships partners are able to recognize each other's rights while asserting their own, and to be sensitive to each other's needs. There is no need to use power. With these couples their equality reflects the balance of their esteem. But

often, consciously or unconsciously, we may employ tactics to get our own way. These may be subtle ones like dropping hints, flattering, acting helpless, or sulking; or more obvious ones like threatening, becoming violent, pleading, asserting authority or bargaining. The tactics we use will depend partly on our personality and partly on our culture and upbringing. Remember Scarlett O'Hara coquetting to get her way in "Gone With The Wind" as southern belles were schooled to do?

There are also sex differences in the kinds of tactics people use. Men tend to be more direct. They coerce, use authority or claim expertise — all high risk tactics. For example, when Donald wants his wife Marlene to entertain some business colleagues he may say: "If we don't invite them I can't see how I can ask them to sign a new contract," or, "I earn the money that buys the food you would cook so I think it only right that you should pull your weight." If Donald succeeds, he feels pleased. If he does not, his self-esteem could be eroded.

▲ **Making the final choice** in a car showroom, a man sits behind the wheel while his partner looks on. Who makes the decisions in a marriage may depend on who earns the money. In traditional marriages major decisions are often a male prerogative, but modern dual-career couples favor a more equal balance of power. Female-dominated relationships usually prove less satisfactory to both partners than arrangements where men dominate or where partners share decision-making. If your partner is too controlling, it may be necessary to increase your influence by consciously employing tactics to get your own way.

Are you satisfied with your share of control over the things that matter? ■ *In the best relationships, partners are sensitive to each other's needs and they are able to recognize each other's rights while asserting their own.*

Can Marlene refuse in such a way as to allow him to retain his dignity? Perhaps she could suggest that they hire a caterer and explain why she does not have the time to cook an elaborate meal.

Women are usually less direct in trying to get their own way. They may sweet-talk, or act helpless or seductive – all low risk strategies. If they fail they have not lost face although they may lose self-esteem. Loretta might suggest that holidaying at the beach always makes her feel sexy, not because this is true but because it will appeal to Alec, and she wants to go because her friends are going. She may feel uncomfortable about her dishonesty. Far better to understand why Alec needs to be manipulated. Perhaps it is because he was never consulted about anything as

a child and needs to assert himself. He may well be longing to go to the beach but needs to feel he has the power to decide.

In the end the outcome of power is who decides – or who decides who will decide. Traditionally, women have tended to make the more trivial decisions – such as whether to buy salmon or cod – while men have made the bigger decisions, like buying a house. This pattern is changing, although in most cultures it is still men who dominate. Researchers tell us that when female-dominated relationships do exist they are generally less satisfying to both partners than either egalitarian or male-dominated relationships, suggesting an unease with powerful women and explaining why many women prefer that big decisions are taken by men. **DMN**

THE BALANCE OF POWER

■ People who see themselves as powerless may feel there is nothing they can do about it. The woman who puts up with verbal abuse because she loves her man, the man who accedes to his wife's every whim because he married her for her money: these are extreme examples. But in many relationships there are times when one partner feels helpless and resents the feeling. Is there anything they can do to make their lives more tolerable without destroying their partnership?

The first thing to remember is that, as part of a couple, you are probably of value to your partner. You need to discover what this value is and then use it to redress the balance. For example, if a husband is aggressive toward his wife he may still need her to care for him. She needs to find a way of making him aware of her value so that he may then be wary of shouting at her. Similarly, a rich wife may find her husband's opinions or social graces just as important as he finds her money. Or the wife of a successful executive may be the supportive and devoted wife he must have to remain successful. If you both understand this you are recognizing that you are exchanging resources. Your powers are interdependent.

If you cannot resolve your feeling of powerlessness by exchanging resources in this way, the way to restore a balance of power may be for you to look elsewhere for what you need, such as getting a job, having a baby or going out with your own friends. Clearly any drastic measures require discussion with your partner, as they affect the relationship not only emotionally but practically. Often, though, the other partner is supportive when the situation is explained – the powerlessness of

one partner can be the result of the other's ignorance rather than intellectual authoritarianism.

Some unhappy people go so far as to play the power game by withholding or controlling their own realms of power. The rich businessman who is tightfisted may find his wife doing what the ancient Greek women did in Lysistrata – denying their men sex. It is difficult to see how this could have any happy resolution and is dangerous ground to be treading. If you must play the power game it can be done openly and with good humor. "I cannot give you the money for a new dress. I was so miserable that you would not come to the football match with me I spent it by drowning my sorrows."

A further way of rendering power valueless is by learning to do without it. "I do not need your attention anyway. I get plenty of attention from my friends."

In some relationships power is complementary and based on collusion. As one husband in therapy put it: "She always wanted to protect me, thinking I was frail and vulnerable, and I thought she was strong." When the woman went through an emotional crisis her husband was angry at her apparent weakness. For her part, she was shocked to discover that she herself was not so strong, nor was he so weak as they had both believed. When they were forced to choose between "me" and "us" they had a painful split and were only able to come together again once they brought their separate, not collusive, identities to the relationship.

In the end, if you and your partner value your relationship you will need to resolve your power struggles without antagonizing each other, appreciating what each brings to your union.

But many of us need to sit down together and work out a plan. The garbage needs emptying daily, the dog needs walking and the car needs a monthly wash. Can you depend on one or the other of you to do it as the need arises? If so, fine; if not, discuss it. You may find that you both love taking the dog for a walk, both hate washing the car. So how will you work it out? Can you take turns with the dog? Walk him together? Or are you prepared to give up that task in exchange for doing another pleasurable chore? And when you *have* to wash the car, could you listen to a favorite tape to make the task more enjoyable? Or use the time to do some useful thinking? Or allow your child to work with you and have a friendly chat?

Sometimes you will have a clash of schedules – for example your yoga class starts at the same time as your son has to be picked up from football. If your class is really important to you, explain that to your partner and see if they can be available for the pickup after football. You will also need to explain that if they have an occasional business drink you will forgo your class, with good grace. And you will mind the children on your partner's bowling evening unless it clashes with your parent-teacher committee meeting.

During your negotiations you need to be sensitive to what your partner feels strongly about, and tactful, so that you both feel you are sharing the chores as equally as your available time allows.

Can housework be shared?

Throughout history, housework has been the domain of women. Even today, despite changes in gender roles, while husbands may have certain tasks, their wives tend to retain overall responsibility for the household. Full-time house-wives do some 90 percent of the housework, working women between 65 and 80 percent. On average that is around 55 hours a week on household chores for a house-wife, 26 hours a week for wives employed full-time. Men do virtually the same amount of housework whether their wives are employed or not (somewhere between 7 and 11 hours per week).

More and more couples are paying lip service to the idea of a fair division of domestic chores but there are strong reasons why equal responsibility is hard to achieve. Some

▲ **Finding it hard to let go**. *Even couples who realize the importance of achieving an equal and enjoyable division of household chores may find this difficult to put into daily practice. An attempt to strike a balance can become a struggle for control, with the woman, in particular, wanting both to off-load and to retain her traditional role.*

TRYING TO BE SUPERWOMAN

■ *Joyce claimed she liked the challenge of combining career and family. Nicholas was certainly no male chauvinist and when, at the start of their marriage, they discussed how to best organize their life together, they agreed to share all domestic and family responsibilities equally. The pattern they fell into, however, was one where Joyce took on most of the responsibilities and chores during the week, with Nick joining in more at weekends. Though often overtired and sometimes secretly resentful, far from complaining about this unevenness, Joyce encouraged it. She modeled herself partly on happy childhood memories of her competent but nonworking mother, regarding cooking, laundry and fussing after the family as natural expressions of caring. In any case, she enjoyed her reputation within the family for being superwoman. A friend who noticed the strain asked her what she was trying to prove. A long overdue talk with Nicholas helped them both to see how much her self-esteem was linked to keeping up her dual roles. Nicholas was able to convince her that loving her was not dependent on home-baking and being waited on. After a reallocation of household jobs, they discovered he actually likes ironing and cooking. She now has the reserve energy and inclination to share his interests – something he has missed.* **RB**

Most men do some housework but seldom more than 11 hours per week ■ *Having a wife who works does not affect the amount of chores men do* ■ *Compare the prestige value of your domestic responsibilities and your partner's – is it equal?* ■ *Women who feel reluctant to share housework need to learn to delegate.*

men have such an intense dislike of housework that the issue can endanger their marital happiness. And because many of us have had a traditional upbringing, trained from childhood to do certain tasks and not others, many men just do not feel they have the necessary skills to cope with what has always been women's work. They may dislike tackling something they cannot do well.

But all the blame cannot be placed on men. Women, even if they hate housework, are often reluctant to delegate responsibility – particularly because they feel they are more competent than their male counterparts. A woman like this may have to drop her standards so that the quality of her life can improve. She should try to stop worrying that her husband will break something if he is let loose with the duster and vacuum cleaner. Would it really matter if he did? And if she equates femininity with traditional domestic chores, and feels as strongly about losing this role as a man feels when he loses his job, she might ask her partner

whether he finds clean floors and an exhausted wife feminine. She may discover that he would prefer to have a more receptive partner and a little dust. **DMN**

Spending time together

While you are working out your division of labor, remember the enjoyable time you need to make room for: time with your partner. Researchers tell us that time spent together – especially in pleasurable activities – is positively correlated with a couple's happiness.

One study of the schedules of over 300 American couples discovered that single-income parents spend on average only half an hour more together every day than dual-income parents do. This would suggest that the amount of time you and your partner spend together is, to some extent at least, a matter of choice.

But what you do with your time together is even more important. If that half hour is spent sharing chores or watching television, it is unlikely to strengthen the relationship. If you try to spend your joint leisure time in an *active* way – whether eating, playing or talking – this is more likely to increase your satisfaction with your relationship. The key is not only to match your work schedules as closely as possible but to use your time together wisely. **ALW**

195

◄ **Managing leisure** *is as important as managing your day-to-day routine as a couple. Just as you need regular vacations to work efficiently in your job, so your relationship is more likely to be successful if you make time for enjoying hobbies, relaxing or simply having fun with your partner. Spending joint leisure time in the right way is vital, however. Activities that demand a high degree of sharing and joint participation will have the most beneficial effects on your partnership.*

The Difficult Partner

SUCCESSFUL partnerships revolve around adaptability, shared values, expressions of affection, sexual satisfaction, openness, supportiveness, among many other factors. Whether or not these are achieved depends on the personalities of those involved and the circumstances in which they find themselves. Establishing and maintaining an effective long-term relationship can be difficult for any couple, but all the more so if one of the partners is quarrelsome, immature, insecure, domineering or manipulative.

Will the kindness and affection you want to give to a prospective partner really help them to change? Should those who are already committed to difficult partners try to carry on coping? What if unexpected long-term illness or unemployment strains a once happy relationship? How can you improve the situation you have fallen into?

Personality problems

Immature adults find it difficult to plan ahead and, as a result, are frequently surprised by the obvious. They are financially irresponsible, will not accept responsibility for their own actions and do not easily learn from their mistakes. Like children, they tend to blame others for the bad things that happen to them or the bad things they do to others, and make transparent excuses for their behavior.

Feelings of insecurity can fail to manifest themselves openly. Even the most successful of business executives – overtly capable, friendly and charming – can be, beneath this attractive façade, paralyzed with the fear that their partners and friends will abandon them.

They may constantly imagine that they are being criticized, have been found wanting and are unlovable. They

LIVING WITH A QUARRELSOME PARTNER

■ *When a couple quarrel frequently and with increasing bitterness, the chances are that they are facing problems for which no solution can easily be found and which may have nothing to do with what they are actually fighting about. When this happens, they can most usefully ask themselves what it is that they need that they are either not giving or receiving.*

Most frequently, the missing ingredient in the relationship is affection. At the heart of every deeply felt relationship is the quest for love and affection, expressed physically, verbally and through actions. However, with passing time, one partner may forget to reinforce their feelings in these ways. The other partner's desire for them to show their affection may not be apparent in the trivial things over which arguments erupt, but may be there nonetheless.

It is important to ask when was the last time you gave your partner a hug, told them you loved them, thanked them for keeping up their end of the relationship. The traditional practice of buying a bunch of flowers, a box of chocolates or some other present is no substitute for the actual demonstration of affection – it might even be construed as trying to buy them off. It is far better (and cheaper) to spend more time together, showing consideration of each other by what we do and say.

LIVING WITH AN INSECURE PARTNER

Some partners are, at bottom, very insecure, and may react to criticism or any other challenge by flying off the handle or, at the other extreme, refusing to talk. They are too frightened to look inward at themselves and their behavior. If they do, they think, they will find out that they are, indeed, a worthless person; criticism is interpreted as evidence of complete rejection.

Although these situations can be very difficult for partners to deal with, they are not hopeless; they just require special strategies. People as insecure as this can only examine their innermost feelings when they feel safe, and so they need a great deal of reassurance, acceptance and praise. If they are constantly told and made to feel that they are loved, they will begin to lose some of their anxiety about being rejected and will come to accept that they may be responsible for their own behavior and begin to do something about it. **JD**

REPAIR AND RECONCILIATION?

■ *Not all deteriorating relationships can or should be repaired. If you feel that your partner's behavior is seriously damaging your well-being or seriously abusing your self-respect, ending the relationship may be the only option. However, many problems can be resolved, provided that you can persuade your partner to help in finding a solution.*

There are usually five main stages of relationship breakdown (see Ch 12). At each point, there is something that can be done to repair the damage or at least make the breakup more bearable.

1 When your relationship is turbulent or dissatisfying, both of you should try to improve the communication and enhance the intimacy between you. Social skills courses, couples therapy and relationship enrichment programs may prove beneficial.

2 When one or both of you is privately critical or offended, you need to make a positive effort to think more favorably about your partner, to consider whether you are blaming them unfairly, and to re-evaluate the benefits of staying and the costs of leaving the relationship.

3 When you have reached the point of open criticism, it is important to confront your problems together. Consider whether you could improve your

Is your partner quarrelsome, immature, insecure, domineering, violent, addicted?
■ *Allowing unacceptable behavior to go unchallenged is a recipe for disaster* ■ *Be understanding, but be prepared to leave.*

may be frequently wracked by jealousy, worry about their partners' faithfulness and whereabouts, and need constant reassurance that their worth is recognized and that they are wanted and accepted.

Alternatively, this fear, worry and lack of self-worth can turn people into trembling shadows, too frightened to voice

their concerns in case they are abandoned. If their partners are unfaithful, they rush to blame themselves and go to great lengths to re-establish the relationship, sometimes suffocating it as a result.

Those who feel particularly insecure may try to mask it by becoming domineering, exercising control over everyone around them, including their partners. They demand immediate approval of all they do or say, expect others to jump to comply with their every wish and do what they are told.

Such powerful figures may initially seem very attractive to those who are themselves either immature or insecure, but usually they are gradually seen for what they are – tyrants – and their partners find it increasingly difficult to tolerate such arrogance and self-centered behavior.

Certain substances have the capacity to cause physical addiction – alcohol and drugs such as heroin are the most common. However, there is also what is known as the "addictive personality," where a person's immaturity, insecurity, their upbringing and other psychological factors

▲ **The domineering partner** *may at first seem very attractive to someone who is looking for a strong sense of security in marriage. However, tyrants usually* *reveal themselves in the long run to be particularly insecure themselves.*

MUTUAL PROBLEM-SOLVING

■ *One way to deal with a situation in which you find your partner's behavior unacceptable is to use constructive problem-solving skills. A summary of widely recognized and endorsed skills is represented in the Mutual Problem-Solving Program devised by the American psychologist Carl Ridley and his associates. Below are the major steps that they suggest.*

1 Understand just what the problem is. Talk with your partner about your perceptions of the issues, and listen to what they think about them until you both understand what is troubling you.

2 Understand how the problem affects your relationship. Share your experiences of how unhappiness or dissatisfaction affects you and your partner. Discuss the improvements each of you would like to see.

3 Understand how each of you contributes to the problem. You may feel that your partner is mainly at fault, but in fact, rarely is one person completely responsible.

4 Agree on a goal. Describe the goal in terms of actual behavior or conditions that need to be changed.

5 Offer alternative solutions. The more you identify, the better the odds that you will find a good one.

6 Analyze and evaluate the alternatives. Decide whether each would be consistent with your and your partner's personal values and resources, and whether it would actually help you to achieve the goal that you have agreed on.

7 Choose the best solution.

8 Implement the solution. Decide what each of you must do, then do it. Set a trial period during which you will monitor the results.

9 After the trial period, evaluate the outcome. Discuss how well the solution has worked and whether you need to make any modifications to it. **BMM**

197

ationship by changing roles, havior or routines.

If your problems are known to her people, you could make use these others to help one or th of you to solve the difficulty. he breakup has gone beyond e point of reconciliation, your ends and relations can help to ake the transition easier for you th of you.

5 When the relationship is over, each of you will need to understand and interpret the breakup. You will find it helpful to talk to friends, giving them your own account of the relationship and its ending. By listening, offering their own perspectives and accepting your need to grieve, your friends can help you to move on. **ALW**

make it more likely that they will succumb to an addiction. This can be to alcohol or a drug or to unacceptable and damaging behavior such as gambling or buying on credit.

Avoiding difficult partners

There is ample evidence that people who are aggressive, drink heavily, take drugs or gamble will continue to do so even after establishing a long-term relationship. Many people, especially women, believe that all their partners need is plenty of kindness and affection and they will change. Unfortunately, this does not usually happen. It is far better to persuade a loved one to alter his or her behavior before setting out on life together, than to hope for change in the future.

It is also very important to be sure of your feelings before you get deeply involved with someone. Many people who later have difficulties with their partners say that they were not in love with them before they got married or started to

▲ "I hate you! Don't ever come back!" *shouts a boy at his father as police in Minneapolis, Minnesota, arrest the man for beating his wife. Studies* show a persistent reluctance by both men and women to intervene or endorse police intervention when a man is hitting his partner. However, Minnesota is one of 13 American states with a policy of arrest and prosecution for domestic assault – the state can press charges even if the victim does

> *Is yours a love-hate relationship?* ■ *Physical violence is a factor in more than one-third of divorces* ■ *If your partner feels the urge to assert control over you by hitting you, you should seek shelter, therapy, or both.*

live with them, but hoped that love would come with time. This, too, does not often happen.

Coming to the realization that you do not love your partner and revealing this to him or her can be extremely upsetting to those involved, but it can be much worse later, especially if children are affected.

Living with a difficult partner

For those who have not avoided choosing a difficult partner, allowing unacceptable behavior to go unchallenged is a recipe for disaster. Something should be done as soon as you realize that your partner's behavior is making you unhappy. The most positive step is to talk it over. It is important to do this in such a way that you communicate your concern: hints may not be enough and are, in any case, easy to shrug off or put down to nagging. Too many partners complain ineffectually over a long period and then simply leave when life becomes too much.

not want to. Sentencing batterers to jail terms or re-education programs has dramatically reduced levels of violence in the home.

VIOLENT RELATIONSHIPS

■ *Aggression and violence are found in many homes, particularly when one partner has been drinking. Domestic violence has been around for a long time, but it has only come out into the open in the relatively recent past. For example, in the late 1960s, it was found that 22 percent of middle-class and 40 percent of working-class divorces in the United States were sought because of physical violence.*

LOVE-HATE RELATIONSHIPS

The balance between the emotions of love and hatred is a delicate one, and in a close relationship, romance can sometimes turn to conflict – a conflict that can get frighteningly out of hand.

In one survey, about 22 percent of American college students reported that they had been either the victim or the perpetrator of an aggressive act in a close relationship. Almost one-third of the people interviewed said that they interpreted the abuse they had experienced in the relationship as "love."

Some people apparently use violence in loving relationships as a way of controlling their partners, in much the same way as parents use physical punishment to control their children. They tell themselves that they are punishing their partner because they love them.

Another reason for abuse could be the idea that there is no alternative to the present partner.

The abuser, fearing that they may be losing their partner and terrified of being left alone, will lash out in violent frustration. The abused partner may put up with unreasonable aggression because they can see no possibility of finding someone else. **RMC**

BATTERERS: WHO ARE THEY?

The vast majority of those inflicting serious violence on their partners are men, and studies have shown that they are most likely to be younger men. Although they are found in all social classes, batterers predominately belong to the lower socio-economic groups. Similarly, they are found in all occupations, but those who have an inferior education or are in jobs with a lower status than their partners' are more likely to get violent.

Such men of violence have often experienced violence themselves when they were children. Psychologically, they are often anxious, easily frustrated and compulsive. They have low self-esteem, which means that they find it difficult to accept any criticism or rejection. When under stress, they do not argue but lash out, although some, because of their own insecurity, will take fright and yield if seriously challenged over their behavior. Battering sometimes lessens with age, but it often continues right through middle age. **JD**

199

DRINKING AND VIOLENCE

■ *A pattern common the world over is the man who goes out drinking, on his return demands sex (which is refused) and then becomes abusive and aggressive.*

When a woman is faced with such a drunken partner, her best immediate course of action is to humor him and persuade him to go to sleep, not to seek explanations or to remonstrate. The next day, the man will often not remember anything about the night before, and when confronted with an account of what happened, he will feel very guilty and promise to improve. The time to seek professional guidance is just as soon as you realize there is a problem. **JD**

What if you are angry about your partner's impulsive spending, naive handling of financial matters, neglecting to consult you about what is going where as, all the while, he or she is leading you both down the road to ruin? Here, both short- and long-term strategies are needed. In the short term, it may be essential for you to take over the family finances, however much the pride of your partner suffers. When things are on an even keel again, you can begin to consult about how much to spend on what, until you achieve a balanced joint responsibility for finances.

It is worth remembering that your partner's motives for overspending may have been generous – for example, a wish to give you and your family a better lifestyle. However, it may be important to seek professional help in other cases. One of the symptoms of manic-depressive illness is an almost gleeful irresponsibility with money, and this is something that is impossible to handle on your own.

Even if you and your partner are able to talk to each other about what is going wrong with your relationship, you may still need the support of somebody else. Talking over your problems with a close friend or family member can be a great relief, and they can often give you a fresh view of your

THE VICTIMS: WHO GETS BATTERED?

■ *Although men are occasionally the victims of physical abuse, the vast majority of those who suffer are women. Often they remain with a violent man without taking any action. They may complain about their treatment, but inwardly accept it as their due.*

There are other factors that may be responsible for women remaining in what can only be an intolerable situation. They may worry that, if they do not accept the violence, it will be inflicted on their children. They may also be completely without funds to make an escape, and can also be isolated, far from friends and family who might be able to render assistance. In addition, even in supposedly advanced Western societies there is still a prejudice against women who suffer violence, and many hide away their bruises rather than expose themselves to the gossip and dis- *belief of others. It is also only recently that the law and the police have taken the part of the battered woman.*

It has been shown that violence can occur at any time but is most often concentrated between the hours of 5pm and midnight, the hours when the male partner is most likely to be at home. Violence is more likely to occur in some parts of a home than others. Men tend to be violent in the bedroom, women in the kitchen, the living room is equally chosen by both – and the bathroom is the safest part of the home.

CONFRONTING THE PROBLEM

No woman should ever tolerate violence against herself – for any reason. There are warning signs: if violence is apparent in the early stages of a relationship, it is highly likely that it will continue even when a couple have settled down together.

When there is violence, every step should be taken to eliminate the factors that may provoke it. This does not mean that the woman (the usual victim) should

◄ **Taking refuge** *in a shelter for battered women in St Paul, Minnesota, a mother and her children recall the once ideal family they appeared to be: "This is what we looked like," say the children, "before the police came and arrested Daddy for hurting Mommy." With practical advice from staff and emotional support from other victims, women in shelters may rebuild the self-esteem they need in order to avoid future violence – in particular, the confidence to live without their partner.*

> *Are you to blame for the way your partner behaves?* ■ *If it really is a fact that you are contributing to the problem, then change – but you will perpetuate a bad situation if you fail to reject unfair and irrational accusations.*

situation. However, those close to you may be tempted to take your side no matter what, and this can be less than helpful when what is needed is a change of perspective. It may only be possible to get this through someone outside your own family or circle of friends, and in this case, you might do well to seek the professional advice of your doctor or of a psychiatrist or marriage counselor (see *Ch 25*).

There are many other areas of daily life in which irre-

sponsibility can damage a relationship – children (caring for them recklessly or insufficiently) and employment (working too much or too little) are just two examples. They demand quick treatment and correction.

Beyond irresponsibility

All of these kinds of unacceptable behavior can be modified to some extent, provided the two partners want this and can work together. There are, however, other kinds that cannot be altered easily or at all. Persistent violence, cruelty, addictions – none of these can ultimately be tolerated.

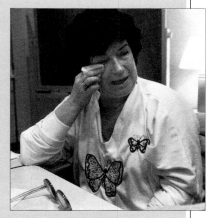

■ **Why do women tolerate violence?** *Some may interpret violence as a sign of love. However, research has shown that many battered women do not feel worthy of affection, nor capable of escaping.*

◄ **"He fights all the time, but it's never been this bad,"** *sobs a battered mother while police arrest the boyfriend who earlier in the evening threw her against the bathtub, knocking her unconscious.*

▼ **"It wasn't his fault"** *insists a 24-year-old woman as hospital staff checking on her heart rate uncover tire marks on her abdomen. After three years of previous physical abuse, she fell out of her boyfriend's moving van during an argument. The back wheels passed over her and the boyfriend did not stop.*

▲ **Driven to kill**. *A battered wife serving an eight-and-one-half year sentence in Minnesota's Shakopee Prison for killing her husband, Jo Ann Hennum says "The hellhole I came from was a prison much worse than this could ever be."*

201

live in fear and trepidation of saying or doing something wrong. It does mean taking positive steps to understand why the batterer feels so inadequate and to improve the self-esteem of both parties.

If these methods do not work, the man should be warned that his behavior will not be tolerated. If he pays no heed to this, the woman should leave him, if only temporarily. Although it is far better to remove the aggressor from the family home than for his victim or victims to have to move out, this is more easily said than done. At least at first, most victims of physical abuse are forced to flee. There is no room for compromise: what is at stake is the woman's life and that of her children. **JD**

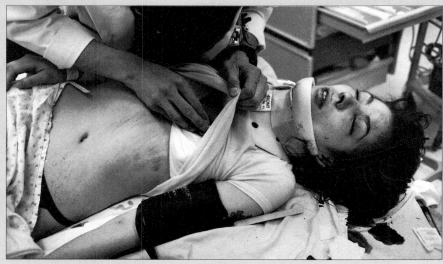

You may find that, when you warn your addicted partner that you will not tolerate the behavior generated by their alcoholism, drug abuse or gambling, they deny that there is a problem, and the unacceptable behavior escalates. It is a good idea to turn to your doctor or a voluntary organization such as Alcoholics Anonymous as soon as you realize that your partner is addicted. There, you will get good advice on how to cope in the way that is best for your partner and, just as importantly, best for yourself and your family.

Accepting the repeated promises of a partner that they will reform is a mistake; it is usually wise to seek outside help. You must also avoid colluding with your partner by pretending that there is no problem or by assisting in the continuation of the addiction through, say, giving money. Any kind of collaboration will be interpreted as tolerance and there will be no change in behavior.

Coping with a partner's illness

Sometimes good, solid relationships are wrecked through circumstances completely outside the couple's control.

When one partner falls ill or is seriously injured in an accident, it is usually a simple matter of adjustment for the other to take over more of the responsibilities of family life until the person's health is restored. However, if the illness is a chronic one or the adverse effects of the accident are long-term ones, all the burdens of running the home, looking after the invalid and the children and ensuring that there is enough money fall on the shoulders of the healthy partner. Many people manage all this, and while their lives could be a great deal better, they somehow learn to cope and their relationships with their partners remain intact. Others, however, buckle under the load, and they develop feelings of hopelessness that are compounded by their understandable fatigue and worry. They may also find them-

selves blaming their partners for their predicament, and then feel guilty for blaming someone who is ill and patently not responsible for what has happened.

When one partner becomes mentally ill, the same problems can occur, especially since the carer-partner may have to cope with difficult or unacceptable behavior, and may

▲ **Preparing for the loss of her partner.** *Maria Ribeiro married her husband David knowing that he was dying because of AIDS. Unexpected illness and death can be harder to adapt to, but the most important factors influencing how well you cope are your personality – how well you cope with stresses of any kind – and the degree of support you receive from your social network and the wider community.*

THE STRAIN OF UNEMPLOYMENT

■ *Unemployment can have a devastating effect on a person and on a family. Even if the person is out of work for only a short time, there can still be a lingering fear that it could happen again, a perhaps unexpressed belief that the loss of job was the person's own fault (even when there was a general layoff) and a pervasive lack of self-worth. Long-term unemployment can magnify these feelings, especially if the other partner is in work. In some families the stress of unemployment results in*

lower marital satisfaction and decreased communication or, at worst, verbal abuse and physical violence.

Relationships can also be damaged when a partner who remains at home (usually the woman) is suddenly faced with sharing the long-established independent part of her life and sorting out who does what around the house. As well as the emotional problems that unemployment can bring, the financial strains should not be underestimated.

How can you prevent a partner's illness from straining your relationship? ■ *Take advantage of outside help and social services* ■ *Join respite schemes and support groups to reduce your sense of isolation* ■ *Resist any conscious or unconscious attempt by your partner to use helplessness to dominate you.*

also find that the relationship he or she had with the other person has disappeared because of the toll that the mental illness has taken.

Taking advantage of outside help is important. Having some help with lifting, nursing, going to and from doctors and hospitals can take some of the effort out of coping. Respite schemes, in which someone else looks after your partner while you have some time to yourself, can make all the difference. Joining a support group where others with the same problems as yours meet and keep in touch can be a good way of finding out helpful hints and reducing your sense of isolation.

It is also important to help prevent your partner turning into what is known as a "painful patient." Pain clinics have discovered that many who suffer chronic pain use this to get rewards and to get their way – learning to love what hurts them. It is only human nature to employ (usually quite unconsciously) whatever behavior causes others to be sympathetic and pay attention. However, these "rewards" can make the pain even more chronic and make it less likely that the person will learn to cope. Techniques have been devised in some clinics to ignore groans of pain and similar behavior, and to talk to patients only when they begin to take part in the world around them. This may seem heartless, but it is something that those in pain get used to in a short time and with very positive results. **JD**

203

▶ **Living with a long-term disability.** *Most disabilities leave the partners still capable of exchanging the emotional support that is central to their sense of closeness and their mutual well-being. This ability is often undermined, however, when the carer-partner buckles under the load, usually when finances are difficult, and/or the disabled partner finds it unacceptable to be dependent.*

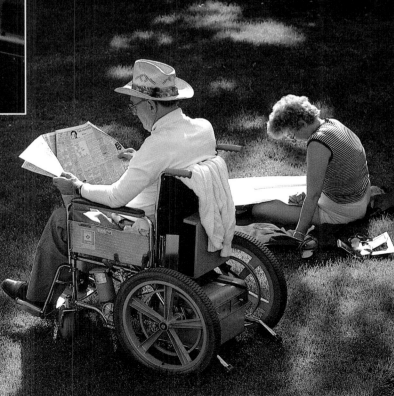

Getting Therapy

ALL TOO OFTEN we wait until the last minute before seeking professional help with relationship problems. We expect this area of our lives to look after itself or believe that common sense is all that is needed to set it right. Also, it is not easy to talk about our most private matters with strangers or to admit that our closest tie is something less than perfect.

Popular misconceptions about marriage therapy are partly responsible for this reluctance to seek advice. Individual therapists vary in their approaches but it is not the case – as some believe – that they tell people what to do or pronounce judgment on who is to blame when a marriage goes wrong.

Another widely held belief is that marriage counseling is there to save marriages, but it can also be about easing the process of parting for a couple who cannot agree to remain together. Married couples are not the only suitable clients. Singles – divorced, widowed or nevermarrieds – and unmarried couples can also be helped.

Why do people go for help?

Typically, one or both partners decide to look for outside help when, after months or possibly years of misery, events suddenly seem to be reaching a crisis. Perhaps it is their legal adviser or doctor who makes the suggestion. Partners may have a specific idea of what they want from therapy but very often they just have the vague hope that their relationship will be improved in some way. Sometimes a particular event – such as discovering a partner's infidelity – is the trigger for making the first appointment. In other cases,

REPAIRING AND STRENGTHENING RELATIONSHIPS

■ *The most common tasks of counselors are prevention of marital breakdown and, when this is not possible, helping couples to separate with as little psychological damage as possible. But* LEFT *couples with stable relationships also seek help. Higher expectations of marriage, especially among women, are encouraging them to explore ways of maximizing the success of their shared life. Marital enrichment sessions cater for partners wishing to inject new interest into their relationships and increase their mutual understanding.*

ABOVE Strain leads to marital conflict for a young couple coping at the same time with a new baby and with unemploy-

people decide to seek help because they are unsure about what to do next, depressed about the marriage, or dread the prospect of a future without (or with) their partner.

Therapists are also available for preventive help before there are serious problems – perhaps at the first sign of trouble. They can also help new partners wanting to strengthen their relationship; this is sometimes called "marital enrichment" and may be associated with a program that couples attend as part of a group to develop relationship skills. More specific help is provided by sex therapy (see p212), divorce counseling and conciliation services.

Helping you to help yourself

Someone who gives advice to an unhappy friend may remark jokingly that they ought to go in for marriage counseling. A common but mistaken view of couple therapists is that they give out advice or instructions and provide magical solutions to relationship problems. Practical information may indeed be a vital part of the helping process, and strategies for maintaining and improving relationships are likely to be learned during counseling. However, therapists generally try to discourage you from expecting instant answers and introduce you to the idea that you yourself will be actively involved in finding solutions. Relationship therapists have to be knowledgeable, but this is in order to be more understanding rather than to instruct their clients.

Marriage counseling aims to help clients understand and then resolve their problem. The extent to which the therapist

ment. Events such as an extra-marital affair or even retirement from work can also be stressful turning points in the life of a marriage. Discussing the situation with a counselor may clarify their problems and suggest solutions.

WHO SEEKS THERAPY?

■ *The individual circumstances and unique history of each couple are vital to therapists. However, experienced helpers come to recognize familiar patterns in couples' motives for seeking help and in the ways they respond to their difficulties. The following are common profiles of candidates for counseling:*

The drifting couple *seem to be avoiding the issue. Perhaps one of them wants the relationship to end, but has not yet been able to admit this to their partner – or perhaps not even to him- or herself.*

Partners with a hidden agenda *conceal their true intentions. For example, a partner may declare that the object is to work toward a reconciliation, but secretly believes the meetings will reveal that parting makes more sense, so that they can then go ahead with a new, separate life, reassured by the knowledge that they tried to salvage the relationship.*

The "identified" client *: one of the partners is presented by the couple as the one with the problem (for example, her phobias, his drinking). The other (who may regard himself or herself as a blameless victim) goes along to see what they can do to help.*

Partners with incompatible goals *: one of them wants to end the relationship and the other wants to repair it. Both want therapy but for different reasons.*

Partners with impossible goals *feel their relationship is unsatisfactory because it does not live up to their expectations – but these turn out to be unattainable. For*

instance, a couple may set out intending never to argue, or never to feel attracted to another person.

Partners who set conditions *: both partners go along for help, but one of them agrees to remain involved only on their own terms. They might, for example, make it a condition that they are not criticized, or that their partner promises not to see or discuss someone they have been having an affair with.*

The angry, arguing couple *constantly attack and accuse each other. Often they take offense at everything the other says. Sitting down and talking about their relationship sometimes provokes furious arguments: they may then cite this bad experience as evidence that talking is pointless or makes matters worse.*

The withdrawn couple *have got into a habit of suppressing thoughts and feelings about their predicament. They avoid conflict by restricting their communication with each other, and, consequently, when they go for therapy this limits the range of subjects they are prepared to discuss. Meetings are full of pauses and silences and both partners are restrained in their answers to the counselor's questions.*

Partners with opposite reactions *: one is "demanding," the other "withdrawn." One reacts with frustration and demands, the other by reducing communication and self-expression, and by avoidance. The differences in their response to disappointments may reinforce a sense that they are in fact incompatible.*

structures the discussion and interprets what the clients say varies. Many therapists follow a "person-centered approach" (promoted by Carl Rogers and therefore sometimes called Rogerian). In its purest form, the quality of the counseling relationship is all that matters in this approach.

Instead of diagnosis, techniques and treatment, it is the relationship between counselor and client that is seen as therapeutic. Key characteristics of this relationship are the counselor's empathy, acceptance and warm regard for the client. In other words, the counselor responds to the client as a likable equal, does not criticize or judge and makes every effort to understand the client's concerns and feelings. Empathy and acceptance are also basic counseling principles for many therapists adopting alternative approaches.

Another characteristic of "person-centered" counselors is that they are nondirective. The counselor respects the clients' right to make their own decisions and choices and does not presume to know what is best for them. Instructions are avoided. Even if the therapist has an informed opinion about what clients should do, it is not offered as a solution because this would be close to assuming responsibility for the clients. The nondirective therapist avoids coming up with answers so that clients can maintain responsibility for their own actions. Provided all the options are thoroughly explored during counseling sessions, this approach helps to build clients' confidence and self-reliance. In its most extreme form, nondirective therapy is restricted to listening, open questions that encourage clients to talk, occasional understanding remarks and rephrasing of what clients have just said.

However, to some clients this approach, in which they are given the reins, may seem rather self-defeating – "If I am going to have to do most of the talking and make the decisions, why bother to go?" – after all, one of the main reasons people turn to a helper is because they do not know what to do next. They keep hoping or even asking for directives – "What do we do about it?".

A complete absence of advice may discourage such clients from seeing the therapist again. Men in particular are likely to want practical advice. Outcome studies, investigat-

WHAT IS ON THE AGENDA?

■ *If your partnership has problems and you turn to counseling for help, the agenda is complicated by the fact that there are two of you. You probably have different interpretations, and you might have different goals. Perhaps one of you believes that the rapport you once had is gone for ever and that the best outcome would be for you to part on friendly terms, while the other believes you can work together to overcome the present deadlock and recapture the loving, cooperative feeling of an earlier time. You will have to share the therapist's attention.*

Therapists will usually be happy to see people separately or as a couple, whichever is preferred, but some insist on "conjoint sessions" (couples seen together with one therapist). Others offer "collaborative therapy" (each partner is treated by a different therapist) or even *"collaborative combined therapy" (where all four sometimes meet together for joint sessions). Some couples make separate visits to begin with, and then go together. If your partner made the first contact and you were invited to go along subsequently, you should not feel that the helper is going to be on your partner's side and could already have formed a negative view of you. Couple counselors are trained to resist such biases. It is not even a case of reserving judgment until hearing your side of things. Helpers are not there to apportion blame and in any case the helper's possible opinion about who has been most at fault is irrelevant. Much more important is for each partner to recognize for themselves the nature (not the amount) of their contribu-*

EXPLORING AND CLARIFYING

● *Each of you puts forward your position.*
You let off steam, give your account of the relationship, how you feel, what you want. As well as telling the helper, you are also telling each other.
● *Getting to the underlying issues.*
Having given a rounded picture, you then begin to concentrate on the main complaints and issues as you see them – what is missing for you, what behavior you are finding unacceptable and what you would like to change.
● *Reviewing.*
With the therapist's help, you summarize the issues. This leads to a clearer view and perhaps alternative interpretations. Either way, it adds insight.

SETTING GOALS

● *Decide on areas of improvement.*
You have already begun to do this, but now need to be more specific and selective. Where could you start? What can you agree on? What changes are practicable?
● *Work out possible goals.*
This involves looking a bit further ahead. Each partner needs to accept some responsibility about their own contribution. You will need to negotiate feasible goals.
● *Final choice and commitment to goals.*
There may be one specific problem that looms large. Alternatively, if there is a range of goals, the task is to sort out what needs most attention.

> *When it seems like there is nothing more to say, how can anyone help?* ■ *Even in the opening stages of therapy, many couples feel they are back in contact: you may hear your partner saying things you never knew they felt* ■ *The therapist's understanding and respect for both partners bolsters their self-esteem.*

ing clients' views of the help they received, show that some are frustrated if they feel a meeting has lacked structure and direction, and some want more interpretation and suggestions from the helper. On the other hand, most would resist being told what to do.

Sometimes a nondirective approach is combined with a "contract-making" approach. Here, counselor and clients agree on what the aims of working together are to be. They identify the difficulties and decide on strategies to improve the situation.

In the case of a couple temporarily separated after the wife has had an affair, for example, the husband might aim to include her more in his social life now he knows how excluded she has felt.

The wife might aim to be more demonstrative toward her husband now she is aware of his doubts about how much she enjoys being with him.

For both, an important goal in discussions with the counselor might be to understand how significant childhood experiences continue to influence their reactions to events in the present. A plan is evolved and specific targets set after clients have decided what changes are desirable and possible.

A room with a view

Therapy may last over a prolonged period and has several stages (see box), but the first exploratory stage can bring immediate changes to the relationship – even before any goals have been set. How can this happen? In the exploratory stage each partner gets to hear the other's position. It may be the first time they have listened, or the first time they have heard the other's case so fully or so objectively spelt out. This can put them back in contact ("I didn't know you felt that way"; "You have never told me this before"). Each has the gratification of being understood in detail and without prejudice by an unbiased third party. The therapist's understanding of and respect for each partner's point of view bolsters self-esteem. Just gaining some moral support helps to restore a more positive approach to life and to the relationship.

People going for therapy are often confused. However, the counseling room is a safe place where they can begin to sort out the muddle. One expert describes therapy as a "room with a view," providing a place for couples to look at their predicament and gain new insight. It cannot give out easy answers to relationship problems but at its best it leads to increased self-awareness and gives partners a new appreciation of each other.

207

tion to the difficulties. There is no consistent order in which issues are covered, though generally the helper has some kind of master plan – a scheme along which to structure the meetings. You will not need to concern yourself with such a program: that is the helper's job. But you may be reassured to know that the discussion is not as meandering as it may sometimes seem. The order of tasks and issues and the amount of time spent on each will vary depending on what you bring to the meetings and what you decide together to be most appropriate. The program below is just an approximate guide. Set out that way, it suggests a neat, orderly progression, but it is likely that the discussions in your meetings will go backward and forward and that the stages will overlap.

CARRYING OUT A PROGRAM OF ACTION
● *Think of strategies for achieving goals.*
  For instance: exchange requests and favors with each other.
  Have a week's trial with some new pattern (for example, being more cooperative, sharing tasks).
  Try role-playing in order to see how behavior can be changed.
● *Choose the best strategy.*
  It may be worth trying each before making your final decision.
● *Act on your decision.*
  Do it (with the support of the therapist – it helps to have encouraging feedback) and show appreciation for each other's efforts.

What therapists can do

Listening is a key part of the therapist's role. The experienced therapist is bound to recognize familiar stories but is also careful to hear whatever is unique about each person or couple. For many clients it is a rare experience to have someone listen in such an attentive, uninterrupted way and having time personally reserved for this purpose. Prospective clients might object to the idea of paying someone just to listen, but listening involves many other skills.

The therapist needs to take in a great deal of information that they will then use in several ways: to show that they have understood; to help their clients see their relationship in a new light; to give feedback and offer interpretations; and to provide structure so that discussions are more purposeful and focused on areas that the clients identify as useful. Other tasks include making it easier for the clients to cope with anger – recognize it, communicate it in a non-destructive way and learn from it – and helping them to confront their own negative feelings or behavior. After the initial talks, partners and therapist can agree on their goals and on an agenda of issues for discussion during subsequent visits.

Explaining their relationship to someone else may suggest solutions or make priorities apparent to a couple with problems. Explanation can take away the sense of desperation, anger or deep hurt. Often we avoid confronting potentially painful areas of difficulty: talking forces us to face these buried issues but at the same time clarifies and suggests next steps. The therapist comments on what the clients have just said in order to reflect back the feeling or point that has been conveyed. The clients then know that the therapist has understood them and feel encouraged to

Structurin
discu

Listening

G
encourage

BRIDGING THE COMMUNICATION GAP

■ *ABOVE When communication breaks down, couples may continue for many years in an unhappy relationship without talking out their problems. Counseling may help them to confront the issues they have long been avoiding. When, in the first session, each partner puts forward their own case, it may be a revealing experience. Each will probably be surprised at points the other makes. Re-* *establishing contact in this way is an important first step toward removing the barriers to openness that have built up. RIGHT Negative communication is potentially as destructive as noncommunication. In a counseling setting such as this one, however, a couple can air their grievances under the direction of a professional. Counselors can help partners cope with anger and teach them to* *express it nondestructively, for example admitting "I'm angry with you" instead of abusing each other. They often act as interpreters, stopping partners at key points in a discussion. This enables a couple to identify important issues that they may have overlooked. Counseling techniques for promoting effective communication include "reflecting," where the therapist comments on what a* *client says, and summarizing. These allow partners to listen to what they have said and clarify or elaborate it. Feedback and interpretation from the counselor will help them understand their communication style and why it fails. Clients and counselor can then agree together on strategies for improving the relationship.*

> *Why should you talk to a stranger about private matters?* ■ *By keeping your deepest concerns hidden, you may be isolating yourself emotionally, and missing opportunities to improve your self-understanding.*

discuss the particular issues that are making them unhappy.

In the vital self-exploration that takes place in therapy the clients are autobiographers and the therapist is like a historian. It is easy to lose track, especially in joint sessions. Not everyone is equally articulate, and the therapist can feed back the right expression or piece of information to help

THE HELPERS

■ *Marriage counseling specialists include private practitioners and others attached to clinics and organizations. There are also other people who may offer marital therapy as part of their main occupational role — such as members of the clergy or social workers.*

It was a few clergymen who first started calling themselves marriage counselors in the 1890s. Since then, associations have developed in many countries, including RELATE in the United Kingdom and the American Association of Marriage and Family Therapists. These organizations, as well as offering personal help, are increasingly working with industry.

Unhappiness in the home is a major cause of absenteeism and low motivation at work — many companies now arrange for marriage counseling, and personnel officers may be trained in counseling skills.

each partner put forward their point of view. The summarizing that therapists do from time to time enables partners to check that they have made their position clear. Rephrasing can provide elaboration or greater precision.

The talking treatment

Talking about problems you have not discussed before can be rewarding in a number of ways. It can lead to self-discovery, fresh understanding and clarification of difficulties. We often keep hidden our deepest and most personal concerns, and this may result in feelings of isolation. The opportunity to share our private world brings a temporary release from aloneness, and this in itself can be a very heartening experience. Indeed, if there has not previously been an opportunity to share feelings and worries in this way, just being able to tell someone might be all the help that is needed.

Putting thoughts, feelings, hopes and priorities into words is also an organizing process. Explaining is a way of thinking things through and improves our understanding of problems. The very act of self-disclosure, of sharing so much personal information, can provide an outlet for pent-up emotions. It was because of such powerful effects that Freud gave psychoanalysis the description "talking treatment." Most psychotherapies that are derived from psychoanalysis have this crucial element: the client talks about his or her feelings and problems. Couple counseling is no exception, though it becomes more complicated when both partners are present. **RB**

nneling

Providing feedback

ng
retations

WHICH THERAPY IS BEST FOR US?

■ *Lynne and John have decided to go for therapy because they are making each other miserable. They alternate between angry arguments, avoiding each other and strained attempts to act normal. For the past few weeks, Lynne has been so depressed that she has taken sick leave from her part-time job. Both are anxious about the effect their strained relationship may be having on their eight-year-old daughter. John feels they must either do something to get on better terms or else agree to part. What should they expect from their counseling sessions? There are four main approaches that the therapist may adopt.*

STUDYING PAST EVENTS

If their therapist takes a "psycho-dynamic" approach, they will each be encouraged to spend time focusing on their past.

Many of their disputes arose because each of them felt unsupported and under-valued in their career efforts. The therapist will want them to consider whether these needs and disappointments reflect child-hood experiences.

Perhaps, as children, both partners experienced competitive relationships with clever sisters and brothers. Comparisons made by themselves and their parents may have been painful, so they are still competing (though now with each other) in order to resolve lingering doubts about their own worth and ability.

Alternatively, Lynne may be trying to cope with conflicting roles: being a good mother and being a competent profess-ional. Much of the conflict here might be linked to how, as a girl, she imagined her future would be. John only had brothers, so he may not appreciate Lynne's emotional struggle.

SHARING THE RESPONSIBILITY

A therapist with a "systems" approach is more likely than other therapists to expect both partners to attend together, treating them as a unit. Lynne's difficulties will be seen as a symptom of John's, and John's as a symptom of Lynne's. The therapist will also be interested in how their daughter is reacting to, and perhaps contributing to,

the difficulties between them. The couple will be encouraged to recognize that just as John is frustrated by Lynne's tendency to moodiness and depression, Lynne's emotional problems are a response to his irritability and impatience. John has won-dered if Lynne should get psychiatric treat-ment for her depression, since she is so listless and is letting everything go. How-ever, a therapist who uses the systems approach will resist any suggestion that she is the one who is "sick." The couple will be encouraged to see that they are both responsible for their marital position, and that the situation is circular: John has a brusque, impatient manner that has acted as a constant "put down" for Lynne, caus-ing her to withdraw. In turn, Lynne's failure to communicate her feelings, plus her obvious unhappiness at times, cause John to feel helpless, inadequate, angry, and ultimately overwhelmed by the situation. They will also be encouraged to see that there are secondary benefits in the way they typically react to these conflicts: the tears and the temper are ways each of them chooses to gain the other's attention and also obtain a release from tension.

LEARNING NEW BEHAVIOR

A therapist taking a "behaviorist" approach will aim, as the name suggests, for changes in behavior. This will involve finding out what bad habits each partner has fallen into, what they do to upset each other and how they would really like each other to act. If John says he misses the affection Lynne used to show, and Lynne complains that John is not interested enough in her and in their daughter, the therapist will help them to identify more specifically what they miss or would like to change in each other. It may then emerge that, without realizing it, Lynne has gradu-ally become much less physically demon-strative (spontaneous hugs, good-bye kisses each morning, snuggling-up when watching TV). She may discover that she misses those moments of contact too. John, for his part, sees himself as "a family man" whose daughter and wife have every claim to his interest, so he may not under-stand what Lynne means. She might explain that he brings work home and is

▲ **A child faces a bewildering world**. *Learning to understand your childhood may help you to relate better to your partner.*

> **How will a therapist help us get over our problem?** ■ *There are four main approaches: uncovering hidden problems from the past, understanding your family as a whole, learning new behavior, thinking again about expectations.*

▲ **Incompatible activities** that undermine togetherness are the target of behaviorist approaches to therapy.

▼ **Learning a more flexible approach** to marital roles may help a couple avoid conflict. Partners should be realistic about what they expect from themselves and from each other.

often engrossed in novels or busy fixing things, so that although they are together a lot, he seems indifferent to their personal concerns, which leaves Lynne feeling lonely. If John wants to put this right, they will be encouraged to set aside some time each week when they can share news and family events. The behaviorist approach is based on learning principles and the idea of positive reinforcement. Each partner is helped to become more aware of what pleases the other so that each has a means of encouraging the other to become a better partner.

REDEFINING EXPECTATIONS

If the couple meet a marital therapist taking a "rational-emotive" approach, the emphasis will be on what each believes and expects with regard to themselves and their relationship. This therapist will focus on any unrealistic ideas they may hold about their marital roles. Lynne, for example, may see herself as responsible for the care of their daughter and only feel able to ask John to take this over as a favor. She will be encouraged to accept that nowadays we should not have this double standard, especially when partners share the "breadwinning" role.

John may say he has as much to cry about as Lynne but he never can, because he was told quite firmly as a boy that men should not cry. If they visit the rational-emotive therapist, the couple will be encouraged to question their "must not" and their "must" beliefs ("Why must the woman always care for the children?" "What is so terrible about a man crying?") The therapist will want them to identify the absolute or extreme views they hold in order to see that they are unreasonable and therefore worth modifying. The couple will go for therapy with their "shoulds," "musts," "oughts," and "I can't stand it as it is," and will be helped to be more rational and compromise their tough expectations of themselves. They will be encouraged to be more tolerant of each other's imperfections instead of constantly blaming each other.

WHICH IS BEST FOR US?

None of these approaches is better than the others. Some therapists find one particular framework so valuable that they use it all the time, becoming experts in that approach. Others describe themselves as "eclectic": they will pick and choose from the range of theories according to what seems most applicable to each client. Quite often different approaches have features in common. Most approaches, for example, would focus on the feelings underlying what a couple says. Similarly, common strategies include identifying when partners are not really hearing each other or are not understanding each other, and pointing out how their experiences and their perspectives differ.

The extent to which therapists give instruction and advice – that is, are directive or nondirective – varies from therapist to therapist and does not simply depend on which approach they prefer. However, a psychodynamic therapist is likely to be the least directive – individuals are helped to see for themselves any changes or practical implications suggested by the exploration of their past histories.

Anyone going for therapy might want to ask their therapist about their particular orientation and approach. Perhaps more significant than any of these distinctions, however, is that the helper should be genuinely concerned for the clients' welfare and committed to helping them achieve a more fulfilling relationship. **RB**

SEX THERAPY

■ If you feel unhappy about sex you are not alone: most people experience sexual problems or anxieties at some time in their lives (see Ch 9). Nevertheless, we often think of sex as a "natural" area of life that should come easily to us.

Consequently, if you feel anxious about your sex life or dissatisfied with it, it is easy to conclude that you are somehow abnormal. In fact, sex is something we need to learn about, whether it is from books, through discussions with friends, or simply through experience.

In most cases sex problems are dealt with by the partners themselves. We can learn slowly – by love, patience, experimentation, persistence and common sense – how to help each other when things go wrong. Even quite serious difficulties can often be dealt with by a caring and truly loving couple. However, many people have problems that cannot be resolved by self-help. Of all those who claim to have a sex problem only a small fraction seek professional help. The couples who do so may realize that they lack the ability to sort things out, or perhaps they are more demanding than those who do not turn to therapists.

Whatever the reason for seeking help with a sex problem – and they are many and complex – there are several different types of therapy available. Some conditions can be improved with drug treatment. Someone who is depressed, for example, might need an antidepressant. The improvement in their depression should allow their sex life to return to normal. Anxiety too, can adversely affect sex and can be relieved by drugs. Psychotherapy and other forms of "talk therapy" are useful, especially if the sexual problem originates from events in childhood or adolescence. Most people, however, do not need "depth psychology" approaches – simple information or advice can work wonders.

All these kinds of help could be called "sex therapy" but the term is usually reserved for those therapies that deal with sex problems in a specific way. This kind of sex therapy started in the 1960s with two American researchers, William Masters and Virginia Johnson, who applied behavior techniques to sex problems. Behavior therapy works from the belief that all behavior is learned. This means that disadvantageous behavior can be **un**learned. In the Masters and Johnson program, couples unlearned old, negative habits that were producing sex problems and learned new, more helpful ways of behaving.

Much of this work was based on laboratory research that showed, for the first time, exactly what happened to men and women during sexual arousal and intercourse. With this knowledge Masters and Johnson were able to teach couples techniques to increase their arousal and make sex more enjoyable. Their book "Human Sexual Inadequacy" enabled couples, and indeed professional counselors, to deal with sex problems in a new way. Clinics soon sprang up all over the United States and within a few years the methods became popular in many other countries. Sex problems that until then had been either dealt with privately by couples or left alone, were given professional treatment. Since Masters and Johnson, other experts have devised new approaches to sex problems.

WHAT TO EXPECT

One of the biggest problems about going for sex therapy is actually starting. It requires a lot of courage to take very personal and often embarrassing problems to a professional for help. Once you have overcome the initial embarrassment, though, things usually go well. A skilled therapist quickly puts clients at their ease and will spend some time at the start of the first consultation taking a detailed sexual and personal history from the couple. The couple is usually dealt with as a unit (whether they are seen together or separately) because on many occasions the partner who presents the problem is not actually the "patient." Often the couple's relationship is the patient – conflicts in their emotional life are having an adverse effect on their sex life.

What happens after this sorting-out phase varies from therapist to therapist. Some use only talk therapy. Some use films and other visual material to help the

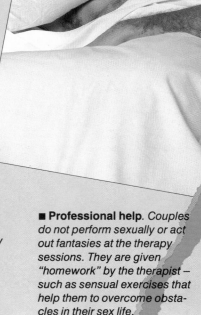

■ **Professional help**. Couples do not perform sexually or act out fantasies at the therapy sessions. They are given "homework" by the therapist – such as sensual exercises that help them to overcome obstacles in their sex life.

Should your sex life just happen "naturally?"
■ *Although experience, books and talk with friends are enough to teach most people all they want to know about sex, therapy may be worth considering, even for seemingly minor difficulties.*

■ **Self-help**. *Partners can often overcome their problems through love, patient experimentation and common sense.*

couple feel less anxious about highly erotic subjects. The majority of sex therapists actually do very little that is directly sexual.

WORKING THINGS OUT AT HOME

Many people thinking of consulting a therapist imagine that they will have to masturbate, have intercourse or act out fantasies in the consulting room, but anything physical is almost always done by the couple at home alone. As with any therapy based on learning, homework is given and is done by the couple – or one or other partner – in the week between therapy sessions. The feedback from these homework assignments is very useful both to the therapist and to the clients as they start to become more at ease with their sexuality.

The practical homework may involve "sensate focusing" where couples gradually learn to touch each other effectively, using massage. Each partner focuses on the pleasure felt from being touched and clients are encouraged to tell each other what they enjoy. At first, the massage is not sexual but gradually it develops into mutual genital massage and, later, intercourse.

Related to this is "desensitization." A couple may have to avoid touching each other because it makes them anxious. Massage can help reduce this anxiety. At first the couple must avoid foreplay or intercourse and only touch each other nonsexually. This prohibition on

sexual contact is vital: it takes the pressure off them to perform and to be "good lovers." They will be able to relax and to enjoy looking, feeling and holding in ways that were previously neglected. Repeating the massage several times helps them to communicate more confidently (see Ch 26). Some couples thus come to realize that intercourse is not an essential part of their enjoyment.

Bookwork is also used by some therapists if a lack of factual knowledge or understanding is the problem. But whatever the approach, the majority of the work is done by the couple between therapy sessions as they learn and grow together. Just how many sessions they will need and how long the whole process will take depends on the problem itself, the background of each partner, the state of their relationship at the time, the skills and style of the therapist, and much more. Sex therapy is, however, usually short-lived – couples usually experience improvements within weeks rather than months.

There are always cases that do not respond well to therapy and call for more in-depth psychological work. Such intervention will usually be necessary for those suffering from serious and persistent sexual problems such as perversions, extreme sexual tastes and needs, and criminal sexual problems.

Most day-to-day sex problems and disorders can be dealt with by a competent sex therapist, however, especially when the couple is well-motivated and willing to change and learn. **AS**

213

LEARNING ABOUT SEX

■ *M, a company director in his late thirties, met D while working abroad. After three years of otherwise happy marriage, the couple decided to consult a sex therapist. Both felt that their sex life was unrewarding. They enjoyed kissing and foreplay but intercourse gave them little pleasure. M ejaculated too quickly, leaving D inadequately stimulated. After the birth of their first child, D met other mothers in hospital and discussed sex with them. She had never been able to reach orgasm and began to feel that she was somehow missing out on the pleasure of sex.*

Therapy proved a great success, teaching the couple more about their sexual responses. D learnt to masturbate and M discovered how to stimulate her clitoris manually to bring her to a climax after he had ejaculated. Eventually M learnt to control his excitement and hold back his orgasm. He felt reassured that if he failed to do this he could always stimulate D with his hands – she preferred this technique in any case. Both were surprised to find that learning simple new methods improved their lovemaking. Feeling more confident about sex also brought them closer emotionally. **PG**

Enjoying Sex

MOST OF US want sex to be richly fulfilling, yet fail to understand just how we can achieve this. An important first step is to realize that practice and experiment can mean the difference between mechanical sex and an experience involving our whole personality. Many couples start a physical relationship without really having discovered each other sexually. Such hastiness may set a pattern that becomes ingrained, predictable and boring. The resulting dissatisfaction can become a major cause of infidelity, as one partner looks for sexual gratification elsewhere. Yet there is no need for that to happen. Thoughtful couples can quite easily escape the boredom trap, finding sexual adventure and developing interpersonal sensitivity within their existing partnership.

The secret of transforming the sex act into true lovemaking lies in learning, or relearning, the lessons of early sexual encounters between courting couples. When partners first meet and develop intimacy they tend to take steps one at a time, learning about sex together gradually. Experience in marital therapy shows that following a number of specific steps to mutual sexual discovery puts most couples on the right track. Some take a few hours, others a few weeks. There is no norm – be guided by what feels right for

you both – but slow rather than rapid progress should be your aim. In general, it is best to avoid intercourse until both partners have reached the appropriate stage.

Learning more about each other's bodies

Stage 1: Learning about his body. When the couple is alone, relaxed and happy, they should set aside some time for the woman to explore her partner's body. Both partners should be naked and warm, and the light should be left on. With her hands she can work her way around his body – but without genital contact at this stage – finding out which parts he likes caressed, and how. This exploration reveals the kinds of contact that give her partner pleasure, and those she should avoid. The couple can end this session kissing and cuddling – and afterward masturbate if strong sexual arousal is sparked off.

Stage 2: Learning about her body. Another day the couple can repeat Stage 1, but with the man exploring the woman's body. Breasts and genitals should be avoided. These first two stages will help you to feel relaxed and happy together – naked and in the light. You will have learned what gives you both pleasure and will feel comfortable with each other's warmth, touch, sound and taste.

Stage 3: Sensual massage. By now you should feel enough at ease to start learning sensual massage. This simply means using the hands to give your partner pleasure, without genital involvement or sexual arousal. Each of you

◄ **During courtship,** *the stages by which two people get to know each other physically are often over-hastily negotiated. Instead of studying each other's particular sexual make-up and special needs, the couple fall into narrowly pre-conceived patterns of petting, foreplay and intercourse – and these become habitual. For many couples the way forward to sexual happiness is to pause and recapitulate the original stages of mutual physical discovery – but this time in a way that is more considered and more considerate.*

Just how well do you and your partner know each other sexually? ■ *Consider a step-by-step program of sexual rediscovery* ■ *Begin by familiarizing yourselves with each other's bodies, genitals excluded* ■ *Go slowly.*

should take turns to be the giver and receiver. (In a loving relationship both are inseparable of course, as by giving you receive, and vice versa.)

The first step is arranging the setting. Make sure that the room is warm, and privacy assured. Some couples like to warm some massage oil, then settle down on a sheet laid on the floor; others simply prefer a bed. You can systematically learn massage techniques from instruction manuals or discover various methods for yourselves. Either way is equally rewarding provided that the atmosphere is relaxed enough to avoid any embarrassment.

The guiding principle in pleasurable massage is for the receiver to tell the giver what the massage feels like, and how to make it even better. Early on, you might find it helpful to rate the quality of massage on a scale from 1 through 5.

Mutual massage of this kind not only helps each partner intimately understand the other's body; it builds confidence in the receiver that the giver will not hurt them. These sessions also improve communication and this benefits everyday interaction as well. Most partners become more open with each other and more sharing once they start to massage in this way. Mutual massage can make couples feel so close that quarrels largely disappear from daily life. And as their technique improves with practice, many individuals sense a deepening bond between them and their partner.

STIMULATION THERAPY

■ *Marital therapists offer sexual enhancement programs designed to raise the level of sex interest lowered, perhaps, by childbirth, illness, marital friction or the routine of married life. The therapy helps improve the quality of sexual relations, too. One such program starts with various suggestions for heightening awareness of the senses. Here are some of them:*

While concentrating intently, with your eyes closed, try running your fingertips back and forth over surfaces with contrasting textures. Try slowly rubbing oil into your skin as you take a bath, constantly varying your touch. Make time to enjoy the sensations you produce, and search out the most pleasurable.

Sounds can be erotically stimulating – certain tones of voice or pieces of music, for instance. Different people will be aroused by different sounds and you and your partner may not always find the same sounds exciting. Consciously experiment.

Become aware of the subtly-different summery smells of warm, healthy skin on different parts of the body. Perfume users could experiment with new fragrances based on flowers or spices. Or they might choose a pleasantly scented joss stick, and burn incense as they summon up a sexual fantasy.

Before or during sex some people feel most aroused if their partner is not entirely naked but is partly clad – especially if what they are wearing has a special look or feel. Many men like women in black underwear, for example. Some women feel more aroused if their man wears a stylish bathrobe. Maybe you and your partner could try such clothes for fun. **P G**

215

◀ **Unself-conscious nudity** *in each other's presence, welcomed by both partners, is assumed to apply as the adventure of sexual rediscovery begins. But for many couples this cannot be taken entirely for granted. After perhaps years of avoiding total nakedness and undimmed lights (for self-conscious rather than romantic reasons), they may first need to* accustom themselves to these conditions by degrees, at the same time talking through any misgivings either partner may have about their own physical self-image.

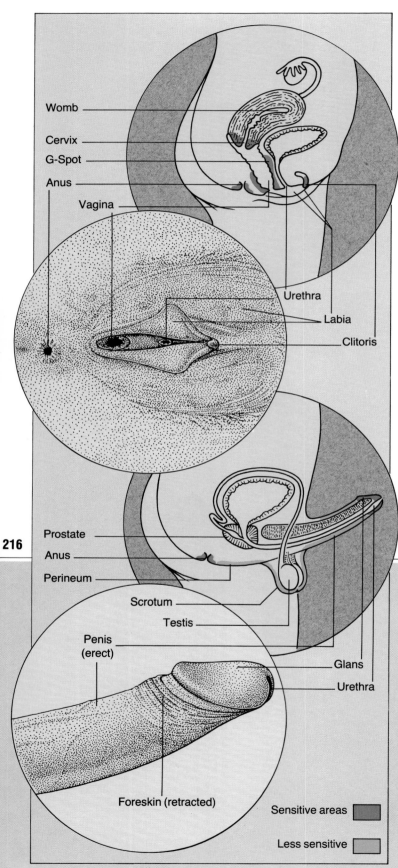

Womb
Cervix
G-Spot
Anus
Vagina
Urethra
Labia
Clitoris

Prostate
Anus
Perineum
Scrotum
Testis
Penis (erect)
Glans
Urethra
Foreskin (retracted)

Sensitive areas

Less sensitive

Stage 4: Genital anatomy. Once you and your partner can happily and confidently perform sensual massage for an hour, you are ready for more intimate sexual activity. Now you should take turns examining each other's sexual organs. If all this arouses you, cuddle and kiss each other and masturbate yourself afterward.

Learning more about arousal

Stage 5: She learns his arousal pattern. Once successfully past stage 4 of the course in mutual sexual rediscovery, a couple is ready for direct genital stimulation – but not yet sexual intercourse. At this stage the man shows the woman the kind of genital manipulation he finds arousing. In a clear enough light, she watches while he masturbates. Some people still frown on masturbation; but doctors are now generally agreed that it is a harmless way of relieving tension, while marital therapists unhesitatingly recommend touching one's own genitals as a good means of gaining confidence in one's sexuality. The woman should pay close attention to what her partner is doing. This means noticing the position of his body, where he puts his hands, how he caresses his genitals and other parts of his body, the rate and type of movement used, how he grips his penis, and what happens as his state of arousal peaks just before and at ejaculation. Then she notes the length and force of the first and later spurts of semen, when he stops self-stimulation, and how the attitude of his body returns to normal.

Once a woman has studied her man demonstrating this several times, she will better understand his pattern of arousal. That understanding helps to banish a common complaint among men that their partner cannot masturbate them in ways they enjoy. Also, understanding what arouses him is likely to make her more prepared to show him what arouses her.

SEXUAL ANATOMY AND AROUSAL

■ *As the precise shape, layout and sensitivity of the genitals can differ somewhat from one individual to another of the same sex, it is important to know how the generalized pattern relates to your partner and exactly what responds how to touch and manipulation. Although during orgasm the keenest pleasure seems to radiate from somewhere along the shafts of clitoris and penis alike, the hood of the clitoris and the looser skin covering the penis are not themselves all that sensitive. During arousal it is normally the tip of the clitoris* and the glans of the penis that are most sensitive – so much so that indirect stimulation is usually essential. Other highly sensitive areas in women may include the vaginal entrance, the area of the fabled G-spot, the cervix – and the breasts. Stimulation of the nipples of the breasts and the perineal area in both men and women can also be highly arousing. Arousal is never purely physical, however. It is the interpreted significance of what is happening – or imagined – that mainly determines whether physical stimulation turns you "on" or "off."

Do you really know enough about your partner's sexual anatomy? ■ *This is the stage of mutual familiarization: show and describe to each other your preferred way or ways of arousing yourself to orgasm.*

Stage 6: He learns her arousal pattern. Many women are shy about showing their partner how they stimulate their own genitals, yet this understanding is another vital landmark in a couple's journey of sexual rediscovery.

The man now takes his turn as pupil – learning exactly how the woman caresses herself to orgasm. He learns the answers to many questions. First, what is the position and attitude of her body? How does she stimulate her body, apart from the genitals themselves? Then, how does she touch her vulva before concentrating on the clitoris? How does she caress that – what movements, rhythms, pressures and positions does she use? How does her behavior alter as she becomes increasingly aroused? Does she insert anything in her vagina? If so, what and when? Meanwhile, what changes are there in her face, breasts, abdomen and skin? Is her stimulation continuous or does it stop from time to time?

Several sessions of detailed observation should help the man to answer all these questions and make him increasingly expert in appreciating his woman's arousal pattern. However, a woman's arousal pattern may change from time to time within her monthly menstrual cycle, and it may therefore take him longer to learn about arousal in her case than vice versa.

Learning what excites your partner most

Stage 7: Sharing fantasies. Fantasies often accompany self-stimulation in adolescence and later life. Most adolescent boys imagine having intercourse with girls they either know or see in photographs. For girls romance and emotional attachment generally matter more than unqualified erotic imagery. As part of the process of sexual rediscovery, you might tell each other about your adolescent fantasies and how these related to early masturbation. This can lead to discussions about your present fantasies. While you share these private secrets, you should cuddle each other tenderly.

Sharing present fantasies can prove more difficult than talking about the past. One partner might mistake the other's lightly thought-up fancies for deeply felt desires. The listener may then feel wounded or upset, especially when fantasies involve sex with someone else or sexual activity the listener dislikes. So you should go cautiously, withholding any fantasies likely to be misunderstood or cause distress.

218

BRINGING EACH OTHER TO ORGASM

■ Although the immediate purpose of the rediscovery program is to extend your knowledge of each other's sexuality and improve your techniques of arousal, how well your approach suits the mood of the moment – tender, abandoned, playful, serious, bawdy or collusively theatrical – remains as important as ever.

◄ **Mutual masturbation** can powerfully reinforce your partner's confidence that, for you, making love is as much a matter of giving pleasure as of taking or receiving it. This sensitive drawing conveys something of the tenderness and generosity

involved – in both directions – as one partner skillfully arouses the other to a peak of physical excitement.

► **"Let us roll all our strength and all our sweetness up into one ball."** Seeming to echo these famous words by the 17th-century poet Andrew Marvell, this deeply compassionate drawing emphasizes the unity, intensity and generative potential of fully reciprocated sexual love.

Both these drawings are by noted American artists.

Now begin to apply the knowledge you have gained ■ *Manually practice bringing each other to orgasm* ■ *Coach your partner, indicating what you like most, not what you dislike* ■ *Then try pleasuring each other simultaneously.*

Talking about fantasies may prove less successful than giving them some kind of indirect expression. One way of doing this is to play a game in which each partner writes a page-length outline for the script of an imaginary sex video. Each person includes whatever situations and events they find the most sexually exciting. Then they exchange scripts. As the partners learn which fantasies arouse each other, they can whisper stimulating little stories as they embrace, caress and mutually masturbate.

Giving each other more pleasure

Stage 8: Bringing each other to climax. Once you know your partner's arousal pattern, you can both learn to relieve each other's sexual tension by mutual masturbation. First comes scene-setting. You should warm the room, perhaps drink a little alcohol and play your favorite music. You might also enjoy reading a sexy book or magazine together or watch a video. Plenty of cuddling and maybe mutual bathing helps. Leave the light on because watching each other can be both instructive and exciting.

Lubricating the penis or clitoris is an important prelimin-

ary as dry skin can give rise to discomfort. As the woman grows aroused, the vaginal fluids she produces can be drawn up to the clitoris. Alternatively, KY jelly or saliva can be used.

You should settle into a comfortable face-to-face position, with genitals adjacent. Throughout this stage it is important to tell each other which sensations please you most, not which you most dislike – reward spurs learning and builds confidence much more effectively than punishment. One of the things you will probably discover is that stimulating just the penis or clitoris is not all you can do; simultaneously caressing a woman's nipples or vaginal entrance or a man's scrotum, anal area or nipples can often add greatly to the pleasure.

Once both of you can confidently masturbate each other in turn, you can learn to do this at the same time. Mutual masturbation enables each partner to give and receive pleasure simultaneously – after all, that is how most couples enjoy actual intercourse. However, there should be no stressful seeking after simultaneous orgasm – just mutual pleasure-giving where both climaxes arrive fairly close together. Concentrating adequately on your partner's needs when your own orgasm is imminent is not easy and may require some practice.

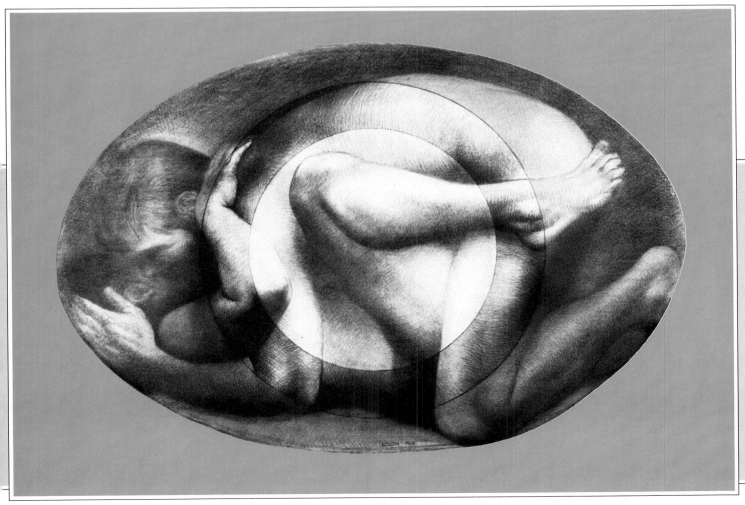

Controlling orgasm

Stage 9: Improving orgasm. While climaxing together can be very satisfying, most couples do not consider that a goal worth striving for. Yet many men complain that they climax much too soon for their partner's liking, and many women wish they could reach orgasm faster than they do. Stage 9 on the path to intercourse through mutual rediscovery involves controlling orgasms, so that the timing of them is more mutually satisfying.

Various techniques can speed up or slow down one partner's climax. Bathing or showering together and creative use of sex books, magazines and videos can help to syn-

chronize arousal. With her guidance, he may discover new stimulation patterns that help her to achieve repeated orgasms; in turn she can learn ways to slow him down (by varying her rhythm or by manually squeezing his penis, for example). Merely thinking unerotic thoughts may help him to delay ejaculation.

Stage 10: Intercourse. You are now ready for full sexual intercourse. You should avoid sexual gymnastics: the aim is simply sharing pleasure with help from your newly learned abilities to communicate and your willingness to experiment together.

Stage 11: Variety and development. After some weeks' successful intercourse you might try role swapping – for example, the partner who is usually more passive could lead the lovemaking. Taking turns like this lets both of you explore your whims and fantasies, perhaps revealing needs and possibilities unsuspected by the partner who is normally the most active.

Once a couple has achieved a mutually fulfilling and varied pattern of intercourse, they will usually find that their relationship has greatly strengthened and is much more likely to go on developing and to endure. Sexual partners who have forged a truly mutual bond are responsive to each

---

SETTINGS FOR LOVEMAKING

■ *Unusual settings can prove stimulating, although only those which offer guaranteed seclusion are suitable for more than mild foreplay.*

Making love outdoors appeals to many couples – and can be fun, if jagged surfaces, prickly plants and biting insects are avoided. Some couples enjoy lovemaking on a beach or mountainside, though most would regard such open sites as far too exposed to public gaze. Other couples find "forbidden" public settings in cities especially arousing when no one else seems to be about, and pride themselves on their skill at concealing or disguising what they are doing.

Some couples continue to enjoy the traditional adolescent pastime of teasing sex play in the back-row seats at the movies. Here, they come under no performance pressure, for unchecked responsiveness and actual intercourse are both barred.

Spontaneous lovemaking in unexpected indoor settings – in the kitchen or garage or on the stairs – is the most usual way of adding spice to a relationship. Indoor fantasy settings offer further, highly individual possibilities, including arranging the furniture and the lighting to create settings that you find romantic or exciting. For some, wearing fantasy costumes can heighten the illusion. **P G**

► **Sunlight and water in a secluded garden**. *You do not have to be a naturist to enjoy the special pleasures of open-air nudity. If the idea appeals and you are discreet enough, the experience of unhurried alfresco lovemaking can be immensely rewarding – as many couples have discovered.*

Think about varying your normal pattern, once sexual intercourse is resumed ■ *Do not be in too much of a hurry* ■ *Jointly plan ways of introducing variety* ■ *Allow pleasurable anticipation to heighten your response.*

other in many ways. Illness, business worries, bereavement, even the threat of a casual affair, are less likely to undermine a partnership where each knows that the other offers greater emotional and physical security and comfort than they could ever find elsewhere.

Erotic holidays

A sensual vacation – when you and your partner escape day-to-day routine to devote time to developing your lovemaking repertoire – can help consolidate the gains made by a course of mutual sexual rediscovery. The holiday could last an evening or a week: how long it lasts is less important than spending it on what you most enjoy together, both in and out of bed. Just quietly being together – perhaps cuddling silently in bed, or listening to music, or walking in the country – is as meaningful as lively sexual activity.

You should plan such treats ahead – anticipation is half the fun. Each of you could take turns in choosing events or situations that stimulate you most; then both of you could choose together. Before each holiday, the planner lets fall

tidbits of information to raise the other's level of anticipation. The couple could also exchange love tokens to be redeemed on holiday for, say, a sensual massage, breakfast in bed, lovemaking in a new location of the planner's choice, a new sexual position or pleasure or acting out a favorite fantasy. Exchanging such tokens daily for some time ahead builds up excitement and helps the lovers to prepare. One partner's tokens might contain instructions for an erotic game that calls for special toys or other articles. The other then has the fun of getting these together. Small personal touches matter just as much as genital events on an erotic holiday. The planner could have flowers sent to

221

■ **An erotic vacation?** *Therapists often advise couples to spend some time each year entirely on their own, well away from family and business worries and distractions. This gives them a rare opportunity not only to communicate at all levels without interruption but also to absorb themselves totally in each other's physical presence.*

the hotel room, and might also buy a small, inexpensive, sexy present as a first-night gift.

A weekend vacation gives time to develop a variety of sexual delights. You could agree to ban actual intercourse until the second day – such a ban itself can prove arousing. Meanwhile, you would indulge in nonpenetrative sexual delights: perhaps undressing for each other; taking sexy polaroid snapshots; making a sexy video; or performing prolonged erotic massage ending in mutual masturbation.

Genital lovemaking will probably be the focal activity of an erotic holiday, but you should also spend time getting to know each other again, as if you were still courting. An important part of that is talking intimately and candidly. Women in particular like their partners to reveal themselves as emotionally responsive and vulnerable.

Above all an erotic holiday should give scope for getting out of sexual ruts. You should try making love in new positions and locations, share any previously unshared dreams and fantasies, and be prepared to change your habits.

Most couples find that a vacation of this kind recharges their erotic batteries and enhances each partner's appeal to the other. Back home, you can discuss the best and least successful aspects of your outing. In fantasy and love talk you can relive your favorite moments while making love in

the weeks that follow. Some evening, undisturbed, you might even re-enact actual events.

Couples prepared to invest this kind of time and effort in their relationship enormously increase their joy in one another's sexuality. Togetherness then spills over into ordinary life, diminishing the number and intensity of potentially disruptive disagreements.

Communicating about sex

The mutual pleasure of lovemaking depends very much on both partners communicating what they want initially, in foreplay and in sexual intercourse. Many couples do not communicate effectively enough. In societies where women wait for men to make the first move women commonly endure frustration. Most Western women feel confident enough to indicate when they would like some love play, but couples may need practice in sharing. Often one partner wants lovemaking more than the other, who might be feeling tired or be angry about something outside the relationship. It is better to explain this than to let your partner think he or she is causing the difficulty.

Our sexuality is so central to our personality that we often find it difficult to discuss sexual preferences and problems with each other. This is especially true for people inhibited

EROTIC WORDS AND PICTURES

■ *Sexually exciting books, photographs and movies can play an important role in stimulation therapy. Sex therapists use such aids to teach understimulated people how to fantasize effectively as a way of heightening response.*

Kinsey's research in the 1940s and 1950s suggested that explicitly erotic items aroused men rather than women, who seemed to find romantic material much more titillating. However, modern laboratory studies show that women's sexual arousal increases as they look at sexually explicit pictures or listen to

erotic stories. Women in fact respond more strongly than men to stories with a sexual content, and as much as men to visual stimuli, especially when these show women taking the initiative. **PG**

▲ **A lighthearted but intimate moment** *is often a good time to mention a perhaps unexpected sexual need or whim. A mood of affectionate playfulness can*

itself be highly conducive to sexual experiment, especially if a mutually interesting item of erotica happens to be the focus.

Can you and you partner discuss your sexual preferences openly? ■ *Do you avoid topics that either of you finds difficult to talk about?* ■ *Do sexual disagreements ever prompt you to direct hurtful comments at your partner?*

by being brought up to think of sex as an intensely private matter. Even well-balanced couples can find sex discussions difficult, especially if things are going wrong in the relationship. The best course is to get into the habit of discussing sex openly and in a trusting way from the start.

Sex therapists find the following guidelines helpful:

First, learn to recognize and discuss subjects that either of you finds particularly hard to talk about. Her figure or his impotence are possible examples. Commonly, whenever one partner raises such a subject the other refuses to discuss it, and conversation stops or degenerates into a quarrel. Willingness to talk openly over any problem topic can soon cut down to manageable size even the most formidable barriers. If your partner has a problem, consider this with sympathy so that they end up feeling understood.

Never forget that your partner is also probably your best friend. Avoid damaging the friendship by hurtful comments sparked off by sexual disagreements. In any argument avoid scornful generalizations such as "How would you understand, you're only a man?" or "You're like all women, totally impossible." Such retorts can cause long-lasting damage.

Avoid assuming that your partner should automatically share your own enthusiasm or dislike of some sexual activity. Manipulative and unfeeling statements like "A woman who really loved me would have oral sex with me" are likely to arouse resentment – and distress in women who would much prefer expressing the love they feel in other ways.

Never use threats to get your own way. One day your partner might call your bluff. Moreover, emotional blackmail will damage your partner's sense of security and this could affect both of you for years. Few of us really want to lose our one-to-one love bond, so if you feel desperate enough to say something like "If you have another affair, I'm leaving you," seek professional help to solve the underlying problems.

Never punish your partner. When some people fail to win a sexual argument, they resort to sulking, silence, sexual withdrawal or become aggressive. This sort of behavior does not prove you were right. None of us treads an infallible path through the sexual minefield of myths, half-truths and misunderstandings.

Finally, bear in mind that separated couples cite poor communication as one of the major problems culminating in divorce. Lifelong sexual enjoyment is only possible between two people able to communicate their gradually changing needs and feelings. **AS**

223

BEING TACTFUL

■ *Most people are not mindreaders – it is up to each of us to communicate our sexual needs.*

Perhaps a woman dislikes making love when her man has a stubbly chin. Perhaps he finds her pajamas unattractive. tactful words ("I love it when your face feels smooth," or "It's much more exciting for me when you're naked") could make intercourse far more enjoyable. "It's lovely when you hold me close," encourages cuddling – itself an excellent aid to better sexual communication.

There is no need for either partner to endure easily pre- *ventable bad breath or body odor in silence. Dropping clear but kindly hints – with a smile – helps more than irritated protests.* **PG**

▲ **Open-mouth kissing,** *widely believed to be one of the hallmarks of heartfelt lovemaking. Although passion will often override physical "put-offs" like* *bad breath or body odor, enjoyable sex normally demands considerate attention to personal hygiene.*

Room For Other People

THE CHANGE from being a single person to being one of a pair is a dramatic shift from one way of life to another, but additional important relationships still continue. Family and friends do not cease to exist, and, if you stay in the same town or neighborhood, you will continue to have contact with your old acquaintances. As they become more committed to each other, and perhaps marry, partners are bound to experience some changes in the kind and degree of contact they have with other people. What changes can they expect in their social lives? How will old and new friends, relatives, in-laws and more casual acquaintances fit into their life as a couple?

Sometimes you want company, somewhere to go, a change of scene and activity. At other times you would rather stay at home and shut out the world. On the one hand, being part of a couple gives you greater choice. You can pursue activities that do not involve your partner (being with your own friends, for example, going to club meetings or playing a sport) or you can enjoy the security of having a special person with whom to share your leisure time. On the other hand, you may find that having a partner restricts your social activities. Your partner may have different ideas about how much socializing you both should do and about the friends you include in these activities.

Socializing as a team

The clear bonus of being one of a couple for anyone who enjoys an active social life is that their social circle more than doubles in size. A couple is likely to socialize as a unit. Invitations are generally sent to both (even if only one of the couple is known) and they are expected to show up together. This may occasionally be a disadvantage – for example, if you find your partner's office parties boring.

Partners may also function as a team with regard to their style of socializing or in coping with the more obligatory functions. If one person is an extrovert and the other more introverted, the more extroverted partner can enjoy being entertaining, or can communicate on behalf of both, leaving the shy partner feeling less pressured and more able to relax. A couple can take turns or divide the burden of being civil and attentive to less easy acquaintances. The one who finds it less irksome can patiently listen to an overtalkative

▲ **Doubling their enjoyment.** *Couples and friends go places and do things together because it enhances the experience.*

Whether you are watching a play or a movie or meeting new people, the fact that your companion can share or at least

understand your reactions makes them easier and more satisfying to express. As couples, we reinforce each

other's confidence at social gatherings and, by telling strangers about each other, we improve our self-presentation.

Can you let others into your life without damaging your relationship? ■ *Socializing as a couple calls for sensitivity and compromise, but it shares the rewards between two and spreads the burden of difficult obligations.*

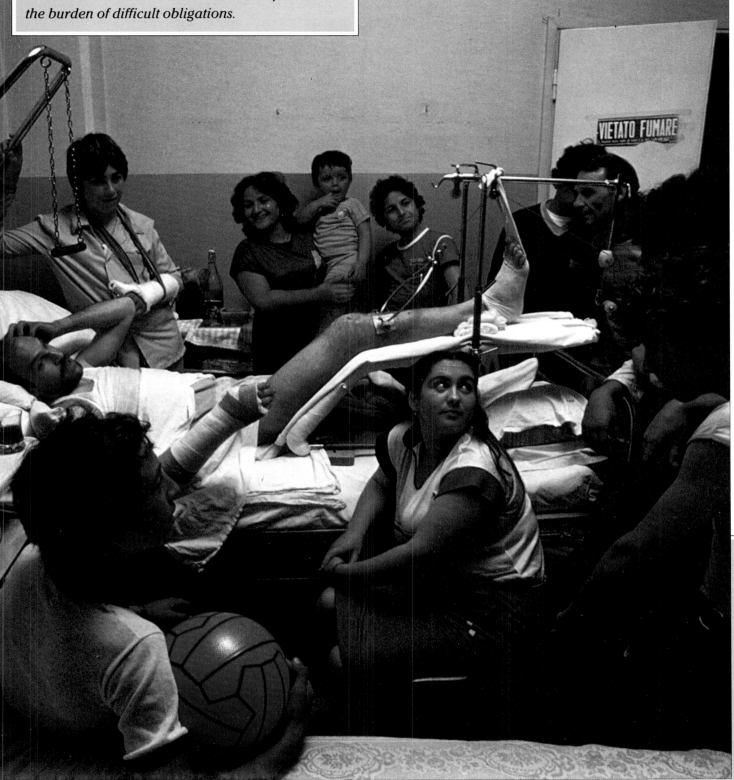

▲ **Welcome support or an invasion of privacy?** *This hospital room is crammed with friends and family in a public* statement of affection and caring. But how are the patient and his wife responding? Perhaps they would have preferred a quiet time together for mutual reassurance? Are the couple buoyed up by the group, or is the strain of reacting to others increasing their anxiety in an already tense situation?

neighbor. On another occasion they may request the return favor of being counted out from an uninspiring social call that does not require both to be present. In this way couples share their social responsibilities. Dinner party invitations can be tactfully declined when one partner is overstretched at work and needs an uneventful evening in which to recuperate. There are two to share the obligations of keeping in touch, two to fulfill expectations not easily met by one, and there are several times more options.

Can couples keep their friends?

Many modern couples regard each other as best friends as well as lovers but this does not mean that other friends suddenly become unnecessary. Experts have emphasized

the psychological need for everyone to have a variety of different relationships. Friendships can become even more important after marriage, because the togetherness of being in a couple tends to subdue individuality. Close contacts outside the marriage help to foster the growth of aspects of yourself that you do not express with your partner or your partner does not help you to develop. The psychotherapist Lillian Rubin makes the contrast between "we" and "me." Within the couple relationship a person finds comfort and security by being part of "we." But having other friends, some shared and some separately, is invaluable for each partner's separate and personal development, as a "me." This is not to say that being in a couple is always detrimental to self-development. To some extent partners

MAINTAINING YOUR IDENTITY AS A COUPLE

■ Could you guess what the relationships are between the five people in this group? They seem clearly to be friends, but are any two of them a couple? Even when merging with the crowd at parties partners tend

to maintain their identity as a couple by a subtle use of "tie signs" – body language signals by which they reaffirm to each other and advertise to the rest of the company that although there is room in their relation-

ship for other people, they remain special to each other. We also use tie signs to express friendship, but the particular way in which two people hold hands or stand beside each other can express a closeness

and an exclusivity that is more intense than friendship.

Lovers and best friends — will they clash or should they be the same person? ■ *How will your new partner affect your long-standing friendships?* ■ *Should you always put your partner first, or is there a way to manage both successfully?* ■ *How do friendships with other people increase your own potential for loving?*

promote each other's potential and can be flexible enough to allow each other far greater opportunity for new experiences.

Love relationships can be especially hard on single friends. Partners come first, and even very close, long-term friendships are liable to be treated as secondary. Single friends and couples can be an uneasy mix. Friendships between women in particular may encounter difficulties since they are often highly charged emotionally and involve a high level of mutual self-disclosure. With a new partner around, contact becomes three-way and this is likely to restrict communication. A married woman's loyalties to her husband may cause her to feel inhibited about discussing more intimate aspects of her life that she has previously been accustomed to share with her friends. Single friends in their turn may feel that their married friend's new role as a wife has changed her.

How friendship choices change

The number of friends a couple maintains during their life together varies to some extent. Newlyweds usually have about seven close friends, middle-aged couples have about

HOW FRIENDS CAN HELP

Help us develop new aspects of our personalities

Allow us independence from our partners

Introduce more variety into our social activities

Provide support if our partner is unavailable

Allow our partner time out from the relationship

▲ **Couples are part of a socially cooperative network** *that helps to make their life function smoothly and satisfyingly.*

227

■ **Can couples and singles mix?** *ABOVE Married people often find it difficult to socialize with unmarried friends. Even formerly close single friends may find themselves on the periphery of couples' lives. LEFT Female friends frequently talk to each other about their feelings and their relationships. When a woman marries and acquires a new "best friend" in her husband, she is less likely to confide in her single friends.*

three or four, and older couples have about six friends. This suggests that couples have different friendship needs at different stages of their lives. After marriage, for example, friendships tend to be curtailed in number and to become less intense. During the middle years of our lives, family relationships and obligations tend to come before our need for friendship. At this time, especially if our children are still quite young, they may be demanding a large amount of our time and attention, leaving less for other people. In later years, when the children are grown or when our partner has died or is retired, friendships tend to become more important again.

FRIENDS FOR THE UNHAPPILY MARRIED

■ *Talking to a friend about our feelings and experiences, whether they are trivial or serious, helps us to see them in perspective and evaluate them. This can be particularly important when we have problems – for example when a major life change, such as unemployment or even the birth of a baby, has strained our marriage. Friendships are beneficial to everyone and it is obvious that an unhappily married person will be helped by having close friends to confide in. More surprisingly, per-* *haps, if the marriage is a good one a close relationship between one partner and a friend can sometimes be harmful. A happily married person may feel resentful and even threatened if their partner spends a lot of time with and confides in another person.*

How many friends do you need as a couple?
■ *How do work, children and growing older change your needs and your abilities to make new friends together?* ■ *Why do couples instinctively relate better to other couples, and what do you look for in another couple's relationship?*

The places and situations where married couples first meet their friends may also vary according to their time of life, and their family commitments. During the early stages of the marriage, friendships typically develop with work colleagues, whereas during the middle stages, couples are more likely to develop friendships with their neighbors and with the parents of their children's friends. In the middle years, couples also spend a great deal of time with other family members, in comparison with the earlier and later years of marriage. As a couple enters old age, relationships are probably most difficult to establish because opportunities may not be so frequent. During this period, people who

▲ **Couples attract couples**. *Spending time with other married people helps to reinforce your chosen lifestyle. But unless both couples have a strong common interest, joint* *outings can be difficult to plan as men and women tend to want different things from friends. Men usually want company while women prefer to talk.*

live nearby or long-standing friends are the main sources of companionship.

When couples look for friendships it is often with other couples rather than with single friends. One explanation is that being with others who have also opted for a marital relationship is more reassuring for all the partners than spending time with single friends who have a different way of life. The newly married couple can see their commitment to each other mirrored in the commitment of other married couples, and they may benefit from watching others experiencing similar ups and downs. This may encourage them to think, "If they can sort out their difficulties so can we."

■ Do we always need friends?
ABOVE When a couple gets married it is important for them to feel confident and secure in their new role. As they are adjusting to the relationship it is common for them to isolate themselves, socializing less frequently. RIGHT In later years, when our children are grown up, and we may be retired, we have more time for friends.

229

However, finding compatible couples may pose problems since it is necessary for each member of the group to get on well with everyone else. Conflict may arise if a couple cannot agree on who are acceptable as friends. In addition, the partners in a foursome may have different preferences. One solution would be to do several activities in one evening: going to a restaurant and then seeing a movie, for example, might satisfy the tastes of all four individuals.

Research suggests that being friends with both members of another couple can have a positive effect on your marriage. Joint activities allow partners to share time together while at the same time benefiting from the company of other people. Much less satisfactory, however, is an arrangement where a foursome breaks down into pairs of friends, since this reduces the interaction between partners.

Gaining a partner, gaining a family

How well you and your partner get on with each other's relatives can have important implications for your life together. Relatives can, at best, be a vital source of love and support or, at worst, they may be endlessly troublesome. After a couple marries, relationships with their families are likely to change. Conflict may develop, for example, because of the need for the couple to maintain links with two families instead of one and to divide their time equally between them. The question often arises of where the couple should spend holidays and traditional family times like Christmas. In some cases relatives may undermine a couple's relationship, for example, if marital problems develop, relatives may not be supportive of the marriage and

How will relatives fit into your life as a couple? ■ *What lies behind the traditional in-law jokes and how can grandchildren help?* ■ *A good relationship with your partner's family can provide an extra source of support.*

may consider one partner to be solely responsible.

On the positive side, however, gaining a partner can mean gaining an extra support system in the shape of the partner's family. The years following marriage are often a time when family ties are re-established or built stronger. For many people relatives represent security, warmth and an increased number of people to rely upon. Relatives may provide both emotional support and functional support –

ARE RELATIVES A HELP OR A HINDRANCE?

■ *ABOVE Some newlyweds remain over-attached to their parents, frequently telephoning them for guidance. Bypassing their partners in this way can place a strain on the relationship. LEFT While many couples enjoy social activities with their in-laws, joint vacations can be difficult when the couples have few common interests. But family gatherings on special occasions are often very rewarding RIGHT. Children's birthday parties are an opportunity for three generations to get together in an undemanding way, increasing their sense of family solidarity.*

HINTS FOR HAPPIER SOCIALIZING

■ *Even if a couple find other close attachments problematic, it is still important to share your time with other people.*

● *Accept the fact that you and your partner will not always like the same people. Having friends you do not share is fine.*

● *Allow time for each of you to see your own friends and family.*

● *If you socialize with another couple, activities in which you can all participate equally are the most successful.*

● *If the members of your foursome have different interests, plan a balance of activities so that all of you are satisfied.*

● *Do not be surprised if you and your partner want different things from friendships: women are more likely to talk about their feelings with friends, while men are more likely to share a mutual interest in sports and activities.*

such as contributing money or extra help with jobs or children. Research has shown that young mothers, in particular, often benefit from the instructional and moral support of their own mothers. Children can provide additional links between the couple and the couple's parents: many grandparents draw great pleasure from their grandchildren, while the new parents benefit from their practical help with tasks like baby-sitting.

Although in some cases there is an element of truth behind the comic stereotype of in-laws as annoying people who either make too many demands on you or regard you as "not good enough" for their son or daughter, many people do get along extremely well with their partner's family and grow to love them dearly. The family may share some of the characteristics that attracted you to your partner. If you have never been close to your own parents and siblings, you may find that in-laws allow you a second chance to build warm, supportive family bonds. Similarly, if parents-in-law had children of only one sex, they may treat you as the daughter or son they had always wanted. Whether or not you are close to your own family, your in-laws can provide extra support if you can build on initial mutual regard and find a

way of setting aside any discrepancies in your values and priorities. In general, it is the wife who maintains ties with both her own and her husband's family. Wives report having most contact with family members of the same sex – for example, they feel closer to their mothers or mothers-in-law than to their fathers or fathers-in-law.

People often feel uncertain as to how they should address their parents-in-law: failure to clarify this from the outset may have an adverse effect on the relationship. Addressing in-laws as "you" sounds impersonal and even impolite, but calling them "Mom" or "Dad" may be too familiar. Some people reach an agreement before the marriage to call in-laws by their first names.

How do casual acquaintances fit in?

However self-sufficient a relationship may seem, no one lives in a social vacuum. Couples often find that they are expected to play a greater role in the community than a single person would and this can provide them with many social rewards. Local parks, shopping malls, libraries and recreation centers extend the arenas of private life and bring partners into contact with a large number of similar people living all around them. If we want to preserve the local amenities we enjoy, or to improve on the facilities that we find unsatisfactory, we can reinforce our sense of identity as a member of the community by supporting campaigns or serving on committees. Running youth clubs, collecting for charities, canvassing for local politicians or setting up crime-watch schemes – all these activities allow partners, either separately or as a pair, to enjoy social contact with those around them.

Research has shown that frequent contact with congenial neighbors may improve your chances of being a happy and healthy person. An intimate partner, good friends and supportive relatives, however, are by far the most beneficial kinds of relationships both physically and psychologically. Common activities shared by neighbors include talking, entertaining, helping out with practical matters – for

▲ **The impact of children on parents' leisure.** *When we have children we find ourselves going to different places and doing things at a different pace. Most couples report great satisfaction from family-based activities. Parents enjoy introducing their children to their own interests; they may also get unexpected fun from doing the things they used to do when they were children themselves.*

▶ **Being on good terms with neighbors** *reduces the potential for friction that comes with living side by side. It can also make important practical help available, especially in a crisis.*

How can you maximize the social rewards of being a couple? ■ *Getting involved in community affairs and sharing activities with neighbors can give your life a new dimension* ■ *Most couples value family-based leisure pursuits but it is important to balance shared time with time for yourselves.*

example, looking after pets or watering plants while one couple is away from home and providing essential food items in emergencies.

Sharing your leisure

Traditionally, we regarded leisure as something left over after we have spent a day at the office, done the housework, seen to the children, made sure elderly parents were managing and so on. Increasingly, however, leisure is being regarded as an integral part of our daily routines, encompassing activities which feed into our relationships and enhance them. As people have more choice and take more responsibility for the quality of their lives, so leisure

becomes central to our daily activity, rather than something that is squeezed in between work and chores.

For couples, leisure is not something that can only be achieved away from each other – football and beer for the men, coffee mornings or shopping expeditions for the women – but is increasingly linked to work and family life. Ideally, occupations and domesticity need not be so demanding that alternative pursuits are required as a necessary therapeutic escape route.

In a recent study of leisure pursuits in North America, it was found that informal, family-based pursuits like reading or talking to each other are the most highly valued. Other favorite pursuits tend to involve the children and relatives. Couples increasingly regard leisure and family pursuits as one and the same thing. Being together and having fun can coincide. Social life may require some time apart or at least the freedom to "do your own thing" if that is desired (see box), but modern relationships between couples tend to emphasize shared pleasure and recreation. **FD-M**

TIME OUT FOR RECREATION

■ *However close you are as a couple, now and again you may want "personal space" to enjoy hobbies or join clubs without your partner. Even if common interests were part of your original attraction to each other you will probably not share all the same recreational interests. Keeping up with separate leisure pursuits requires some time out from the relationship.*

Partners usually enjoy spending time with friends of the same sex. Even modern couples who have crossed the old sex-role boundaries tend to value the extra dimension that they find in friendships with someone of the same sex. This might be due to some special camaraderie, a common interest topic, distinctive kinds of male or female self-expression, or just being able to relax more easily when the opposite sex is not around.

Periods of leisure spent apart from each other can provide a channel for preserving your individuality and adding interest to your relationship. You should not feel guilty at developing your own interests. Nor should you go along with your partner's interests, if they do not appeal to you, from a belief that "togetherness" demands it. Allowing each other to have fun alone may keep the relationship alive better than always doing everything together. However, sharing an interest need not cramp

your individual style. There is obviously no harm in relaxing in the same pool or at the same hobby workbench. Even couples who are doubles partners in tennis or who act in the same dramatics group still have their separate parts to play. **RB**

▲ **Spending time with your own friends.** *It is a mistake to feel guilty about not sharing all your partner's interests: some separate recreation enhances rather than weakens the relationship.*

233

Shared Parenting

THE TRADITIONAL nuclear family – mother at home with the children, father out breadwinning – is rapidly becoming the exception rather than the rule in industrialized societies. Increasingly, women are part of the work force, and couples have to find new solutions for raising their children. Some opt for a co-parenting arrangement, with the husband and wife sharing the day-to-day care of the children – no longer a boss and a helper, but two equal parenting partners. They may decide mutually on this arrangement before the birth of their first child or negotiate it after the children arrive and old agreements no longer seem desirable.

What are the benefits?

Many women who work find that they still have full-time parenting responsibilities. They are doing two busy jobs without the time needed or the relevant financial reward. Having a husband share the burden of the children's daily care reduces the overload and allows the woman to establish another identity outside mothering.

For a man, shared parenting provides the opportunity for a closer relationship with his children. As traditional sex roles have loosened, a man now has the freedom to nurture and care for a child with no threat to his male identity. This involvement with his children can help a man to repair what may commonly be a wound from his own childhood – that he felt he never really knew his father (see *Ch18*).

For the children, co-parenting allows them to develop a close, intimate relationship with parents of both sexes. They can see themselves as either like father or like mother without being as restricted as children in more traditional families in their choice of adult models.

Growing up can offer the same diversity for them as it seems to have provided for both their parents. This is especially the case if both parents are earning incomes in addi-

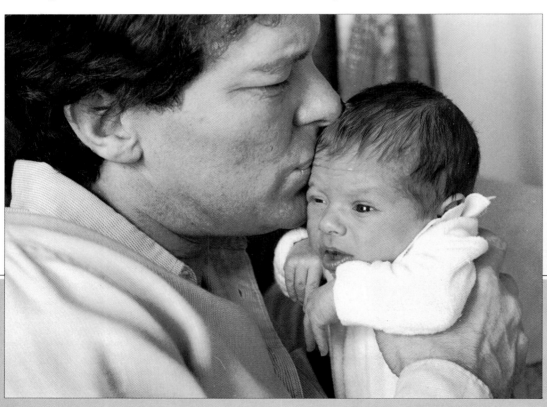

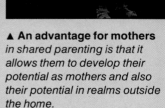

▲ **An advantage for fathers** in shared parenting is a closer relationship with their children. An advantage for children is that their education about the male sex role does not begin with the more usual male image of remoteness and lack of involvement.

▲ **An advantage for mothers** in shared parenting is that it allows them to develop their potential as mothers and also their potential in realms outside the home.

"I SAW THE NERVOUS LOOK IN HER EYES"

■ When Tim was born, David loved to hold him. But when he tried to change Tim's diaper he was all thumbs. Nancy, he felt, seemed to find it all so easy. He started to feel quite desperate every time the diaper leaked and the pins fell out. Then one day they went to visit a friend of Nancy's who had just had a baby. David saw the nervous look in her eyes as she attempted to put the baby's tiny arm into a woolly sleeve. "I know how to do that," he thought and after that he did. It was all a matter of confidence.

How involved with his children should a father become? ■ *A couple that is suited to the challenge can enhance their intimacy by sharing roles* ■ *Fathers benefit from being closer to their children, mothers from the opportunity to find self-expression outside the home, children from a wider pool of parental resources.*

tion to both taking turns to mind the baby. There is also safety in numbers. The children of a co-parenting couple will have the insurance of another equally competent carer should one be unavailable for any reason.

Can men and women share their roles?

Is it really possible for a woman and a man to share parenting? Biologically, of course, pregnancy, birth and breastfeeding cannot be experienced by a man, although this can be partially offset if the father takes an active part at the birth and helps care for the new baby.

New mothers today will not have had much more experience with babies than their husbands have. However, most cultures still, to some extent, expect certain roles of men and women – boys are sent outside to play but girls are psychologically prepared for motherhood with dolls.

The early family experience of today's mothers and fathers, who were themselves all raised primarily by women, also creates unique personality styles in males and females that affect their preparation for parenthood. The American psychologist Nancy Chodorow suggests that little girls raised by their mothers never develop a full sense of separateness from their female parenting figure. Mothers, for their part, perceive their female children as like them and even as an extension of themselves. This is why they may have greater difficulty in letting go of their daughters. The result is that a girl grows up very connected to another person. Out of this sense of connectedness come those attributes that will in turn make girls good candidates for mothering: empathy, nurturance and intuition about people's thoughts and feelings.

Boys follow a different course of development, precisely because they, too, are typically brought up by a woman who, for them, is an opposite-sex parenting figure. A mother

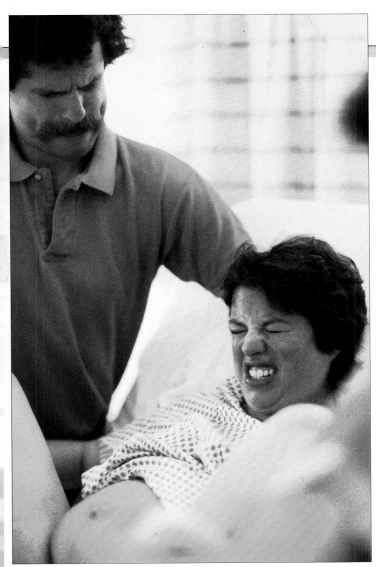

◀ **Shared labor**. Men who help at the birth of their children feel less excluded during the weeks of intense mother-infant bonding that follow. They are more likely to become intimately involved with the baby at an early stage. Most infants show outward signs of emotional attachment to their mothers by about eight months, to their fathers about a year later. Co-parented children may show attachment to their fathers by about one year, or earlier.

HOW INVOLVED CAN MEN BE?

■ *Pregnancy, birth and breastfeeding are the barriers which prevent a man from mothering like a woman. How do co-parenting couples deal with this?*

Make sure the father is present at the birth.
Supplement breastfeeding with bottles.
Let the father carry, rock and cuddle the baby.
Encourage the father to get actively involved with the baby immediately after the birth, taking advantage of his greater alertness and physical energy.

One research study has shown a direct correlation between reduced jealousy in the father about the mother's involvement with the baby and the success of the shared parenting arrangement.

WHAT DR SPOCK SAID

As early as 1958 the American physician Benjamin Spock in his highly influential books of advice to parents said: "A man can be a warm father and a real man at the same time...The time to begin being a real father is at the start." By 1979 he recognized that the father's responsibility should be as great as the mother's: "It will be a great day when fathers consider the care of their children to be as important to them as their jobs and careers."

perceives her son, quite early in his life, as very different from herself. Consequently, she raises him as an *other* to relate to, not an extension of herself. The boy, in turn, has the hard task of having gradually to disengage himself from his mother, who is there all the time, and turn to a more distant father to establish his identity or sense of himself as a male in the world. Unlike his sister he will grow up with a sense of being separate from his most familiar parent, the mother.

This separateness and the need to individuate himself from mother's daily influence in order to become a man, gives rise to a somewhat different set of personality attributes. Instead of empathy, nurturance and intuition, the male is likely to develop the more rational traits, such as thinking clearly, being analytic and objective, keeping emotions in check. These attributes do not prepare him for relationships and mothering. When a man and a woman decide to share parenting, it helps if they remind themselves of their different preparations for the role of caretaker, so that each can be sensitive to the other's gender experience.

Sex differences in parenting

Beyond everyday caretaking, parenting is also a very deep part of personal identity. Becoming a parent changes your view of yourself and your role in life. In this respect the psy-

DISCOVERING A DIFFERENCE

■ *Jeff and Louise are a shared parenting couple. Jeff recalls two incidents from their daughter's infancy. In one, Rachel was about to roll off the changing table. Both Jeff and his wife were present, but it was she who ran to catch the baby. In the other, their car skidded off an icy road. Jeff emerged from the car, dazed. He completely forgot about the baby in the back seat, while Louise went straight for her. In both instances they behaved without thinking. Jeff admitted later that he and Louise acted so differently because their daughter was simply more a part of Louise's life than of his. It was not that he was any less committed to his daughter than Louise, but that parenting was something that he did, and therefore something he could stop doing. With Louise, there was no such stopping, for a mother was something she was all the time.*

SEPARATE BUT EQUAL

*Men and women may approach parenting differently because of their own upbringing. This is true even for mothers and fathers who decide to co-parent. To assess whether a couple is successful in co-parenting it is best to use the "separate but equal" approach. That is, fathers will see parenting as an **activity they do**, mothers will see being a parent as **who they are**. Neither is right or wrong, better or worse. Marital harmony will be enhanced if couples can remember this separate but equal gender difference.*

On balance, shared parenting couples are the most likely to be successful in their relationships with one another and with their children. Fathers, watching mothers, learn to be more emotionally accessible to the children; mothers, watching fathers, learn to do parenting with a little more separateness. The better blend of styles can reduce distance between partners and create two highly successful parents.

236

LOOKING TO THE FUTURE

■ *What will happen to the children who grow up in the shared parenting family? According to the British psychologist John Bowlby, infants will usually attach to only one caretaking figure, which serves the infant best in his or her social-emotional development.*

Yet babies in shared parenting families attach quite well to two parents without any negative results. They achieve a sense of trust and stability in a world where more than one person is committed to and involved in their daily welfare.

And when the children grow up, we should expect a better balance within each of them, with men having better nurturing and emotional capacities and women more prepared to assert separate identities.

▲ **Time for fathering.** *Most men can and do give some of their time to parenting. However, the time is usually not spent on basic care but on shared recreation and on teaching their children skills. When they are not parenting, fathers find it easier than mothers to concentrate on other activities.*

Studies have found that, in spite of much more intense involvement with their children, co-parenting fathers, too, find it easier than mothers to put their children out of their minds.

Even full co-parents have male and female styles ■ *Even if you each give equal time to parenting, you should be prepared to find fathering a more detached activity, mothering a more totally absorbing commitment.*

chological experience of parenting is different for each co-parenting partner. One study found that men and women do not experience co-parenting in the same way. Because of their stronger sense of separateness men *do* parenting, while women, because of their stronger sense of connectedness, *are* parents.

Parenting is something that men *can* do and – it follows –

something they can stop doing. As one father explains, when it comes to leaving his child and going to work: "Out of sight is out of mind. I have no more thoughts about the kids throughout the day." His wife, in contrast, reports: "I can't do the on and off stuff. It's like my children are with me throughout the day." When she goes to work, she is still parenting.

Fathers' and mothers' co-parenting styles highlight these differences. Mothers are far more involved in buying and choosing clothes for their children. Mothers see to more of

MOTHER GUILT

■ *Shared parenting mothers try to blend a mothering identity with an extramarital role or career. But they find they are also mothers all the time. Their own early training for motherhood and the cultural message that women should be home with their children, help mothers who share parenting to feel more ambivalent about having two identities than the fathers do.*

One mother's lament about her son echoes that of many others when she says that sometimes she wants to rush back to the day-care center, scoop him up, and take him home. Other days she wishes she could just barricade herself in her office. The precarious physical and emotional balancing act may create a strong sense of guilt. The woman worries about her ability to be both a mother and something else without harm to her child.

Men do not feel this. No father guilt surfaces to match the mother guilt, because sharing fathers find that parenting is only one of the things they do, and since they do more than most men in the culture around them, they feel no cause for alarm.

237

SEPARATE MALE, CONNECTED FEMALE

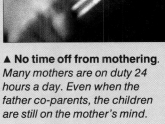

▲ **No time off from mothering.** *Many mothers are on duty 24 hours a day. Even when the father co-parents, the children are still on the mother's mind.*

◄ **In his first relationship,** *a baby boy feels no distinction between his mother's identity and his own; then he learns,* between one and two, that there is a difference between males and females. He learns to accentuate the separateness of his identity. Girls allow their sense of connectedness to continue much longer. This may be part of the reason why the boy will find it easier as a father to be apart from his children.

the psychological management of child rearing – making lists, keeping track of both functional and emotional needs of the child, carrying their child around in their heads. Fathers worry about their children less than mothers do and they handle separations from the children more easily. Fathers also seem better able to mind the baby while attending to something else, such as reading a book.

Why co-parenting may be difficult

It is unfortunately still true that women generally earn far less than men in the work force and these economic barriers may deter some parents from sharing. It tends to make more financial sense for the woman to stay home and for the man to go out to work. Another deterrent to fathers who wish to co-parent is lack of suitable provision in men's contracts of employment, such as flexi-time, paternity leave and leave to take care of sick children. This is bound to act as a disincentive.

Yet, despite all these influences pushing men and women into separate roles, research shows that any human being who can provide psychological and physical care and respond appropriately to a child's signals can nurture a child. Studies have shown that men can be as emotionally responsive and as capable as women. Increasingly, they are playing key roles in bringing up their children. The criteria for success are based less on the gender of the parenting figure, as on the availability, ability and desire of the person to do these things.

The image of a "real" man taking care of small children is increasingly popular. Advertisements with big bare-chested men cradling tiny babies appear on billboards and television screens, and there is wide acclaim for movies on the subject.

But, despite the rewards, there are also drawbacks for co-parenting fathers in real life. While some mothers and mothers-in-law of co-parenting men delight in becoming mentors to these "mothering" sons, this group also includes the harshest critics of the new arrangement – one that violates every norm of their own parenting career.

Neighbors and bystanders may still not be psychologically prepared to accept a man pushing a baby carriage. One father in a conservative American town recalls the hostile comments he received while strolling with his young

238

▲ **Parents need patience,** *stamina and, above all, ample self-esteem: as an occupation, parenting earns little social status. Men who can take great satisfaction from it are ones who know how to set and live by their own standards of achievement.*

▶ **"The model husband"** *is the satirical caption for this 1886 cartoon from "Harper's Monthly." Prestigious publications no longer ridicule men who share in domestic tasks, but many co-parenting fathers meet social criticism more directly, especially from members of the older generation of their own and their wives' families.*

daughter down the street. Male friends often feel they have lost their comrade to the world of women and children. The man taking his baby to a coffee morning with other new parents feels ill at ease as the only male parent in the company. Moreover, an employer may question the commitment of a male employee who misses a board meeting to attend a school play.

Successful role-sharing

To co-parent is in part to share the *role* of caretaking. Rearing a child includes the tasks and responsibilities of care, nurturing and socializing. Recent studies of American co-parenting couples found both men and women to be highly successful in role-sharing. The first requirement is that both parents should be available for a reasonable amount of time. A parent who wants to do shared parenting

THE BEST PEOPLE FOR THE JOB

■ *Who are the couples who stand the best chance of making a shared parenting option work? Research shows that they are:*
● *partners committed to gender equality.*
● *partners who already share household chores.*
● *partners who have mutual respect for each other's ability to parent.*
● *men who are willing to let family intrude in their work lives and who have jobs that would allow them to share parenting.*
● *women who are willing to give up some of the power of the hearth to a man.*
   If these requirements sound too difficult to live up to, it is worth remembering that even if you have to muddle through at first you are likely to improve in the process of sharing.

SHARED PARENTING STYLES

■ *Once a couple feels that they have the correct balance of ingredients for sharing, they can work out their own model to suit their lifestyle. It will probably fit into one of the following categories.*

SPLIT-SHIFT PARENTING
Each day one parent is responsible for the children while the other goes out to work, and then the two parents switch positions. This works best if, for example, both parents have part-time jobs.

ALL-HANDS-ON-DECK
Both parents work each day, while their child is looked after at school, at a day-care program, or by a babysitter. At the end of the day the family is all together, with a fluid sharing of responsibilities by mother and father. For example, whichever parent gets home first might start the dinner, bed and baths routine. When the other partner returns, he or she will read the goodnight story to the children before washing up.

MY TURN/YOUR TURN
One parent takes on the primary parenting for a period of time – in months or years – and then there is a reversal. This may occur when one partner decides to take a course or go back to work after staying home with the child for a year or two.

CATCH AS YOU CAN
The couple negotiates their tasks day by day. Whoever is more available takes on the parenting responsibilities, in the belief it will all even out in the end. This arrangement can only be successful if partners have work schedules that are mutually flexible.

239

◄ **Teamwork parenting** *can only work well if the other responsibilities of each parent allow them the time and the flexibility to be genuinely available. Both parents need a high commitment and a sense of confidence in themselves as carers.*

but is only available four hours a week is not contributing enough. A couple will also need flexibility in order to adjust the parenting schedule to each other's needs. For example, one year the couple may have a strict 50-50 time arrangement whereas the next year the schedule may shift temporarily to 60-40 as one parent enrolls in an advanced training program.

Parenting is also a *psychological* experience. Without the emotional commitment of both parents to the children and to each other as co-parenting partners, the arrangement can easily break down. For example, if a father repeatedly cries "I don't know how to do this 'mothering' stuff," and his wife is willing to take over, shared parenting will not work.

Finally, it is important that each parent should develop confidence in their ability to take care of a child, and a belief in him or herself as a good or good-enough parent. This is especially important for men. A father may feel he lacks expertise, but should realize that there are no child-care skills a man cannot learn.

Is co-parenting good for a marriage?

The reduction of the child-care burden for a woman and the opportunity for a man to be closely involved in his child's life can create greater intimacy in a couple as they both experience the cooperative endeavor of raising a child together.

On the other hand, because of differences in the way they react, sharing parents can create tensions for themselves, as each wants the other to parent "my way." Child rearing is, after all, a very emotional experience.

In the traditional family, conflicts about raising the children can erode a marriage. Often there is a lack of understanding of each other's very different roles in parenting. Tension may grow if one of the children has emotional or physical problems or is going through a difficult stage. The mother may feel consumed by the huge responsibility; the father, feeling helpless to solve the problem, may resent the fact that his wife, too, cannot put things right, and may feel he has lost his partner to the child's all-demanding orbit. However, if they are sharers and can divide between them the care of such a child, both parents not only get a breathing spell but also discover that they can build each other up rather than tear each other down.

With or without difficult children, the feelings that are expressed and shared in the co-parenting family, as husband and wife handle the daily tribulations of parenting, can serve to consolidate their relationship. Such shared experience can provide the psychological glue to bond the couple over time.

Leaving time for each other

Although shared parenting can create bonds it can sometimes threaten intimacy because it requires considerable time and energy. Often 50-50 parenting actually adds up to

DRAWN TOGETHER OR PUSHED APART?

■ *Working closely together can help to consolidate a relationship. However, it can create conflict as differences of opinion emerge about how the work should be done.* TOP *A son has brought home a school report. Will his father, casting a male eye on the facts of the situation, react in harmony with his wife, who is focusing her maternal eye on the child in the situation?* BOTTOM *Sharing the work of parenting can be so time-consuming that partners find no time for their relationship.*

Co-parenting sometimes makes intimacy more difficult ■ *Dangers to watch for include tensions over the right way to do the job* ■ *Be sure to reserve some time for your own relationship – get to know a reliable babysitter.*

100-100 parenting, each partner highly committed to the children. At the end of the day it is not two, but four hands immersed in the tub giving the baby a bath. With both partners facing work and parenting, there is little time left to devote to each other as a couple.

Sharing parents should ensure that time together does not revolve only around parenting discussions or negotiations. If life centers completely around the children all feelings of romance and sensuality can get lost, and the couple may be vulnerable when the time comes for the children to leave home. The husband and wife should avoid the pitfalls of becoming so child-centered that they lose the capacity to be alone with each other.

Some co-parenting couples do this by setting aside time each night after the children are asleep to have a drink, often with the rule "No talk about the kids." Others arrange to have a date for dinner or a concert each week. A weekend away is especially helpful. While someone trusted cares for the children, a couple has enough extended time alone, without the interruptions of child minding, to rediscover and nurture their adult relationship. **DE**

▲ **Shared experiences** provide the psychological glue to bond a couple over time. Sharing recreation, like this pair and their baby setting off for a hike in British Columbia, is fundamental to creating intimacy, but – for the right couple – sharing in addition the work of building the family, rather than dividing it into male and female tasks, can be another part of the togetherness that their relationship achieves.

Revitalizing Your Relationship

NEW relationships are exciting. In the early stages of knowing someone we are interested and attentive and eager to learn about them. We feel that the relationship grows and deepens every day. But as time passes and we get used to each other our initial curiosity and involvement may wane. When our partner speaks, we do not always listen. We stop asking about our partner's experiences, thoughts and feelings. Routine and predictability replace spontaneity and novelty. What has happened to the relationship and what can we do to recapture the interest lost between us? Can we, as a couple, continue to grow and to broaden our horizons together as the months and years go by?

Relationship stagnation

It is more difficult to keep relationships alive and growing today than it was in the past. There are three important reasons for this. First, people live longer now than ever before. Couples who manage to avoid divorce or separation can expect to spend more years together than their ancestors did. Second, because everybody has more leisure time than they used to, couples find themselves with more free time together. Third, our levels of expectation have changed. Modern couples tend to expect their relationships to be more interesting and challenging than couples of earlier generations did. As a result, they view stagnation as a more serious threat to their relationships.

One sure sign that a relationship has stopped developing is boredom. When one or both partners become bored for whatever reason, they begin to dislike each other's company. Interactions with the partner are simply too much effort – are not rewarding enough to be worthwhile.

A second indication that a relationship is no longer thriving is that both partners begin to feel neglected. As long as a relationship is thriving, partners are interested and involved with each other. If it stops growing, the couple sometimes begin to take each other for granted or turn their attentions to other things. The consequence is that one or both feels devalued, unappreciated and ignored by the other. This kind of situation can spiral into one of ever-decreasing interest, communication and satisfaction. For example, if one partner grows tired of the relationship, they

◄ **Is your relationship all that it should be?** *Locked into a boring routine, partners may fail to draw out the vitality they once inspired in each other.*

When intimacy becomes dull familiarity should you just accept it? ■ *From time to time in every relationship there is a need to rekindle the pleasures of anticipation that made courtship a time of excitement.*

may begin to withdraw from it, shifting all their interest and energy to their job, friends and hobbies. The less the couple communicates, the more bored with the relationship the partner becomes. As their boredom increases, they with-

draw further. Not surprisingly their partner feels neglected.

In any relationship, the transition from involved to uninvolved may be so gradual that neither partner is aware it is happening at the time. He may vaguely remember a time when she would ask for and discuss his opinions and stories. Now she does not confide in him the way she used to. He thinks "She's not interested in me any more."

When people feel neglected and bored, they look for stimulation and satisfaction from other sources. Someone who has grown tired of their primary relationship may devote more and more time to their job, to other people or to other activities. But although the new activities may temporarily relieve the tedium, they can also lead to further problems. When things get really bad, one partner may find someone more interested and more interesting than the current partner, and end up having an affair or even leave.

Being realistic

No relationship can keep up a consistently high level of excitement and involvement over a long period. But relationships *can* continue to grow; boredom is not inevitable. If you feel that your relationship may be wilting (see box) the first step is to recognize where the boredom lies. Are you and your partner bored with each other – as individuals – or do you find your way of life tedious?

The second step toward dealing with stagnation is to be realistic about the amount of interest and involvement that you can cope with on a daily basis. Some couples go to

▲ **Playing the fool together,** a couple find light relief. A relationship will quickly regain lost vitality if partners can rediscover a shared sense of humor. Enjoyable times occur often in the early days of a relationship and the happiest couples are those that continue to have fun and make each other laugh. Taking time out from everyday demands of careers, friends and hobbies may also help them to recapture the novelty and excitement of their initial attraction.

243

IS YOUR RELATIONSHIP STAGNANT?

■ *Here are some of the warning signs that your relationship is beginning to stagnate.*
● *Conversations with your partner do not interest you.*
● *You are able to predict everything your partner says and does.*
● *Rather than spending your free time with your partner, you are usually busy with your own friends and engage in activities that do not include your partner.*
● *You make up excuses or find reasons to avoid spending time with your partner.*
● *Romantic times together are few and far between because neither of you makes the effort to plan for them.*
● *If you have children, they are all you and your partner talk about.*
● *When you and your partner spend time together, you are usually engrossed in separate activities (such as reading) or in activities that do not involve much attention (such as watching television).*
● *You begin to consider the possibility of seeing other people.*
● *You spend more time reminiscing about the past than planning for the future with your partner.*
● *You stop thinking of ways to surprise your partner.*

such desperate lengths to inject life into their relationships that their attempts seem false and unnatural. The goal is not to live life at fever pitch. Rather, you and your partner should focus on ways of keeping the relationship vital and growing.

Many people spend far more time each week looking after their cars and lawns than their relationships. But no one can hope to have a growing relationship without devoting some time to maintenance. How much time do you spend each week really working at your relationship – planning times to be together, writing notes, doing thoughtful things, preparing surprises? The first step involves these simple but very important maintenance activities (see *Ch19*).

Talking to each other

However, simple maintenance is not enough. You also need to communicate properly. Some couples find this puzzling. "We talk to each other every day," they may say. But do you have the sort of intimate and lively conversations you had in the early stages of your relationship? And what do you mainly discuss? If you have children are they and their needs the main topic of conversation or do you also talk about wider topics that interest you both? Do you ever talk about yourselves as a couple? One of the topics you and

your partner *should* discuss is the current state of your relationship. Be open about any feelings of stagnation you may have felt, and share ideas for invigorating the relationship. Unfortunately, research has shown that any discussion about the state of the relationship is taboo with many couples. Some people find it so difficult to talk about their feelings that they refuse to discuss their relationship at all. Others may do it so easily and so often that their partners accuse them of "pulling up the plant to see how the roots are growing," and resist their efforts at communication. Each couple needs to find a level of communication that is comfortable for both partners. It is important for us to recognize that keeping a relationship thriving over a prolonged period of time is difficult. Often what is needed is a certain amount of candid discussion and conscious planning when the time is right for both partners.

How a couple communicates is at least as important as how much they communicate or what they talk about. Are you a sympathetic listener? Partners who make an effort to be attentive, truly interested in the other and emotionally expressive do have more intimate and interesting discussions; and their discussions all help to keep their relationship growing. One American study found that chronic, self-centered complaining is among the most disliked characteristics in a partner and can stultify a relationship. Partners should of course feel that they can discuss their difficulties with each other but constant grumbling is different from confiding in a partner and being responsive to the advice or sympathy they can offer.

People also become bored when their partners only talk about trivial or superficial things. Paradoxically, we often

HOW TO BROADEN YOUR HORIZONS

Flirt with each other. Teasing and touching can restore the warmth and involvement you enjoyed during the early days of the relationship.

Use humor positively. You do not need to be a stand-up comedian with a running patter of one-liners. Rather, look for the humor in everyday situations.

Try new things together. Do things neither of you has done before. Develop new joint interests. You may have far more fun than you ever imagined.

Surprise your partner. Do thoughtful things. Break routines with spontaneity and unexpected plans. Keep your partner guessing (but not about your feelings!)

Set aside time to talk. It is all too easy to put jobs, children, social events and hobbies ahead of your partner. But regular two-way conversations are vital.

Share enjoyable activities. This not only provides opportunities for interaction, but makes the relationship more enjoyable and rewarding.

Nurture individual growth. Pursue independent interests. Two continually developing people combine to create a more vital relationship.

Stay attractive. Take care of your physical appearance and reward your partner for doing the same. It is much easier to remain interested in a partner we find attractive.

◄ **Strategies for relationship growth** *focus on the couple's development as individuals as well as partners.*

HOW TO AVOID BEING A BORE

■ *Here is what you can do to make sure you are an interesting partner.*
● *Try not to be preoccupied with yourself or to complain constantly about your own difficulties.*
● *Show interest in and sensitivity to your partner's problems and point of view.*
● *Avoid talking only about the few topics that interest you, particularly if your partner is not very interested in them.*
● *Do not be passive and withdrawn when your partner tries to engage you in conversation.*
● *Become involved, express your opinions and emotions and be enthusiastic.*

have our least intimate interactions with the people closest to us, and with whom we are supposedly most intimate. Someone whose obsession with football makes him dominate conversations, recounting the course of each game, lecturing about game strategy, and detailing the personalities and abilities of the players, is bound to make his partner feel alienated. Similarly, partners whose contributions to conversations involve repetition of old stories and stale jokes are unlikely to hold the other's attention. What seems to be most important in the art of conversation is providing substance and variety.

Play together and stay together

In the early stages of their relationship, couples do a lot together. They go to movies, concerts and restaurants, they take walks together and spend endless hours just talking. Often, as the relationship develops, they seem to do less together. This not only limits the sheer amount of contact the partners have, but very much reduces the amount of fun for them both. One survey of American couples showed that 40 percent of them felt they had too little time together. There are many reasons why this is so, among them are the demands of work, domestic chores and children.

■ **Joint activity**. *For this Italian couple and their children it can mean a family outing TOP. Family activity can bring partners close (see Ch10) but* allowing children to dominate conversations or activities may result in parents neglecting their relationship with each other. BOTTOM LEFT *An elderly* couple express intense enjoyment at the races. Shared interests not only contribute to partners' initial attraction for each other but may continue to draw them together throughout their life. BOTTOM RIGHT *A German couple have fun making pasta.*

It is not leisure time in itself but *shared* leisure activities involving interaction that determine whether a couple is satisfied or not. Quality – rather than quantity – is what counts. Simply spending time together in apparently shared but independent activities (such as watching television) is not satisfactory to a lot of couples. This does not mean that couples have to avoid those kinds of activities. But it does suggest that activities that involve both partners may be better for the relationship.

Because many things can interfere with leisure time, couples need to make a conscious effort to do enjoyable things together. This need not mean extravagant spending on vacations or an expensive evening out. The important thing is to have pleasant experiences together, away from the hassles of everyday life. An occasional lunch or walk together or a time set aside for conversation at the end of the day are inexpensive and valuable ways of enjoying each other's company. Many busy couples are able to schedule a special time each week for these kinds of activities. They may have lunch together every Wednesday or reserve Monday nights for conversation, as a change from household chores.

Unfortunately, many people have not learned to value their leisure. We may feel guilty about taking time out for other things. Or we may simply not recognize how important leisure is for our well-being and that of our relationship. We may not have learned how to make the most of free time. Although many couples have a lot of free time to spend with each other, they often waste it on understimulating activities that involve little interaction or communication.

ENRICHING YOUR RELATIONSHIP

■ *There are many ways of enriching relationships. Couples can plan activities that help them to get to know each other, stimulate mutual growth and rejuvenate their relationship. For example, some couples might want to choose a stimulating book to read each month, then spend an hour or two a week discussing it. Others might plan an ongoing joint project on which they can work together – such as building a new patio, serving on a community fund-raising committee or taking skiing lessons. You and your partner should work out together what joint activities feel "right" for you.*

Another approach to relationship enrichment is to attend workshops and retreats designed to help couples to invigorate their relationships. The first programs of this kind were a result of the marriage-enrichment movement, but many are now available for nonmarried couples. In these programs the focus is on healthy rather than troubled couples. Instead of counseling couples who are already unhappy and dissatisfied, enrichment programs are designed for couples who are generally satisfied with their relationship, but who feel a need to explore ways of making it even more interesting and rewarding.

> ***Grow and develop together*** ■ *Research finds that relationships are more dynamic when each partner has a strong sense of individuality, making it stimulating to be with them and to share their continuing sense of personal growth.*

Although shared leisure activities are important, this does not mean that couples have to spend every available moment together. On the contrary, overexposure to our partners can become very stifling. It can also hinder our individual growth and self-fulfillment. A stimulating relationship requires togetherness, but we need to strike a balance between spending time together and doing things separately.

This "balancing act" poses a challenge for many couples. Each of us has our own ideas about what proportion of free time we should devote to our partner and what proportion to our own interests.

Conflicts can occur when partners disagree on the amount of time they should spend together. Often one partner feels that as a "couple" they should spend virtually all of their free time in joint activities.

The other may want time to perform with a local theater

▲ **Fulfilled as individuals, fulfilled as partners**. *Li Shuang, a Chinese artist who fell in love with a French diplomat, triumphs in creativity as well as love. After being sentenced to two years in a re-education camp, she was allowed to join her partner in France in 1984. Here they appear together in Paris at an exhibition of her paintings. Pursuing an interest in which your partner does not participate need not undermine your relationship. Achieving the right balance between togetherness and individuality, you can stay interested in your partner and keep them interested in you.*

troupe, or to become involved in civic activities, for example. When couples are faced with this common problem, negotiation and compromise are essential.

Individual growth

Researchers have found that relationships are more dynamic when each partner has a strong sense of *self*. Recognizing that neither of us is wholly responsible for the other's happiness – but that each of us is responsible for our own – can be a very liberating insight.

This may sound paradoxical. It suggests that the strongest relationships are those in which the two partners have the greatest individuality. But research seems to indicate that people who are unfulfilled *as individuals* will be unhappy and unfulfilled as partners in a relationship.

If this is the case people may be able to enrich their relationships through continuing to grow and develop as individuals. Many experts believe that the best starting point is for each partner to encourage the other's sense of personal fulfillment. It may help if they discuss ways in which they would like to improve as individuals.

A relationship is less likely to go stale when the two people are committed to continued personal growth for themselves and each other. Although many people seek opportunities for their own personal growth, some fail to recognize that the promotion of individual growth in a relationship works both ways. Partners do and should continue to expand their own personal horizons, but they must also encourage and reward the other for doing the same. This helps to preserve the relationship from sameness.

Sometimes growth and change in a partner can seem threatening. People may feel neglected and become jealous and insecure because of individual pursuits if they are afraid that their partners will grow away from them. Often too, one partner's interests and activities mean that the other has to make sacrifices and adjustments. Even so, the alternatives – stagnation, lack of self-fulfillment and dissatisfaction – are far more likely to undermine a relationship in the long run. Individual growth is not a threat to partners who are committed to their relationship. As each partner brings new experiences back to the other, the relationship is infused with novelty and growth. **MRL ATJ**

▶ **The bond of intimacy** *makes each couple special. Knowing each other more thoroughly than anyone else does, we develop unique patterns of communication, sharing and caring. The most vital relationships are between partners who constantly renew this sense of being special for each other.*

READERS may want information about other aspects of a subject, or detail on particular topics that have aroused their interest. Some generally available books and periodicals suggested for further reading are listed below. The main published sources consulted by the contributors to this book follow the further reading suggestions.

1 Needing a Special Person
Duck, S 1983 *Friends, for Life: the Psychology of Close Relationships* Harvester, Brighton; Haddon, C 1985 *The Powers of Love* Michael Joseph, London; Lynch, J J 1979 *The Broken Heart* Harper and Row, New York.

2 What Makes a Couple
Davis, K E 1985 "Near and Dear: Friendship and Love Compared" *Psychology Today*, 19, pp22-4; Hatfield, E 1988 "Passionate and Companionate Love" in Sternberg, R J and Barnes, M L (eds): *The Psychology of Love* Yale University Press, New Haven and London; Sternberg, R J 1988 "Triangulating Love" in Sternberg, R J and Barnes, M L (eds): *The Psychology of Love* Yale University Press, New Haven, CT and London.

3 Finding, Matching and Attracting
Murstein, B I 1986 *Paths to Marriage* Sage, London; Duck, S 1988 *Relating to Others* Dorsey Press, Chicago, IL.

4 Pairing Off
Brehm, S 1985 *Intimate Relationships* Random House, New York; Duck, S 1986 *Human Relationships* Sage, London.

5 Love and Commitment
Alberoni, F 1983 *Falling in Love* Random House, New York.

6 Maintaining Individuality
Cargan, L and Melko, M 1982 *Singles: Myths and Realities* Sage, Beverly Hills, CA; Storr, A 1963 *The Integrity of the Personality* Penguin, Harmondsworth.

7 Opting for Marriage
Blumstein, P and Schwartz, P 1983 *American Couples* Morrow, New York; Gillis, J R 1985 *For Better, For Worse: British Marriages, 1600 to the Present* Oxford University Press, Oxford; Newcomb, M D 1987 "Cohabitation and Marriage: A Quest for Independence and Relatedness" *Applied Social Psychology Annual*, 7, pp128-56; Stephenson, J 1986 *Women's Roots* Diemer, Smith, Napa, CA.

8 How Couples Have Changed
Coverman, S and Sheley, J F 1986 "Change in Men's Housework and Child-Care Time, 1965-1975" *Journal of Marriage and the Family*, 48, pp413-22; Kenrick, D T and Trost, M R 1987 "A Biosocial Model of Heterosexual Relationships" in Byrne, D and Kelly, K (eds): *Males, Females and Sexuality* State University of New York Press, Albany, NY; Marshall, M 1984 *The Cost of Loving* G P Putnam's Sons, New York; Schwartz, P 1987 "The Family as a Changed Institution" *Journal of Family Issues*, 8, (4), pp455-9.

9 Making Love
Cauthery, P and Stanway, A 1985 *The Complete Guide to Sexual Fulfillment* Century Hutchinson, London; Comfort, A 1972 *The Joy of Sex* Mitchell Beazley, London; Dixon, A 1985 *For Yourself; A Woman's Guide to Sexual Fulfillment* Fontana, London; Stanway A 1988 *A Woman's Guide to Men and Sex* Century Hutchinson, London.

10 Thinking of Parenthood
LeMasters, E E and DeFrain, J 1989 *Parents in Contemporary America: A Sympathetic View* Wadsworth, Homewood, IL; Menning, B E 1977 *Infertility: A Guide for the Childless Couple* Prentice Hall, Englewood Cliffs, NJ; Pfeffer, N and Woollett, A 1983 *The Experience of Infertility* Virago, London; Stanway, A 1984 2nd edn *Infertility: A Common-Sense Guide For the Childless* Thorsons, Wellingborough, Northamptonshire; Veevers, J E and Figley, C R 1980 *Childless by Choice* Butterworths, Toronto; Whelan, E M 1980 *A Baby?...Maybe* Bobbs-Merrill, New York.

11 Extramarital Affairs
Atwater, R 1982 *The Extramarital Connection* Irvington, New York; Buunk, B and Van Driel, B 1989 *Variant Lifestyles and Relationships* Sage, Newbury Park, CA; Lake, T and Hill, A 1979 *Affairs, The Anatomy of Extramarital Relationships* Open Books, London.

12 Falling Out
Brehm, S S 1985 *Intimate Relationships* Random House, New York; Kingma, D R 1987 *Coming Apart: Why Relationships End, and How to Live Through the Ending of Yours* Conari Press, Berkeley, CA; Phillips, D with Judd, R 1978 *How to Fall Out of Love* Warner Books, New York; Weiss, R S 1975 *Marital Separation* Basic Books, New York.

13 Contemplating Divorce
Price, S J and McKenry, P C 1988 *Divorce* Sage, Newbury Park, CA; Krantzler, M 1973 *Creative Divorce: A New Opportunity for Personal Growth* M Evans, New York.

14 Starting Again
Pasley, K and Ihinger-Tallman, M (eds) 1987 *Remarriage and Stepparenting* Guilford Press, New York; Wallerstein, J S and Kelly, J B 1980 *Surviving the Breakup* Basic Books, New York.

15 The Mature Years
Hatfield, E and Walster, G W, 1982 *A New Look at Love* University Press of America, Lanham, MD; Wasow, M 1976 *Sexuality and Aging* School of Social Work, University of Wisconsin, Madison, WI.

16 A Sense of Intimacy
Hendrix, H 1988 *Getting the Love You Want: A Guide for Couples* Henry Holt, New York; Marsh, P (ed) 1988 *Eye to Eye. How People Interact* Salem House, Topsfield, MA; Rubin, L 1983 *Intimate Strangers* Harper and Row, New York.

17 Ideals and Realities
Mansfield, P and Collard, J 1988 *The Beginning of the Rest of Your Life? A Portrait of Newly-Wed Marriage* Macmillan, Basingstoke; Scarf, M 1987 *Intimate Partners: Patterns in Love and Marriage* Century, London; Skynner, R and Cleese, J 1983 *Families and How to Survive Them* Methuen, London.

18 Expectations of the Opposite Sex
Osherson, S 1986 *Finding Our Fathers* Free Press, New York; Rubin, L 1983 *Intimate Strangers* Harper and Row, New York.

19 Sustaining Your Relationship
Duck, S 1988 *Relating to Others* Dorsey Press, Chicago, IL; Hendrick, C and Hendrick, S 1983 *Liking, Loving, and Relating* Brooks/Cole, Monterey, CA; Mace, D and Mace, V 1974 *We Can Have Better Marriages If We Really Want Them* Abingdon Press, Nashville, TE.

20 Better Communication
Blumstein, P and Schwartz, P 1983 *American Couples* Morrow, New York; Duck, S 1986 *Human Relationships* Sage, London; Folger, J and Poole, M S 1984 *Working Through Conflict* Scott, Foresman and Company, Glenview, IL; Gottman, J, Notarius, C, Gonso, J and Markman, H 1976 *A Couple's Guide to Communication* Research Press, Champaign, IL.

21 Understanding Each Other
Berenson, F 1981 *Understanding Persons: Personal and Impersonal Relationships* Harvester Press, Brighton; Fromm, E 1957 *The Art of Loving* Allen and Unwin, London; Mischel, T (ed) 1974 *Understanding Other Persons* Blackwell, Oxford.

22 A Sound and Happy Marriage
Dindia, K and Baxter, L A 1987 "Strategies for Maintaining and Repairing Marital Relationships" *Journal of Social and Personal Relationships*, 4, pp143-58; Duck, S 1988 *Relating to Others* Dorsey/Open University Press, London and Chicago IL; Fitzpatrick, M A and Badzinski, D 1985 "All in the Family: Interpersonal Communication in Kin Relationships" in Knapp, M L and Miller, G R (eds): *Handbook of Interpersonal Communication* Sage, Newbury Park, CA.

23 Managing Together
Blumstein, P and Schwartz, P 1983 *American Couples* Morrow, New York; Brehm, S 1985 *Intimate Relationships* Random House, New York; Hertz, R 1986 *More Equal Than Others: Women and Men in Dual-Career Marriages* University of California Press, Berkeley, CA.

24 The Difficult Partner
Carter, S and Sokol, J 1988 *Men Who Can't Love* Berkley, New York.

25 Getting Therapy
Dominian, J 1984 *Make or Break: An Introduction to Marriage Counselling* SPCK, London; Knight, L 1986 *Talking to a Stranger: A Consumer's Guide to Therapy* Fontana, London.

26 Enjoying Sex
Gillan, P 1987 *Sex Therapy Manual* Blackwell Scientific Publications, Oxford; Heiman, J and Lopiccolo, J 1977 *Becoming Orgasmic: A Sexual Growth Program for Women* Prentice Hall, New York; O'Connor, D 1987 *How to Make Love to the Same Person for the Rest of Your Life* Bantam, London/New York; Stanway, A 1988 *A Woman's Guide to Men and Sex* Century Hutchinson, London.

27 Room for Other People
Bell, R R 1981 *World of Friendship* Sage, Beverly Hills, CA; Block, J D 1980 *Friendship: How to Give it, How to Get it* Macmillan, New York; Rubin, L B 1985 *Just Friends: the Role of Friendship in Our Lives* Harper and Row, New York.

28 Shared Parenting

Ehrensaft, D 1987 *Parenting Together: Men and Women Sharing the Care of Their Children* Free Press, New York; Kimball, G 1987 *50/50 Parenting: Sharing Family Rewards and Responsibilities* Lexington Press, Lexington, MA.

29 Revitalizing Your Relationship

Broderick, C 1979 *Couples: How to Confront Problems and Maintain Loving Relationships* Simon and Schuster, New York; Curran, D 1983 *Traits of a Happy Family* Winston, Minneapolis; Laurence, L T 1982 *Couple Constancy: Conversations with Today's Happily Married People* Research Press, Ann Arbor, MI.

CONTRIBUTORS' SOURCES

1 Needing a Special Person Argyle, M and Henderson, M 1985 *The Anatomy of Relationships* Penguin, Harmondsworth; Bowlby, J 1965 2nd edn *Child Care and the Growth of Love* Penguin, Harmondsworth; Broadhead, W E et al 1983 "The Epidemiologic Evidence for a Relationship Between Social Support and Health" *American Journal of Epidemiology*, 117, pp521-37; Duck, S 1983 *Friends, for Life: the Psychology of Close Relationships* Harvester, Brighton; Erikson, E H 1980 *Identity and the Life Cycle* Norton, New York and London; Harré, R, Clarke, D and De Carlo, N 1985 *Motives and Mechanisms: an Introduction to the Psychology of Action* Methuen, London; Kelly, H H and Thibaut, J W 1978 *Interpersonal Relations: A Theory of Interdependence* Wiley, New York; Lewis, M and Rosenblum, L A (eds) 1974 *The Effects of the Infant on its Caregiver* Wiley, New York; Richards, M P M 1974 "First Steps in Becoming Social" in Richards, M P M (ed): *The Integration of a Child into a Social World* Cambridge University Press, London; Rusbult, C E 1980 "Commitment and Satisfaction in Romantic Associations: A Test of the Investment Model" *Journal of Experimental Social Psychology*,16, pp172-80; Stern, D 1977 *The First Relationship: Infant and Mother* Fontana, London; Wright, P 1984 "Self-Referent Motivation and the Intrinsic Quality of Friendship" *Journal of Social and Personal Relationships*, 1 (1), pp115-30.

2 What Makes a Couple Davis, K E 1985 "Near and Dear: Friendship and Love Compared" *Psychology Today*, 19, pp22-4; Blumstein, P and Schwartz, P 1983 *American Couples* Morrow, New York; Hatfield, E 1988 "Passionate and Companionate Love" in Sternberg, R J and Barnes, M L (eds): *The Psychology of Love* Yale University Press, New Haven and London; Sternberg, R J 1988 "Triangulating Love" in Sternberg, R J and Barnes, M L (eds): *The Psychology of Love* Yale University Press, New Haven, CT and London; Wright, P H 1985 "The Acquaintance Description Form" in Duck, S and Perlman, D (eds): *Understanding Personal Relationships: An Interdisciplinary Approach* Sage, Beverly Hills CA; Wright, P H and Bergloff, P J 1984 "The Acquaintance Description Form and the Study of Relationship Differentiation" Paper presented to the 2nd International Conference on Personal Relationships, Madison, WI.

3 Finding, Matching and Attracting Adelman, M and Bankoff, E (in progress) *A Study of Personal and Relational Needs of Jewish Singles* Department of Communication Studies, Northwestern University; Austrom, D and Hanel, K 1981 "Psychological Issues of Single Life in Canada: An Exploratory Study" *International Journal of Women's Studies*, 8, pp12-23; Buss, D M and Barnes, M 1986 "Preferences in Human Mate Selection" *Journal of Personality and Social Psychology*, 50, pp559-70; Dillard, J P 1987 "Close Relationships at Work: Perceptions of the Motives and Performance of Relational Participants" *Journal of Social and Personal Relationships*, 4, pp179-93; Folkes, V S 1982 "Forming Relationships and the Matching Hypothesis" *Personality and Social Psychology Bulletin*, 8, pp631-6; Guttentag, M and Secord, P F 1983 *Too Many Women? The Sex Ratio Question* Sage, London; Lynn, M and Bolig, R 1985 "Personal Advertisements: Resources of Data About Relationships" *Journal of Social and Personal Relationships*, 2, pp377-83; Lynn, M and Shurgot, B A 1984 "Responses to Lonely Hearts Advertisements: Effects of Reported Physical Attractiveness, Physique, and Coloration" *Personality and Social Psychology Bulletin*, 10, pp349-57; Mainiero, L A 1986 "A Review and Analysis of Power Dynamics in Organizational Romances" *Academy of Management Review*, 11, pp750-62; Murstein, B I 1986 *Paths to Marriage* Sage, London; Spreitzer, E and Riley, L E 1974 "Factors Associated with Singlehood" *Journal of Marriage and the Family*, pp533-42; Walster, E et al 1973 "'Playing Hard to Get': Understanding an Elusive Phenomenon" *Journal of Personality and Social Psychology*, 26, pp113-21.

4 Pairing Off Baxter, L and Wilmot, W 1985 "Taboo Topics in Close Relationships" *Journal of Social and Personal Relationships*, 2, pp253-69; Baxter, L and Wilmot, W 1984 "Secret Tests: Social Strategies of Acquiring Information About the State of the Relationship" *Human Communication Research*, 11, pp171-202; Bell, R and Daly, J 1984 "The Affinity-Seeking Function of Communication" *Communication Monographs*, 51, pp91-115; Cate, R, Henton, J, Koval, J, Christopher, F and Lloyd, S 1982 "Premarital Abuse: A Social Psychological Perspective" *Journal of Family Issues*, 3, pp79-90; Cate, R, Huston, T and Nesselroade, J 1986 "Premarital Relationships: Toward the Identification of Alternative Pathways to Marriage" *Journal of Social and Clinical Psychology*, 4, pp3-22; Cate, R M and Lloyd, S A 1988 "Courtship" in Duck, S (ed): *Handbook of Personal Relationships: Theory, Research and Interventions* Wiley, London and New York; Christopher, F and Cate, R 1985 "Premarital Sexual Pathways and Relationship Development" *Journal of Social and Personal Relationships*, 2, pp271-88; Duck, S 1988 *Relating to Others* Open University Press, UK and Brooks/Cole, Monterey, CA; Jessor, R, Costa, F, Jessor, L and Donovan, J 1983 "Time of First Intercourse: A Prospective Study" *Journal of Personality and Social Psychology*, 44, pp608-26; Kerckhoff, A C 1974 "The Social Context of Interpersonal Attraction" in Huston, T L (ed): *Foundations of Interpersonal Attraction* Academic Press, New York; Markman, H 1981 "Predicting Marital Distress: A 5-year Follow-Up" *Journal of Consulting and Clinical Psychology*, 49, pp760-2; Murstein, B I 1976 *Who Will Marry Whom?* Springer, New York; Peplau, L, Rubin, Z and Hill, C 1977 "Sexual Intimacy in Dating Relationships" *Journal of Social Issues*, 33, pp89-109; Winch, R E 1958 *Mate Selection: A Study in Complementary Needs* Harper and Row, New York.

5 Love and Commitment Berscheid, E and Walster, E 1974 "A Little Bit About Love" in Huston, T (ed): *Foundations of Interpersonal Attraction* Academic Press, New York; Kelley, H H 1983 "Love and Commitment" in Kelley, H H et al (eds): *Close Relationships* Freeman, New York; Lee, J L 1973 *Colours of Love: An Exploration of the Ways of Loving* New Press, Toronto; Marston, P J, Hecht, M L and Robers, T 1987 " 'True Love Ways': The Subjective Experience and Communication of Romantic Love" *Journal of Personal and Social Relationships*, 4, pp 387-407; Plato 1969 *The Symposium* transl Joyce, M in *Plato: The Collected Dialogues* Princeton University Press, Princeton, NJ; Rubin, Z 1973 *Liking and Loving: An Introduction to Social Psychology* Holt, Rinehart and Winston, New York; Sartre, J P 1957 *Existentialism and Human Emotions* Philosophical Library, New York.

6 Maintaining Individuality Adams, M 1976 *Single Blessedness: Observations on the Single Status in Married Society* Heinemann, London; Blumstein, P and Schwartz, P 1983 *American Couples* Morrow, New York; Cargan, L and Melko, M 1982 *Singles: Myths and Realities* Sage, Beverly Hills, CA; Erikson, E H 1980 *Identity and the Life Cycle* Norton, New York; McAdams, D P 1988 "Personal Needs and Personal Relationships" in Duck, S (ed): *Handbook of Personal Relationships* Wiley, London; Maslow, A 1962 *Toward a Psychology of Being* Van Nostrand, London; Rogers, C R 1961 *On Becoming a Person* Houghton Mifflin, Boston, MA; Spreitzer, E and Riley, L E 1974 "Factors Associated with Singlehood" *Journal of Marriage and the Family*, 36, pp533-42; Stein, P J 1976 *Single* Prentice-Hall, Englewood Cliffs, NJ; Storr A 1963 *The Integrity of the Personality* Penguin, Harmondsworth; Storr, A 1988 *The School of Genius* André Deutsch, London.

7 Opting for Marriage Aronson, E and Linder, D 1965 "Gain and Loss of Esteem as Determinants of Interpersonal Attractiveness" *Journal of Experimental Social Psychology*, 1, pp156-71; Blumstein, P and Schwartz P 1983 *American Couples* Morrow, New York; Gillis, J R 1985 *For Better, for Worse: British Marriages, 1600 to the Present* Oxford University Press, Oxford; Hafner, R J 1986 *Marriage and Mental Illness: A Sex-Roles Perspective* Guilford, New York; Martinson, F M 1970 *Family in Society* Dodd, Mead, New York; Miller, H L 1972 *Loving: A Psychological Approach* Wiley, New York; Newcomb, M D 1981 "Heterosexual Cohabitation Relationships" in Duck, S and Gilmour, R (eds): *Personal Relationships 1: Studying Personal Relationships* Academic Press, London; Newcomb, M D 1987 "Cohabitation and Marriage: A Quest for Independence and Relatedness" *Applied Social Psychology Annual*, 7, pp128-56; Scanzoni, J 1979 "A Historical Perspective on Husband-Wife Bargaining Power and Marital Dissolution" in Levinger G and Moles, O C (eds): *Divorce and Separation* Basic Books, New York; Stephenson, J 1986 *Women's Roots* Diemer, Smith, Napa, CA.

8 How Couples Have Changed Campbell, J 1988 *The Power of Myth* Doubleday, New York; Coverman, S and Sheley, J F 1986 "Change in Men's Housework and Child-Care Time, 1965-1975" *Journal of Marriage and the Family*, 48, pp413-22; Davidson, B, Balswick, J and Halverson, C 1983 "The Relation Between Spousal Affective Self-Disclosure and Marital Adjustment" *Home Economics Research Journal*, (11), pp381-91; Davidson, B, Balswick, J and Halverson, C 1983 "Affective Self-Disclosure and Marital Adjustment: a Test of Equity Theory" *Journal of Marriage and the Family*, (45), pp93-102; Kenrick, D T and Trost, M R 1987 "A Biosocial Model of Heterosexual Relationships" in Byrne, D and Kelly, K (eds): *Males, Females and Sexuality* State University of New York Press, Albany, NY; Mace, D 1979 "Marriage and Family Enrichment – a New Field?" *The Family Coordinator*, (28), pp409-19; Marshall, M 1984 *The Cost of Loving* G P Putnam's Sons, New York; Mishkind, M E, Rodin, J, Silberstein, L R and Striegel-Moore, R H 1986 "The Embodiment of Masculinity" *American Behavioral Scientists*, 29, (5), pp545-62; Rubin, L 1983 *Intimate Strangers* Harper and Row, New York; Rubin, Z 1973 *Liking and Loving* Holt, Rinehart and Winston, New York; Schwartz, P 1987 "The Family as a Changed Institution" *Journal of Family Issues*, 8, (4), pp455-9; Waring, E M and Chelune, G J 1983 "Marital Intimacy and Self-Disclosure" *Journal of Clinical Psychology*, (39), pp183-90.

9 Making Love Bancroft, J 1983 *Human Sexuality and its Problems* Churchill Livingstone, London; Cauthery, P and Stanway, A 1983 *The Complete Book of Love and Sex* Century Hutchinson, London; Cauthery, P and Stanway, A 1985 *The Complete Guide to Sexual Fulfillment* Century Hutchinson, London; Masters, W H and Johnson, V E 1966 *Human Sexual Response* Little Brown & Co, Boston, MA; Potts, M and Diggory, P 1983 *Textbook of Contraceptive Practice* Cambridge University Press, Cambridge; Stanway, A 1988 *A Woman's Guide to Men and Sex* Century Hutchinson, London; Stanway, A 1988 *Preparing for Life* Viking, London; Stuart, R 1980 *Helping Couples Change* Guildford Press, New York.

10 Thinking of Parenthood Clark, A M and Clark, A D B (eds) 1976 *Early Experience: Myth and Evidence* Open Books, London; Hill, M, Lambert, L and Triseliotis, J 1989 *Achieving Adoption with Love and Money* National Children's Bureau, London; Hoffman, L W, Thornton, A D and Manis, J D 1978 "The Value of Children to Parents in the United States" *Journal of Population*, 1, pp91-131; Kadushin, A 1971 2nd edn *Adopting Older Children*

CONTRIBUTORS' SOURCES CONTINUED

Columbia University Press, New York; LaRossa, R and LaRossa, M 1981 *Transition to Parenthood: How Infants Change Families* Sage, Beverly Hills, CA; Miller, B C and Myers-Walls, J 1983 "Parenthood: Stresses and Coping Strategies" in McCubbin, H and Figley, C (eds): *Stress and the Family I: Coping with Normative Transitions*, pp54-73, Bruner/Mazel, New York; Miller, B C and Sollie, D L 1980 "Normal Stresses During the Transition to Parenthood" *Family Relations*, 29, pp29-35; Rowe, J 1982 *Yours by Choice* RKP, London; Sollie, D L and Miller, B C 1980 "The Transition to Parenthood As a Critical Time for Building Family Strengths" in Stinnett, N, Chesser, B, DeFrain, H and Knaub, P (eds): *Family Strengths: Positive Models for Family Life*, University of Nebraska Press, Lincoln, NE; Tizard, B 1977 *Adoption: A Second Choice* Open Books, London; Triseliotis, J 1973 *In Search of Origins* RKP, London; Triseliotis, J and Russell, J 1984 *Hard-to-Place: The Outcome of Adoption and Residential Care* Heinemann/Gower, London.

11 Extramarital Affairs Bartell, G D 1971 *Group Sex* Wyden, New York; Buunk, B 1980 "Sexually Open Marriages" *Alternative Lifestyles*, 3, (3), pp312-28; Buunk B and Bringle, R 1987 "Jealousy in Love Relationships" in Perlman, D and Duck, S (eds): *Intimate Relationships: Development, Dynamics and Deterioration*, pp123-45, Sage, Newbury Park, CA; Hite, S 1976 *The Hite Report* Macmillan, New York; Hupka, R B, Jung, J and Silverthorn, K 1987 "Perceived Acceptability of Apologies, Excuses and Justifications in Jealousy Predicaments" *Journal of Social Behavior and Personality*, 2, (3), pp303-13; Jowell, R and Airey, C (eds): 1984 *British Social Attitudes: the 1984 Report* Gower Publishing, Hants, UK; Stone, L 1977 *The Family, Sex and Marriage in England, 1500-1800* Weidenfeld and Nicolson, London.

12 Falling Out Blumstein, P and Schwartz, P W 1983 *American Couples* Morrow, New York; Braiker, H B and Kelley, H H 1979 "Conflict in the Development of Close Relationships" in Burgess, R L and Huston, T L (eds): *Social Exchange in Developing Relationships*, pp135-68, Academic Press, New York; Brehm, S S 1985 *Intimate Relationships* Random House, New York; Duck, S 1982 *Personal Relationships 4: Dissolving Personal Relationships* Academic Press, London; Duck, S 1984 *Personal Relationships 5: Repairing Personal Relationships* Academic Press, London; Hatfield, E, Utne, M K and Traupmann, J "Equity Theory and Intimate Relationships" in Burgess, R L and Huston, T L (eds): *Social Exchange in Developing Relationships* Academic Press, New York; Kingma, D R 1987 *Coming Apart: Why Relationships End, and How to Live Through the Ending of Yours* Conari Press, Berkeley, CA; Kyle, S O and Falbo, T 1985 "Relationship Between Marital Stress and Attributional Preferences for Own and Spouse Behavior" *Journal of Social and Clinical Psychology*, 3 (3), pp339-51; Phillips, D with Judd, R 1978 *How to Fall Out of Love* Warner Books, New York; Rubin, M J 1982 "Non-engagement, Failure to Engage, and Disengagement" in Duck, S (ed): *Personal Relationships 4: Dissolving Personal Relationships* Academic Press, London; Weber, A L, Harvey, J H and Stanley, M A 1987 "The Nature and Motivations of Accounts for Failed Relationships" in Burnett, R, McGhee, P and Clarke, D D (eds): *Accounting for Relationships* Methuen, London; Weiss, R S 1975 *Marital Separation* Basic Books, New York; Wills, T A, Weiss, R L and Patterson, G R 1974 "A Behavioral Analysis of the Determinants of Marital Satisfaction" *Journal of Consulting and Clinical Psychology*, 42, pp802-11.

13 Contemplating Divorce Hetherington, E M, Cox M and Cox R 1978 "The Aftermath of Divorce" in Stevens, J H and Matthews, M (eds): *Mother-Child, Father-Child Relations* National Association for the Education of Young Children, Washington, DC; Hozman, T L and Froiland, D J 1977 "Children Forgotten in Divorce" *Personnel and Guidance Journal*, 55, pp530-33; Hunt, M and Hunt, B 1977 *The Divorce Experience* McGraw-Hill, New York; Kessler, S 1975 *The American Way of Divorce: Prescriptions for Change* Nelson Hall, Chicago, IL; Kitson, G C and Sussman, M 1982 "Marital Complaints, Demographic Characteristics and Symptoms of Mental Distress in Divorce" *Journal of Marriage and the Family*, 44, pp87-101; Kubler-Ross, E 1969 *On Death and Dying* MacMillan, New York; Levinger, G 1965 "Marital Cohesiveness and Dissolution: an Integrative Review" *Journal of Marriage and the Family*, 27, pp19-28; Wallerstein, J S and Kelly, J B 1980 *Surviving the Breakup: How Children and Parents Cope with Divorce* Basic Books, New York; Weiss, R S 1975 *Marital Separation* Basic Books, New York; Weitzman, L J 1985 *The Divorce Revolution: The Unexpected Social and Economic Consequences for Women and Children in America* Free Press, New York.

14 Starting Again Ahrons, C R and Rodgers, R 1987 *Divorced Families* Norton, New York; Ambert, A, (forthcoming) *Ex-Spouses and New Spouses* JAI Press, Greenwich, CT; Arendell, T 1986 *Mothers and Divorce* University of California Press, Berkeley, CA; Burgoyne, J and Clark, D 1984 *Making-A-Go-Of-It: A Study of Stepfamilies in Sheffield* Routledge and Kegan Paul, London; Furstenberg, F F Jr and Spanier, G B 1984 *Recycling the Family. Remarriage After Divorce* Sage, Beverly Hills, CA; Luepnitz, D A 1982 *Child Custody. A Study of Families After Divorce* Lexington Books, Lexington, MA; Weitzman, L 1985 *The Divorce Revolution: The Unexpected Social and Economic Consequences for Women and Children in America* Free Press, New York.

15 The Mature Years Argyle, M 1987 *The Psychology of Happiness* Methuen, London; Carlson, J and Hatfield, E (in press) *The Psychology of Emotion* Dorsey Press, Chicago, IL; Hatfield, E, Traupmann, J, Sprecher, S, Utne, M and Hay, J 1984 'Equity and Intimate Relations: Recent Research' in Ickes, W (ed): *Compatible and Incompatible Relationships*, pp1-27, Springer Verlag, New York; Rapson, R L 1971 *The Cult of Youth in Middle-Class America* D C Heath and Co, Lexington, MA; Satariano, W A, Syme, S L 1981 "Life Changes and Disease in Elderly Populations: Coping With Change" in McGaugh, J L and Kiesler, S B (eds): *Aging: Biology and Behavior* Academic Press, New York; Wasow, M 1976 *Sexuality and Aging* School of Social Work, University of Wisconsin, Madison, WI.

16 A Sense of Intimacy Acitelli, L and Duck, S 1987 "Intimacy as the Proverbial Elephant" in Perlman, D and Duck, S (eds): *Intimate Relationships: Development, Dynamics and Deterioration* Sage, Beverly Hills, CA; Franzoi, S L, Davis, M H and Young, R D 1985 "The Effects of Private Self-Consciousness and Perspective Taking on Satisfaction in Close Relationships" *Journal of Personality and Social Psychology*, 48, (6), pp1584-94; Hatfield, E 1984 "The Dangers of Intimacy" in Derlega, V (ed): *Communication, Intimacy, and Close Relationships* Academic Press, New York; Hendrix, H 1988 *Getting the Love You Want: A Guide for Couples* Henry Holt, New York; L'Abate, L and Sloan, S 1984 "A Workshop Format to Facilitate Intimacy in Married Couples" *Family Relations*, 33, pp245-50; McAdams, D 1984 "Human Motives and Personal Relationships" in Derlega, V (ed): *Communication, Intimacy, and Close Relationships* Academic Press, New York; Rubin, L 1983 *Intimate Strangers* Harper and Row, New York.

17 Ideals and Realities Baucom, D 1987 "Attributions in Distressed Relations: How Can We Explain Them?" in Duck, S and Perlman, D (eds): *Intimate Relationships: Development, Dynamics and Deterioration* Sage, London; Blumstein, P and Schwartz, P 1983 *American Couples* Morrow, New York; Cowan, C and Kinder, M 1985 *Smart Women, Foolish Choices: Finding the Right Men, Avoiding the Wrong Ones* Bantam, New York; Davis, K E and Todd, M J 1982 "Friendships and Love Relationships" in Davis, K E and Mitchell, T O (eds): *Advances in Descriptive Psychology*, (2), JAI Press, Greenwich, CT; Livingstone, S M 1987 "The Representation of Relationships in Television Drama" in Burnett, R, McGhee, P and Clarke, D D (eds): *Accounting for Relationships: Explanation, Representation and Knowledge* Methuen, London; Mansfield, P and Collard, J 1988 *The Beginning of the Rest of your Life? A Portrait of Newly-Wed Marriage* Macmillan, Basingstoke; Scarf, M 1987 *Intimate Partners: Patterns in Love and Marriage* Century, London; Rusbult, C E 1987 "Responses to Dissatisfaction in Close Relationships: The Exit – Voice – Loyalty – Neglect Model" in Duck, S and Perlman, D (eds): *Intimate Relationships: Development, Dynamics and Deterioration* Sage, London; Shotter, J 1987 "The Social Construction of an 'Us': Problems of Accountability and Narratology" in Burnett, R, McGhee, P and Clarke, D D (eds): *Accounting for Relationships: Explanation, Representation and Knowledge* Methuen, London; Skynner, R and Cleese, J 1983 *Families and How to Survive Them* Methuen, London.

18 Expectations of the Opposite Sex Belenky, M F et al 1986 *Women's Ways of Knowing* Basic Books, New York; Bergquist, W 1988 *Developmental Stages of Couples* Center for Developmental Studies, San Francisco, CA; Brown, R 1986 "Some Issues of Sexual Liberation" in *Social Psychology: The Second Edition* Free Press, New York; Erikson, E 1959 "Identity and the Life Cycle" *Psychological Issues*, 1, pp1-171; Gilligan, C 1982 *In a Different Voice* Harvard University Press, Cambridge, MA; Levinson, D et al 1978 *The Seasons of a Man's Life* Knopf, New York; Osherson, S 1986 *Finding Our Fathers* Free Press, New York; Rubin, L 1983 *Intimate Strangers* Harper and Row, New York.

19 Sustaining Your Relationship Baxter, L 1987 "Symbols of Relationship Identity in Relationship Cultures" *Journal of Social and Personal Relationships*, 4, pp261-80; Bell, R, Daly, J and Gonzalez, M C 1987 "Affinity-Maintenance in Marriage and its Relationship to Women's Marital Satisfaction" *Journal of Marriage and the Family*, 49, pp445-54; Dindia, K and Baxter, L 1987 "Strategies for Maintaining and Repairing Marital Relationships" *Journal of Social and Personal Relationships*, 4, pp143-58; Duck, S 1986 *Human Relationships* Sage, London; Fisher, B and Sprenkle, D 1978 "Therapists' Perceptions of Healthy Family Functioning" *International Journal of Family Counseling*, 6, pp9-17; Hatfield, E and Sprecher, S 1986 *Mirror, Mirror. . . The Importance of Looks in Everyday Life* State University of New York Press, Albany, NY; Helgeson, V, Shaver, P and Dyer, M 1987 "Prototypes of Intimacy and Distance in Same-Sex and Opposite-Sex Relationships" *Journal of Social and Personal Relationships*, 4, pp195-233; LaFollette, H and Graham, G 1986 "Honesty and Intimacy" *Journal of Social and Personal Relationships*, 3, pp3-18; Mace, D and Mace, V 1980 "Enriching Marriages: The Foundation Stone of Family Strength" in Stinnett, N, Chesser, B, DeFrain, J and Knaub, P (eds): *Family Strengths: Positive Models for Family Life*, pp89-110, University of Nebraska Press, Lincoln, NE; Montgomery, B 1989 "Interactants' Views of Flirtatious Communication: Motives, Messages, and Consequences" Unpublished Research Report; Ridley, C and Nelson, R 1984 "The Behavioral Effects of Training Premarital Couples in Mutual Problem Solving Skills" *Journal of Social and Personal Relationships*, 1, pp197-210.

20 Better Communication Alberts, J K 1988 "An Analysis of Couples' Conversational Complaints" *Communication Monographs*, 55, pp184-97; Bateson, G 1972 *Steps to an Ecology of Mind* Ballantine, New York; Burgoon, J 1985 "Nonverbal Signals" in Knapp, M and Miller, G (eds): *Handbook of Interpersonal Communication*, pp344-90, Sage, Beverly Hills, CA; Canary, D and Cupach, W 1988 "Relational and Episodic Characteristics Associated With Conflict Tactics" *Journal of Social and Personal Relationships*, 5, pp305-27; Gottman, J 1979 *Marital Interaction* Academic Press, New York; Gottman, J, Notarius, C, Gonso, J and Markman, H 1976 *A Couple's Guide to Communication* Research Press, Champaign, IL; Montgomery, B 1988 "Quality Communication in Personal Relationships" in Duck, S (ed): *Handbook of Personal Relationships*, pp343-59, Wiley, London; Noller, P 1985 "Negative Communications in Marriage" *Journal of Social and Personal Relationships*, 2, pp289-301; Norton, R 1979 *Communication Style* Sage, Beverly Hills, CA; Zietlow, P and Sillars, A 1988 "Life-Stage Differences in Communication During Marital Conflicts" *Journal of Social and Personal Relationships*, 5, pp223-47.

21 Understanding Each Other Acitelli, L and Duck, S W 1986 "Intimacy as the Proverbial Elephant"in Perlman, D and Duck, S (eds): *Intimate Relationships: Development, Dynamics and Deterioration* Sage, Beverly Hills, CA and London; Baxter, L A and Wilmot, W A 1985 "Taboo Topics in Close Relationships"*Journal of Social and Personal Relationships*, 2, pp253-69; Burnett, R 1986 *Conceptualisation of Personal Relationships* D Phil thesis, University of Oxford; Burnett, R 1987 "Reflection in Personal Relationships" in Burnett, R, McGhee, P and Clarke, D D (eds): *Accounting for Relationships: Explanation, Representation and Knowledge* Methuen, London; Clarke, D D 1987 "Emotion, Decision and the Long-term Course of Relationships" in Burnett, R, McGhee, P and Clarke, D D (eds): *Accounting for Relationships: Explanation, Representation and Knowledge* Methuen, London; Fincham, F D 1985 "Attributions in Close Relationships" in Harvey, J H and Weary, G (eds): *Attribution: Basic Issues and Applications* Academic Press, London; Fromm, E 1957 *The Art of Loving* Allen and Unwin, London; Hinde, R A 1984 "Why Do the Sexes Behave Differently in Close Relationships?" *Journal of Social and Personal Relationships*, 1, pp471-501; Peters, R S 1974 "Personal Understanding and Relationships" in Mischel, T (ed): *Understanding Other Persons* Blackwell, Oxford; Wilkinson, S 1987 "Explorations of Self and Other in Developing Relationships" in Burnett, R, McGhee, P and Clarke, D D (eds): *Accounting for Relationships: Explanation, Representation and Knowledge* Methuen, London; Zajonc, R B 1984 "On the Primacy of Affect" *American Psychologist*, 39, pp117-23.

22 A Sound and Happy Marriage Argyle, M and Henderson, M 1985 *The Anatomy of Relationships* Penguin, Harmondsworth; Davis, K E and Todd, M J 1982 "Friendships and Love Relationships" in Davis, K E and Mitchell, T O (eds): *Advances in Descriptive Psychology*, (2), JAI Press, Greenwich, CT; Dindia, K and Baxter, L A 1987 "Strategies for Maintaining and Repairing Marital Relationships" *Journal of Social and Personal Relationships*, 4, pp143-58; Duck, S 1988 *Relating to Others* Dorsey/Open University Press, London and Chicago, IL; Fitzpatrick, M A and Badzinski, D 1985 "All in the Family: Interpersonal Communication in Kin Relationships" in Knapp, M L and Miller, G R (eds): *Handbook of Interpersonal Communication* Sage, Newbury Park; Lauer, R H and Lauer, J C 1987 "Factors in Long-Term Marriages" *Journal of Family Issues*, 7, pp382-90; Lund, M 1985 "The Development of Investment and Commitment Scales for Predicting Continuity of Personal Relationships" *Journal of Social and Personal Relationships*, 2, pp3-23; Noller, P 1984 *Nonverbal Communication and Marital Interaction* Pergamon, Oxford; Schwartz, P 1988 "The Family as a Changed Institution" *Journal of Family Issues*, 8, pp455-9; Surra, C A, Asmussen, P and Arizzi, L 1988 "The Association Between Reasons for Commitment and the Development and Outcomes of Marital Relationships" *Journal of Social and Personal Relationships*, 5, pp47-64.

23 Managing Together Beech, R 1985 *Staying Together. A Practical Way to Make Your Relationship Succeed and Grow* Wiley, Chichester; Bernard, J 1982 1973 *The Future of Marriage* Yale University Press, New Haven, CT; Brenner, H 1976 *Estimating the Social Costs of National Economic Policy: Implications for Mental and Physical Health and Criminal Aggression* Joint Economic Committee, 92nd Congress, October 26, 1976. U.S. Government Printing Office, Washington, DC; Coleman, J C 1988 *Intimate Relationships, Marriage and Family* Macmillan, New York; Cromwell, R E and Olson, D H 1975 *Power in Families* Wiley, New York; Davidson, L and Gordon, L K 1979 *The Sociology of Gender* Rand McNally, Chicago, IL; Emerson, R 1962 "Power-Dependence Relations" *American Sociological Review*, 27, pp31-41; Eshelman, J R 1988 *The Family: An Introduction* Allyn and Bacon, Boston, MA; Haas, L 1980 "Role Sharing Couples: A Study of Egalitarian Marriages" *Family Relations*, 29, pp289-94; Hayghe, H 1982 "Dual-Earner Families: Their Economic and Demographic Characteristics" in Aldous, J (ed): *Two Paychecks: Life in Dual-Earner Families* Sage,

Beverly Hills, CA; Newman, D 1988 *Gender and Power in Intimate Relationships: Dyadic Structure and Cognitive Processes* Doctoral Dissertation, University of Washington; Nye, F I et al 1976 *Role Structure and Analysis of the Family* Sage, Beverly Hills, CA; Voyandoff, P and Kelly, R F 1984 "Determinants of Work-Related Family Problems Among Employed Parents" *Journal of Marriage and the Family*, 46, pp881-92.

24 The Difficult Partner Dicks, H V 1967 *Marital Tensions* Routledge and Kegan Paul, London; Dominian, J 1980 *Marital Pathology* Darton, Longman and Todd, London; Gelles, R J and Cornell, C P 1985 *Intimate Violence in Families* Sage, London; Mattinson, J 1988 *Work, Love and Marriage* Duckworth, London; Norton, A J and Moorman, J E 1987 "Current Trends in Marriage and Divorce Among American Women" *Journal of Marriage and the Family*, 49, (1) pp3-14; Ramprakash, D (ed) 1985 *Social Trends 15* HMSO, London; Thompson, E J 1976 *Social Trends 7* HMSO, London.

25 Getting Therapy Barker, R L 1984 *Treating Couples in Crisis: Fundamentals and Practice in Marital Therapy* The Free Press, New York; Cauthery, P and Stanway, A 1985 *The Complete Guide to Sexual Fulfillment* Century Hutchinson, London; Clulow, C F 1985 *Marital Therapy: An Inside View* Aberdeen University Press, Aberdeen; Dominian, J 1984 *Make or Break: An Introduction to Marriage Counselling* SPCK, London; Dryden, W (ed) 1985 *Marital Therapy in Britain: 1, Context and Therapeutic Approaches* Harper and Row, London; Egan, G 1986 *The Skilled Helper: A Systematic Approach to Effective Helping* Brooks/Cole, Pacific Grove, CA; Knight, L 1986 *Talking to a Stranger: A Consumer's Guide to Therapy* Fontana, London; Masters, W H and Johnson, V E 1966 *Human Sexual Response* Little, Brown and Co, Boston, MA; Masters, W H and Johnson, V E 1970 *Human Sexual Inadequacy* Churchill, London; Mearns, D and Thorne, B 1988 *Person-Centred Counselling in Action* Sage, Beverly Hills, CA; Nelson-Jones, R 1983 *Practical Counselling Skills* Cassell, London; Rogers, C 1951 *Client-Centred Therapy* Houghton Mifflin Co, Boston, MA; Wile, D B 1981 *Couples Therapy: A Nontraditional Approach* Wiley, New York.

26 Enjoying Sex Cauthery, C and Stanway, A 1985 *The Complete Guide to Sexual Fulfillment* Century Hutchinson, London; Chang, J 1977 *The Tao of Love and Sex* Wildwood House, Aldershot; Comfort, A 1972 *The Joy of Sex* Mitchell Beazley, London; Douglas, N and Slinger, P 1982 *Sexual Secrets* Arrow Books, London; Friday, N 1973 *My Secret Garden* Quartet Books, London; Heiman, J and Lopiccolo, J 1977 *Becoming Orgasmic: A Sexual Growth Program for Women* Prentice Hall, New York; Kitzinger, S 1985 *Woman's Experience of Sex* Penguin, Harmondsworth; Kolbenschlag, M 1981 *Kiss Sleeping Beauty Good-bye* Bantam, London/New York; Malone, P and Malone, T 1987 *The Art of Intimacy* Simon and Schuster, New York/London; Montagu, A 1971 *Touching: The Human Significance of the Skin* Harper and Row, San Francisco, CA; Nicholson, J 1984 *Men and Women: How Different are They?* Oxford University Press, Oxford; O'Connor, D 1987 *How to Make Love to the Same Person for the Rest of Your Life* Bantam, London/New York; Stanway, A 1988 *A Woman's Guide to Men and Sex* Century Hutchinson, London; Yorke, A 1988 *The Art of Erotic Massage* Javelin Books, London.

27 Room for Other People Argyle, M M and Henderson, M 1985 *The Anatomy of Relationships* Penguin, Harmondsworth; Bott, E 1971 2nd edn *Family and Social Networks* Tavistock, London; Cowen, E, Gesten, E, Boike, M, Norton, P and Wilson, A 1979 "Hairdressers as Caregivers: A Descriptive Profile of Interpersonal Help-Giving Involvement" *American Journal of Community Psychology*, 7, pp633-48; Dickson-Markman, F 1986 "Social Support and Health Among Married Individuals" Paper presented at the Speech Communication Association, Illinois; Dickson-Markman, F and Markman, H 1988 "The Effects of Others on Marriage: Do They Help or Hurt?" in Noller, P and Fitzpatrick, M A (eds): *Perspectives on Marital Interaction* Multilingual Matters, Philadelphia; Julien, D 1986 "Patron dyadiques des perceptions

d'interactions sexuelles chez des couples maritaliment satisfaits et insatisfait" Unpublished dissertation, University of Quebec, Montreal; Hess, B 1972 "Friendship" in Riley, M W, Johnson, M and Fonner, A (eds): *Aging and Society*, pp357-93, Russell Sage, New York; Hirsch, B J 1981 "Social Networks and the Coping Process: Creating Personal Communities" in Gottlieb, B H (ed): *Social Networks and Social Support* Sage, London; Kelly, J R 1983 *Leisure Identities and Interactions* Allen and Unwin, London; Petrowsky, M 1976 "Marital Status, Sex, and the Social Networks of the Elderly" *Journal of Marriage and the Family*, 38, pp743-56; Rubin, L B 1985 *Just Friends: the Role of Friendship in Our Lives* Harper and Row, New York; Titus, S L 1980 "A Function of Friendship: Sound Comparisons as a Frame of Reference for Marriage" *Human Relations*, 33, pp409-31.

28 Shared Parenting Bowlby, J 1969 *Attachment and Loss*, 1, Basic Books, New York; Chodorow, N 1978 *The Reproduction of Mothering: Psychoanalysis and the Sociology of Gender* University of California Press, Berkeley, CA; Ehrensaft, D 1987 *Parenting Together: Men and Women Sharing the Care of Their Children* Free Press, New York; Kimball, G 1987 *50/50 Parenting: Sharing Family Rewards and Responsibilities* Lexington Press, Lexington, MA; Russell, G 1983 *The Changing Role of Fathers* University of Queensland Press, St Lucia, Australia; Winnicott, D W 1970 *Playing and Reality* Basic Books, New York.

29 Revitalizing Your Relationship Broderick, C 1979 *Couples: How To Confront Problems and Maintain Loving Relationships* Simon and Schuster, New York; Curran, D 1983 *Traits of a Happy Family* Winston, Minneapolis; Duck, S 1988 *Relating to Others* Dorsey, Chicago, IL; Gottman, J, Notarius, C, Gonso, J and Markman H 1976 *A Couple's Guide to Communication* Research Press, Champaign, IL; Hof, L and Miller, W R 1981 *Marriage Enrichment: Philosophy, Process and Program* Robert J Brady Co, Bowie, MD; Holman, T B and Epperson, A 1984 "Family and Leisure: A Review of the Literature with Research Recommendations" *Journal of Leisure Research*, 16, pp277-94; Iso-Ahola, S E and Weissinger, E 1987 *Journal of Social and Clinical Psychology*, 5, pp356-64; Laurence, L T 1982 *Couple Constancy: Conversations with Today's Happily Married People* Research Press, Ann Arbor, MI; Leary, M R, Rogers, P A, Canfield, R W and Coe, C 1986 "Boredom in Interpersonal Encounters: Antecedents and Social Implications" *Journal of Personality and Social Psychology*, 51, pp968-75; Luthman, S G and Kirschenbaum, M 1974 *The Dynamic Family* Science and Behavior Books, Palo Alto, CA; Nickols, S Y and Abdel-Ghany, M 1983 "Leisure Time of Husbands and Wives" *Home Economics Research Journal*, 12, pp189-98; Orthner, D K 1975 "Leisure Activity Patterns and Marital Satisfaction Over the Marital Career" *Journal of Marriage and the Family*, 37, pp91-102; Ramey, E R 1974 "Boredom: The Most Prevalent American Disease" *Harper's* November Issue, pp12-22.

PICTURE AGENCIES/SOURCES

ASp Allsport UK Ltd.
B Bubbles Photo Library, London.
BAL Bridgeman Art Library.
B/C Black Star/Colorific.
C Colorific Photo Library Ltd, London, New York.
C/D Colorific/DOT.
COM/SGA Comstock/Susan Griggs Agency.
F Format Photographers, London.
FI Fotomas Index.
FSP Frank Spooner Pictures, London.
G/FSP Gamma/Frank Spooner Pictures, London.
H The Hutchison Library, London.
HS Homer Sykes, London.
I Impact Photos, London.
ILN The Illustrated London News Picture Library.
KC The Kobal Collection, London.
L/FSP Liaison/Frank Spooner Pictures, London.
ME Mary Evans Picture Library, London.
MG Magnum Photos Ltd, London, Paris, New York.
N Network Photographers, London.
P/SGA Photofile/Susan Griggs Agency, London.
PFL Popperfoto, London.
PI Pictor International.
R Rex Features Ltd, London.
R/S Rex/Sipa, London.
S Stern, Hamburg.
SGA Susan Griggs Agency, London.
SM/Z Studio Mike/Zefa, London.
SRG Sally and Richard Greenhill, London.
ST Stockphotos, London.
TCL Daily Telegraph Colour Library, London.
TIB The Image Bank, London.
TIB/G+J The Image Bank/G and J Images, London.
TIB/JA The Image Bank/Janeart Ltd, London.
TSW Tony Stone Photo Library, London.
V Viewfinder Colour Photo Library, Bristol.
WP/C Wheeler Pictures/Colorific, London.
Z Zefa, London.
Z/A Zefa/Alex, London.
ZP/TIB Zao Productions/The Image Bank, London.
Z/S Zefa/Stockmarket, London.

252

KEY TO PHOTOGRAPHERS

A Abbas. **AEa** Andrew Eames. **AEr** Alain Ernoult. **AGd** Al Gardner. **AR** Alon Reininger. **AS** Anthea Sieveking. **AT** Arthur Tilley. **AV** A Venzago. **AWe** Alex Webb. **Be** Bendel. **BGl** Burt Glinn. **BL** Barry Lewis. **BMcN** Burton McNeely. **BPo** Bob Pizaro. **Cz** Constellaz. **CFi** Chuck Fishman. **CFB** Charlotte Fuller-Bourdier. **CK** Chuck Kuhn. **CT** Christopher Tordai. **CV** C Voigt. **CW** Cary Wolinsky. **DB** David Burnett. **DBa** D Barnes. **DF** Donna Ferrato. **DG** David Gilliland. **DL** David Levenson. **DMz** Doug Menuez. **DSc** David Schultz. **DV** David Vance. **EB** Eric Bouvet. **EF** Enrico Ferorelli. **EL** Elyse Lewin. **ELe** Elisa Leonelli. **ESa** Eric Sander. **EZ** E Zeschin. **FB** F Bouillot. **FS** F Scianna. **FSr** Faustino Sirven. **FSW** Frank "Shorty" Wilcox. **GBa** Gio Barto. **GBr** Gerald Brinacombe. **GCl** Geoffrey Clifford. **GCr** Gary Craller. **GPe** Gilles Peress. **GQK** G Quentin Kimball. **GSo** Gaby Sommer. **HCB** Henri Cartier Bresson. **HHD** Huntley Hedworth. **HK** Heinz Kluetmeier. **HS** Homer Sykes. **IBr** Ian Bradshaw. **IG** Ian Giles. **IL** Ian Lloyd. **JBa** J Barlow. **JDs** John Dominis. **JGl** J Globus. **JGt** John Garrett. **JH** Jim Howard. **JHu** Jeff Hunter. **JM** John Moss. **JMa** Jenny Matthews. **JMe** Joel Meyerowitz. **JOB** Joanne O'Brien. **JP** Jim Pickerell. **JPN** Jean-Paul Navicet. **JT** John Troha. **JU** Jay Ullal. **JW** Jenny Woodcock. **JY** John Yates. **Ki** Kiedrowski. **KB** K Benser. **KBr** Ken Brown. **KD** Karim Daher. **KK** Klaus Kerth. **KP** Kate Pattullo. **LF** Leonard Freed. **LG** Louise Gubb. **LT** Liba Taylor. **LTh** Loisjoy Thurstun. **MA** Mike Abrahams. **MBr** Marcus Brooke. **MCa** Monique Cobral. **MFk** Martine Franck. **MG** Mike Goldwater. **MGo** Michael Going. **MMs** Michel Maïofiss. **MMI** Michael MacIntyre. **MN** Michael Nichols. **MPa** Martin Parr. **MS** Michael Salas. **MY** Mike Yamashita. **NBe** Nathan Benn. **NDMcK** Nancy Durrell McKenna. **PCo** Peter Correz. **PFu** Paul Fusco. **PM** Peter Marlow. **PT** Penny Tweedie. **PZ** Patrick Zachmann. **RBa** R Barnes. **RBl** Ron Blakeley. **RFa** R Faber. **RFs** Robert Francis. **RHz** R Huntzinger. **RK** Richard Kalvar. **RM** Robert McFarlane. **RN** Richard Nicholas. **RRe** Roger Ressmeyer. **RSt** Richard Steedman. **RWo** Rafaël Wollmann. **RWr** R Wagner. **SBo** Steve Benbow. **SC** S Corrodi. **SG** Sheila Gray. **S/L** Schmid/ Langsfeld. **SMk** Stephen Marks. **SMe** Susan Meiselas. **SN** Steve Niedorf. **SPo** Steve Powell. **SRG** Sally and Richard Greenhill. **SSp** Sandy Spink. **ST** Susan Turvey. **TB** Tim Brown. **TH** Thomas Hoepker. **WB** Werner Bokelberg. **WM** Wayne Miller. **WMcB** Will McBride.

PICTURE LIST

Page number in **bold** type. Photographer's initials in parenthesis.

Frontmatter

2 On beach (AT) TSW. **10** In swimming pool, TSW. **13** Intimate couple, Z.

Part title Couples

14-15 Couple by lake (PM) MG.

1 Needing a Special Person

16 Party (PZ) MG. Kiss at station (JOB) F. **17** Couple lying down, COM/SGA. **18-19** Cuddle on grass (JW) V. **19** Under boardwalk (CFB) C. Man and dog (MFk) MG. **20** Cuddle (NDMcK) H. Couple at table (MPa) MG. **21** Couple in bed (DV) TIB. **22** Couple, England (MCa) F. **23** Seaside, Z/A. Chinese newlywed (CW) C.

2 What Makes a Couple

24 Young man looking out of window (Cz) H. **25** Young woman looking out of window (Cz) H. **26** Society dinner (TH) MG. **27** Lovers on pavement (LF) MG. Couple walking (GBa) TIB. In café, Paris (RK) MG. **28** Two young men (HHD) V. **29** Young couple (JM) C. Middle-aged couples dancing (RK) MG.

3 Finding, Matching and Attracting

30 Art gallery (AV) MG. **31** In pool (RBl) C. **32** Older woman marries younger man (NDMcK) H. Younger woman and older man (BMcN) TIB. Satirical print, Longitude and Latitude of St Petersburgh, 18 May 1813, by Cruikshank, FI. **33** New York Stock Exchange, PFL. **34** Dance hall (RFs) H. **35** Couples greeting (JMe) TIB. At work (PM) MG. **36** Dating, PFL. Soldier and girl on stairs, H. **37** Bachelors Festival, Spain, R/S. **38** International Marriage Travel Agency (GSo) G/FSP. Meeting Asian partner (GSo) FSP. **39** Aids-free dating service, L/FSP.

4 Pairing Off

40 Six young people (CV) Z. **40-41** On train, Rumania (HCB) MG. **41** Funfair (BL) N. On beach, Brazil (MMI) N. **42** Disco (Be) Z. **43** On park bench, ME. Lying on grass, Z. **44** Coney Island, Z.

45 Art Museum (MY) C. **46** By river bank, Z. **47** Couple in bed (S/L) TIB.

5 Love and Commitment

48-49 Young couple, PFL. **49** Elderly couple, TIB/JA. **50** Lovers, Ludlow, England (KBr) V. **53** Engagement rings, R.

6 Maintaining Individuality

54 Painter and windmill, Spain (MY) C. Pearly king and queen, England (DB) C. **55** Ultralite (AEr) I. Mass wedding, Singapore (IL) H. **57** Club, Italy (FS) MG. Dancing class (IBr) C. **59** Carthusian monk, R. Garden, R. **60-61** Couple (RHz) Z/S. **61** Allotment, picture by Jason Shenoi/courtesy of Company Magazine.

7 Opting for Marriage

62 Indian wedding (ELe) C. **63** Marriage, Beirut (JU) S. **64** Signing wedding documents (LT) H. **65** Hot air balloon wedding (CFi) C. Underwater wedding, R. **66** Sophia Loren, R. Couple with trophy (JMe) TIB. **67** Black/white couple, South Africa (LG) C. **68** The cake (A) MG. **68-69** Throwing confetti, R. **69** The garter (EZ) R. Bridesmaid (MG) N. Gifts, China (CW) C.

8 How Couples Have Changed

70 American family 1957, PFL. The Village Wedding by Luke Fildes (1844-1927), BAL. **71** Spencer Tracy and Katherine Hepburn in "Without Love" 1945, G/FSP. **72** Hop harvesters, England, PFL. Young professionals, New York City (JDs) WP/C. **72-73** Parents and baby group, London (SRG) SRG. **73** "Hippy-Flower Party" Berlin 1967, PFL. **74** Assembling barrage balloon, World War II, PFL. Germaine Greer, R. **75** Executive father and baby (MGo) TIB.

9 Making Love

76 Making love (PFu) MG. **77** Mother and daughter, TSW. **79** Lovers, top left, ST. Lovers, top right (WM) MG. **80** Resting couple, Z. **81** Disappointed couple, Z. **82** Couple caressing (NDMcK) H. **84** Diana Rigg and Douglas Sheldon in "The Avengers", KC. Dynasty, KC. **85** Contraceptives (RN) Z. Aids billboard, R.

10 Thinking of Parenthood
86 37 weeks pregnant (NDMck) H. 87 Counseling (JH) C. 88 Couple in bed with child (SC) TIB/G+J. 89 Mountain bike riders (DSc) TSW. Mother and baby (AS). 90 Empty cradle (JW). 91 6 babies in 19 months (AGd) C. 92-93 Family (JMa) F.

11 Extramarital Affairs
94 Still from film "Bob and Carol and Ted and Alice", KC. 95 Anguish, PI. Happy couple at table, PI. 96 Afternoon love (NDMcK) H. 97 Computer widow (RRe) C. At work (PM), MG. 98 Couple in restaurant (CK) TIB. 99 Aids victim, R/S. 100 Carmen, G/FSP. 101 Apologies, PI.

12 Falling Out
102 Harmony before marriage, FI. 103 Matrimonial harmonics, FI. 104 Argument over money (ST). 104-105 Painting new home (JHu) TIB. 106-107 Argument at home, PI. 108 River bank, Z. 109 Crying (JP) C.

13 Contemplating Divorce
110-111 Outside divorce court (FB) TCL. 112 The Prince of Wales and Mrs Simpson, Biarritz, August 1934, ILN. 112-113 Jewish family (MMs) G/FSP. 113 Anti-divorce demonstration, Argentina, 1986 (RWo) G/FSP. 114 Woman at window (KP). Man and his dog (SBo) C. 115 Mother and son (JP) C. 116 Marriage breakup (ST). 117 Couple, Paris, R. 118 Divorced mother at work (GPe) MG. Divorced mother at home (GPe) MG.

14 Starting Again
120 Café, Vienna, SM/Z. 121 Father and son (NDMcK) H. Picnic (CT) H. 122 Roller skating (AR) H. 123 The Burtons, R. 124 Visiting father (ST). 124-125 Binuclear family (Ki) Z. 125 Loving stepmother (DG) V.

15 The Mature Years
126 Young couple, ZP/TIB. 127 Parents with teenager (ST). Elderly couple, Essex, England (JW) V. 128 Teenage couple (NDMcK) H. 129 Older couple embracing, Italy (FS) MG. 130 60th wedding anniversary, France (ESa) G/FSP. 131 Couple on beach (GCr) TIB. Looking at photo album (SRG) SRG.

Part title Greater Intimacy
132-133 Lovers kissing (RFa) TIB.

16 A Sense of Intimacy
134 Young couple (HS) HS. 135 Dancing (MN) MG. 136 Father changing diaper (NDMcK) H. 137 Talking (HS) I.

17 Ideals and Realities
138 At the ball (HS) HS. Gondola, Venice (SG) F. 138-139 On beach (PCo) TSW. 139 Breakfast (Cz) H. Scene from "Dynasty" (JGl) R. 140 The Lion in Love by Abraham Soloman (1824-1862), Roy Miles Gallery, London, BAL. Newlyweds, Z/S. 141 On dance floor (PZ) MG. 143 Sharing problems (LTh) B. 144 Chelsea Flower Show, England (HS) HS. 145 Côuple (KK) Z. 146 Elaine and Sir Lancelot, Andromeda. 146-147 Tarzan and Jane, KC.

18 Expectations of the Opposite Sex
148 Departure (PZ) MG. 149 Vietnam veteran (SMe) MG. Mother and 13 year-old son (NDMcK) H. 150 Bart Conner, Peter Vidmar, USA (SPo) ASp. Friends, Morocco, H. 151 Beauty and the Beast by Walter Crane, by kind permission of the Hornby Library, Liverpool and The Whitworth Art Gallery, Manchester, England. 152 Doing the accounts (CW) C. 154 Executives (TB) TSW. 155 House husband (DMz) C.

19 Sustaining Your Relationship
156 Flower stall (HS) HS. 157 Jogging across bridge, R. 158 Couple dancing (PFu) MG. Kissing goodbye (HS) I. 159 Elderly couple celebrating, MG. 160 Couple on sofa, TIB. Opening champagne (AEa) H. 161 Walking with flowers (MS) TIB. 162 Looking at jewelry (FSr) TIB. 163 Couple laughing (JBa, RBa) TSW.

20 Better Communication
164 College students (BPo) Com/SGA. Couple in restaurant (NBe) SGA. 167 Car trip (SMk) ST. In the kitchen (PZ) MG. 169 Champagne on lawn, Glyndebourne, England (HS) HS. Couple, Ireland (HS) HS. 170-171 In woods, Northern Virginia, USA (JH) C.

21 Understanding Each Other
172 On phone, COM/SGA. 173 Couple reading, COM/SGA. 174 At window (DBa) TCL. 177 Man at desk, TSW. 178-179 In woods, P/SGA. 179 Tennis (RSt) TIB.

22 A Sound and Happy Marriage
180 Couple under umbrella, TIB. 181 Dancing, Miami (AWe) MG. 182 Breakfast in bed (S/L) TIB. Lovers, Paris (KD) G/FSP. 183 In park (SSp) B. 184 Gorbachev, R/S. 185 Pizza parlour, London (MA) N. 187 Shopping, Z. Couple dancing (SRG) SRG. Couple painting outdoors (MBr) C.

23 Managing Together
188 Couple outdoors (S/L) TIB. 189 Paying bills (EL) TIB. 190 Police (PM) MG. Bedtime story (SN) TIB. 192-193 Buying car (JP) C. 194 Cooking (JM) C. 195 On footbridge (RFs) H.

24 The Difficult Partner
197 Getting into car (LTh) B. 198-199 Family violence (DF) I. 200 Mother and daughters (DF) I. 200-201 Mother crying (DF) I. 201 Battered woman (DF) I. Woman crying (DF) I. 202-203 Wife and sick husband (AR) C. 203 Couple in garden, Canada (PT) I.

25 Getting Therapy
204 Therapy session, Z. Young couple (WB) TIB. 204-205 Unemployed family (SBo) N. 207 Therapy group (JT) B/C. 208 Breakfast (ST). 209 Argument (KB) Z. 210 Young girl in doorway (SRG) SRG. 210-211 Fixing lamp (CW) C. 211 Watching TV (CW) C. 212-213 Couple in bed, Z.

26 Enjoying Sex
214 Couple on sofa, Z. 215 Nude couple, R. 217 Nude couple on bed (RM) SGA. 218 The Lovers 1969, Lithograph by Gerald Gooch, Hansen Fuller Gallery, San Francisco. 219 Target in the Night 1968, Charcoal by Betty Dodson, Collection of Mr and Mrs Carleton Varney. 220 In garden pool (PFu) MG. 221 Couple on beach (JBa, RBA) TSW. Couple in bath (GQK) R. 222 Couple on bed (WB) TIB. 223 Kiss (PFu) MG.

27 Room for Other People
224 Charity dinner (AWe) MG. 225 Hospital visit (WMcB) S. 226 Party (HS) HS. 227 Roof top café, Italy (EF) C/D. Women under tree (JM) C. 228 Young men on wall (HS) HS. Stately home, Paris (BGI) MG. 229 Royal Academy art exhibition, England (HS) HS. Japanese women, H. 230 Skiing group (FSW) R. On phone (KP). 231 Birthday party (GBr) TIB. 232 Tobogganing (JGt) B. Neighbors (LTh) B. 233 River Cam, Cambridge, England (MY) C.

28 Shared Parenting
234 Father and son (NDMcK) H. Graduation, USA (JY) SGA. 235 Giving birth (HK) C/D. 236 Family on motorbike, Ho Chi Minh City (GCl) WP/C. 237 Mother and children (AS). 238 Father and son (AS). The Model Husband from Harper's Monthly 1886, ME. 239 Feeding twins (NDMcK) H. 240 School report (SRG) SRG. Family in living room (JP) C. 242 Family by lake, Canada (NDMcK) H.

29 Revitalizing Your Relationship
242 Couple on sofa (IG) Courtesy of Gloworm Ltd. 242-243 Couple cycling, TIB/JA. 245 Italian family (EF) C/D. Making pasta (RWr) Z/S. At the races, England (DL) C. 246-247 Chinese artist Li Shuang exhibits in Paris, 1984 (EB) G/FSP. 247 Skiing together (JPN) C.

253

Bold numbers indicate fuller information. Where information continues over more than one page, the number of the beginning page only is given.

abortion 74, 92
  as contraception 85
acquaintances 232
addiction 197, 202
"addictive personality" 197
adolescence 136, 152
  extended 74
adoption **92**
adultery **94**
adulthood 70
advertisements, marriage 34, 37
affairs, extramarital **94**
  benefits of 99
  costs of 99
  frequency of 95
  length of 100
  reasons for 96
  secret and open 96
affection 76, **158**
  lack of 196
  maintaining **156**
"affinity maintenance strategies" 156
age
  at marriage 32
  and fertility 90
  of first intercourse 47
aggression 199
aging 126
  and love **126**
  and sexual activity 83, 128
AIDS (Acquired-Immune Deficiency Syndrome) 39, 75, 85, 95, 99
Alcoholics Anonymous 202
alimony 118
American Association of Marriage and Family Therapists 209
androgyny 153
anger, coping with 208
anorgasmia 80
Argyle, Michael 184
arousal 78, **216**
artificial insemination 91
assault, domestic 198
attachment
  behavior in babies 18, 236
  to extramarital partner 99
attention, mutual 185
attraction **30**
  of likes 45
  of opposites 45
attractiveness, maintaining 156, 244

babies
  adopting 92
  attachment behavior 18
banns 68
batterers 199
behavior, unacceptable **199**
behavior therapy 210, 212
bereavement 21, 130
betrothal 67
birth control, natural 85
  see also contraception
births
  men helping at 235
  to single women 32
body awareness 74
  mutual 214
body language 166

boredom 141, **242**
  avoiding 244
Bowlby, John
  infant attachment 236
"broken heart syndrome" 130

cervical cap 85
cervical diaphragm 85
child care, sharing – *see* co-parenting
child sexuality 77
child rearing – *see* parenting
childbearing, limiting 89
childless couples 89
  after divorce 121
childlessness – *see* infertility
children
  adopting with special needs 92
  and commitment 71
  decision to have **86**
  and divorce 111, 113, 115, 118
  place in family 89
  reactions to divorce **119**
  telling about adoption 93
Chodorow, Nancy
  on daughters and mothers 235
climax – *see* orgasm
closeness 21, 24, 134
  levels of 60
  ways of achieving **40**
co-parenting 75, **234**
  difficulties of 238
  and marital satisfaction 240
cohabitation – *see* living together
coitus interruptus 85
commercial introductions 37
commitment 21, 25, 26, 181
  assessing 52
  children and 71
  fragmentation of 53
  love and **48**
  love with and without 52
  in marriage 181
  self-expression and 59
communication 106, 161, 244,
  about sex 222
  bridging the gap 208
  coordination of 165
  in courtship 47
  improving **164**
  lack of 53
  of love 49
  negative 208
  positiveness in 165
  skills 42
  styles **164**
  verbal and nonverbal 164, 169
commuter couples 75
companionate love **50**, 126
compatibility 30
complaints 166, 170, 244
compromise 185, 225
conciliation services 205
condoms 85
confessions 170
confidences, gender differences in handling 230
conflict **102**
  about sex 46, 103
  constructive 102
  in courtship 44
  destructive 102
  marital 204
  over child-rearing 240
  in partnership 163
  physical 199

  reactions to 103
  unresolved 106
connectedness 237
contraception 46, 74, 84, **85**, 92
conversation 245
  habits to avoid **168**
counseling, candidates for 205
counselor, client's relationship with 206
couples **24**, **70**, 74
  angry, arguing 205
  committed 26
  divergence in views 144
  drifting 205
  independent 105
  older **126**, 130
  relationships with other couples 228
  separate 105
  and singles 227
  standards for 28
  traditional 105
  typical 29
  unhappy staying together 181
  withdrawn 205
  without children 89
couples therapy 196
courtship 40, **44**
  industry 36
  patterns 43
  time of 44
creativity, and androgyny 155
criticism 196
cunnilingus 83

dating **40**
  after divorce 118
  computer 36
  designer 39
  services 34
death 202
decision-making 191
dependence 61
  baby's 89
  see also interdependence
depression 151
  after divorce 114
  post-natal 90
  and sex therapy 212
"desensitization" 213
disability, living with long-term 203
dishonesty 163
disillusionment 138
divorce 21, 73
  and adultery 99
  contemplating **110**
  coping after 115, **120**
  counseling 205
  economics of 118
  escalating rate 75
  health and 60, 116
  obstacles to 112
  and religious beliefs **113**
  threatening with 175
  see also separation
domestic division of labor 105, 194
domination 197, 203
Down's Syndrome 87
  adopting a child with 92
dowry 69
drifting apart 175
drinking, and violence 199
drugs 120
  fertility 91
  treatment in sex problems 212

Duck, Steve
  on breakdown of relationships 107

emotional patterns, understanding each other's 179
emotional space 173
emotional styles, gender differences in 149
emotional support 65, 158, 182
empathy 176, 179
engaged partners 29
engagement 67
equality
  in marriage 105
  passion and 72
  of the sexes 148
erotic holidays **221**
erotic words and pictures 222
eternal triangle 100
Exchange Theory 23
expectations
  in courtship 45
  for emotional fulfillment 177
  of intimacy 103, 141
  in later years 129
  of marriage **65**, 67, 182, 204
  of openness 171
  of the opposite sex **148**
  redefining 211
  in relationships 20, 26, 30, 242
  and sexual myths 83
  in use of introduction agencies 37
  women's 75
explanation 208, 209
eye contact 136, 169, 171

falling out **102**
Fallopian tubes, blockages of 90
familiarity 137, 141, 173
families
  binuclear 124
  blended 73
  executive 73
  single-parent 73
family
  activities as a 232, 245
  effect of working mothers on 190
  end of the traditional 73
  starting a **86**
  two-income **190**
family bonds 231
family income 104, 190
family life, intimacies of 136
fantasies 81, 217
fate, love and 176
fathering 75, 235
fathers, executive 75
feelings 143
  of being in love 51
  communicating negative 42
  expressions of true 175
  and marriage therapy 211
  in parenthood 88
  role in relationships 178
  sensitivity to the other's 163
fellatio 83
femininity 148, 195
  level of 154
  see also gender differences
feminist movement 74
fertility
  and age 90
  overabundant 91
fertilization **78**
fidelity, sexual 50, 182

fighting 166
finding a mate **30**
flirting 97
  with your mate 159, 244
foreplay 83
Freud, Sigmund
  child sexuality 77
  psychoanalysis 209
friends
  relationship with in
    marriage 185, **226**
  and separation 121
friendship 19, 22, 24, 181
  how choices change 227
  in love 50
  plus sex 25
  same sex 233
fun 215, 243, 245

games 49
gender differences
  in attitudes to work 60
  in coping with adultery 101
  in coping after divorce **116**
  in emotional styles **149**
  in expression of love 107
  in extramarital sex 95
  in parenting **236**
  in perspectives 176
  in tactics 192
  in thinking styles **153**
  see also femininity; masculinity
gender roles, sharing 235
gender stereotyping 73
genetic counseling 87
gifts, wedding 69
give-and-take 22, 161
Gottman, John
  conversational habits 168
grandchildren 233
grandparents 111, 231
grief, in divorce 115
guilt
  and commitment 52
  in divorce 113
  mother 237
  and sex 83

happiness, in marriage **180**
health
  and divorce 116
  and intimate relationships 20
  and marriage **20**, 58, 65
helplessness, used to dominate 203
Henderson, Monika 184
history, and changes to couples 74
Hite Report 96
homosexual love relationships 28
honesty, wisdom of **162,** 170
"house husbands" 155
housework, sharing 105,**194**
humor 140, 167, 243, 244

ideals, and realities **138**, 146
"identified" client 205
identity
  and adoption 93
  crises in adolescence 152
  and parenthood 87
  and parenting 236
  and relationships 17,**54**
  and sex roles 152
  shared 67
illness
  after divorce 120

coping with a partner's **202**
  and intimate relationships 20
illusions 145
immaturity 196
in vitro fertilization 91
in-laws, coping with 230
income, family 104, 190
independence 54, 61, 189
independent approach to
  marriage 105, 186
individuality 24, 183, 226, 233
  in marriage 67, 142
  and relationships 246
  retaining **54, 59**
industrialization and marriage 73
infants – *see* babies
infertility 86, **90**
  causes of **90**
  male 90
  treatment of **91**
infidelity 53, **94**, 204
insults 170
interdependence 24, 28, 102,
  110, 189, 193
intimacy
  and adultery 95
  becomes familiarity 242
  limits to 134
  need for 54
  openness and 166
  perils of **102**, 183
  and personal growth 58
  physical and emotional 135
  problems 136
  sense of **134**
introduction services 36, **38**
  AIDS-free 39
irresponsibility 201
isolation 36
IUDs (intrauterine devices) 85

jealousy **100**

karyotype 87
kin relationships 28
Kinsey Report 96, 128

languages of love 107, 185
leisure 185, 195
  with children 232
  shared activities 233, 246
libido, loss of 77
listening 165, 168, 208, 244
living together 28, 58, **71**
  contract for 71
  economics of 188
  or marriage 62
  transition to marriage 66
loneliness 16, 21
  emotional 16
  long-term 114
  social 16
love
  and acceptance 172
  and commitment **48**
  companionate 50
  creates illusions 145
  lasting 48
  passionate 50
  romantic 48, 51, 52
  showing 49
  and stability of marriage 182
love-hate relationships 199
lovemaking **76**
  disappointment after 81

phases of 78
  settings for 220
loving
  active 51, 52
  collaborative 49, 51
  committed 50, 51
  expressive 49, 51, 52
  intuitive 49, 51
  styles of 46, **51**
  traditional romantic 51, 52

manic-depression 200
marital enrichment programs 204
marital relations
  infertility and 91
  and parenting stresses 90
marital relationship – *see* marriage
marital satisfaction 88
  in later years 126
  and parenthood 88
marriage
  adjustment to 66
  as affirmation 62
  arranged 182
  choice of 57, **62**
  disillusionment with 102
  dual-career 75
  economics of 64
  ending a **110**
  happiness in **180**
  and health 20, 58, 65
  in history 70
  ideal stereotype 139, 186
  impact of adultery on 95, 101
  "open" 25, 97, **98**
  parents as model 141
  and personal growth **54**
  rules for happy 182, **184**
  second **122**
    see also remarriage
  and security 65
  and social pressure 62
  social trends in 33, 57
  stability **180**
marriage ceremony 62, 65
  see also wedding customs
marriage contracts 64, 118
marriage counseling 201, 205, 209
marriage squeeze **33**
marriage therapy **204**
marriage travel agencies,
  international 38
masculinity 148
  level of 154
  see also gender differences
massage, in sex therapy 81, 213
Masters and Johnson
  sex therapy 83, 91, 212
masturbation 21, 83
  mutual 81, 218
  myths about 83
matchmaking 30, 38
mate-swapping 97, 99, 101
maturity **126**
  and parenthood 87
  rewards of 130
media, influence on partnership
  images **138**
meeting places 34
memories 160
men
  after divorce 116
  and emotions 150
  need to change 74

and premarital sex 46
  work-centered 60, 176
menstruation, and sexual desire 79
mental illness
  coping with partner's **202**
  and intimate relationships 20
misunderstanding 173
"Mittelschmerz" 79
mobility 72
money
  conflicts over **104**
  and divorce 113, 121
  management **188**
  and marriage 181
  marrying for 64
monogamy 58, 94, 99
  "serial" 66
moods 106, 179, 185
mother and child interaction 18
mothering 237
mothers
  age of 87
  new 90
  relationship with sons and
    daughters **235**
mourning, in divorce 115
Mutual Problem-Solving Program **197**

needs
  attending to partner's 159,
    176, 192, 217
  basic human 17, 22, 54
  neglect, feelings of 242
neighbors 20, 232
noncommunication 208
Norton, Robert
  communication styles 165
nudity 215
nullity, decree of 113

old age, contentment in 130
openness 165, 182
  wisdom of 170
oral sex 83
orgasm 78,**79**, 217, 218
  controlling 220
ovulation, failure of 90

"painful patients" 203
pairing off **40**
parenthood **86**
  timing of 87
  see also adoption
parenting
  benefits **86**, 88
  during divorce 119, 121
  gender differences in **236**
  negative side of 88
  "parallel" 124
  shared **234**, 239
  styles **236**, 239
  teamwork 239
  weekend 124
parents
  and marriage 230
  new 89
  older 87
parents-in-law 232
partner
  choosing a 180
  the difficult **196**
  hoping to change behavior of 198
  the ideal 31
  idealizing your 51, 146
  taking for granted 175

partners
  cautious 43
  counseling profiles 205
  former 123
partnership 22
  images of **138**, 146
  managing your **188**
passion
  and equality 72
  in love 50, 126
  romantic 48
passionate love **50**
pelvic inflammatory disease (PID) 90
personal growth 18, 61, 244, **247**
  and divorce 113, 115
  and intimate relationships 55, 58
  and marriage 71, 143
  and parenthood 87
personal space 233
personality problems 196
perversions 213
pets, friendship with 17, 19
pheromones 136
physical attributes 30
physical contact
  and closeness 43
  nonsexual 159
physical symbiosis 18
pill, contraceptive 46, 85
play 245
pledges of love 51
PMT – see premenstrual tension
polygyny 177
post-natal depression 90
poverty trap 118
power 104, 188, 193
  marital **192**
premarital sex **46**
premenstrual tension, and sexual
  desire 79
privacy 135, 137, 171
problem-solving 106
  mutual **197**
problems, learning to
  acknowledge 176
professional help for relationship
  problems 204
professional people, and advertising
  for a mate 36, 39
promiscuity 46, 85, 94
psychoanalysis 178, 209
psychotherapy 209, 212

quarreling **102**, 205

racial prejudice, and adoption 93
rapport **30**
realism, in marriage 186
reality
  ideals and **138**
  interpreting 143
reconciliation 196
recreation – see leisure
"reflecting" 208
RELATE 209
relationship
  celebrating the 160
  enrichment 196, 246
  examining state of 174, 177
  the first 18
  forming a **40**
  maintenance strategies **156**, 244
  patterns of development 43
  problems in 106, 160, 204
  professional help for problems **204**

readjusting the **142**
repair **196**
revitalizing your **242**
rewards from **17**, 24
rules for a happy 184
seriousness of 43
stagnation 143, 242
standards 26, 28, 138
relationship breakdown **106**
  coping after 109, **120**
  stages 108, 196
relatives, in marriage 230
religion
  and divorce **112**
  and marriage 62, 181
  and sex 21
remarriage 113, **120**, 142
  likelihood of for women and for
    men 122
respect, mutual 130, 159, 183
respite schemes for carers 203
responsibility
  household 189, 195
  in parenting 90
  in therapy 210
responsiveness 171
retirement 205
Richards, Martin 18
Ridley, Carl
  Mutual Problem-Solving
    Program 197
rights, recognition of partner's 192
rites of passage 69, 87
rituals, marriage – see wedding
  customs
Rogers, Carl
  "person-centered" approach 58,
    206
role, playing a romantic 145
role expectations, adjusting your **140**
role strain 190
role-sharing 105, 239
roles, changes in male and female 74
romantic love 48
Rubin, Lillian 226

Schwartz, Pepper
  the modern family 73
self-deception 145
self-disclosure 135, **183**
  mutual 173
  pace of 175
  women's in friendship 227
self-esteem 18, 101, 194, 200, 207, 238
  your partner's **183**
self-expression 56, 59
self-knowledge 23, 178, 209
semen-donor fathers 91
"sensate focusing" 213
sensuality 136
separateness
  in parenting 236
  within marriage 105, 187
separation
  anxiety 18
  coping after 120
  health and 60
  makes the heart grow fonder 42
  pain of 114
  professional help in 204
  questions to ask about 111
  see also divorce
"seven-year itch" 99, **142**
sex
  casual 21

and conflict 46
in courtship 46
enjoying **214**
learning about 213
with one chosen partner 21
plus friendship 25
self-stimulation – see masturbation
sex drive 76
sex roles 151
  changing 75
  in marriage 140
sex stereotypes 152
sex therapy 77, 205, **212**
  and infertility 91
sexual anatomy, and arousal 216
sexual arousal **216**
sexual behavior, in later years 126
sexual desire
  roots of 77
sexual enhancement programs 215
sexual exclusivity 25
sexual fantasy 81
sexual intercourse 220
  frequency of 77
  mutual satisfaction in 79
  role swapping in 220
sexual myths **83**
sexual performance anxiety 81
sexual problems **80**, 81
  criminal 213
  help for **212**
sexual relationship, patterns of
  transition to 46
sexual revolution 46, 74, 94
sexually transmitted disease
  (STD) 21, 83, 99
shared interests 41, 45, 172, 244
single, staying 55
singles
  couples and 227
  meeting potential partners 34
  myths and realities **56**
singles clubs 34
"soaps" 139
social change 70, 74
social pressure
  in co-parenting 238
  to marry 62
social skills courses 196
socializing 34, 231
  marriage and **224**
society
  attitude to divorce 110
  attitude to extramarital affairs 94
solitude 55
  see also loneliness
special relationships **16**, 161, 247
spiritual commitment 181
Spock, Benjamin
  advice to parents 235
stability in marriage **180**
standards, relationship 26, 28
Stein, Peter
  choosing married or single life 57
stepchildren, helping them cope 125
stepparenting **124**
sterilization 85
stimulation therapy 215
superwomen syndrome 194
surrogate mothers 91
"swinging" – see mate swapping

taboo subjects, handling 42
tact, in sex 223

talking treatment 209
  see also communication
telephone chat lines 37
"test-tube babies" 91
therapy **204**
  approaches in 206
  choosing appropriate **210**
  stages of 207
thinking styles, gender
  differences 153
togetherness 159, 171, 173, 244, 246
tolerance 173, 196
traditional approach to marriage 186
trial marriage – see living together

understanding
  your partner 176
  common barriers to 174
  mutual **172**, 178, 197
unemployment 202
unity, a couple's sense of 181

victims of battering 200
video dating services 36
violence 151, **199**
  why women tolerate 201
vows, of love 51, 53
vulnerability 53, 175

wedding customs **68**
well-being, and relationships 19
"wild man" 150
women
  after divorce 121
  battered 200
  career or family choice 55, 89, 237
  career or marriage choice 55
  effect of earnings on marriage 104
  new roles for 74, 84
  and premarital sex 46
  relationship-centered 60, 176
  rights of 190
  selectivity in marriage 33
  sexual desire in 79
  working 189
work
  commitment to 60
  happiness at 190
  and marital unhappiness 209
  meeting at 35
  roles and family roles **190**
"wounded father" 152
Wright, Paul
  special benefits of an intimate
    relationship 23